DIVINE FREEDOM
AND
THE DOCTRINE OF
THE IMMANENT
TRINITY

DIVINE FREEDOM

AND

THE DOCTRINE OF THE IMMANENT TRINITY

*In Dialogue with Karl Barth
and Contemporary Theology*

PAUL D. MOLNAR

T & T CLARK
A Continuum imprint
LONDON • NEW YORK

T&T CLARK LTD

A Continuum imprint

The Tower Building
11 York Road, London
SE1 7NX

15 East 26th Street
New York, NY 10010
USA

www.tandtclark.co.uk

www.continuumbooks.com

First published 2002
This paperback edition published 2005

ISBN 0 567 08865 0 (hbk)
ISBN 0 567 04134 4 (pbk)

British Library Cataloguing-in-Publication Data
A catalogue record for this book is available from the British Library

Typeset by Waverley Typesetters, Galashiels

Contents

Preface

A LL Christian theologians realize that the purpose of a doctrine of
the immanent Trinity is to recognize, uphold and respect God's
freedom. Without theoretical and practical awareness of this freedom
all theological statements about the significance of created existence
become ambiguous and constitute merely human attempts to give
meaning to creation, using theological categories. At issue in a proper
understanding of a doctrine of the immanent Trinity is the fact that,
although we obviously have no alternative but to understand God in
the categories available to us in our human experience, it is not anything
within our experience or inherent in those categories that prescribes
who God is *in se* and *ad extra*. This is an extremely important point
and much of the controversy that presently exists regarding the doctrine
of the Trinity concerns just this issue, as we shall see. The paramount
problem here concerns the fact that, since we know the triune God by
grace and through faith, we cannot, as it were, read back our concepts
and experiences into God. And a properly conceived doctrine of the
immanent Trinity, while not designed to prevent this, will indeed do
so to the extent that God's freedom is recognized and upheld through
such a doctrine.

This was essentially the issue in the controversy between Athanasius
and Arius. God is who he is, independent of creation, and while he has
indeed chosen not to remain isolated in himself, the fact remains that
he can be known with certainty only through his own self disclosure.
Or as Athanasius put it: 'It is more pious and more accurate to signify
God from the Son and call him Father, than to name him from his

works and call him Unoriginate.'[1] This is one of the most pressing problems facing contemporary trinitarian theology: how do we speak accurately of God's Fatherhood and Sonship, and about God's relationality and temporality without projecting our limited human relations of fatherhood and sonship and created temporality into the divine life, thus compromising not only God's sovereignty, but our genuine contingent freedom which is grounded in God's freedom for us in the incarnation and at Pentecost? Or to put it another way, how may we know God in accordance with his nature rather than creating God in our own image?

In face of this critical question, this book will be an effort to articulate a contemporary doctrine of the immanent Trinity. First, a contemporary doctrine should eschew irrelevant speculation about God's inner nature, abstracted from God's own self-revelation, in the awareness that this is and has been damaging to theology and practice within the Church. I will therefore avoid both separating and confusing the immanent and economic Trinity and adhere to the economic Trinity for our information about the immanent Trinity. Second, a contemporary doctrine of the immanent Trinity also will be aware of the fact that numerous theologians today either directly polemicize against such a doctrine or simply pay lip-service to it because they know its importance in recognizing and upholding God's freedom and distinction from creation. Neither of these alternatives, as we shall see, does justice to the function and theological importance of a doctrine of the immanent Trinity.

Among twentieth-century theologians Karl Barth was well aware of this difficulty when he wrote that 'the content of the doctrine of the Trinity . . . is not that God in His relation to man is Creator, Mediator and Redeemer, but that God in Himself is eternally God the Father, Son and Holy Spirit . . . [God acting as Emmanuel] cannot be dissolved into His work and activity'.[2] Trinitarian doctrine or trinitarian thinking cannot displace God as the foundation of true knowledge since God's action in revelation is not a dogma, view or principle but the actual Word of God working *ad extra* as creator, reconciler and redeemer.

---

[1] Athanasius, *Contra Ar.* 1.34, in *A Select Library of Nicene and Post-Nicene Fathers of the Christian Church Second Series*, trans. and ed. Philip Schaff and Henry Wace (Edinburgh: T&T Clark, 1987), 326. Cf. also Thomas F. Torrance, *The Trinitarian Faith: The Evangelical Theology of the Ancient Catholic Church* (hereafter: *The Trinitarian Faith*) (Edinburgh: T&T Clark, 1987), 6 and 49.

[2] Karl Barth, *Church Dogmatics*, 4 vols in 13 pts (hereafter: *CD*). Vol. I, pt. 2: *The Doctrine of the Word of God*, trans. G. T. Thomson and Harold Knight (Edinburgh: T&T Clark, 1970), 878–9. Cf. also *Doctrine of the Word*, 35–7 and *CD* II/2, 309, 313.

The doctrine of the Trinity therefore depends on this Word which cannot be reduced to anything within history. It can help to clarify who God is in revelation and is itself the central Christian doctrine, but it is not itself the controlling center of dogmatics. Since God is this center, I will argue that grace, faith and revelation, which include creation in a genuine communion with God from creation to consummation, always remain grounded exclusively in God and never jointly in God and creation. God lives, discloses himself anew and has to be discovered anew because theology has no sovereignty in relation to God. Thus as Barth noted,

> Wherever there is knowledge of Jesus Christ, it takes place in the power of His witness, in the mystery and miracle, the outpouring and receiving, of the gift of the Holy Spirit . . . He is the *doctor veritatis*: He is the finger of God . . . which causes the reason of man . . . to receive the truth . . . Wherever there is Christian *gnosis* it is His work. That is why it has no other sources or norms. That is why it can be had without any demonstrations of its origin.[3]

Unfortunately, however, the way many theologians today employ trinitarian categories actually leads from agnosticism to monism and dualism, and thus compromises divine and human freedom just because they either have simply paid lip-service to God's freedom or because they completely reject the idea that we can or should know the immanent Trinity. Most modern theologians adopt Karl Rahner's axiom that 'the immanent Trinity is strictly identical with the economic Trinity and vice versa'[4] in some form, even if only to move beyond it, to speak about God's involvement with the world. Certainly there is a perfectly non-controversial way to understand this axiom, that is, it may simply mean that the God with whom we are involved in Christ and the Spirit is none other than the eternal Father, Son and Holy Spirit. But a question to be explored in this book will be whether or not this axiom as it stands, and as it actually functions for many modern theologians, can truly respect God's freedom as a doctrine of the immanent Trinity

---

[3] *CD* IV/2, 126. See also Karl Barth, *Evangelical Theology: An Introduction* (hereafter: *Evangelical Theology*), trans. Grover Foley (Grand Rapids, MI: Eerdmans, 1963), 6: 'The separation and distinction of this one true God from all the others can only be continually his own deed.'

[4] Karl Rahner, 'Theology and Anthropology', *Theological Investigations* (23 vols) (hereafter: *TI*), Vol. 9, trans. Graham Harrison (New York: Herder & Herder, 1972), 28–45, 32. See also *TI* 9, 130. Cf. Karl Rahner, *The Trinity* (hereafter: *Trinity*), trans. Joseph Donceel (New York: Herder & Herder, 1970), 22ff.

must. Does the vice versa obscure God's freedom, so that any attempt to reconcile God's freedom with this axiom, as it stands, inevitably underplays God's actual pre-temporal, supra-temporal and post-temporal freedom? Some confusion and reversal of the creature–creator relationship inevitably follows. Several indications of such a reversal today are: (1) the trend towards making God, in some sense, dependent upon and indistinguishable from history; (2) the lack of precision in Christology, which leads to the idea that Jesus, in his humanity as such, is the revealer; (3) the failure to distinguish the Holy Spirit from the human spirit; (4) a trend to begin theology with experiences of self-transcendence, thus allowing experience rather than the object of faith to determine the truth of theology. Exploring these indicators by seeing what a number of prominent contemporary theologians have to say in these areas, I hope, will lead toward a contemporary doctrine of the immanent Trinity that clarifies divine and human freedom and avoids agnosticism, monism and dualism.

Acknowledgments

I would like to thank Professor Iain R. Torrance for his consistent support, encouragement and friendship. At his invitation, I presented what is now Chapter Two at the University of Aberdeen in March 1999. Iain and his wife Morag went to great lengths to make that a wonderfully memorable event. Professor David Fergusson went out of his way to make my visit a success and offered valuable advice as well. I would also like to thank Professor Trevor Hart for his invitation to deliver the same lecture at the University of St Andrews and for his hospitality during my visit. Everyone at both Universities made me feel very welcome and helped me think through important issues related to Barth's Christology. In addition I am grateful to the Very Reverend Professor Thomas F. Torrance for reading and commenting on material contained in a number of chapters and for his encouragement to proceed with this work. Further, his thinking, as especially expressed in his major works on the Trinity, has been extremely helpful to me and his influence will be seen throughout the book. I am also grateful to St John's University for providing me with a research grant during the summer of 1998 and for their support of this work.

This book has developed over many years, and there are dialogue partners, friends and colleagues who have contributed to my thinking; special thanks are due to Professors George Hunsinger, Bruce McCormack and Nick Healy. I would also like to thank George Hunsinger and Walt Lowe for invitations to speak at two meetings of the Karl Barth Society of North America. In November 1994 I presented an abbreviated version of what is now Chapter Five and in November

1998 I presented a version of what is now Chapter Three. I am grateful to the many members of the Barth Society whose intense scholarship makes that one of the most important and rewarding scholarly meetings I attend. Thanks are also due to everyone at T&T Clark who so ably contributed to the production of this book. Finally, I would like to extend a sincere thank you to John J. McCormick who generously gave his time and expertise in reading and re-reading several versions of this manuscript and offering valuable editorial suggestions at each stage. Still, it goes without saying that the sole responsibility for any errors resides with the author.

Also, I am grateful to the following for permission to reprint previously published material: T&T Clark for Karl Barth, *Church Dogmatics*, 4 vols in 13 pts., 1958–81; Paul D. Molnar, 'Robert W. Jenson's Systematic Theology Volume I: The Triune God', *Scottish Journal of Theology* 52 (1999), 117–31; Paul D. Molnar, 'Toward a Contemporary Doctrine of the Immanent Trinity: Karl Barth and the Present Discussion', *Scottish Journal of Theology* 49 (1996), 311–57; Paul D. Molnar, 'God's Self-Communication in Christ: A Comparison of Thomas F. Torrance and Karl Rahner', *Scottish Journal of Theology* 50 (1997), 288–320; Paul D. Molnar, 'The Function of the Immanent Trinity in the Theology of Karl Barth: Implications for Today', *Scottish Journal of Theology* 42 (1989), 367–99; *The Thomist* for Paul D. Molnar, 'Is God Essentially Different from His Creatures? Rahner's Explanation from Revelation', 51 (1987), 575–631; *Theological Studies* for Paul D. Molnar, 'The Function of the Trinity in Moltmann's Ecological Doctrine of Creation', 51 (1990), 673–97; Blackwell Publishers for Paul D. Molnar, 'Some Dogmatic Implications of Barth's Understanding of Ebionite and Docetic Christology', *International Journal of Systematic Theology* 2 (2000), 151–74; Crossroad Publishing for Karl Rahner, *Foundations of Christian Faith: An Introduction to the Idea of Christianity*, trans. William V. Dych. A translation of *Grundkurs des Glaubens: Einführung in den Begriff des Christentums* © Verlag Herder Freiburg im Breisgau 1976.; Fortress Press and SCM Press for Jürgen Moltmann, *The Trinity and the Kingdom* originally published by Harper & Row and by SCM Press, 1981; Darton, Longman & Todd for Karl Rahner, *Theological Investigations, Vol. IV: More Recent Writings*, trans. Kevin Smith. A translation of *Schriften zur Theologie, IV*, published by Verlagsanstalt. Benziger & Co. A.G., Einsiedeln. Translation © Darton, Longman & Todd, 1966 and 1974.

Abbreviations

CD	Karl Barth, *Church Dogmatics*
FCF	Karl Rahner, SJ, *Foundations of Christian Faith: An Introduction to the Idea of Christianity*
GMD	Gordon D. Kaufman, *God – Mystery – Diversity: Christian Theology in a Pluralistic World*
HW	Karl Rahner, SJ, *Hearers of the Word*
IFM	Gordon D. Kaufman, *In Face of Mystery: A Constructive Theology*
SJT	*Scottish Journal of Theology*
ST	Gordon D. Kaufman, *Systematic Theology: A Historicist Perspective*
STI	Robert W. Jenson, *Systematic Theology Volume I: The Triune God*
SW	Karl Rahner, SJ, *Spirit in the World*
TI	Karl Rahner, SJ, *Theological Investigations*
TNA	Gordon D. Kaufman, *Theology for a Nuclear Age*
TS	*Theological Studies*

Chapter One

The Purpose of a Doctrine of the Immanent Trinity and Its Neglect Today

IN this chapter I will explore two important questions which will lead to a more precise understanding of how a doctrine of the immanent Trinity ought to function today. The first concerns the role of experience in theology; the second concerns issues raised by feminist theologians about the *locus* of trinitarian theology. Should anyone's experience, whether male or female, be normative for understanding God? Or should all our experiences, important as they are, be continually assessed by the extent to which their relation to the truth shapes them? I will follow the view held by Karl Barth, and clearly articulated by Thomas F. Torrance, that theology must allow the unique nature of its object to determine what can and cannot be said about the triune God. While both of these theologians rely on the thought of Athanasius, Torrance has made this reliance especially explicit.

The Role of Experience

Among contemporary American theologians, perhaps the most notorious examples of those who at least indirectly have helped to shape trinitarian theology in exactly the wrong way are Gordon Kaufman and Sallie McFague. Their thinking makes it impossible to speak of the immanent Trinity and thus reduces speech about God to our human attempt to give meaning to our existence using theological categories. Their thinking in turn has strongly influenced the trinitarian theology of Catherine LaCugna and the feminist theology of Elizabeth Johnson. I will illustrate how this influence affects the theology of LaCugna and Johnson as the chapter proceeds, with a view toward seeing how experience displaces God's free actions *ad extra* when a doctrine of the immanent Trinity is ignored or compromised.

Both Gordon Kaufman and Sallie McFague are correct to call attention to the important issue of idolatry and to the fact that in the past the Church has misunderstood the faith when it was thought that Christianity could or should be imposed on others, as happened during the Inquisition and the Crusades. Along with many others, I share their concerns about the fact that Christians have often misused Christian symbols. They are also correct to believe that the imagination is part of the theological enterprise. But I disagree with them on two extremely important issues. They think that because theology merely represents our human attempt to give meaning to existence using theological symbols, it should be 'judged in terms of the adequacy with which it is fulfilling the objectives we humans set for it'.[1] Thus when they speak of theology as 'imaginative construction' they mean that its truth is not governed by a unique object (the triune God) who exists independently of the mind, but that *we* are the ones who actually create truth by the way we think and act. They both believe that to speak of a really existing God who is the creator and who, before that, was the eternal Father, Son and Holy Spirit represents what they call a false form of reifying symbols. They therefore believe that any contemporary talk about an immanent Trinity represents irrelevant speculation.

Gordon Kaufman

For Kaufman, theology is essentially imaginative construction, that is, the human imagination uses the image/concept of God as the 'ultimate point of reference', to organize its experiences in the world and to enable humans to come to terms with those things that threaten the survival of civilization, such as potential nuclear holocaust. Any theology that would begin with revelation would be considered 'authoritarian'. Kaufman thus sees two alternatives: (1) we can admit that theology is essentially imaginative construction or (2) we can accept the fact that our terms refer to reality.[2] He insists that if, mistakenly, we were to

---

[1] See Gordon D. Kaufman *Theology for a Nuclear Age* (hereafter: *TNA*) (Philadelphia: Westminster Press, 1985), 19. See also Gordon D. Kaufman, *God – Mystery – Diversity: Christian Theology in a Pluralistic World* (hereafter: *GMD*) (Minneapolis: Fortress Press, 1996), 42.

[2] Gordon D. Kaufman, *In Face of Mystery: A Constructive Theology* (hereafter: *IFM*) (Cambridge, MA: Harvard University Press, 1993), 49. Re: theology as essentially imaginative construction; see also *TNA*, 26ff.

choose the second alternative, we would be guilty of reifying our images, that is, we would have failed to realize that our concepts are simply imaginative constructs governed by the way we think humanity ought to function in community in a movement toward peace. Such a failure would lead us to think that God is an objective reality existing independently of our conceptions.

Because Kaufman thinks that the symbol God is a myth[3] he is unable to acknowledge or describe the Christian God at all. For this reason, although he opposes dualism (any separation of God from the world), he himself is led into the most extreme form of it. For while he insists that 'if genuine revelation is affirmed, the character of God's relating himself to his world must express the inmost essence of his being and will' yet he also insists, 'To the internal *structure* of this innermost essence we have no access in history or revelation; and anything said about it is pure speculation.'[4] Ultimately this truly rigid dualism leads Kaufman to the position that 'God will no longer be pictured or conceived as a personal being in the heavens above who "before the foundation of the world" . . . devised a detailed divine plan . . . we will no longer . . . be able to imagine ourselves as in direct personal interaction with this divine being.'[5]

Catherine LaCugna

It is just this dualistic thinking that structures what Catherine LaCugna thinks about the Trinity. For instance, she approves Kaufman's refusal to make a distinction between the immanent and economic Trinity because she believes, with him, that theology should not accept the fact that the immanent Trinity 'is equivalent to "God as he is in himself" or "God's essence"'.[6] She believes that 'the economy itself does not *necessarily* imply real distinctions "in" God that are of a different ontological order than the distinctions in the economy. There *may be* such distinctions, and it *may be* a legitimate enterprise for a purely speculative theology to posit such intradivine distinctions, but there is no transeconomic perspective from which to establish their existence.'[7]

---

[3] *IFM*, 332, that is, 'this symbol is actually but one feature of a larger mythic map of reality'.

[4] Gordon D. Kaufman, *Systematic Theology: A Historicist Perspective* (hereafter: *ST*) (New York: Charles Scribner's Sons, 1968), 102, n. 9.

[5] *IFM*, 332.

[6] Catherine Mowry LaCugna, *God for Us: The Trinity and Christian Life* (hereafter: *God for Us*) (San Francisco: HarperSanFrancisco, 1991), 226–7.

[7] LaCugna, *God for Us*, 227.

What she quite rightly wishes to avoid is thinking that ignores the economy. But she assumes, incorrectly, that if a theologian argues on the basis of the intradivine distinctions, then the economy *must* be left behind, with the result that the Trinity then would have no bearing on our life or faith. Thus, she supports Schoonenberg's view that on the basis of revelation we cannot know whether or not God would have been a Trinity apart from salvation. Unquestionably we all agree that *we* cannot leave the economy behind without disrupting the important connection between the Trinity and the life of faith. Yet it is precisely on the basis of revelation that we do indeed know that God would still be the eternal Father, Son and Spirit without the world, even though he freely created the world and has acted to save the world in his Word and Spirit. While we are in no position to say anything about God in himself (the immanent Trinity) except on the basis of what is revealed by the economic Trinity, it is imperative, as Thomas F. Torrance never tires of reminding us, that we recognize that all of our theological knowledge is grounded in the fact that God is toward us what he is eternally in himself.

LaCugna's entire trinitarian theology is built upon a foundation of sand precisely because she refuses to acknowledge the importance of the immanent Trinity as the presupposition, meaning and goal of any trinitarian theology. As we shall see later in more detail, it is just this thinking that leads her to reduce God's existence to his existence in the economy: 'The doctrine of the Trinity is not ultimately a teaching about "God" but a teaching about *God's life with us and our life with each other*.'[8] Indeed she believes that 'to speak about God in immanent trinitarian terms is nothing more than to speak about God's life with us in the economy'.[9] It is important to note here that we cannot speak intelligibly about God's life with us unless the God of whom we speak is distinguishable from us and from our life with each other. And this is the very thing that LaCugna is unable to do precisely because of her refusal to allow the doctrine of the immanent Trinity a genuine function in her thinking about God for us.

To be fair, it is quite obvious that she believes that some talk of an immanent Trinity is legitimate – but only if it is nothing more than an analysis of the economy. She is of course ambiguous about this. On the one hand she speaks as if it were extremely important to distinguish God *in se* from God for us in order to avoid the appearance of projection.

---

[8] LaCugna, *God for Us*, 228.
[9] LaCugna, *God for Us*, 229.

But on the other hand she insists that any grounding of the economy in an immanent Trinity represents a separation of God from us. Thus she believes that '*theologia* is not the Trinity *in se* but, much more modestly and simply, the mystery of God . . . *an "immanent" trinitarian theology of God is nothing more than a theology of the economy of salvation*'.[10] And this leads to the idea that divine *perichoresis* should be understood as the 'divine dance' that signifies not 'intradivine communion' but

> divine life as all creatures partake and literally exist in it . . . Everything comes from God, and everything returns to God, through Christ in the Spirit. This *exitus* and *reditus* is the choreography of the divine dance which takes place from all eternity and is manifest at every moment in creation. There are not two sets of communion – one among the divine persons, the other among human persons . . . The one *perichoresis*, the one mystery of communion includes God and humanity as beloved partners in the dance.[11]

By way of summary LaCugna points out that 'The exodus of all persons from God and the return of all to God is the divine dance in which God and we are eternal partners.'[12] But having said that, LaCugna clearly reveals her own inability to distinguish God from creatures precisely because her thinking has already incorporated them under the umbrella of her relational feminist ontology at the outset. No wonder Colin Gunton believes that LaCugna's position seems more like that of John Scotus Erigena, one of the founders of modern pantheism, than the Cappadocians, to whom she frequently appeals.[13] And that is the problem. LaCugna's thinking ultimately leads her into both the pantheism and dualism that she quite obviously attempts to avoid by paying lip-service to God's freedom. But lip-service is not enough for her to avoid making God dependent on us and allowing an abstract concept of relationality to determine her view of God and of Christ. More will be said about this later. Here I simply wish to establish the fact that LaCugna's thinking about the Trinity at the outset is not really dictated by God, Christ or the Holy Spirit just because she allows her theology to be shaped by the historicist,

---

[10] LaCugna, *God for Us*, 223–4.

[11] LaCugna, *God for Us*, 274.

[12] LaCugna, *God for Us*, 304.

[13] See Colin E. Gunton, Review of Catherine LaCugna, *God for Us*, *Scottish Journal of Theology* (hereafter: *SJT*) 47.1 (1994) 135–7. See also Colin E. Gunton, *The Promise of Trinitarian Theology*, second edn (Edinburgh: T&T Clark, 1997), xvii–xix.

Kantian[14] and pantheistic views of Gordon Kaufman. It may be noted here that Kaufman's understanding of God, as dictated by the evolutionary process, is in fact pantheistic because he cannot distinguish God from the evolutionary process itself:

> The symbol 'God' suggests a reality, an ultimate tendency or power, which is working itself out in an evolutionary process . . . God – this whole grand cosmic evolutionary movement – is giving birth, after many millennia, to finite freedom . . . God is here understood as that ecological reality behind and in and working through all of life and history . . .'[15]

Sallie McFague

Sallie McFague reconceives God from generally accessible human experience but does 'not know whether God (the inner being of God) can be described by the models of mother, lover and friend'.[16] Through these significant experiences she describes a God who is dependent upon and *intrinsically* related to the world and thinks the doctrine of the Trinity simply gave dogmatic status to relationality.[17] By describing only our experiences of relationality, however, her pantheism destroys the free basis that our human relations have in God who becomes 'our friend and co-worker', one who needs many saviors[18] instead of our Lord, Savior, Helper and Friend as the Incarnate Word. As the Trinity is 'a summation of . . . ontology or of the Christian experience of God' her models can replace the Father, Son and Spirit;[19] thus, she focuses

> on God's activity in relationship to the world and our talk about that activity. It makes no claims about the so-called immanent . . . trinity, for I see no way that assumptions concerning the inner nature of God are possible. My interest centers on the economic trinity, on the experience of God's activity in relation to the world.[20]

[14] Kaufman believes the idea of God is a regulative idea that we use to order our existence. Cf. Gordon D. Kaufman, *An Essay on Theological Method* (hereafter: *Method*) (Atlanta, GA: Scholars Press, 1990), 24.

[15] *TNA*, 43–5.

[16] Sallie McFague, *Models of God: Theology for an Ecological Nuclear Age* (hereafter: *Models*) (Philadelphia: Fortress Press, 1987), 192.

[17] McFague, *Models*, 112–13. Also, 72, 136, 150 and 166.

[18] McFague, *Models*, 136, 150.

[19] McFague, *Models*, 181.

[20] McFague, *Models*, 224.

This thinking is of a piece with her belief that while she cannot *know* the reality of God, she can still speculate about God's reality by creating new mythologies rather than replicating past traditional mythologies such as were embodied in the doctrine of creation. Hence she writes, 'I do not *know* who God is, but I find some models better than others for constructing an image of God commensurate with my trust in a God as on the side of life.'[21] Thus, she believes that

> through remythologizing the doctrines of God and human beings in light of the picture of reality from contemporary science – through the use of the organic model as a way of reconceiving the relation of God and the world – the appropriate human stance vis-à-vis God and our planet will emerge. Remythologizing . . . is a form of embodied thought combining image and concept that calls forth both a feeling and a thinking response . . . If one uses the model of the universe as God's body . . . one would, or at least might, act differently toward it than if one used the model of creation as a work of art (one possible model from the Genesis story).[22]

Yet the problem with this thinking is that if she cannot know the immanent Trinity, that is, the reality of God, but can only speculate in a mythological way about God by projecting possibilities from our experiences of motherhood, love and friendship, then any claim she might make to actually know God is simply vacuous. All that is really known are our experiences, and our supposed knowledge of God is nothing more than projection. Indeed this projection leads directly to the pantheism, modalism and dualism that mark her reflections.

Her particular modalist idea that we only have to do with an economic Trinity, however, results from the same methodological agnosticism that marks Catherine LaCugna's work and which cannot describe God who really *is* Father, Son and Spirit in eternity and in time. So while Christian prayer, following Jesus' own instruction, has always been related to the coming of the kingdom, McFague sees prayers as a conjuring of images, which will enable *us* to think of the world as special so that we will preserve it as God's body, that is, as something that 'is not something alien to or other than God but is from the

---

[21] McFague, *Models*, 224. McFague thus specifically rejects the idea that we actually can know anything about the immanent Trinity, *Models*, 223–4. It is worth noting that McFague actually describes herself as an erstwhile Barthian in her book *The Body of God: An Ecological Theology* (hereafter: *The Body of God*) (Minneapolis: Fortress Press, 1993), 208, and holds the same view espoused in *Models*: 'The transcendence of God frees us to model God in terms of what is most significant to us' (193).

[22] McFague, *The Body of God*, 81.

"womb" of God, formed through "gestation"'.[23] It is apparent that the very idea of the world as God's body is a panentheistic attempt (which clearly collapses back into pantheism) to bypass the uniqueness of the incarnation as an event in the life of Jesus and to visualize the God–world relation as one in which 'God will therefore need the world, want the world, not simply as dependent inferior (flesh subordinated to spirit) but as offspring, beloved, and companion.'[24] Apotheosis thus issues in self-justification just because for her Jesus is '*paradigmatic of God the lover but is not unique. This means that Jesus is not ontologically different from other paradigmatic figures* ... He is special to us as our foundational figure: he is our historical choice as the premier paradigm of God's love'.[25] McFague's mythological view of the incarnation suggests that

> The world as God's body, then, may be seen as a way to remythologize the inclusive, suffering love of the cross of Jesus of Nazareth ... God is at risk in human hands: Just as once upon a time in a bygone mythology, human beings killed their God in the body of a man, so now we once again have that power, but, in a mythology more appropriate to our time, we would kill our God in the body of the world.[26]

The point here is that McFague is deeply influenced by the thinking of Gordon Kaufman and, for that very reason, she is led to reject what has always been the only sure foundation for Christian knowledge of God, that is, the existence and activity of the eternal (immanent) Trinity. For her, Jesus is one significant example of God's love for us among others and he is this since Christians chose to make him their foundation. Precisely because of her agnosticism with respect to the immanent Trinity, she therefore ascribes true knowledge of God and of Christ to us instead of recognizing that true knowledge of God can only come from God. The triune God does not become who he is based on our choices but can only be known in truth when and if our choices correspond with his choice of us in Christ through the Holy Spirit. Indeed, as Colin Gunton has observed, any compromise of divine freedom means that human freedom is also endangered: 'God's personal otherness from the world is needed if there is to be a true establishing of the world in its own right.'[27]

---

[23] McFague, *Models*, 110.
[24] McFague, *Models*, 112–13.
[25] McFague, *Models*, 136, emphasis mine.
[26] McFague, *Models*, 72–3.
[27] Gunton, *The Promise of Trinitarian Theology*, second edn, xix.

Feminist Concerns/Elizabeth Johnson

In her book *She Who Is: The Mystery of God in Feminist Theological Discourse*, Elizabeth A. Johnson patterns her entire discussion of God methodologically and in terms of content after the theologies of Gordon Kaufman and Sallie McFague. Thus, she argues that the symbol God functions as our 'ultimate point of reference'. Hence, if we speak of God as an arbitrary tyrant or as a war God we will have an aggressive and intolerant community, while if we speak of a loving and forgiving God we will have a community of forgiveness and caring. God is described as a 'matrix' within which human life is lived and understood. Indeed her basic argument is that '[t]he symbol God functions'[28] and that we must make it function today so as not to exclude women. The suggestion clearly is that it is we who invest this symbol with meaning and it is we who thus must change the symbol in order to obtain the desired social results.

Instead of recognizing that the truth of our symbols for God is grounded in God and thus in revelation, Johnson argues that women have been excluded 'from the realm of public symbol formation and decision making' and have thus been subordinated to 'the imagination and needs of a world designed chiefly by men'.[29] While Johnson admits that God is officially seen as spirit and beyond male or female sexuality, nevertheless she argues that the Church's daily language in worship, preaching and teaching conveys the message that 'God is male, or at least more like a man than a woman, or at least more fittingly addressed as male than as female'. Because the symbol God functions and because it has thus functioned to subordinate women, the task of contemporary theology is to make it function so as to enhance women's dignity as equally created in God's image. What is needed, according to Johnson, is a 'creative "naming toward God", as Mary Daly so carefully calls it, from the matrix of their own experience'.[30] As active subjects in their own right, women wish to name God out of their emerging identity. Language for God in female images is thus necessary to overcome any subordination of women and any false domination by men.

There can be no doubt that women frequently have been mistreated and still are mistreated today by men and other women. Further, women are quite justified in reacting against their exclusion from certain

---

[28] Elizabeth A. Johnson, *She Who Is: The Mystery of God in Feminist Theological Discourse* (hereafter: *She Who Is*) (New York: Crossroad, 1992), 4.

[29] Johnson, *She Who Is*, 4.

[30] Johnson, *She Who Is*, 5.

positions in the Church and to some of the rather odd arguments used to explain their exclusion. Even though I am sympathetic to the feminist desire for rights and equality, these cannot mean that theology should now exchange the revelation of God for the experience of women and thus collapse theology into anthropology. This surely will not enhance the stature of women and will ultimately obscure rather than illuminate the truth, which alone can set all of us free in this matter. Since Jesus is the way, the truth and the life, any theological understanding of this issue must begin and end its thinking with him.

Critical Issues

Because Elizabeth Johnson's main concern is to overcome women's subordination, she sees theology more as an imaginative way to achieve that goal politically, socially and religiously, than as an attempt to understand who God really is and what he has actually done and is doing in history. For this reason there are several serious errors and inconsistencies evident in Johnson's thinking which need to be explained and overcome.

Naming God from the Matrix of Women's Experience

As already noted, Johnson argues that, while the Christian God in reality is neither male nor female[31] and so should not be understood as sexually defined, one of her main arguments is that, throughout church history, God, as Father and Son, has been understood to be male and was so named by men in order to subordinate women.[32] This is simply wrong and, as Roland Frye has shown, follows the errant assumptions of Mary Daly's slogan 'Since God is male, the male is God'[33] with the implication that God must be emasculated for women to achieve equality. Neither in scripture nor in the history of dogma has God, as Father and Son, been understood to be male – not even subliminally. In fact the reason why Johnson thinks this way is because her basic theology is grounded

---

[31] Johnson, *She Who Is*, 54.

[32] Johnson, *She Who Is*, 5, 21, 44 and 48ff.

[33] Cited in Roland Frye, 'Language for God and Feminist Language: Problems and Principles' *SJT* 41.4 (1988), 441–70, 443. See also Roland Frye, 'Language for God and Feminist Language: Problems and Principles', *Speaking the Christian God: The Holy Trinity and the Challenge of Feminism*, ed. Alvin F. Kimel, Jr (Grand Rapids, MI: Eerdmans, 1992), 17–43, 19. See Mary Daly, *Beyond God the Father: Toward a Philosophy of Women's Liberation* (Boston: Beacon Press, 1985), 19.

in the experience of women. She is, as she says, naming God from the matrix of women's experience. Thus, while she continues to use the traditional name for God sparingly she ultimately changes its meaning by associating it with metaphors and values 'arising from women's experience'.[34] This, however, is merely an interim strategy, she says, until some new word arises

> for the as yet unnameable understanding of holy mystery that includes the reality of women as well as all creation. On the way to that day, language of God/She is aimed at generating new content for references to deity in the hopes that this discourse will help to heal imaginations and liberate people for new forms of community.[35]

The truth, however, is that in scripture and in doctrine, God was understood from a center in God rather than from a center in human experience, whether male or female. That is the significance of Athanasius's statement mentioned above that 'It would be more godly and true to signify God from the Son and call him Father, than to name God from his works alone and call him Unoriginate.'[36] Here the Father–Son relation has priority over the creator–creature relation in an irreversible way so that God's nature is neither defined nor measured by our own human nature. True knowledge of God in this context could take place *only* through Christ who was and is one in being with the Father. The deity of Christ therefore was central to a proper view of the Trinity. As Thomas F. Torrance remarks, 'The Deity of Christ is the supreme truth of the Gospel, the key to the bewildering enigma of Jesus'.[37] Athanasius thus made it clear that those who would call God the Unoriginate were those who named him only from his works because they did not know the Son who is the very same being as God the Father.[38] Our knowledge of God as creator then is taken from

[34] Johnson, *She Who Is*, 43.
[35] Johnson, *She Who Is*, 43.
[36] Torrance, *The Trinitarian Faith*, 49.
[37] Thomas F. Torrance, *The Christian Doctrine of God, One Being Three Persons* (hereafter: *The Christian Doctrine of God*) (Edinburgh: T&T Clark, 1996), 46. While Douglas Farrow, *Ascension and Ecclesia: On the Significance of the Doctrine of the Ascension for Ecclesiology and Christian Cosmology* (hereafter: *Ascension and Ecclesia*) (Grand Rapids, MI: Eerdmans, 1999), 13, argues that theologians today are more prone to stumble over Christ's humanity than his divinity, I hope to show throughout this book that it is mainly the failure of modern theologians to begin and end their thinking with the man Jesus who was and is the eternally begotten Son of the Father that causes much of the trouble that now exists in connection with our understanding of the immanent and economic Trinity.
[38] Torrance, *The Trinitarian Faith*, 76.

knowledge of God as Father and as Son because all things were created through the Son. As Hilary of Poitiers makes clear

> You hear the name *Son*; believe that He is the Son. You hear the name *Father*; fix it in your mind that He is the Father. Why surround these names with doubt and illwill and hostility? The things of God are provided with names which give a true indication of the realities; why force an arbitrary meaning upon their obvious sense? Father and Son are spoken of; doubt not that the words mean what they say.[39]

What all of this means is that we cannot have precise theological knowledge of God as the almighty creator 'in terms of abstract possibilities and vague generalities – from what we imagine God is not, or from examining what God has brought into being in complete difference from himself'.[40] It was the Gnostic Basileides from Alexandria who, relying on Plato's notion that 'God is beyond all being', taught that 'we cannot say anything about what God is, but can only say something about what he is not'.[41] But Gregory Nazianzen (*Or.* 28:9) held in opposition to this thinking that 'if we cannot say anything positive about what God is, we really cannot say anything accurate about what he is not'.[42] As Thomas F. Torrance rightly explains, Nicene theologians refused to speak of God in empty negative conceptions because, if we do not think of the Father in his relation to the Son but only as creator in relation to creatures, then we will think of the Son himself as one of the works of the Father. And this will mean that we are then speaking of God 'in a way that is not personally grounded in God himself, but in an impersonal way far removed from what he is in himself'.[43] Further, if we try to reach knowledge of God from some point outside of God, then there is no point within God 'by reference to which we can test or control our conceptions of him' and so we 'are inevitably flung back upon ourselves'.[44] In this case our God-talk will be arbitrary and grounded in human experience rather than God himself. And this is just what Athanasius accused the Arians of doing. Hilary was also unhappy with such a procedure, arguing that 'the action

---

[39] Hilary of Poitiers, *On the Trinity*, Book III, 22 (hereafter: Hilary, *Trinity*), in *A Select Library of Nicene and Post-Nicene Fathers of the Christian Church Second Series*, Vol. IX, trans. Philip Schaff and Henry Wace (Grand Rapids, MI: Eerdmans, 1997), 68.
[40] Torrance, *The Trinitarian Faith*, 78.
[41] Torrance, *The Trinitarian Faith*, 50.
[42] Torrance, *The Trinitarian Faith*, 50.
[43] Torrance, *The Trinitarian Faith*, 50.
[44] Torrance, *The Trinitarian Faith*, 51.

of God must not be canvassed by human faculties; the Creator must not be judged by those who are the work of his hands'.[45] Throughout this book it will be noted that whenever and wherever the deity of the man Jesus is undermined or ignored, then and there God is defined *by* human experience rather than *by* revelation and thus *through* human experience.

Divine Incomprehensibility

It is extremely important that this point be made clear because, when Johnson calls God 'holy mystery', an expression taken from Karl Rahner, she is referring ultimately to a God who remains unknown and attempts to ground this thinking in a view of divine incomprehensibility that accords with the basic agnosticism of Sallie McFague and Gordon Kaufman. It is God's incomprehensibility, she believes, that makes it legitimate to speak of God as a 'matrix surrounding and sustaining life'.[46] And yet, as we shall see in more detail below, this is essentially a vague pantheistic description of God employed by theologians who refuse to think from a center in God and who explicitly and implicitly deny the deity of Christ. Johnson believes, with Anne Carr, that because of God's incomprehensibility we need more images of God, and the more we have, the better God's incomprehensibility will be preserved.[47]

While it is certainly true that the triune God is and remains incomprehensible and that no human concept can grasp the divine being, this cannot mean that we may now know God by stepping outside the Father–Son relation in and through which God has actually revealed himself by including us within his own internal relations by grace. Here Johnson follows Gordon Kaufman and argues that we know both God and the world through 'imaginative constructs'.[48] Undoubtedly God can be known through our imagination; but this cannot mean that our imagination is what makes God known. Yet this latter view is precisely the view of Kaufman and McFague who both fall into pantheism and

---

[45] Hilary, *Trinity*, Book III, 26, at 70.

[46] Johnson, *She Who Is*, 45.

[47] See Anne E. Carr, *Transforming Grace: Christian Tradition and Women's Experience* (San Francisco: Harper & Row, 1988), 141: 'the father symbol . . . must be relativized by the use of many other images for God'. Hence 'The use of many images more clearly affirms the fully transcendent and incomprehensible reality of God' (143). Like Elizabeth Johnson, Carr sees the experience of women as a source for theology (145) and mistakenly believes that when Christians refer to God as Father they believe God is male (136ff.).

[48] Johnson, *She Who Is*, 45.

both explicitly deny the deity of Christ in order to affirm their imaginative views of God, Christ and salvation.[49]

Here Johnson follows Tillich's view that symbols point beyond themselves to something else in which they participate. Symbols open depths of our own being and grow from a 'collective unconscious'. They live and die based on their ability 'to bear the presence of the divine in changing cultural situations'.[50] Today she says we have reached the crossroads of dying and rising religious symbols and can see that the 'patriarchal idol is cracking' while female symbols for the divine are emerging. Thus she suggests that the historical reality of women should function as a symbol for the mystery of God. They are to be seen as channels for speaking about God. Johnson resists addressing this situation by adding feminine qualities to God or by finding a feminine dimension in God. Such approaches, she says, might only reinforce the patriarchalism that she wishes to overcome. Instead she will speak of God using female, male and cosmic reality as divine symbols! Her basic point is that if women are created in God's image then 'God can be spoken in female metaphors in as full and as limited a way as God is imaged in male ones'.[51]

Experience as a Source and Norm for Theology

The major problem with this reasoning, however, is the simple methodological fact that it uses human experience, in particular the experience of women, as its source and norm for theology. From revelation, however, we know that the only proper norm for theology is God himself, since God can be known only through God. As Hilary of Poitiers declared, if we are to understand God, we must take our 'stand upon the sure ground . . . of God [we] must not measure the Divine nature by the limitations of [our] own, but gauge God's assertions concerning Himself by the scale of His own glorious self-revelation . . . He Whom we can only know through His own utterances is the

---

[49] See, e.g., *IFM*, 320: 'we were created by cosmic evolutionary and historical processes on which we depend absolutely for our being'. Regarding Christ, Kaufman argues against the idea that Jesus is unique as the 'only begotten son of God' stating that such thinking represents false reification (*IFM*, 390–3). As noted above, Sallie McFague maintains both that God needs the world as 'offspring, beloved, and companion' (pantheism) and denies Jesus' uniqueness by asserting that 'Jesus is not ontologically different from other paradigmatic figures either in our tradition or in other religious traditions.'

[50] Johnson, *She Who Is*, 46.

[51] Johnson, *She Who Is*, 54.

fitting witness concerning Himself'.[52] Of course Karl Barth and Thomas F. Torrance have fundamentally taken over this patristic insight. And it is an indispensable insight for fruitful theological investigation because it begins with the acknowledgment that theology can only take place as faith seeking understanding, that is, the object of faith, God himself, promises to lead those who accept his Word to a true knowledge of himself and his purposes for creation. Thus if our knowledge of God is not grounded in the very being and action of God himself – and consequently in his Word and Spirit – then it is in fact nothing more than our own religious or irreligious speculation grounded in our self-experience. Thinking thus, from a center in God rather than from a center in ourselves yields a very different method and very different conclusions in this matter. This is where contemporary trinitarian theology has something to contribute. As Karl Rahner rightly indicated, trinitarian theology detached from an experience of Christ and the Spirit can easily lead to wild conceptual acrobatics.[53] Yet it would be disastrous for anyone to assume that experience of the self should be the condition for the possibility of experiencing and knowing God or that such experience should be seen as a source or ground for theology. Any such assumption means that, methodologically, one has begun to think theologically from a center in oneself rather than from a center in God; this unfortunately is the legacy of Rahner's transcendental method.[54]

We cannot rehearse the entirety of Rahner's transcendental method here. But we can point out several key ingredients that are picked up and used by Elizabeth Johnson and which lead to her basic view of theology.[55] First, she argues that among possible historical mediations

---

[52] Hilary, *Trinity*, Book I, 18, 19, at 45.

[53] Rahner, *Trinity*, 48.

[54] See Chapter Four below for a discussion of how Rahner's method affects his trinitarian theology. See also Chapter Five below for an exploration of how the theology of Ted Peters is shaped by this method. It is exactly because Ted Peters thinks about the Trinity on the basis of an experience of the beyond and intimate that he finally compromises God's freedom *in se* and *ad extra*.

[55] Francis Martin, *The Feminist Question: Feminist Theology in the Light of Christian Tradition* (Grand Rapids, MI: Eerdmans, 1994), notes that Rahner would most likely not acknowledge Johnson's conclusions drawn from his chapter 'Experience of Self and Experience of God' in his *Theological Investigations*, Vol. 13. Still, Martin believes that Rahner 'must take some responsibility for them. Rahner's transcendentalist foundationalism easily elides from a description of an unthematic experience and its correlate . . . to a quite thematic experience that also finds its correlate in God and his plan of salvation . . . his identification of the necessary background of all thought with being, and then this being with God, neglects a fundamental biblical teaching, namely that God, as creator, is not to be identitifed with the constructs or demands of the structure of the thinking subject', 181.

of encounter with God, 'the experience of oneself has a unique importance'.[56] Second, she believes that Rahner's theological investigation of
the unity between the self and the symbol God sheds light on the way
forward regarding women's experience today. Since we are 'spirit in the
world' an experience of radical questioning and the possibility of free
and responsible action before a constantly receding horizon shows that
humans 'are dynamically oriented toward fathomless mystery as the
very condition for the possibility of acting in characteristic human
ways'.[57] Thus she contends that, in their most personal actions, human
beings display 'an openness toward infinite mystery' as the basis of
their existence, and so they are 'dynamically structured toward God'.[58]
Third, she believes that the experience of God is primordially mediated
'through the changing history of oneself'. God cannot be experienced
directly but 'as the ultimate depth and radical essence of every personal
experience such as love, fidelity, loneliness, and death'. In fact our own
mystery arises in these 'prethematic' experiences and so we thus
experience 'and are grasped by the holy mystery of God as the very
context of our own self-presence. In fact the silent, nonverbal encounter
with infinite mystery constitutes the enabling condition of any
experience of self at all'.[59] Fourth, since the connection between one's
self-experience and the experience of 'holy mystery' is intrinsic in this
way, it follows that if one experience changes, so does the other. Any
personal development will mean development in the experience of God,
while any diminishment of personal identity represents a loss of
experience of God. These can be seen accordingly as 'two aspects of
one and the same history of experience . . . Each mutually conditions
the other'.[60] Fifth, when a person thus has new experiences of freedom
or accepts oneself, this evokes a change in the experience of God. Also
when one rejects an idol, sees some truth about God or transcends
particulars to reach 'toward unfathomable mystery', these experiences
of God belong to one's self-experience. Following Rahner then, Johnson
sums up: 'the personal history of the experience of the self is in its total
extent the history of the ultimate experience of God also'.[61]

While Johnson notes that Rahner's individualism has been criticized
by Metz and others, it is clear that she takes his basic method as

---

[56] Johnson, *She Who Is*, 56.
[57] Johnson, *She Who Is*, 65.
[58] Johnson, *She Who Is*, 65.
[59] Johnson, *She Who Is*, 65.
[60] Johnson, *She Who Is*, 65–6.
[61] Johnson, *She Who Is*, 66.

foundational: self-experience illuminates who God is and indeed the two are mutually conditioning factors. Furthermore, she accepts Rahner's basic conception of God as the 'holy mystery' or the silent term of the experience of transcendence, which everyone experiences in the experiences of love, freedom, loneliness and death.[62] And so she contends that it is in this 'deeply personal-and-religious dimension that women are caught up in new experiences, which when articulated move toward new speaking about God'. As women have new experiences of liberation from male domination, she believes God is being experienced in new ways.

> Through women's encounter with the holy mystery of their own selves as blessed comes commensurate language about holy mystery in female metaphor and symbol, gracefully, powerfully, necessarily . . . speaking about God and self-interpretation cannot be separated. To give but one example, conversion experienced not as giving up oneself but as tapping into the power of oneself simultaneously releases understanding of divine power not as dominating power-over but as the passionate ability to empower oneself and others . . . in the ontological naming and affirming of ourselves we are engaged in a dynamic reaching out to the mystery of God . . .[63]

Clearly, Johnson has not only redefined who God is, but has done so from a center in herself, and so unfortunately calls into question the ultimate authority and freedom of God, of scripture and finally of Christ himself. In her thinking, conversion no longer means accepting God as he exists self-sufficiently and as one who loves us in freedom and by grace. Rather, conversion means self-acceptance. In classical theology, she believes, sin was understood as pride because it was described from the perspective of the ruling male. But today, she contends, sin cannot be seen as pride because, for those whose sense of self has been devalued or those who have been excluded from 'self-definition' by a dominant group, pride is not a pitfall. For these persons any suggestion of turning from self-love or losing oneself functions ideologically to 'rob them of power' and to keep them subordinate. Thus we are told that women's basic temptation is not to pride but to the lack of it! This is why God must be named in female categories today – this is the female call to conversion or to empowerment, according to Johnson.

[62] We will explore the problem with this assumption by Rahner in detail in Chapter Four below.
[63] Johnson, *She Who Is*, 66–7.

One extremely important point, however, is completely overlooked in this analysis. And that is, whether we like it or not, whether we are male or female, whether we have a good sense of self or a poor one, God remains who he is and sin remains the failure to accept God as immeasurably superior to ourselves; sin remains the failure to acknowledge that it is by grace that we are saved and so we cannot in any sense equate self-experience or self-acceptance with experience of God or acceptance of God. By what right can anyone change the definition of sin or of salvation, unless they strip the terms of their theological meaning and invest them solely with a sociological or psychological meaning? Amazingly, those today who would insist that the traditional understanding of sin as pride does not apply to women, because they have been excluded from power and need to take that power back, have in fact shown by their own analysis that the original sin remains pride. For, while it is important to assist people whose sense of self has been devalued, and while it is important to recognize that women should not be dominated or subjected to patriarchal ideology (or any other kind), any appeal to pride in order to solve these difficulties will only make matters worse. Relying on pride to overcome false domination by others will lead one to conclude that it was exactly through one's own self-reliance that a person must overcome such false domination in the first place. Almost without noticing it, then, theological language comes to be used simply to empower women and others who have been falsely dominated, so that they can and must free *themselves* from this enslavement.

But it matters how one is set free. If I can free myself, then I am indeed self-reliant and even God cannot contradict my aims, goals and methods for achieving self-reliance. That is to say God is a symbol that I create and recreate in order to achieve a desired social, political and religious end. On the other hand, if God frees me from false domination, then it is an act of grace that claims me for God's service in such a way that I know that God is other than myself as my creator, savior and lord – one who can be and is my helper and friend, but not on my terms. I then know that God is not some vague and indescribable mystery that can be experienced in experiencing love, freedom and death. Yes, these are experiences that raise questions about existence and ultimately questions about the existence and nature of God. But in order to answer these questions, it is necessary to think from a center in God rather than from a center in myself. And that is precisely the problem of sin. Without the grace of God revealed and active in Jesus Christ and his Holy Spirit, it is impossible to think from a center in

God. Sin means the attempt to commandeer God to the service of my agenda rather than allowing God the freedom to create a new heart in me according to his own purposes and goals.

Agnosticism: Docetic and Pantheistic Implications

Before drawing this chapter to a conclusion, it is important to note that it is precisely Johnson's agnosticism, which is part and parcel of her method, that allows her to change the content of the trinitarian doctrine. This she does by advocating the kind of Docetic Christology that Karl Barth correctly rejected and that will be discussed in detail in the next chapter. It also allows her to change the meaning and content of the resurrection and of Christology itself. Hence she contends that 'Jesus in all his physical and spiritual historicity is raised into glory by the power of the Spirit. What this ringing affirmation precisely means is inconceivable.'[64] Indeed, in a manner not unlike that of Robert Jenson, and also closely allied to that of Gordon Kaufman, she argues that

> the biblical symbol Christ . . . cannot be restricted to the historical person of Jesus . . . but signifies all those who by drinking of the Spirit participate in the community of disciples. Christ is . . . a creation of the Spirit who is not limited by whether one is Jew or Greek . . . male or female . . . the body of the risen Christ becomes the body of the community.[65]

This confusion of Christ and the Church allows Johnson to argue in a way clearly indebted to the thought of Sallie McFague, that Jesus is named Christ in 'a paradigmatic way' but that 'multiple redemptive role models' are available to us! Her ultimate aim of course is to argue that Jesus' maleness must be reinterpreted in light of the 'whole Christ' so that '*Christa* and *Christus* alike' contribute to the Christian story by constituting Christ in his entirety.

Johnson actually believes that she escapes a Docetic interpretation of Jesus. But the fact is it is her unwillingness to accept the truth that the man Jesus from Nazareth is the Christ simply because he is, and not because we think he is an important redemptive role model, that leads her directly into Docetism. She substitutes *sophia* for the eternal Word to argue once more that

---

[64] Johnson, *She Who Is*, 163.
[65] Johnson, *She Who Is*, 162. Jenson's understanding of the Church as Christ's risen body will be discussed in Chapter Three.

> God is not male . . . feminist theological speech about Jesus the Wisdom
> of God shifts the focus of reflection off maleness and onto the whole
> theological significance of what transpires in the Christ event. Jesus . . .
> is confessed as Sophia incarnate, revelatory of the liberating graciousness
> of God imaged as female. Women . . . can freely represent Christ, being
> themselves, in the Spirit, other Christs.[66]

Clearly, Johnson believes that on the one hand God is imaged as male,
in spite of her stated recognition that this is not the case. Indeed she
really believes that in identifying Jesus as male and as logos 'a certain
leakage of Jesus' human maleness into the divine nature' takes place so
that 'maleness appears to be of the essence of the God made known in
Christ'.[67] On the other hand, she believes that by focusing attention on
the Christ event, understood from her feminist analysis of wisdom,
instead of on the man Jesus, she can image God as female. But the
point of this chapter has been to argue that a proper doctrine of the
Trinity begins and ends its reflections with Jesus Christ himself who
alone can enable us to think from a center in God and not from a
center within our male or female experience. This does not discount
our experience but simply acknowledges that the norm for theological
truth is and always remains God *alone*.

It is worth noting here that those theologians, Johnson included,
who use the feminine gender of Wisdom in Hebrew and Greek 'to
suggest something akin to a divine feminine apotheosis or hypostasis'
have ignored the fact that such passages 'should be read as examples of
Hebrew personification'.[68] Gender should not be confused with sex;
thus the mere fact that a word is feminine or masculine in gender does
not necessarily imply reference to an actual male or female being. Those
who elevate Sophia to a divine feminine are in fact 'in line with the
Gnostic heresy, as when Ptolomaeus declared that the "celestial mother
Sophia" bestowed the Logos upon Jesus at his baptism'.[69] Such thinking
also opens the door to polytheism. In addition, those who believe that
Sophia is in some sense divine basically repeat an Arian argument 'for
the subordination of Son to Father by interpreting Jesus Christ as the
incarnation not of God but of God's Wisdom'.[70]

---

[66] Johnson, *She Who Is*, 167.
[67] Johnson, *She Who Is*, 152.
[68] See Roland Frye, 'Language for God and Feminist Language', in Kimel (ed.), *Speaking the Christian God*, 34.
[69] Frye, 'Language for God', 35.
[70] Frye, 'Language for God', 36.

Furthermore, in feminist interpretation, simile and metaphor are often confused so that the occasional biblical comparisons of God's love to that of a mother 'are given the same force as if they were names or identifications'.[71] It is a fact that where God is called Father in scripture, metaphor and naming are used and these are grounded in God's revelation to us, that is, in his naming himself to us. Wherever God is compared to a mother, simile is used. What difference does this make? According to Roland Frye, simile 'states resemblance, while metaphor boldly transfers the representation'.[72] Similes are more restricted than metaphors. Thus, while the Lord is spoken of in scripture as a good shepherd (metaphor), in Isa. 42:13 it is said that 'The Lord goes forth like a mighty man' (simile) and again the Lord says 'now I will cry out like a woman in travail, I will gasp and pant' (simile).[73] God is not here identified as mother any more than God is identified as warrior. These similes are used in a very restricted sense and do not make the same claim to identify God as the metaphoric language of good shepherd or the language that speaks of God as Father and Son does. The upshot of all this is that it is important to recognize the scriptural use of language in order to avoid the kind of polytheism and Gnosticism that follows when it is thought that we can name God from our experiences, whether they be male or female. God is not named Mother in the Bible because God has revealed himself as the Father of Jesus Christ – not as a male, but as a unique Father of a unique Son, who is eternally begotten before all worlds. Revelation is not the projection of human experience into God, but the action of God naming himself to us and including us in a genuine relationship with himself by faith and grace. Therefore, as Elizabeth Achtemeier notes, while Israel was surrounded by people who 'worshiped female deities', the Israelites themselves worshiped one God who, unlike the religions of Israel's neighbors, could not be identified with creation: 'It is precisely the introduction of female language for God that opens the door to such identification of God with the world'.[74]

Finally, it is just because Johnson has failed to respect God's actual freedom for us in the history of the man Jesus of Nazareth and has instead substituted her abstract notion of liberation for Christ's atoning liberation that she reaches what can only be described as the gnostic

[71] Frye, 'Language for God', 34.
[72] Frye, 'Language for God', 37.
[73] Frye, 'Language for God', 39.
[74] Elizabeth Achtemeier, 'Exchanging God for "No Gods"', in Kimel (ed.), *Speaking the Christian God*, 8–9.

conclusion that women can represent Christ because they are in fact other Christs.[75] The truth of the gospel hinges on the fact that there never was and never will be another Christ than the one incarnate Son of God whose name was Jesus of Nazareth. This Christ represents himself in the power of the Holy Spirit. It is no wonder that Johnson's work, like that of LaCugna, is marked by a distinct tendency toward pantheism: Sophia is seen as becoming incarnate because 'Her essence . . . might well be called connectedness, for . . . she is a breath, an emanation . . . The power of relation built into wisdom metaphors comes to unique fruition in the doctrine of Jesus-Sophia, Sophia incarnate. Sophia is present in and with her envoy Jesus'.[76] Here it is obvious that the incarnation is no longer seen as a free act of grace but is conceptualized as a necessary relation dictated by the essence of wisdom with its connectedness and which emanates in and through Jesus, who is no longer the unique mediator, but is reduced to an envoy representing God's love that can be categorized in any one of a number of freely chosen metaphors.

Johnson even argues that 'Jesus' death was an act of violence brought about by threatened human men, as sin'.[77] The clear implication is that only men are implicated in Jesus' death. Are we to suppose that women are exempt from the sin that led to Jesus' death on the cross? The answer seems to be that we are, since Johnson claims that women

---

[75] Elaine Pagels, in her University Lecture in Religion at Arizona State University entitled 'The Gnostic Jesus and Early Christian Politics', 28 January, 1982, asserts that according to the gnostic Gospel of Thomas, Jesus says, '"when you come to know yourselves" (and discover the divine within you) then "you will recognize that it is *you* who are the sons of the living Father" – just like Jesus! . . . The Gospel of Philip makes the same point . . . you are to "become not a Christian, but a Christ".' From this she concludes that the Gospel of Thomas really intends to say that '"you, the reader, are the twin brother of Christ"; when you recognize the divine within you, then you come to see, as Thomas does, that you and Jesus are, so to speak, identical twins' (6). And of course if we are identical twins with Jesus we no longer need to rely on him but may instead rely on ourselves in typically gnostic fashion. As Pagels herself puts it, 'One who seeks to "become not a Christian, but a Christ" no longer looks to Jesus, as orthodox believers do, as the source of all truth' (7). Indeed Pagels argues that it was the Gnostics and not the orthodox Christians who named God mother and father precisely because their norm was not Jesus himself but their own self-consciousness. While Pagels approves of this misguided theology, Roland Frye makes plain why such gnostic thought is antithetical to the Gospel: 'Language for God', *SJT* 454ff. It is worth noting that Ludwig Feuerbach wrote that Christ is 'The consciousness of the species. We are all supposed to be one in Christ. Christ is the consciousness of our unity. Therefore, whoever loves man for the sake of man, whoever rises to the love of the species . . . is a Christ; he is Christ himself', Ludwig Feuerbach, *The Essence of Christianity*, trans. George Eliot, intro. by Karl Barth, foreword by H. Richard Niebuhr (New York: Harper Torchbooks, 1957), xviii.

[76] Johnson, *She Who Is*, 168–9.

[77] Johnson, *She Who Is*, 158.

disciples 'are the moving point of continuity between the ministry, death, burial, and resurrection of Jesus'.[78] What is so astonishing about this analysis is that (1) it divides humanity by separating men from women, and (2) it makes the Docetic claim that women are free of sin while men are the sinners. Tragically, this thinking misses the point of the atonement, which is that what was not assumed was not saved. All humanity is implicated in Christ's death – his rejection manifests the depth of human sin. But since he died for all (women as well as men), all are saved by him alone. Johnson's failure to acknowledge Jesus as the One Mediator clearly leads to a confused view of the atonement.

These christological errors are ultimately traceable to Johnson's own agnosticism, which roots the doctrine of the Trinity in experience. For her, analogy means that, based on the Christian experience of faith which 'is the generating matrix for language about God as triune', one can say, 'the Trinity is a legitimate but secondary concept that synthesizes the concrete experience of salvation in a "short formula"'.[79] Because the Trinity is not controlled from a center in God but from a center within the Christian experience of salvation, Johnson concludes that analogy points to the 'holy mystery'. Indeed this

> language is not a literal description of the inner being of God . . . It is a pointer to holy mystery . . . At rock bottom it is the language of hope. No one has ever seen God, but thanks to the experience unleashed through Jesus in the Spirit we hope . . . that it is the livingness of *God* who is with us in the suffering of history, and so we affirm that God's relation to the world is grounded in God's own being capable of such relation.[80]

Clearly, it is the experience of hope that provides the impetus for what Johnson has to say about the Trinity, and what she says is that we do not know God in his inner essence as Father, Son and Holy Spirit. Rather, God is holy mystery, which can go by many other names such

---

[78] Johnson, *She Who Is*, 159.

[79] Johnson, *She Who Is*, 198. See also *She Who Is*, 173. According to Johnson 'analogy . . . means that while it [human naming of God] starts from the relationship of paternity experienced at its best in this world, its inner dynamism negates the creaturely mode to assert that God is more unlike than like even the best human father'. Of course the analogy of faith starts from Jesus Christ, who encounters us and who alone can liberate us to speak of God in truth. Thus true knowledge of God not only begins and ends with Christ himself as attested in the New Testament but it never claims knowledge of God's fatherhood by negating our human experience of fatherhood. God is revealed as Father in an utterly unique way and is as such the key to understanding human fatherhood. It is never the other way around.

[80] Johnson, *She Who Is*, 201.

as Mother and not just by one name as Father, Son and Holy Spirit. Hence

> the symbol of the Trinity is not a blueprint of the inner workings of the godhead, not an offering of esoteric information about God. In no sense is it a literal description of God's being *in se*. As the outcome of theological reflection on the Christian experience of relationship to God, it is a symbol that indirectly points to God's relationality . . . God is *like* a Trinity . . .[81]

This abstract understanding of God is not at all grounded in the economic trinitarian self-revelation but is instead explicitly grounded in experience so that in the end it is the creature who defines the creator based on experiences of suffering within history. What makes this confusion possible and even necessary is Johnson's failure to distinguish the immanent and economic Trinity – more accurately what makes this confusion possible and necessary is her failure to acknowledge the immanent Trinity as the norm for truth. Instead, she substitutes the experience of salvation, which is supposedly unleashed by Jesus. Jesus, who is the Word incarnate, cannot really be the active subject in relation to us. Rather, he is seen as one messenger or one model among others that we use to try to achieve equality and liberation. Ultimately her agnosticism, like LaCugna's, leads to the dualist conclusion that Jesus is an envoy and not the very presence of God within history in his unique history and subsequently in and through the community of faith. It leads to the dualist conclusion that God is *like* a Trinity rather than the one who is one and three from all eternity. Finally, it leads to the dualist conclusion that holy mystery, which can be known in everyone's transcendental experience, but which, for that reason, cannot be equated with the immanent Trinity (which ultimately remains unknown and unknowable), is the true God and that any literal view of God as Father must therefore be an idol.

In fact, however, the point of this chapter has been to show that wherever and whenever trinitarian theology takes its bearings from a center in human experience and not from a center in God (through Christ himself) it necessarily leads to agnosticism, dualism and finally to pantheism. It cannot lead to true knowledge of the triune God, which can only come to us from God through his Word and Spirit. Naturally enough Johnson's concept of analogy is meant to suggest that calling God mother is not only appropriate but desirable. Yet the

---

[81] Johnson, *She Who Is*, 204–5.

unfortunate result of her failure to appreciate that only God can name God leads to the pantheist idea that, as mother and child have a relation of 'interdependence', so God's relation with creation is one of interdependence.[82] Hence, 'the mother image points to an intrinsic relatedness between God and the world as a loving relationality that belongs to the very essence of being a mother and never ends'.[83] Here relationality has become God while the eternal Father, Son and Holy Spirit has been relegated to the domain of freely chosen metaphor. It goes without saying that whenever God's relations with the world are thought to belong to his essence, then his creative function has absorbed his essence in typically Cartesian fashion. Pantheism always implies that God cannot exist without the world. Johnson's position clearly bears that out.

It is time that contemporary theologians faced this problem squarely. Theology needs to begin and end its task with Jesus Christ as the revelation of God in history. Any other starting point will mean a self-chosen one and thus one that stands in conflict with God's freedom for us exercised in Christ. This is where trinitarian theology is important. A theology of the Trinity recognizes who God is who meets us in Christ and then thinks about various contemporary issues and problems in light of the relation between creator and creatures reconciled by God in Christ. In this first chapter then we have seen how very important it is for theology to think from a center in God. No theology can provide that center for itself. This can only be received from God himself as grace. And thinking that takes place within faith finds that center in Jesus Christ himself, the Son of God. This chapter has shown that contemporary theologians who think about God as a symbol or as a freely chosen metaphor that we use to create a better world have simply missed the essential point about a contemporary doctrine of the immanent Trinity. The point is that, unless God is acknowledged at the outset as the one who alone creates, reconciles and redeems us, then we are left alone with ourselves, and any attempt to find freedom and truth are doomed to the agnostic conclusion that we never truly know God; we only image God in ways that seem appropriate to ourselves. In the next chapter we shall see how this problem arises and takes shape in Christology. And I will continue to suggest that the proper solution to this problem is a return to Jesus Christ himself as the starting point and norm for theology.

---

[82] Johnson, *She Who Is*, 178–9.
[83] Johnson, *She Who Is*, 185.

Chapter Two

Christology and the Trinity: Some Dogmatic Implications of Barth's Rejection of Ebionite and Docetic Christology

ONE of the most vexatious aspects of contemporary Christology is the fact that so many theologians do not begin where Karl Barth began and in so doing miss the importance of distinguishing the immanent and economic Trinity. Hence they end by trying to build a Christology on a historically or idealistically reconstructed Jesus whose uniqueness is more a creation of the community than a reality whose genuine recognition rests upon a simple acknowledgment of his lordship. Barth's starting point for thinking about the person and work of Jesus Christ was, as is well known, the simple fact of Jesus Christ himself who was the Son of God by virtue of his unique relation to the Father. This may sound like a simple or even simplistic point. But it is in fact loaded, because by this statement Barth was not only trying to say that thinking must be determined by the unique object being considered, but he was also asserting that accurate thinking about revelation (and thus about Jesus Christ) could begin neither with our ideas nor with our experiences.[1] At bottom, revelation was not the disclosure of something hidden within history, but the disclosure of God himself who had entered history from outside. Beginning with ideas would lead to what he labeled Docetic Christology, while beginning with experience would lead to what he called Ebionite Christology. In both instances confession of Jesus' deity would be no more and no less

[1] *CD* I/2, 20.

than confession of the power of human ideas or the power of human experience. Such starting points therefore would necessarily deny the content of Christian confession at the outset. They would deny the fact that Jesus is the Son of God, independently of what we may think and independently of our experiences, beliefs or feelings. Ultimately what was at stake for Barth was the difference between genuine Christian insight and a kind of Feuerbachian reversal of divine and human predicates. In the last chapter we saw that this predicament is still a lively issue, because much contemporary Christology and trinitarian theology begins from experience and not from Jesus Christ himself. It should be noted that Barth's starting point does not simply reject or annul human experience and self-determination in some Christo-monistic sense. It merely means that the unique object that determines our thinking is and always remains God, the Father of Jesus Christ, who meets us in and through our experiences in the power of the Holy Spirit, without becoming identical with them or dependent upon them; this God claims our obedience.[2]

Some of the dogmatic implications of Barth's rejection of Ebionite and Docetic Christology and for his concern to distinguish the immanent and economic Trinity then are: (1) Christology must begin with Jesus Christ himself as attested in the New Testament. Any other starting point will necessarily distort who Jesus was and is, precisely because God has indeed exercised his freedom to be for us in Christ and not in some other way. (2) Failure to recognize Jesus' true deity means failure to recognize God as he really is for us. Thus, recognition of Jesus' true deity means acknowledging his antecedent existence as the eternally begotten Son of the Father, and so it has trinitarian implications and suggests an important distinction between the immanent and economic Trinity. (3) Jesus' humanity as such does not reveal because he is veiled in his revelation and thus he causes offense. Revelation thus means the unveiling of what is by nature veiled and it is identical with the power of the resurrection. This means it must be understood as an *exception* and as a *miracle*. (4) Recognition of Jesus' deity is an analytic and not a synthetic statement. Therefore, Jesus' uniqueness is in no way dependent upon the community's recognition of him to be true and valid. And because this is so, there can be no confusion of Christ and Christians and no suggestion of adoptionism or subordinationism in Christology or in trinitarian reflection. Any

---

[2] See *CD* I/1, 198ff.

such suggestion once more implies the reversal of divine and human being and action and thus the collapse of theology into anthropology.

Situating the Question

To focus the issues here, consider, for example, where Jürgen Moltmann begins his Christology in *The Way of Jesus Christ*. He begins his 'pneumatological christology' with the community's experience of discipleship and argues against the traditional christologies on the basis of 'Christo-praxis' or what he calls a 'doxological' Christology, which he says is the 'source from which christology springs'.[3] A doxological Christology is grounded in 'the experience of men and women who follow Christ'.[4] Moltmann's self-stated goal is to overcome traditional metaphysical and more modern anthropological errors. His Christology therefore marks a transition from the metaphysical to the historical and finally to the postmodern type 'which places human history ecologically in the framework of nature'.[5] In other words, he intends to criticize Karl Rahner's Christology as a form of what he calls 'Jesuology' and he intends to criticize Karl Barth's Christology as a metaphysical one that 'de-historicizes' the events of Christ's life while locating his own Christology in a 'cosmological perspective' that 'integrates human history in the natural conditions in which it is embedded'.[6] Some very odd conclusions follow from this. I will just mention two of them.

First, Moltmann argues that 'Jesus *is* the Lord because God *has raised* him from the dead. His *existence* as the Lord is to be found in God's eschatological *act* in him, which we call raising from the dead.'[7] This thinking is of course echoed in the reasoning of very many prominent contemporary theologians among whom are Wolfhart Pannenberg and Robert Jenson. And the most unfortunate part of this thinking concerns the fact that it does not begin with the simple fact that Jesus is the Lord simply because he *is*. Thus it negates his antecedent existence as the pre-existent Word which is so critically important for a proper trinitarian understanding of divine–human relations. It is interesting to note, as we will see shortly in more detail, that Barth's rejection of Ebionite and

[3] Jürgen Moltmann, *The Way of Jesus Christ: Christology in Messianic Dimensions* (hereafter: *The Way*), trans. Margaret Kohl (San Francisco: HarperSanFrancisco, 1990), 41. For analysis and critique, see Paul D. Molnar, 'Moltmann's Post-Modern Messianic Christology: A Review Discussion', *The Thomist* 56.4 (October 1992), 669–93.

[4] Moltmann, *The Way*, xiv.
[5] Moltmann, *The Way*, xvi.
[6] Moltmann, *The Way*, xvi.
[7] Moltmann, *The Way*, 40.

Docetic Christology led him to argue that 'The resurrection can give nothing new to Him who is the eternal Word of the Father; but it makes visible what is proper to Him, His glory.'[8] And in connection with his trinitarian theology Barth insisted that

> we have to accept the simple presupposition on which the New Testament statement rests, namely, that Jesus Christ is the Son because He is (not because He makes this impression on us, not because He does what we think is to be expected of a God, but because He is). With this presupposition all thinking about Jesus, which means at once all thinking about God, must begin and end.[9]

It is also interesting to note the importance of the hiddenness of revelation. Jesus' being as the Word incarnate meant that as the Word he was completely hidden[10] to those who met the man Jesus and to us, and indeed he was an offense to those who encountered him, as he is to us. For Barth, nothing could be more hidden than revelation, and we must be offended at it precisely because it is something completely new and contrary to what would normally be acceptable to our thinking and experience.[11] As we shall see, it is this offending element in revelation that theologians like Karl Rahner have obviated with their attempts to find an a priori way of approaching the study of Christology.

Second, Moltmann's own understanding of Jesus' pre-existence and resurrection is flawed. He argues that, in their mutual experience, the child Jesus and Abba 'discover themselves . . . In his relationship to Jesus, God becomes "Abba" . . . this mutual relationship is constitutive for both persons and precedes the history they share'.[12] From this it follows that 'Jesus' personhood does not exist in isolation, *per se*; nor is it determined and fixed from eternity. It acquires its form in living relationships and reciprocities'.[13] Hence

> The divine power of healing does not come from his side alone . . . The healings are stories about faith just as much as they are stories about Jesus. They are stories about the reciprocal relationships between Jesus and the faith of men and women. *Jesus is dependent on this faith*, just as the sick are dependent on the power that emanates from Jesus.[14]

---

[8] *CD* I/2, 111.
[9] *CD* I/1, 415.
[10] Cf. *CD* I/2, 41–4.
[11] Cf. *CD* I/2, 61.
[12] Moltmann, *The Way*, 143.
[13] Moltmann, *The Way*, 136.
[14] Moltmann, *The Way*, 111–12, emphasis mine.

In connection with the resurrection, Moltmann reached the Docetic conclusion that 'Resurrection means not a *factum* but a *fieri* – not what was once done, but what is in the making: the transition from death to life.'[15] This, because

> The early Christian faith in the resurrection was not based solely on Christ's appearances. It was just as strongly motivated . . . by the experience of God's Spirit . . . Believing in Christ's resurrection therefore does not mean affirming a fact. It means being possessed by the life-giving Spirit . . .[16]

What is actually described by resurrection language then is not really an event in the life of Jesus that is independent of the disciples' faith and our faith. Rather it is something grounded in 'visionary phenomena' which have as their foundation the 'inner experience' of those who had them. Thus the controlling factor here for Moltmann is not Jesus, risen bodily from the dead, but the fact that 'The "seeing" of the risen Christ became faith.'[17] And it is just this Ebionite explanation of the resurrection and Moltmann's Docetic conclusions that are at odds with Barth's emphasis on the importance of Jesus' bodily resurrection as the factor that gives meaning to faith without becoming dependent upon faith. Far from de-historicizing the events of Christ's life, as Moltmann believed, Barth decisively maintained the historicity of the resurrection as an event in Jesus' life that could be as little proven from history as the event of revelation could. As we will see below, it is Moltmann's panentheism, which starts from experience and reconstructs theology in process terms, that cannot allow for an 'an immanent Trinity in which God is simply by himself, without the love which communicates salvation'.[18] Thus, Moltmann must 'surrender the traditional distinction between the immanent and the economic Trinity', and affirm

> Rahner's thesis that 'the economic Trinity *is* the immanent Trinity, and vice versa' . . . The thesis about the fundamental *identity* of the immanent and the economic Trinity of course remains open to misunderstanding as long as we cling to the distinction at all . . . The economic Trinity not only reveals the immanent Trinity; it also has a retroactive effect on it.[19]

---

[15] Moltmann, *The Way*, 241.

[16] Moltmann, *The Way*, 218.

[17] Moltmann, *The Way*, 218.

[18] Jürgen Moltmann, *The Trinity and the Kingdom: The Doctrine of God* (hereafter: *Trinity and Kingdom*), trans. Margaret Kohl (New York: Harper & Row, 1981), 151.

[19] Moltmann, *Trinity and Kingdom*, 160.

This thinking opens the door to the mutually conditioned relationship Moltmann sees between Jesus and those he heals. As we shall see, Moltmann uncritically enlists the principle of mutual conditioning and eliminates any need to conceptualize a God truly independent of creatures.[20] Any real notion of lordship applying to God's love revealed in Christ is simply reinterpreted by the experience of suffering, drawing God into the vicissitudes of creation itself.[21]

Karl Barth was able to avoid these and other difficulties simply because his starting point for Christology was Jesus Christ himself: 'The explanation of their [Palestinian Jews of Jesus' time] statement that Jesus is Lord is to be sought only in the fact that for them He was the Lord, and was so in the same factual and self-evident and indisputable way as Yahweh was of old Israel's God.'[22] What led Barth to this conclusion? It was his consideration of 'God the Son' in § 2 of *CD* I/1 where he wrote, 'The one God reveals Himself according to Scripture as the Reconciler . . . As such He is the Son of God who has come to us or the Word of God that has been spoken to us, because He is so antecedently in Himself as the Son or Word of God the Father.'[23] It is in this part of his trinitarian theology that Barth first discusses Ebionite and Docetic Christology as ways of thinking that are excluded by the simple fact of revelation, namely, by the fact that Jesus Christ is truly God and truly human at the same time.[24]

In *CD* I/1, Barth begins by noting that 'What God reveals in Jesus and how He reveals it, namely, in Jesus, must not be separated from one another according to the New Testament'.[25] Without denying Jesus' distinction from the Father, Barth then considers 'the unity of the Son with the Father attested . . . and therefore the deity of Jesus Christ . . . as definitive, authentic and essential'.[26] For this reason, and

---

[20] Moltmann, *Trinity and Kingdom*, 4, 32ff., 38ff. and Jürgen Moltmann, *God in Creation: A New Theology of Creation and the Spirit of God* (hereafter: *Creation*), trans. Margaret Kohl (New York: Harper & Row, 1985), 13ff., 86–9, 101ff. and 204ff.

[21] For Barth, God was deeply affected by creatures but not *because* of any mutually conditioning relationship between himself and another. See, e.g., *CD* II/1, 307ff., 312, 496, and esp. 510–11.

[22] *CD* I/1, 405.

[23] *CD* I/1, 399.

[24] Of course without using the designations Ebionite and Docetic Christology, similar thinking already appears in *The Göttingen Dogmatics*. See Karl Barth, *The Göttingen Dogmatics: Instruction in the Christian Religion*, Vol. 1, ed. Hannelotte Reiffen, trans. Geoffrey W. Bromiley (hereafter: *The Göttingen Dogmatics*) (Grand Rapids, MI: Eerdmans, 1991), 115–16.

[25] *CD* I/1, 399.

[26] *CD* I/1, 400.

unlike Bultmann in his book *Jesus*, Barth insists that we cannot understand the Jesus of the New Testament one-sidedly by focusing only on his sayings and excluding his miraculous actions. Both must be seen together as is evidenced in Mk 2:1–12 in the story of the paralytic. If the two are seen together, then Jesus will be acknowledged in his essential and authentic deity as the eternally begotten Son of the Father. Thus, for Barth,

> The New Testament statement about the unity of the Son with the Father, that is, the deity of Christ, cannot possibly be understood in terms of the presupposition that the original view and declaration of the New Testament witnesses was that a human being was either exalted as such to deity or appeared among us as the personification and symbol of a divine being.[27]

This statement is a direct rejection of the manner in which M. Dibelius formulated the problem of New Testament Christology, that is, 'as the way in which "knowledge of the historical figure of Jesus was so quickly transformed into faith in a heavenly Son of God"'.[28] Barth rejects this thinking because it leads to a blind alley; it leads to modern historical versions of what he calls Ebionite and Docetic Christology.

And it may be noted that John Macquarrie, in his book *Jesus Christ in Modern Thought*, echoes the very perspective that Barth here rejects when he claims to find, following J. D. G. Dunn, 'a unifying idea amid the diversity of the New Testament, an idea which he [Dunn] expresses as the conviction that the historical figure, Jesus the Jew, becomes an "exalted being"'.[29] Interestingly, it is just this thinking that leads Macquarrie to argue that the term Christ should not be restricted to the man Jesus of Nazareth, but should instead describe the Christ-event, that is, 'Jesus and the community as together embraced in the Christ-event'. Thus, for Macquarrie 'there is no sharp dividing line between Jesus and the community'.[30] The Christ-event refers to 'something larger than the career of Jesus of Nazareth. In that larger reality there were joined inseparably the career of Jesus and its impact on the believing community'.[31] This is of a piece with his belief that

[27] *CD* I/1, 402.

[28] *CD* I/1, 402.

[29] John Macquarrie, *Jesus Christ in Modern Thought* (hereafter: *Jesus Christ*) (Philadelphia: Trinity Press International, 1990), 12.

[30] Macquarrie, *Jesus Christ*, 21.

[31] Macquarrie, *Jesus Christ*, 20.

there are 'two sources for the knowledge of Jesus Christ – the testimony of the past and the experience of the present'.[32]

All of this thinking steadfastly refuses to begin from Jesus Christ who was the Son of God. And the result is a form of Ebionite Christology that sees the relation between Jesus and the community as one that is mutually conditioned.[33] Indeed it leads exactly to the notion that it is an idea rather than Jesus himself that unifies the New Testament. Strangely, while Macquarrie mistakenly criticizes Barth for being unhistorical in his Christology, it is this very thinking that fails to respect the fact that it is precisely Jesus the man from Nazareth who is the Christ and so is itself quite unhistorical and thus Docetic in the end.

Moreover, this thinking leads Macquarrie to argue that the resurrection 'is one element in that potentiality for being that was given to the human race as created in the image and likeness of God'.[34] Instead of seeing that the resurrection is the miraculous power of divine action itself which unveils the true meaning of Jesus as the incarnate Word, Macquarrie believes that 'Those whose lives had been deeply influenced by Jesus spoke of a "resurrection"',[35] and that to assert that Jesus is risen does not 'mean an actual rising from the dead' in a historical sense. Rather the historical event is 'the rise of the Christian church ... considered as part of the Christ-event and not only something in the career of Jesus'.[36] What then is the historical fact that empowers the Church to be the body of Christ? According to Macquarrie 'There is a solid historical fact here, namely, that the birth of the church depended on the belief of the disciples that Jesus had been resurrected.' Thus only 'a belief in the resurrection provides anything like a sufficient reason for the rise of Christianity after the death of Jesus'.[37] But does Macquarrie believe that Jesus rose bodily from the dead or not? According to Macquarrie 'what is resurrected is not the dead body that has been laid in the grave' because he believes that this would lead to the idea that resurrection was only the resuscitation of a corpse. Hence Macquarrie suggests that 'Perhaps resurrection is transcendence to a new level in the being of the human person, a level which eludes our understanding so long as we are seeing it only from below.' And because he follows a trend also evident in the thought of Karl Rahner

---

[32] Macquarrie, *Jesus Christ*, 6.
[33] Macquarrie, *Jesus Christ*, 22–3.
[34] Macquarrie, *Jesus Christ*, 66.
[35] Macquarrie, *Jesus Christ*, 5.
[36] Macquarrie, *Jesus Christ*, 406.
[37] Macquarrie, *Jesus Christ*, 406.

to explain reality through the concept of self-transcendence, he insists that we are not restricted 'to these visionary experiences recorded in the New Testament'.[38]

Here it is clear that it is not and cannot be Jesus himself risen bodily from the dead who gives meaning to the faith of the Church. He has instead been absorbed into the faith of the Church under the idea of the Christ-event. And this just misses the main point that Barth correctly insisted upon, that is, that the power of the resurrection is identical with the power of the Word and Spirit evident in Jesus' life from Christmas to Good Friday to Easter and beyond; a power over which we have no conceptual, existential or ontological control.

Ebionite Christology

What then is Barth rejecting and affirming here with his opinion about M. Dibelius, whose views, as we have just seen, are alive and well in the theology of John Macquarrie? He rejects any suggestion that Christ's deity can be 'taken individualistically as the apotheosis of a man' whose effect on others led to 'the impression and idea that He was a God'.[39] Barth is here repudiating all forms of adoptionism and all notions that a hero figure (Jesus included) could be 'idealised upwards as God . . . This is Ebionite Christology, or Christology historically reconstructed along the lines of Ebionitism.'[40] There are then at least two problems that Barth identifies here for us.

First, reading the New Testament or the dogmatic tradition with the assumption that we first know Jesus as a historical figure and then, supposedly like the disciples, we believe in him as Son of God suggests that his deity is grounded in and results from the experience (the response) of the community of faith.[41] In *CD* I/2, more light is shed on this when Barth says, 'As Docetism starts from a human conception to which it logically returns in due course, so does Ebionitism start from a human experience and impression of the heroic personality of Jesus of Nazareth. On the basis of this impression and experience, divinity is ascribed to this man.'[42] Barth never ceased to emphasize this fact in all his dogmatic reflections. Hence, in the doctrine of reconciliation, when Barth considered the important topic of human vocation he insisted

---

[38] Macquarrie, *Jesus Christ*, 408–9.
[39] *CD* I/1, 402.
[40] *CD* I/1, 403.
[41] Thomas F. Torrance makes a similar point in *Preaching Christ Today: The Gospel and Scientific Thinking* (Grand Rapids, MI: Eerdmans, 1994), 8ff.
[42] *CD* I/2, 20.

that 'we must maintain at all costs that the living Jesus Christ is the subject acting in it [vocation] here and now in the allotted time of the lives of specific men . . . [instead of speaking] more or less abstractly of the structure of the experience of the man who is called. To be realistic at this point, we must speak quite concretely and unequivocally of Jesus Christ Himself.'[43] Interestingly, Barth goes on to note that the Holy Spirit must not be seen as in any sense independent of Christ but as 'His Spirit, as the power of His presence, work and Word' if we are to speak properly of vocation.

In fact, it is not too much to say that all Barth's thinking about Christology and trinitarian theology is unmistakably structured by his positive and negative assertions developed in relation to the categories Ebionite and Docetic Christology both in *CD* I/1 and I/2. As we shall see, the resurrection plays a decisive role in Barth's understanding of revelation and reconciliation. And his view of the resurrection stands in stark contrast to the views of Moltmann, Pannenberg, Jenson, Rahner and others. While Barth insists that the resurrection discloses who Jesus was and is as the Son of God, these theologians and others argue, in different ways, that the resurrection to some extent constitutes his being as the eternal Son.

Second, such Ebionite thinking is individualistic and adoptionistic and thus further suggests that Jesus was not the eternally begotten Son of the Father but had to become this by virtue of his ministry, the effect he had on others or by God's adopting him as his Son either at his birth, transfiguration or at his resurrection.[44] This is certainly a major problem in contemporary Christology. Thus, while Barth is extremely clear that we must be precise in emphasizing Christ's centrality and uniqueness in accordance with the precision of Chalcedon, Wolfhart Pannenberg is notably vague and positively ambiguous when he says that Jesus' eternal sonship

> precedes his historical existence on earth and must be regarded as the creative basis of his human existence. If the human history of Jesus is the revelation of his eternal sonship, we must be able to perceive the latter in the reality of the human life. The deity is not an addition to this reality. It is the reflection that the human relation of Jesus to God the Father casts on his existence, even as it also illumines the eternal being of God.[45]

---

[43] *CD* IV/3, 502.

[44] *CD* I/1, 402–3.

[45] Wolfhart Pannenberg, *Systematic Theology Volume 2* (hereafter: *Systematic Theology 2*), trans. Geoffrey W. Bromiley (Grand Rapids, MI: Eerdmans, 1994), 325. Chapter 10 concerns the deity of Christ.

Thus for Pannenberg, 'Apart from Jesus' resurrection, it would not be true that from the very beginning of his earthly way God was one with this man. That is true from all eternity *because* of Jesus' resurrection.'[46] It is not surprising that Barth's own reaction to Pannenberg's *Jesus – God and Man* was one of horror.[47] Pannenberg continues to insist that 'Only the Easter event determines what the meaning was of the pre-Easter history of Jesus and who he was in his relation to God.'[48] By contrast of course Barth held that in the resurrection 'the man Jesus appeared to them . . . in the mode of God . . . He had always been present among them in His deity'.[49]

And Pannenberg is not alone. According to Robert Jenson, '"the Son" in trinitarian use [does not] first denote a simply divine entity. Primally, it denotes the claim Jesus makes for himself in addressing God as Father . . . this Son is an eternally divine Son only in and by this relation.'[50] Obviously if Jesus is only the eternal Son in and by this relation, then his antecedent existence, which alone gives meaning to his historical existence is compromised. Barth very clearly countered this kind of thinking when he wrote that

> 'Begotten of the Father before all time' means that He did not come into being in time as such . . . That the Son of God becomes man and that He is known by other men in His humanity as the Son of God are events, even if absolutely distinctive events, in time . . . *But their distinction does not itself derive or come from time* . . . because the power of God's immanence is here the power of His transcendence, their subject must be understood as being before all time, as the eternal Subject . . .'[51]

---

[46] Wolfhart Pannenberg, *Jesus – God and Man*, trans. Lewis L. Wilkins and Duane A. Priebe (Philadelphia: Westminster Press, 1977), 321, emphasis mine.

[47] *Karl Barth Letters 1961–1968*, ed. Jürgen Fangmeier and Hinrich Stoevesandt, trans. and ed. by Geoffrey W. Bromiley (Grand Rapids: Eerdmans, 1981), 178. Barth wrote to Pannenberg: 'My first reaction on reading your book was one of horror when . . . I found you rejecting M. Kähler in a way which led me to suspect that, like others, you . . . intended to pursue a path from below to above . . . Is not this to build a house on the sand – the shifting sand of historical probabilities . . . *In its positive content is your christology – after the practice of so many modern fathers – anything other than the outstanding example and symbol of a presupposed general anthropology, cosmology, and ontology?*' emphasis mine.

[48] Pannenberg, *Systematic Theology 2*, 345.

[49] *CD* III/2, 448; cf. also 451.

[50] Robert W. Jenson, *Systematic Theology Volume I: The Triune God* (hereafter: *ST1*) (New York: Oxford University Press, 1997), 77.

[51] *CD* I/1, 426–7, emphasis mine.

Docetic Christology

Here it is important to note that in Barth's thinking Ebionitism does not stand on its own but is closely related to what he labels Docetism: 'There was and is a counterpart and extension of Docetism in the shape of an equally arbitrary Christology of Ebionitism.'[52] From another point of view, then, one could take the New Testament statement of Jesus' deity in a collective sense suggesting that 'In Him . . . we have the personification of a familiar idea or general truth, e.g., the truth of the communion of deity and humanity or the truth of the creation of the world by God's word and wisdom'.[53] Importantly, this view pays little attention to the historical Jesus, who is more or less dispensable. 'He was believed in as theophany or myth, as the embodiment of a general truth . . . As and to the degree that the symbol of this idea was seen and venerated in Jesus of Nazareth, He was called Kyrios'.[54] In other words, 'what was in view was the idea, not the Rabbi of Nazareth, who might be known or not known as such with no great gain or loss either way, whom there was at any rate a desire to know only for the sake of the idea. This is Docetic Christology, or Christology historically reconstructed along the lines of Docetism.'[55] It will be recalled that John Macquarrie, for instance, begins his thinking about Jesus with the community's experience of transcendence and ends by displacing Jesus, God and man with the idea of an exalted being.

What both of these views have in common is that 'strictly speaking the New Testament statement about Christ's deity is a form of expression that is meant very loosely and is to be interpreted accordingly'.[56] More importantly, what both of these views have in common is their refusal to begin thinking about the 'problem of Christology', or about Jesus Christ, from Jesus himself as we meet him in the New Testament witness. The Jesus we meet in the New Testament witness is one who really is true God and true man and whose mystery cannot be resolved by thinking of him as one or the other or as some *tertium quid*. 'As the true humanity of Christ is ultimately dispensable for Docetism, so is the true divinity of Jesus for Ebionitism – in fact, in the last resort it is a nuisance.'[57] Of course for Barth one could hardly say that

---

[52] *CD* I/2, 19.
[53] *CD* I/1, 403.
[54] *CD* I/1, 403.
[55] *CD* I/1, 403.
[56] *CD* I/1, 403.
[57] *CD* I/2, 20–1.

Docetic thinking had recognized true divinity, since the divinity alleged by that viewpoint is dictated by an idea of divinity conjured by people apart from and in contradiction of the particular God revealed in Jesus Christ.

In *CD* I/2 Barth argues that, however important the incarnation may be – and it is important – 'we ought not to say that the incarnation is the proper content of the New Testament', since all religions and myths can produce the idea of an incarnation. What is central to the New Testament and only to the New Testament is the fact that 'the Son of God is called Jesus of Nazareth, and Jesus of Nazareth the Son of God'.[58] The name of Jesus of Nazareth signifies the reality of revelation, that is, that God has entered history in the person of his Son in order to save humanity from sin, suffering, evil and death. For Barth knowledge of the triune God meant knowledge of a force that was disturbing to and destructive of 'the advance of religion, its life and richness and peace' and that it was bound to be so because

> Olympus and Valhalla decrease in population when the message of the God who is the one and only God is really known and believed . . . No sentence is more dangerous or revolutionary than that God is One and there is no other like Him . . . Let this sentence be uttered in such a way that it is heard and grasped, and at once 450 prophets of Baal are always in fear of their lives . . . Beside God there are only His creatures or false gods . . .[59]

But the most important point to be noted here is that 'to gain a real understanding of Christ's God-manhood, does not rest upon our choice or goodwill, for the decision concerning whether it is reached or not depends not upon us, but upon the object whose reality is here to be seen and understood'. For Barth the discovery that Jesus is God's Son and that God's Son is Jesus 'is not to be conceived of as though those who thus thought and spoke had first a definite conception of God or of a Son or Word of God, of a Christ, and then found this conception confirmed and fulfilled in Jesus. That would be an arbitrary Christology, docetic in its estimate and in its conclusions'.[60] As we shall see, Rahner begins his questing Christology just this way and thus falls foul of this Docetic Christology. As we have seen in Chapter One, Elizabeth Johnson interpreted Christology from the matrix of women's experience and both substituted Sophia for the Word incarnate and saw Jesus as

---

[58] *CD* I/2, 14.
[59] *CD* II/1, 444.
[60] *CD* I/2, 15–16.

an envoy and model of God's love alongside others. Barth's decisive thinking is also in marked contrast, say, to the popular view espoused by Sallie McFague when she writes,

> Jesus' response as beloved to God as lover was so open and thorough that his life and death were revelatory of God's great love for the world. His illumination of that love as inclusive of the last and the least, as embracing and valuing the outcast, is *paradigmatic of God the lover but is not unique. This means that Jesus is not ontologically different from other paradigmatic figures* either in our tradition or in other religious traditions who manifest in word and deed the love of God for the world. He is special to us as our foundational figure: he is our historical choice as the premier paradigm of God's love.[61]

While McFague's thinking is intended to reject Christ's uniqueness, Barth's thinking also diverges sharply from Wolfhart Pannenberg's more sophisticated attempt to ground his understanding of Jesus as God's Son in the experience of anticipation.[62] Of course it must be emphasized that Pannenberg, Moltmann and Rahner all were trying to explain and to maintain Christ's uniqueness in a way that would make sense to modern people. Thus they differ in that important way from such theologians as Sallie McFague and Gordon Kaufman, whose wider Christology, as we shall see, is an almost classic case of Docetic Christology which, like McFague's, does not intend to acknowledge Jesus' uniqueness.

From what has been said so far, it appears that the key problem with much modern Christology is its inability to admit, with Barth, that 'among the realities of this cosmos there is not one in which God would be free for man. In this cosmos God is hidden and man blind'.[63] This is exactly why revelation meets us as a mystery and a miracle, that is, 'an exception from the rule of the cosmos of realities that otherwise encounter man'.[64] It contradicts what the phenomena seem to be saying.[65] Thus God's hiddenness itself can only be known from revelation. Several crucial points that are instructive for us today follow from this thinking and set Barth apart from much contemporary Christology.

First, God can and indeed did cross the boundary between himself and us in the incarnation; his nature does not prevent him from being

---

[61] McFague, *Models*, 136, emphasis mine.
[62] Cf. Paul D. Molnar, 'Some Problems with Pannenberg's Solution to Barth's "Faith Subjectivism"', *SJT* 48.3 (1995), 315–39.
[63] *CD* I/2, 30.
[64] *CD* I/2, 28.
[65] *CD* I/1, 166.

'God within the sphere indicated by this nature of ours'. While we are limited to and by our nature, as a flame must shoot upwards and is bound to its nature as a sign of its creatureliness, 'It corresponds with the greatness of God . . . not to be tied down and limited by His own nature.'[66] The fact that deity became human without ceasing to be divine is thus a miracle.

Second, God is free for us in such a way that God the Son or Word becomes man – not God the Father or the Holy Spirit. Yet 'God in His entire divinity became man.' And for those who accuse Barth of modalism it should be noted that he says here, 'it is not the one nature of God as such with whose operation we have to do here. It is the one nature of God in the mode of existence of the Son which became Man.'[67] While we cannot understand how this can be so, it is a fact that Jesus Christ is the incarnate Word. There is no absolute necessity here and so Barth approves the fact that Aquinas grants that the Father or the Spirit could have become incarnate. This is a thought that would be abhorrent to Karl Rahner, who repeatedly rejects this very idea.[68] While Rahner's positive intention is to avoid an abstract consideration of the Word as one of a non-numerical three, it is also clear that there is a certain logical necessity to the way Rahner conceives the Word, in accordance with his theology of symbolic expression. This leads him to compromise God's freedom in various ways, as we shall see more explicitly below. While Barth here acknowledges God's freedom, he nonetheless argues that we must accept the factual necessity attested by scripture that Jesus is the incarnate Word.

Third, while God assumes a form knowable to us and so can be known 'by analogy with other forms known to us',[69] it is still true that God's entry into history is a veiling of the eternal Word, that is, a kenosis that will lead to an unveiling, even in the veiling. But, and here is the key difference between Barth's thinking and that of many contemporaries, what is known here can be known only by grace and not at all by nature – 'not on the ground of an *analogia entis* already visible to us beforehand'.[70] This means that we can neither seek nor will we find any possibility of knowing God's revelation by exploring

---

[66] *CD* I/2, 31.

[67] *CD* I/2, 33.

[68] See, e.g., Rahner, *Trinity*, 11, and Karl Rahner, SJ, *Foundations of Christian Faith: An Introduction to the Idea of Christianity* (hereafter: *FCF*), trans. William V. Dych (New York: A Crossroad Book, Seabury, 1978), 214.

[69] *CD* I/2, 35.

[70] *CD* I/2, 37.

human experiences of self-transcendence, even if we argue that such experiences are graced at the outset. For Barth, grace as grace exposes us as those who continually bypass Jesus Christ and thus are in conflict with grace by nature since the fall.[71] Revelation shows us the 'factual resistance of man to the divine act of lordship, a resistance in which he who makes this statement will be aware that he participates, and shares in its guilt'. For Barth, God's revelation is genuinely hidden and offensive. This can be seen in his analysis of God's time and our time: 'God in Himself is not offending. Time in itself is also not offending. But God in time is offending because the order of rank mentioned is thereby set up, because we are thereby gripped by God . . . in the delusion that we possessed time.'[72] The problem is that we want to destroy or render innocuous or conceal this fulfilled time, the time of Jesus Christ, which can only be known from itself. In connection with our knowledge of God Barth insists that our life in the Holy Spirit is a life of faith, that is,

> the temporal form of [our] eternal being in Jesus Christ and therefore in truth . . . Our truth is not the being which we find in ourselves . . . [this] will always be the being in enmity against God . . . Our truth is our being in the Son of God, in whom we are not enemies but friends of God, in whom we do not hate grace but cling to grace alone, in whom therefore God is knowable to us.[73]

Seen in this light, Barth argues that the crucifixion can be viewed as a very primitive form of self-preservation and self-defense that includes Israel and the nations. Barth insists that it was not just the Jews who were offended by Jesus but also the Gentiles. In fact he notes that the very man who thought he was the exception here, Peter, had to submit to being told that he would deny Jesus. This, because offense is inevitable at the servant form of revelation, that is, at 'God in time'. This is a hiddenness contrary to nature. It is because we seek ourselves and resist God that we take offense at revelation. We thus contradict and resist it. The cross represents our attempt to get clear of the offense of revelation

---

[71] Thus Barth writes, 'To believe means to believe in Jesus Christ. But this means to keep wholly and utterly to the fact that our temporal existence receives and has and again receives its truth, not from itself, but exclusively from its relationship to what Jesus Christ is and does as our Advocate and Mediator in God Himself . . . in faith we abandon . . . our standing upon ourselves . . . for the real standing in which we no longer stand on ourselves . . . but . . . on the ground of the truth of God . . . We have to believe; not to believe in ourselves, but in Jesus Christ' (*CD* II/1, 159).

[72] *CD* I/2, 61.

[73] *CD* II/1, 158–9.

and to make God's time the same as ours – to level up the order of rank. We think we can set aside the offense in revelation but in fact we cannot. That is why the fact that revelation nevertheless takes place is a miracle and an offense. That God has time for us, that 'there is a divine time in the midst of our time' is a miracle. It cannot be explained 'otherwise than by the special direct new act of God'. A miracle is

> the special new direct act of God in time and in history. In the form in which it acquires temporal historical actuality, biblically attested revelation is always a miracle, and therefore the witness to it, whether direct or indirect in its course, is a narrative of miracles that happened. Miracle is thus an attribute of revelation.[74]

So the most important point to make here is that there is no loss of majesty on God's part when he condescends to become man and to suffer and die on our behalf. There is a veiling of his majesty but not an abandonment of or a lessening of his divinity. 'He who the third day rose from the dead was no less true God in the manger than on the cross.'[75]

Fourth, the Word became flesh means that he assumed our sinful alienated flesh and thus became everything that we are and also experienced death; but he could not sin because God cannot be untrue to himself. While we cannot explain how this mystery can be so, it remains the case that Jesus' humanity is both a barrier (a veil) and also 'a door that opens'.[76] It is a problem to us but a solution as well because, while Jesus died as man, he also rose from the dead. This thinking explains why Barth insisted that Jesus, in his humanity as such, was not the revealer. His humanity 'receives its character as revelation and its power to reveal solely from the Word and therefore certainly cannot in itself . . . be the object of faith and worship'.[77] There is therefore no divinization of his human nature.[78]

Contemporary Examples of Ebionite Christology

Let us explore further examples of what Ebionite Christology might look like today in order to set in relief the positive and negative

---

[74] *CD* I/2, 63–4.
[75] *CD* I/2, 38.
[76] *CD* I/2, 41.
[77] *CD* I/2, 138. We will discuss the important christological question of whether or not Jesus' humanity as such reveals in more detail later.
[78] *CD* IV/2, 72.

insights to be gained from Barth's position. Regarding the problem of Christology, Paul F. Knitter believes that John Hick 'works out a solution that allows Christians to continue to adhere to Christ as *their* unique savior without having to insist that he is necessarily unique or *normative* for others'.[79] Belief in Christ's divinity is thus considered mythical. Hence, it must be reinterpreted to get to the reality of Jesus. Hick believes it is understandable that early Christians spoke of the Father–Son relation and of Jesus' consubstantiality with the Father. But, this view is no longer possible today he thinks, because it leads to all the 'uncomfortable "onlys" in Christian self-consciousness: Christ is the "only Savior" or the "only final norm" for all other religions'.[80] Thus, Hick concludes, 'the real point and value of the incarnational doctrine is not indicative but expressive, not to assert a metaphysical fact but to express a valuation and 'evoke an attitude'.[81] For Hick 'Christians can declare that God is *truly* to be encountered in Jesus, but not *only* in Jesus . . . Such a Christology lays the foundation not only for the possibility but the necessity of interreligious dialogue.'[82]

This is an almost classic contemporary expression of what Barth categorized as Ebionite Christology simply because both Knitter and Hick refuse to begin their thinking about Jesus Christ from the fact that Jesus himself is the unique incarnate Son of the Father. Thus, they refuse to acknowledge that he alone must be the proper object of thought in Christology. Instead Paul Knitter and John Hick change the very nature of truth by arguing that Christians can accept Christ as unique and normative for themselves but not for others. What kind of truth is

---

[79] Paul F. Knitter, *No Other Name? A Critical Survey of Christian Attitudes toward the World Religions* (hereafter: *No Other Name?*) (New York: Orbis Books, 1985), 132, emphasis mine. For more analysis and critique of Paul F. Knitter, see Paul D. Molnar, 'Some Dogmatic Consequences of Paul F. Knitter's Unitarian Theocentrism', *The Thomist* 55.3 (July 1991), 449–95.

[80] Knitter, *No Other Name?*, 150.

[81] Knitter, *No Other Name?*, 151. Also see John Hick, *The Metaphor of God Incarnate: Christology in a Pluralistic Age* (Louisville, KY: Westminster/John Knox Press, 1993). Incarnation is a metaphor that describes in Jesus 'the ideal human life lived in openness and response to God . . . In so far as Jesus lived a life of self-giving love . . . he "incarnated" a love that is a finite reflection of the infinite divine love' (105). This idea continues to express Hick's basic Ebionite view, which is closely allied to his Docetic Christology, which sees Jesus as one instance of divine love among others at work in the world. For Hick, no metaphysical claim can be made here because Jesus' being as God is nothing more than the expression of a personal value judgment, or a 'historical judgment' (110) on the part of people who saw in him a special human openness to God. Thus, for Hick anyone could be an incarnation of God: 'To the extent that a man or a woman is to God what one's own hand is to oneself, to that extent God is "incarnate" in that human life' (106).

[82] Knitter, *No Other Name?*, 152.

it that is not objectively the same for every one? Paul Knitter explains that

> truth will no longer be identified by its ability to exclude or absorb others. *Rather, what is true will reveal itself mainly by its ability to relate to other expressions of truth and to grow through these relationships* – truth defined not by exclusion but by relation . . . The new model reflects what our pluralistic world is discovering: no truth can stand alone; no truth can be totally unchangeable. Truth, by its very nature, needs other truth . . . Truth, without 'other' truth, cannot be unique, it cannot exist . . . the model of truth-through-relationship allows each religion to be unique . . .[83]

This relativistic understanding of Christ and of truth follows from the fact that both theologians are uncomfortable in interreligious dialogue when it comes to acknowledging Christ's uniqueness precisely because they assume that the New Testament meant to affirm Christ's deity only in a mythological sense. That is to say, Christians were only expressing the fact that they valued Jesus and they were trying to engender similar reactions in others. Thus Hick argues that the point of the incarnation was to express a valuation and evoke an attitude and definitely not to describe a metaphysical fact.[84] It is precisely the Ebionite assumption at work here that leads to Paul Knitter's non-normative Christology, the hallmark of which is to assert that Jesus is one savior among others.[85]

This particular Ebionite thinking has definite implications for how the resurrection itself is interpreted. Knitter argues that 'Belief in the resurrection originated from a deeply personal faith experience, which can be described as a "revelation" or "conversion" experience.' Hence the appearance accounts and the empty tomb are seen 'as attempts to express and give more tangible form to these conversion

---

[83] Knitter, *No Other Name?*, 219, some emphases mine.

[84] Hick, *The Metaphor of God Incarnate*, 104ff.

[85] See Knitter, *No Other Name?*, 171ff. For Knitter 'Jesus *is* unique, but with a uniqueness defined by its ability to relate to – that is, to include and be included by – other unique religious figures. Such an understanding of Jesus views him not as exclusive or even as normative but as *theocentric*, as a universally relevant manifestation (sacrament, incarnation) of divine revelation and salvation . . . such a nonnormative, theocentric christology does not contradict the New Testament' (172). For Knitter neither Christ's incarnation nor his resurrection are to be seen as 'one and only'. That is why other saviors are possible and necessary for him as well. It goes without saying that both his initial assumption and his further explanation of Jesus' supposed uniqueness are completely at variance with the New Testament witness. See also Hick, *The Metaphor of God Incarnate*, 89–98 where he explicitly argues for 'Plural Incarnations'.

experiences' and the New Testament account of the resurrection is seen 'as a richly mythic account ... of experiences that could never be photographed'. This leads Knitter to assert that the reality behind the Easter stories need not be limited to an experience of Jesus just because the particular conversion experience on the part of the disciples is not much different from the conversion or faith experiences of countless others after the deaths of their archetypal religious leaders. Consequently, in Paul Knitter's opinion, this fact shows that 'The resurrection of Jesus, in all its authentic mystery and power, does not necessarily imply "one and only".'[86]

But has Knitter thought about Jesus' resurrection as attested in the New Testament at all with this analysis? Is Jesus' personal resurrection from the dead the factor determining what Knitter has to say about this matter? I am afraid the answer has to be that Paul Knitter has substituted the conversion or faith experiences of the disciples for the event that the Gospels and Paul claim took place in the life of Jesus as the basis of their faith. Thus, for Knitter, resurrection language is not only mythological but it describes an experience that is universally accessible without faith in the risen Jesus. And it is this Ebionite thinking that leads him to believe first that what happened to Jesus could have happened to others, and second, that who he is as the risen savior derives its significance from the impression he made on the disciples rather than from who he was and what he did in his own life history. Moreover, Knitter assumes that the origin from which resurrection language sprang was a deeply personal faith experience or a conversion experience.[87]

This is in conflict with the New Testament understanding of the matter because in the Synoptics and in John and Paul the assumption is that the origin of their descriptions was the man Jesus himself who had risen from the dead and in his glorified existence really encountered the disciples during the Easter history as the Lord of history. As Barth put it, 'The Easter story, Christ truly, corporeally risen, and as such appearing to His disciples, talking with them, acting in their midst – this is, of course, the recollection upon which all New Testament

---

[86] Knitter, *No Other Name?*, 198–200.

[87] It should be noted that for John Hick, *The Metaphor of God Incarnate*, the resurrection refers 'to the transitional event or events in virtue of which the Jesus movement survived the death of its founder ... Precisely what this transitional event was we cannot now discern with confidence' (23). This conclusion would have come as quite a surprise to Paul who argued that, without Christ's resurrection, his preaching and their faith would be without substance (1 Cor. 15:14–15). In any case Hick prefers to speak of 'an experience essentially similar to Paul ... of a supernatural light' (24) instead of an actual event in the life of the historical Jesus which gave meaning to Paul's faith.

recollections hang'.[88] 'What happened here according to the witness of the New Testament cannot, by its nature, cease to be, any more than it cannot yet exist. This witness has in view a being immune from dissolution and above the need of coming into being. And yet this being is the object of recollection.'[89] Indeed Barth astutely insists, in the doctrine of reconciliation, that attempts to explain Jesus' appearances with the notion of visions subjectively or even objectively interpreted (as for instance John Macquarrie and Moltmann do)

> smacks . . . of an apologetic to explain away the mystery and miracle attested in the texts . . . The texts do not speak primarily of the formation of the Easter faith as such but of its foundation by Jesus Christ Himself, who met and talked with His disciples after His death as One who is alive (not outside the world but within it), who by this act of life convinced them incontrovertibly of the fact that He is alive and therefore of the fact that His death was the redemptive happening willed by God . . . its objectivity, not taking place in their faith but in conflict with their lack of faith, overcoming and removing their lack of faith and creating their faith . . .[90]

Contemporary Examples of Docetic Christology

What about contemporary examples of Docetic Christology? Remembering that Ebionite and Docetic Christology are closely connected and seem to run into each other, I will briefly discuss two examples. Gordon D. Kaufman is an almost classic example of Docetic Christology while Karl Rahner, though far more serious and orthodox than Kaufman, has what could be considered a Christology that more noticeably combines both the Ebionite and Docetic tendencies.

Gordon Kaufman

Gordon Kaufman explicitly maintains that, when speaking of Christ and salvation, the New Testament texts 'do not in fact refer exclusively to the man Jesus of Nazareth'. The term Christ is sometimes applied to Jesus but other times applied to the community and its transformation. Thus, when Paul says that 'In Christ God was reconciling the world to himself' (2 Cor. 5:19) he cannot have meant that God's relationship to

---

[88] *CD* I/2, 114.
[89] *CD* I/2, 115.
[90] *CD* IV/1, 340–1.

the world had changed in the man Jesus. For Kaufman this is unintelligible! Instead the term Christ points us to the 'complex of events and new relationships that grew up in and around this man'. Therefore it is wrong to suggest that God was incarnate in this man since the New Testament meant to say that God was incarnate in the larger community, that is, in its spirit of love, freedom, mutual caring and forgiveness. 'It is in this new order of interpersonal relationships that the incarnation of God is to be found.'[91]

It is not surprising then that Kaufman thinks that Muslims and Jews were right in criticizing Christians for compromising God's absoluteness (oneness) with their erroneous belief in the deity of the man Jesus.[92] Kaufman therefore argues for what he terms this wider Christology. He believes it will have the advantage of avoiding Christian chauvinism and the oppression and weirdness associated with the archaic traditional belief in the incarnation. For Kaufman then 'the humaneness of God – the tendency toward the human and the humane (toward "Christ") in the ultimate nature of things – has existed from the very beginning'. So the term Christ refers to 'this new order of human relationships'.[93]

Christians reconceived the ideals of justice, love and peace 'in the light of the vision of the human and the humane which had become visible in Christ'. For Kaufman 'Any reification of Christ ... into a kind of absolute standard to which all human ideas and values and conduct must conform is clearly a confusion and mistake which should be forthrightly rejected today.' Any belief that Jesus is the 'only begotten son of God' is to be rejected as false reification.[94]

The obvious problem with this thinking is both its Ebionite and Docetic perspectives. On the one hand Kaufman really believes that Christian recognition of Christ's deity represents the objectification of Christian self-consciousness and the projection of certain attitudes such as triumphalism onto what he calls the story of the man Jesus, who simply suffered for others. Such an Ebionite stance prevents him from acknowledging that Jesus Christ himself is utterly unique in such a way

---

[91]   *IFM*, 382–3.

[92]   *IFM*, 392. See also *GMD*, 11 and 40. See also 119: 'From early on Jews and Muslims realized that Christians were falling into idolatrous attitudes toward Christ (and the church), and they criticized these in the name of the One High God. But to this day most Christians have failed to acknowledge this quite proper theological critique of the ways in which they employed their central religious symbols.'

[93]   *IFM*, 387–8.

[94]   *IFM*, 390–1.

that his uniqueness is in no way grounded in the community's response to him. On the other hand, Kaufman is clearly redefining who Jesus really was as reported in the New Testament in order to make him conform to his own process idea of divinity which sees God as a 'serendipitous creativity' at work in the world. Thus Jesus is seen by him as one manifestation of divine love among others and indeed the term Christ itself is not dictated by who Jesus was and is, but by a wider Christology that is defined by the community's ideas of God and the process of humaneness that it thinks it has found in Jesus. But, like all Docetic Christology, it is not bound to Jesus, the man from Nazareth. It can equally make these assertions from the perspective of many other religions and even from the perspective of humanism itself, as Kaufman himself insists. Unfortunately, Kaufman's perspective leads him to conclude that 'The resurrection was preeminently an event in the *history of meaning*'[95] rather than an event in the life of Jesus. And of course the meaning is identical with the transformations evident within the community of faith.

Karl Rahner

In *Foundations of Christian Faith* Rahner begins his Christology by calling attention to the fact that there is an 'anonymous Christianity'. By this he means that anyone can be a 'justified person who lives in the grace of Christ' even if that person has no specific, historical contact with 'the explicit preaching of Christianity'. Such a person 'possesses God's supernatural self-communication in grace not only as an offer, not only as an existential of his existence; he has also accepted this offer and so he has really accepted what is essential in what Christianity wants to mediate to him: his salvation'.[96]

And it is extremely significant that Rahner began his theology in *Foundations* insisting that we cannot start our thinking with Jesus Christ. Although Rahner notes that the Second Vatican Council said that theologians should be introduced to the mystery of Christ right at the beginning of their study, he wishes to avoid a

> *too narrowly Christological approach* . . . [because] a too narrow concentration of the foundational course on Jesus Christ as the key and the solution to all existential problems and as the total foundation of faith would be too simple a conception . . . Today Jesus Christ is himself a

---

[95] *ST*, 433, emphasis in original.
[96] *FCF*, 176.

problem . . . Hence we cannot begin with Jesus Christ as the absolute and final datum, but we must begin further back than that.[97]

So where does Rahner choose to begin? He begins with 'a knowledge of God which is not mediated completely by an encounter with Jesus Christ'.[98] He begins with our transcendental experience which he claims mediates an 'unthematic and anonymous . . . knowledge of God'.[99] He thus claims that knowledge of God is always present unthematically to anyone reflecting on themselves so that all talk about God 'always only points to this transcendental experience as such, an experience in which he whom we call "God" encounters man in silence . . . as the absolute and the incomprehensible, as the term of his transcendence'.[100] This term of transcendence Rahner eventually calls a holy mystery because he believes that, whenever this experience of transcendence is an experience of love, its term is the God of Christian revelation.[101]

It is worth noting that Rahner does not insist, as Barth does, that true knowledge of God begins only at the place where God has freely made himself known, that is, where God has become 'God for us'. For Barth, as we have already seen, any attempt to begin theology by bypassing Jesus Christ, true God and true man, means that we have failed to acknowledge revelation in its uniqueness. It means the failure to recognize grace as grace. It is amazing that Rahner, who is so famous for having reoriented Catholic theology toward the importance of the doctrine of the Trinity, has himself methodologically ignored the most significant point of that doctrine completely. Instead of allowing his thought about God and Christ to be governed by the Father of Jesus Christ known in faith through the Holy Spirit, Rahner begins with transcendental experience. This Ebionite starting point leads to his conclusions about Christ and grace which are disastrous just because they manifest all the difficulties associated with Ebionite and Docetic Christology.

In connection with his view of the incarnation, Rahner understands God first as 'that nameless mystery which is the vehicle of all under-standing' and 'the incomprehensible mystery — which is . . . the

---

[97] *FCF*, 13.

[98] *FCF*, 13.

[99] *FCF*, 21.

[100] *FCF*, 21.

[101] For more on this, see Paul D. Molnar, 'Is God Essentially Different from His Creatures? Rahner's Explanation from Revelation', *The Thomist* 51.4 (October 1987), 575–631, and Chapter Four below. We have already seen how Elizabeth Johnson exploits the expression 'holy mystery' in Chapter One.

condition of possibility of grasping and comprehending anything, the all-encompassing incomprehensibility of the Whole, no matter how it is named'.[102] By contrast, Barth argued that the content of revelation cannot be separated from the form: 'The form here is essential to the content, that is, God is unknown as our Father, as the Creator, to the degree that He is not made known by Jesus.'[103] Clearly, Rahner's abstract understanding of God as the term of our transcendental dynamisms yields a concept of God that is at variance with the very heart of what is or should be understood in light of the trinitarian self-revelation of God the Father. And although Barth is today frequently criticized for overstressing the *analogia entis* as a problem, the fact is that it is the *analogia entis* or the attempt to find God apart from Christ that really is the problem here.

Beginning with our unthematic experience, Rahner is led to conclude, in his treatment of the incarnation, that self-acceptance is the same as accepting Christ. Answering his own question about what it means to say that God became man, Rahner says, 'Man . . . is . . . an indefinability come to consciousness of itself' and indeed one can only say what man is by describing what he is concerned with, that is, 'the boundless, the nameless'.[104] Since we are a mystery in this way, Rahner concludes that 'Our whole existence is the acceptance or rejection of the mystery which we are'.[105] What could be more logical a conclusion once one assumes that our confession of Christ is grounded in our transcendental experience? In fact in his Christology in *Foundations* Rahner insists that transcendental theology 'must develop in a general ontology and anthropology an a priori doctrine of the God-Man, and in this way try to construct the conditions which make possible a genuine capacity to hear the historical message of Jesus Christ'.[106] In his mind this then is joined with the historical testimony regarding Jesus' life, death and resurrection. Rahner insists that such an a priori doctrine could not in fact be developed prior to the actual appearance of the God-man or prior to an encounter with him.

But given the facts that Rahner believes in an anonymous Christianity, he rejects a too narrowly christological starting point, and he begins Christology in Ebionite fashion with transcendental experience, how can Rahner possibly avoid reducing theology to

---

[102] Karl Rahner, 'On the Theology of the Incarnation', *TI* 4, 106.
[103] *CD* I/1, 390.
[104] *TI* 4, 107–8.
[105] *TI* 4, 108.
[106] *FCF*, 176–7.

anthropology? I believe he cannot. For in the end Rahner argues that 'the transcendence which we are and which we accomplish brings our existence and God's existence together: and both as mystery'.[107] And in this respect Rahner believes that, in light of this understanding of our indefinable human nature, we can better understand the incarnation. When God assumes this human nature then it 'simply arrived at the point to which it always strives by virtue of its essence'.[108] Human nature must disappear, Rahner says, into the incomprehensible. This happens strictly speaking 'when the nature which surrenders itself to the mystery of the fullness belongs so little to itself that it becomes the nature of God himself. The incarnation of God is therefore the unique, *supreme*, case of the total actualization of human reality, which consists in the fact that man *is* in so far as he gives up himself.'[109] It is difficult to avoid the conclusion that, on the one hand, Rahner is suggesting that the incarnation is the result of the human achievement of ultimate self-transcendence.[110] On the other hand it is hard to avoid the conclusion that Jesus is only the highest instance of this anthropological achievement.[111] The former insight is almost classically Ebionite while the latter insight is almost classically Docetic, because the former suggests the apotheosis of a man while the latter suggests that it is Rahner's idea of God as the mysterious nameless incomprehensible Whole that determines his thought about Jesus.

Therefore, the problem with Rahner's thinking is enormous. He believes that the incarnation must be the end and 'not the starting point of all Christological reflection';[112] yet he argues that God's revelation or self-communication 'in the depths of the spiritual person is an a priori determination coming from grace and is in itself unreflexive

---

[107] *TI* 4, 108.
[108] *TI* 4, 109.
[109] *TI* 4, 109–10.
[110] After explaining how Rahner's theology of the symbol influences his view of the incarnation, one Rahner commentator actually writes, 'In the light of Rahner's evolutionary view of Christology, this process wherein the Word becomes flesh is identical with the process wherein flesh becomes the Word of God', William V. Dych, SJ, *Karl Rahner* (Collegeville, MN: Liturgical Press, 1992), 79.
[111] This is why Colin Gunton criticizes Rahner's Christology as a form of *degree* Christology. See Colin E. Gunton, *Yesterday and Today: A Study of Continuities in Christology* (Grand Rapids, MI: Eerdmans, 1983), 15ff. Though John Hick, *The Metaphor of God Incarnate*, differs from Rahner by explicitly rejecting Chalcedonian Christology, his is also a degree Christology: 'We are not speaking of something that is in principle unique, but of an interaction of the divine and the human which occurs in many different ways and degrees in all human openness to God's presence' (109).
[112] *FCF*, 177.

... it is not something known objectively, but something within the realm of consciousness'. This is what Rahner calls transcendental revelation, that is, 'God's gift of himself, the gratuitously elevated determination of man'.[113] It is mediated categorically because we exist in history; but it is not identical with this categorical knowledge. This 'non-objective and unreflexive self-revelation in grace must always be present as mediated in objective and reflexive knowledge'.[114]

Given these presuppositions, Rahner is literally unable to conceptualize the two things that were most important to Barth – the two things that in my opinion acknowledge grace as grace and the incarnation as a free, miraculous and utterly unexpected act of God for us.

1. *His thinking does not reflect the fact that revelation is an exception and a miracle and thus the occurrence of something utterly new in history.* This failure leads to a very odd interpretation of the resurrection as 'an inevitable part of the interpretation of my existence imposed on my freedom . . . The message of Jesus' resurrection says in addition that his definitive identity, the identity of his bodily history, has victoriously and irreversibly reached perfection in God'.[115] Thus Rahner actually believed that 'the knowledge of man's resurrection given with his transcendentally necessary hope is a statement of philosophical anthropology even before any real revelation in the Word'.[116] Such a statement clearly reflects the fact that for Rahner it is our transcendental experience of hope that is the determining factor in his thinking and not the man Jesus who rose from the dead and enabled the disciples' faith.[117] It could hardly be otherwise because, as one Rahner commentator puts it, 'Faith sees meaning and significance in the data which history provides, and sees it in an act of recognition of that for which it had been searching.'[118] Thus, for Rahner, without a transcendental experience of hope, it would be impossible for us to share in the disciples' experience of the risen Jesus. Objective and subjective elements are here mutually dependent.

Indeed one of Rahner's own disciples, Dermot Lane, attempts to deal with the resurrection by following Rahner and concludes that we

---

[113] *FCF*, 172.

[114] *FCF*, 173.

[115] Karl Rahner and Karl-Heinz Weger, *Our Christian Faith: Answers for the Future*, trans. Francis McDonagh (hereafter: *Our Christian Faith*) (New York: Crossroad, 1981), 111.

[116] *TI* 17, 18.

[117] For more on this, see Chapter Six below for how Thomas F. Torrance and Karl Rahner interpret the resurrection differently because of their contrasting understanding of God's self-communication in Christ.

[118] Dych, *Karl Rahner*, 56.

cannot be overly objective or overly subjective in our interpretation of the resurrection. So, attempting to avoid what he views as a kind of fundamentalism on the one hand and Bultmann's reduction of the Easter event to the rise of faith on the other, Lane formulates the view, based on an interpersonal model of a 'person-to-person trans-forming experience' that 'The issue here cannot be reduced to either "faith creates resurrection" or "resurrection creates faith". Rather, these are *intrinsically* related dimensions of the *same transforming experience.*'[119] And Lane really believes that this obvious confusion of 'cause' (resurrection) and 'effect' (the apostles' experiences of the risen Lord) adequately presents the resurrection as the actual foundation of the Church and the sacraments. This finally leads to his belief that what happened in Christ's death and resurrection was already anti-cipated in our experiences of the world. Thus, the resurrection is seen as reasonable:

> Is it not reasonable to ask whether there is any point within the history of mankind in which these deeply-rooted aspirations and hopes of mankind have been fulfilled and realised? . . . Within such an horizon the resurrection appears not as some exception or isolated incident but rather as the *realisation and crystallisation of man's deepest aspirations* . . . nor is it a violation of the laws of nature . . . the resurrection is, in the case of Jesus, the full realisation and actual fulfilment of those *seeds of indestructibility* which exist within the heart of every individual.[120]

It is obvious from this reasoning that the seeds of indestructibility within the heart of every person are the basis of and foundation for both the reality of and meaning of Jesus' own resurrection. The horizon, constructed on this foundation, leads to a denial of the miraculous element in the resurrection of Jesus; it blurs the distinction between his activity and our experiences and aspirations; and finally it makes Jesus' resurrection a particular instance of the general experience of hope found within everyone.

---

[119] See Dermot A. Lane, *The Reality of Jesus* (hereafter: *The Reality*) (New York: Paulist Press, 1975), 60–1, emphasis mine. Compare this to Rahner: 'There is such a thing as Easter faith. Those possessing it are beyond all reckoning. It is present first in the disciples of Jesus, and the witness *which they bear to their Easter experience* and their Easter faith is to acknowledge him who was crucified . . . It may be that we of today cannot draw any clear distinction within the Easter event as understood here between Easter itself (precisely the fact of the risen Christ) and the Easter experience of the disciples . . . In the case of Jesus' disciples their Easter faith and their Easter experience (their belief and the grounds for that belief) are already blended into each other indissolubly', *TI* 7, 164, emphasis mine.

[120] Lane, *The Reality*, 64, emphasis mine.

2. *Rahner's thinking does not allow for the fact that revelation, which is identical with Jesus Christ, actually causes offense.* It is not something for which we have any a priori capacity whatsoever just because it is and remains identical with the risen Christ. And when revelation is accepted for what it really is, then we actually know that we lack this capacity. However, Rahner insists upon this capacity just because of his belief in our obediential potency and supernatural existential, which structure his notion of transcendental revelation. This very belief is the motor that runs his transcendental method. Thus these categories compel him to reflect first upon human experience, which he assumes is an experience of God and of Christ, and only then upon the meaning of revelation. Rahner's conclusions are more than a little problematic.

First, he concludes that revelation is at least in some sense identical with our transcendental dynamisms. Hence, Rahner conceives the universal offer of grace as 'always and everywhere and primarily to the transcendentality of man as such' which is accepted and justifying 'when this transcendentality of man is accepted and sustained by man's freedom'. Indeed, Rahner believes that 'the universality of the factuality of grace from the outset [is] . . . an existential of man's transcendentality as such'.[121] And these beliefs undergird his anonymous Christianity. But given what we have shown above, it also confuses the universal lordship of the man Jesus with our own transcendental experience and thus allows Rahner to direct us to accept ourselves instead of directing us away from ourselves toward Christ. This was exactly the conclusion that Barth sought to avoid and actually did avoid by defining and rejecting both Ebionite and Docetic Christology; such thinking in the end is both Pelagian and compromises Christ's uniqueness.

Second, Rahner concludes that Christology and anthropology are mutually conditioning because he will not begin his Christology with 'the Church's official Christology as such', that is, with the Church's acknowledgment of Jesus as the eternal Word of God. As Rahner puts it,

> we are not starting out from the Christological formulations of the New Testament in Paul and John . . . we are not assuming the impossibility of going behind such a 'late' New Testament Christology to ask about a more original and somewhat more simple experience of faith with the historical Jesus, in his message, his death, and his achieved finality that we describe as his resurrection.[122]

[121] *TI* 18, 182.
[122] *TI* 18, 145.

He really believes his starting point in transcendental experience, with what he calls a 'questing Christology', will lead to what the Church teaches regarding Jesus. Since for Rahner 'all theology is . . . eternally an anthropology'[123] he believes that 'Christology is the end and beginning of anthropology'[124] and that 'anthropology and Christology mutually determine each other within Christian dogmatics if they are both correctly understood'.[125] By contrast, Barth argued that 'There is a way from Christology to anthropology, but there is no way from anthropology to Christology'.[126] Indeed, Barth consistently insisted that there was an order of priority or rank that remained even in the incarnation because he started and ended his reflections with the man Jesus who was the Word incarnate. Thus, the relationship between grace and nature remained an irreversible one that was not conditioned by human belief or unbelief. Further, Barth believed that the incarnation was best understood by saying that the Logos assumed flesh while Rahner believed that the Logos 'empties himself' because God expresses himself. This validates Rahner's belief that the humanity as such is God's self-utterance. But Barth believed that 'One cannot subsequently speak christologically, if Christology has not already been presupposed at the outset, and in its stead other presuppositions have claimed one's attention.'[127]

Third, Rahner concludes that one can be a Christian without specifically hearing about Christ or knowing him. But for Barth one cannot believe in the God of Christian faith without knowing about him through the articles of the creed which specifically refer to the Father, the Son and the Holy Spirit. As Barth put it:

> what gives faith its seriousness and power is not that man makes a decision, nor even the way in which he makes it . . . On the contrary, faith lives by its *object*. It lives by the call to which it responds . . . The seriousness and the power of faith are the seriousness and power of the *truth*, which is identical with God Himself, and which the believer has heard and received in the form of definite truths, in the form of articles of faith . . . In believing, man obeys by his decision the decision of God.[128]

---

[123] *TI* 4, 116.
[124] *TI* 4, 117.
[125] *TI* 9, 28.
[126] *CD* I/1, 131.
[127] *CD* I/2, 123.
[128] Karl Barth, *Credo*, trans. Robert McAfee Brown (New York: Charles Scribner's Sons, 1962), 2.

For Barth a person

> might suppose himself appointed and able to set divinity in motion in his life, or possibly to create it . . . Such presumptuous faith might befit a pious Hindu . . . but it should not represent itself as Christian faith [which] occurs in the *encounter* of the believer with him in whom he believes. It consists in communion, not in identification with him.[129]

Fourth, Rahner believes that self-acceptance in our transcendental experience is the same as acceptance of God and Christ. Thus,

> Anyone therefore, no matter how remote from any revelation formulated in words, who accepts his existence, that is, his humanity . . . in quiet patience, or better, in faith, hope and love – no matter what he calls them, and accepts it *as* the mystery which hides itself in the mystery of eternal love and bears life in the womb of death: such a one says yes to something which really is such as his boundless confidence hopes it to be, because God has in fact filled it with the infinite, that is, with himself, since the Word was made flesh. He says yes to Christ, even when he does not know that he does . . . Anyone who accepts his own humanity in full . . . has accepted the son of Man . . .[130]

Here the container concept of space determines Rahner's view in accordance with his theology of the symbol and thus tends to compromise God's freedom with the inference that human nature can be filled with divine grace and that the humanity of Jesus is filled with the Logos in its self-emptying or self-expression, as a symbol is full of the thing symbolized.[131] For Rahner, Jesus is the supreme symbolic presence of God in history, and because of the nature of symbolic reality, 'the finite itself has been given an infinite depth and is no longer a contrast to the infinite, but that which the infinite himself has become'.[132] This is the basis of Rahner's assertion that Jesus, in his humanity as such, is the revealer and it stands in stark contrast with Barth's consistent emphasis on the fact that our lives are hidden with Christ in God – really hidden.

---

[129] Barth, *Evangelical Theology*, 99.

[130] *TI* 4, 119. Joseph Cardinal Ratzinger, *Principles of Catholic Theology: Building Stones for a Fundamental Theology*, trans. Sister Mary Frances McCarthy, SND (San Francisco: Ignatius Press, 1987), astutely argues that this very thinking compromises the newness of Christianity by resolving the particular into the universal and by reducing 'Christian liberation into pseudoliberation . . . Self-acceptance – just being human – is all that is required [to be a Christian]' (167). Ratzinger properly rejects this kind of thinking as a type of rationalism that fails to come to grips with the particularity of Christianity that calls for conversion and not self-acceptance.

[131] *TI* 4, 239, 251. See below, Chapter Five, for more on this point.

[132] *TI* 4, 117.

Thus, Barth argues that God separates himself from us in uniting himself to us in Christ, and that Jesus' humanity actually conceals his uniqueness as the Son of God and that this must be miraculously revealed or unveiled by God himself if we are truly to know it at any given time. Barth thus rejected the idea that Jesus in his humanity as such reveals because he does not believe that God's majesty is diminished in the incarnation and he believes that created reality is not infinitely extended by virtue of the incarnation because Christ remains distinct from the rest of history as one who is utterly unique.

Conclusion

Karl Barth is often criticized today for overdoing his attack on an *analogia entis*, which he supposedly invented to some degree in order to attack it. Yet, what Barth was trying to avoid in his rejection of the *analogia entis* was *any* attempt to understand God which bypassed Jesus Christ as the *only* possible starting point. This procedure denies and subverts God's grace and thus manifests the fact that fallen humanity is indeed in conflict with grace and revelation. This is the real problem that affects much modern Christology, and I believe that Barth's original development of what he labeled Ebionite and Docetic Christology helps us to see a bit more clearly through this problem today by focusing on Jesus himself and on no one and nothing else in order to understand that God really is 'for us'. Because it is God himself who is 'for us' we must make a clear and sharp distinction between the immanent and economic Trinity, a distinction that Rahner and many who follow him do not make. The consequences of this were discussed throughout this chapter. In the next chapter we will see exactly how a number of prominent contemporary theologians wrestle with the implications of Christ's pre-temporal existence as this relates to the doctrine of the immanent Trinity. It will be my contention that any outright rejection of a *logos asarkos* would compromise God's freedom with the implication that the economy, rather than God himself, defines his eternal being. One of those theologians, Robert Jenson, accepts Rahner's axiom of identity and goes beyond what Rahner would have maintained in order to understand the person and work of Christ. As a result of that, his failure to distinguish properly the immanent and economic Trinity leads him to compromise God's freedom and to misunderstand some key aspects of Christology in ways similar to Rahner. But he is not alone. Bruce McCormack and Douglas Farrow, each in their own way, blur the distinction between the immanent and the economic Trinity by failing to appreciate the function of the *logos asarkos* in Barth's theology. It will be instructive to see exactly how failure to appreciate the proper relation between the immanent and economic Trinity affects many aspects of theology including how to understand Christ's humanity, his resurrection, his relation with the Church, and the proper relation between time and eternity.

Chapter Three

Christology, Resurrection, Election and the Trinity: The Place of the Logos Asarkos in Contemporary Theology

SINCE the relevance of the *logos asarkos* is so important to a proper understanding of the relation of the immanent and economic Trinity it will be helpful to begin by considering two contemporary proposals that will open the door to a wider analysis and critique of the theology of Robert Jenson with the help of distinctions made by Karl Barth. First, we will explore the views of Bruce McCormack and then the views of Douglas Farrow.

Bruce McCormack

Recently Bruce McCormack has considered the conception of the *logos asarkos* in relation to Barth's theological ontology and election, acknowledging that Barth did not wish to 'deny the propriety of the distinction between the *Logos asarkos* and the *Logos ensarkos* altogether'.[1] Contrary to Douglas Farrow's view, which will be discussed shortly, McCormack correctly indicates that, for Barth, Jesus' human nature did not exist until a particular time in history: 'It was not eternal; the Logos did not bring it with him, so to speak, in entering history. Hence there could be no denying the reality of a *Logos asarkos* prior to the incarnation.'[2]

---

[1] Bruce McCormack, 'Grace and Being: The Role of God's Gracious Election in Karl Barth's Theological Ontology', in *The Cambridge Companion to Karl Barth*, ed. John Webster (Cambridge: Cambridge University Press, 2000), 96.
[2] McCormack, 'Grace and Being', 96.

McCormack grapples with the implications of Barth's doctrine of election, namely, that God's decision to establish a covenant of grace also meant a self-determination on God's part to be God for us in Jesus Christ. This raises the question of whether or not the incarnation should be construed as being '*constitutive*' of God's eternal being. McCormack carefully distinguishes Barth's position from Hegel's insisting that, for Barth, in opposition to Hegel, the incarnation is God's free act, that Barth sharply distinguished the creator–creature relation, that Barth insisted that God pre-existed creation, and that God's eternal actions could not be collapsed into history. Hence, 'The immanent Trinity is complete, for Barth, before anything that has been made was made (including time itself).'[3] Still, McCormack wishes to argue that both the incarnation and outpouring of the Holy Spirit are in some sense 'constitutive' of God's eternal being, by way of anticipation. But will such an interpretation of Barth respect God's freedom, which indeed is the basis for human freedom and for human self-determination?

Here McCormack asks about the logical relation of God's election to his triunity, arguing that 'If election is an eternal decision, then it has never not taken place.'[4] But if God's election has always taken place, how then can it be construed as a decision; does it not then become a necessity (a logical necessity at that), that is, the very opposite of what Barth intended with his doctrine of the immanent Trinity?

Strangely, McCormack believes that Barth's mature doctrine of election required him to retract some of his earlier views about the relation of revelation and triunity. For instance, McCormack asserts that Barth rejected the idea that God was triune only for the sake of his revelation in *CD* I/1; yet McCormack also argues that this previously rejected thinking seems to be implied by Barth's later doctrine of election. Hence, McCormack thinks, that if we place election logically prior to the doctrine of the Trinity, this inconsistency will be overcome. And he cannot understand why Barth did not pose this question and attempt to overcome it himself. The only conclusion that McCormack can reach 'is that Barth either did not fully realize the profound implications of his doctrine of election for the doctrine of the Trinity, or he shied away from drawing them for reasons known only to himself'.[5] How then does McCormack 'correct' Barth's theology here? He argues that we must understand God's triunity

---

[3] McCormack, 'Grace and Being', 100.
[4] McCormack, 'Grace and Being', 101.
[5] McCormack, 'Grace and Being', 102.

logically as a function of divine election . . . the eternal act of Self-differentiation in which God is God 'a second time in a very different way' . . . and a third time as well, is *given in* the eternal act in which God elects himself for the human race. The *decision* for the covenant of grace is the ground of God's triunity and, therefore, of the eternal generation of the Son and of the eternal procession of the Holy Spirit from the Father and Son . . . the works of God *ad intra* (the trinitarian processions) find their ground in the *first* of the works of God *ad extra* (viz. election). And that also means that eternal generation and eternal procession are willed by God; they are not natural to him if 'natural' is taken to mean a determination of being fixed in advance of all actions and relations.[6]

McCormack therefore argues that this thinking is compatible with Barth's view of the doctrine of the Trinity and that the doctrine might have been 'subordinated in the order of treatment to the doctrine of election'.[7]

This thinking once again highlights the importance of a proper doctrine of the immanent Trinity. For Barth, God exists eternally as the Father, Son and Holy Spirit and would so exist even if there had been no creation, reconciliation or redemption. Thus, the order between election and triunity cannot be logically reversed without in fact making creation, reconciliation and redemption necessary to God. It is precisely this critical error that is embodied in McCormack's proposal. Barth insisted that the Trinity exists eternally in its own right and thus even the electing God is not subject to any necessities, especially a necessity that would suggest that the ground of his triunity is the covenant of grace. It is exactly the other way around. The covenant of grace is a covenant of *grace* because it expresses the free overflow of God's eternal love that takes place in pre-temporal eternity as the Father begets the Son in the unity of the Holy Spirit. None of this is subject to a principle of love, and God's being is not the result of his will. Rather, his will to elect expresses his freedom to be God in a new way as God for us. It expresses the fact that, as we shall see in more detail in Chapter Five, God is Lord of his inner life as well as of his actions *ad extra*. But none of this is required by his essence, and his essence most certainly is not contingent upon his works *ad extra*. Indeed, as we shall see below, God's will cannot be played off against his nature here because his free will expresses his nature as one who loves in freedom. We will explore the limited way in which the *logos asarkos* was advocated by Barth when

---

[6] McCormack, 'Grace and Being', 103, emphasis in original.
[7] McCormack, 'Grace and Being', 103.

we consider Robert Jenson's outright rejection of the concept; Barth was certainly leery of the concept if it suggested any attempt to think of God by going behind the God revealed in Christ, but he insisted upon its necessity in connection with the doctrine of the Trinity and Christology.

Here is where a clear and sharp distinction between the immanent and economic Trinity is essential. While McCormack admits that such a distinction is necessary, it plays no conceptual role at this point in his argument. Consequently, it is just because McCormack failed to make such a distinction at this important point, that he is misled into believing that God became the triune God only by virtue of his self-determination to be our God. The reason Barth never changed his view on this matter is because he consistently recognized and maintained God's freedom, without which the doctrine of the Trinity becomes nothing more than a description of our relations among ourselves, which we then dubiously attribute to the God of our own invention. Paramount here, as we shall see below in more detail, is Barth's insistence that we cannot explain the *how* of the mystery of God's triunity, election and incarnation – we can only accept election and incarnation as facts grounded in God's primal decision to be God for us. But election is a decision of the living God, and thus, while it is irreversible, once made, it still was freely made, and therefore we cannot simply equate the immanent and economic Trinity in the manner suggested by McCormack, without actually making God dependent on the world in precisely the Hegelian way that he recognizes is so mistaken in this regard. This important example should serve as a warning that we cannot simply dispense with a *logos asarkos*, as McCormack apparently wishes to do in the end. For Barth, as we shall see in more detail shortly, the *logos asarkos* is a necessary concept in the doctrine of the Trinity and Christology that recognizes and maintains God's freedom. One might ask at this point whether Barth is not more concerned with God's freedom here than God himself might be. But the simple answer to such a question is that he plainly recognizes that a compromise of God's freedom here means dissolution of human freedom and ultimately the collapse of theology into anthropology.

Douglas Farrow

In his important book *Ascension and Ecclesia*, which I will discuss in more detail in Chapter Nine, Douglas Farrow praises Barth for his apparent thoroughgoing rejection of a *logos asarkos* without paying attention to the fact that this concept performed a significant but limited role in Barth's theology. Farrow indicates that Irenaeus similarly rejected such a concept and links Barth to Irenaeus in a positive way.[8] Farrow himself believes that such a concept brings 'us dangerously near to the gnostic conviction that Jesus himself is somehow incidental to the Word. Flirtation with that idea was and is common enough, of course, preserving even among orthodox theologians traces of the gnostic bias against the redemption of the material world'.[9] Indeed Irenaeus too, when he referred to Jesus as 'God of God; Son of the Father; Jesus Christ; King for ever and ever', and so thought of him as the one 'who sailed along with Noah, and who guided Abraham; who was bound along with Isaac', causes Farrow to ask 'whether so much has been claimed for Jesus that his humanity must be crushed after all under the weight of these claims'.[10] Moreover, Farrow argues that Karl Barth, in spite of his supposed thoroughgoing rejection of a *logos asarkos*, has a difficulty similar to that of Irenaeus: 'Is not *our* reality somehow threatened if we take such statements about Jesus too seriously?'[11] This leads Farrow to conclude that Barth 'has spoken the name of Jesus so loudly that other names cannot even be heard; that once again humanity is being swallowed up, if not by God directly then by "the humanity of God"'.[12]

The simple answer to these reflections is that for Barth one can never stress God's freedom too strongly as long as it is properly understood as his freedom disclosed and active in the history of Jesus Christ and the outpouring of the Holy Spirit. This is the case because it is precisely God's freedom for us in Christ that establishes and maintains human freedom itself.[13] The mystery of Jesus Christ indeed consists in the fact that he was both the eternal God and a contingent human being at the same time – one did not in fact overwhelm the other; but, by the grace of God, Jesus lived as a man of his time and was at the same time Lord of history. This is indeed the heart of the Christian faith. But Farrow is in search of 'Jesus-history' which is defined as 'the sanctification of our humanity through the life and passion and heavenly intercession of Jesus',[14] and so emphasizes his humanity that no decisive function is allotted to Jesus as God incarnate. That is why for Karl Barth the *logos*

---

[8] See Farrow, *Ascension and Ecclesia*, 53ff. and 243.
[9] Farrow, *Ascension and Ecclesia*, 54.
[10] Farrow, *Ascension and Ecclesia*, 83.
[11] Farrow, *Ascension and Ecclesia*, 83.
[12] Farrow, *Ascension and Ecclesia*, 243.
[13] See, e.g., *CD* IV/3, 378ff.
[14] Farrow, *Ascension and Ecclesia*, 6.

asarkos was a necessary and important trinitarian insight that recognizes and helps us to maintain God's freedom. As we have been seeing, it allows him to recognize that the Trinity exists in its own right and that our trinitarian thinking can never substitute historical relations for the relations of the Father, Son and Spirit that are decisive for the events that take place within the economy.

Farrow concludes that there were two types of pre-existence attested in the New Testament, that is, Jesus' pre-existence as a man and as God. Like Barth, he stresses the importance of the immanent Trinity, but unlike Barth he refuses to acknowledge that there ever was a *logos asarkos*. Referring to John's Gospel, Farrow contends '*That* he [Jesus] goes [ascends] makes him the way [to the Father]'.[15] But wasn't Jesus the way, the truth and the life precisely because, as Son, he was eternally *homoousion* with the Father from the beginning? Doesn't the entire gospel hinge on this fact – a fact which, as we have been seeing, becomes unrecognizable whenever Jesus' pre-existence as God is obscured? Does Farrow's belief in Jesus' human pre-existence take due cognizance of the need to distinguish the immanent and economic Trinity and of election as a free act of grace as Barth did? As we shall see below in Chapter Five, Barth accepted the fact that God once existed in isolation from us even though he elected us in Jesus Christ as the beginning of his ways and works and executed that election in his life, death, resurrection, ascension and session at the Father's right hand. Thus, the doctrine of the immanent Trinity clearly recognizes God's freedom to exist as the eternal Father, Son and Spirit without need of creation. That is precisely why election is God's covenant of grace – it is freely exercised on our behalf. Further, Barth argued that one's vocation, like one's justification and sanctification,

> prior to its actualisation in his own history it has its basis as we must say first and supremely, in his election in Jesus Christ 'before the foundation of the world' (Eph. 1:4). It has as the seed and root of its historical reality, truth and certainty the absolutely prevenient 'history' which as the *opus Trinitatis internum ad extra* is in God Himself the eternal beginning of all His ways and works, namely, the election of grace of the God who loves in freedom and is free in love, in which the Son, thereto ordained by the Father and obedient to the Father, has elected Himself for sinful man and sinful man for Himself. In light of this, the one true God is the true God of man in . . . His pre-temporal, supra-temporal and post-temporal eternity.[16]

---

[15] Farrow, *Ascension and Ecclesia*, 36.
[16] *CD* IV/3, 483f. See also *CD* III/4, 595–646.

Does Farrow's own understanding of 'Jesus-history' not become his theological criterion, with the result that the living Lord is kept from acting decisively in this context? Indeed, noticeably missing throughout Farrow's book is any notion of Christ's active lordship, namely, of his ability, as the Word incarnate, to interact with us now through the power of the Holy Spirit.

One wonders whether Farrow's search for a 'eucharistic world-view'[17] indicates that in the end he is not as reliant on the living Lord as he intends. Wasn't Barth right to observe that *all* world-views represent human attempts to avoid the lordship of Jesus Christ?[18] Indeed, far from advancing some sort of Christomonism, Barth very clearly argued that, because God in Jesus Christ has become our brother, 'man has become the brother of God in Jesus Christ, and as such cannot adopt an attitude of hostility, neutrality or passivity in relation to the name and cause of God'.[19] For Barth we are set free for our active life and our vocation in Jesus Christ. But Barth insists that our active life in freedom is a participation in the life of the man Jesus by being disciples and allowing ourselves 'to be claimed by Him for an active life under his leadership'.[20] Still, for Barth 'Man neither is nor can be a second Jesus Christ . . . His freedom, activity and achievements will always be very different from the freedom, activity and achievements of God.'[21] Our relation with Christ then takes place in an unlikely miracle in which we participate in his freedom while remaining active ourselves: 'it is the miracle of miracles that man may be genuinely active as a subject in this sense where God acts and speaks . . . Yet it is true because in Jesus Christ it is revealed and commanded that it should continually become real.'[22] For Barth then there can be no Christomonism because our union with Christ 'does not mean the dissolution or disappearance of the one in the other, nor does it mean identification. It does not mean a conjunction of the two in which one or the other, and perhaps both, lose their specific character, role and function in relation to the other, the reciprocal relation being thus reversible.'[23] Instead our union with Christ preserves the independence, activity and uniqueness of each.

---

[17] Farrow, *Ascension and Ecclesia*, 73, 88.
[18] *CD* IV/3, 254ff.
[19] *CD* III/4, 482.
[20] *CD* III/4, 482.
[21] *CD* III/4, 482.
[22] *CD* III/4, 483.
[23] *CD* IV/3, 540.

By contrast, is it not Farrow's very understanding of 'Jesus-history' that tends toward the Docetism he thinks he finds in Barth with the idea that Jesus humanly pre-existed his birth, life, death, resurrection and ascension? How can Jesus truly share our humanity if his is a humanity that pre-existed his birth on earth, even if this is only understood retroactively?[24] It is one thing to say that Jesus' humanity existed one way in God's primal decision to be God for us in Jesus Christ. But it is quite another to say, as Farrow does, that there is a 'pre-existence of a *man*, a pre-existence which is disclosed to us and interpreted for us chiefly through the ascension'.[25] Once again Farrow's complete rejection of any notion of a *logos asarkos* leads him to project Jesus' eternal existence after the resurrection and ascension into pre-temporal eternity with the result that he is unable to distinguish the immanent and economic Trinity at that point. This leads him to suggest that the historical events of Jesus' life somehow contribute to his unique existence in precisely the Hegelian manner that we have seen is so problematic in contemporary theology.

Robert Jenson

Robert Jenson's *Systematic Theology Volume 1: The Triune God* is very important because it intends to show that contemporary theology must find its meaning in the triune God or else it will in fact contradict the gospel. Many theologians find Jenson's approach to the doctrine of the Trinity just the answer that is needed by contemporary theology in its attempts to avoid modalism, dualism and pantheism. Jenson's positive contribution rests on his insistence that reflection about God cannot take place except on the ground of the gospel and that such reflection ought to be faithful to the God of the gospel rather than to anyone's particular tradition, whether Roman Catholic, Lutheran or Reformed. While tradition certainly is important to Jenson, he is very clear that the norm for theological truth must always be the triune God himself, who is present to us as event or, as he puts it toward the end of the book, as a fugue! Jenson strongly emphasizes the importance of Jesus' resurrection, the necessity of the Church and the sacraments as the sphere in which we experience our inclusion in God's own self-knowledge and love, and the importance of not understanding God, with Greek metaphysics,

---

[24] See Farrow, *Ascension and Ecclesia*, 297.
[25] Farrow, *Ascension and Ecclesia*, 283.

as timeless and impassible or in a modalist or subordinationist way. Jenson seeks to plot the narrative of Jesus' life, death and resurrection in contrast to the Greek and medieval thought forms in which this story was told so that the reader can see that the concerns of the gospel were in conflict with the concerns of Aristotle and Plato. Without doubt, Jenson makes every effort to start and end his reflections with the gospel in such a way that Israel and the Church are bound together in their dependence on the very same God who raised Jesus from the dead. This important point shows that, while Jesus the Son is at the center of his thinking, Jenson feels free to allow the living Christ, the risen Lord, to continue to exercise his mediatorial function in the world today. Unlike many contemporary theologies of the Trinity, Jenson's presentation sets out to make room for Christ's active mediation of himself to us today and does so with a renewed emphasis on the Holy Spirit that deliberately does not separate the Holy Spirit from Jesus himself or the Father.

Despite his positive intentions, however, Jenson's trinitarian theology as articulated in *Systematic Theology Volume 1* and *The Triune Identity* raises serious questions that center on four important interrelated areas: (1) the proper relation of the immanent and economic Trinity; though, as far as I am aware, while Jenson deliberately adopted Rahner's axiom and gave it an eschatological twist in his previous book, *The Triune Identity*, this question does not even arise in *Systematic Theology Volume 1*; (2) the person and work of Jesus Christ, the Son of God; (3) the proper significance of Jesus' resurrection from the dead, including how we ought to understand Jesus' glorified body; and finally (4) Jenson's understanding of the relation between time and eternity.

The Proper Relationship between the Immanent and Economic Trinity

As I have stated throughout this book, a properly conceived doctrine of the immanent Trinity aims to recognize, uphold and respect God's freedom. As Jenson himself insists, God must have been free to remain himself had there been no creation or salvation. Nonetheless, Jenson also accepts, with Rahner, the identity of the immanent and economic Trinity.[26] Now, as we have begun to see already, the problem with Rahner's axiom as it stands is that it tends to blur the distinction between God and history, especially in terms of Christology, as Rahner explicates

---

[26] Robert W. Jenson, *God According to the Gospel: The Triune Identity* (hereafter: *The Triune Identity*) (Philadelphia: Fortress Press, 1982), 139.

matters from within his philosophy and theology of the symbol. Thus, for example, as we have already seen, Rahner contends that Jesus, in his humanity *as such* reveals God.[27] In a similar way Jenson argues that 'Jesus' human action and presence is without mitigation God's action and presence, with whatever that must do to and for creatures.'[28] Here we must insist, however, that, while it is true that God did not merely come in the man Jesus but *as* man, it is still necessary to make the Chalcedonian distinction at this point or else the revealing power that comes from the Word and is not transferred to Jesus' humanity will be merged with history and then become dependent upon it.[29] Jenson's thinking leads to such puzzling statements as: 'the events in Jerusalem and on Golgotha are themselves inner-triune events' and 'the Spirit who will raise the Son finds his own identity only in the *totus Christus*, in the Son who is identified with us'.[30] Such suggestions seem to blur the distinction between events in God and events in history and further suggest that the Spirit does not eternally have his identity but must find it through events within history.

The Person and Work of Jesus Christ, the Son of God

In answering the question of whether or not Jesus in his humanity as such is revelation, Karl Barth, noting that it is one of the hardest problems of Christology,[31] rejected this idea because he insisted, correctly in my view, that revelation involved both a veiling and an unveiling. He was relying here upon the Chalcedonian formulation of the two natures as unmixed (and therefore not identical), distinguished but also not separated.[32] Thus, Barth insisted upon a clear and sharp distinction between the immanent and economic Trinity in order to avoid ascribing to history or humanity as such what can only become real within and

---

[27] For more on this see Chapter Five below.

[28] *STI*, 144.

[29] Thomas F. Torrance, *Theology in Reconciliation* (London: Geoffrey Chapman, 1975), 151ff. and 201ff. follows Athanasius and Cyril of Alexandria and presents a positive understanding of Christ's vicarious humanity that neither falls into Apollinarian substitution of divinity for his humanity nor into Nestorian separation. Thus, 'since the Son of God did not just come into man but came *as man*, yet without ceasing to be God, the same subject in the Incarnation occupies two roles that are not just two roles or modes but real natures' (155). See also Torrance, *The Christian Doctrine of God*, 40–1.

[30] *STI*, 191.

[31] *CD* I/1, 323. More will be said about this in Chapter Five below.

[32] *CD* IV/2, 63ff. For more on the Chalcedonian character of Barth's Christology see George Hunsinger, *Disruptive Grace: Studies in the Theology of Karl Barth* (Grand Rapids, MI: Eerdmans, 2000), chapter 6.

for history and humanity by the grace of God active in Christ and the Spirit. Barth argued that 'the Godhead is not so immanent in Christ's humanity that it does not also remain transcendent to it, that its immanence ceases to be an event in the Old Testament sense, always a new thing, something that God actually brings into being in specific circumstances'.[33]

Barth also maintained the importance of the *logos asarkos* within the strict doctrine of the Trinity and within Christology. He believed this abstraction was necessary because God acting for us must be seen against the background of God in himself who could have existed in isolation from us but freely chose not to. He rejected a *logos asarkos* in his doctrine of creation if it implied a 'formless Christ' or 'a Christ-principle' rather than Jesus who was with God as the Word before the world existed; he rejected it in connection with reconciliation if it meant a retreat to an idea of God behind the God revealed in Christ; but he still insisted it had a proper role to play in the doctrine of the Trinity and in Christology, describing it as 'indispensable for dogmatic enquiry and presentation'.[34] In stark contrast, Jenson rejects such a concept, because history (creation) is allowed to determine God's eternal existence in his thinking; it is noteworthy that in his book *The Triune Identity*, Jenson was indeed trying to reconcile God's freedom with Rahner's axiom as it stands (with the vice versa).[35] Barth refused to discredit this 'antecedently in himself' as 'untheological metaphysical speculation'.

---

[33] *CD* I/1, 323.

[34] *CD* III/1, 54. Cf. *CD* IV/1, 52. Cf. also *CD* I/2, 168ff. and *CD* III/2, 65f., 147f. and *The Göttingen Dogmatics*, 160, where Barth wrote, 'The Son is both *logos ensarkos* and *logos asarkos*. Do we not have to say this afresh and for the first time truly the moment we speak about the union of God and man in revelation lest we forget that we stand here before the miracle of God? Can we ever have said it enough?' Cf. also, *CD* I/2, 136 where Barth writes, 'The Word is what He is even before and apart from His being flesh'.

[35] Cf. *The Triune Identity*, 138–41. Jenson believes any concept of a *logos asarkos* prevents the procession of the Son from being the same as Jesus' mission. And indeed it does; precisely in order to prevent God's eternal freedom from being confused with his freedom for us. This is not to suggest a separation of Jesus' humanity and divinity but to say that, unless his mission is seen against the background of his being *in se* before the world was, then his deity will be equated with or seen as the outcome of history. Jenson, following Wolfhart Pannenberg, sees it this way. Thus, 'the Trinity is simply the Father and the man Jesus and their Spirit as the Spirit of the believing community' (*The Triune Identity*, 141). What happened to the eternal Trinity, which pre-existed, exists now and is also future? This Trinity is banished into a future: 'This "economic" Trinity is eschatologically God "himself"', an "immanent" Trinity' (*The Triune Identity*, 141). Hence, Jenson substitutes Jesus' resurrection for God's *ousia* (168) and argues that 'The divine *ousia* is no longer our first concern. It is the work, the creative event done as Jesus' life, death, resurrection' (113); here historical events displace God's eternal being and action. This is the major problem that follows Rahner's axiom of identity with its vice versa.

Christ's deity has to do with 'the distinction between the Son of God in Himself and for me. On the distinction between the "in Himself" and "for me" depends the acknowledgment of the freedom and unindebtedness of God's grace, that is, the very thing that really makes it grace.'[36]

What happens in *Systematic Theology Volume 1* is instructive. What Jenson seeks to interpret 'is a birth of the *Logos* as God that enables and therefore must be somehow antecedent to his birth as man'. On the one hand we are told that 'There must be in God's eternity – with Barth, in his eternal decision – a way in which the one Jesus Christ as God precedes himself as man, in the very triune life which he lives eternally as the God-man.' On the other hand he argues that 'What in eternity precedes the Son's birth to Mary is not an unincarnate *state* of the Son, but a pattern of movement within the event of the incarnation, the movement to incarnation, as itself a pattern of God's triune life.'[37] While Jenson notes that he inadequately made this distinction in his earlier work, he nevertheless believes that his rejection of a *logos asarkos* preceding the incarnation was correct. Now the problem with this reasoning is that it leads directly to the idea that history constitutes God's eternal being, that is, to the idea of a dependent deity. And that in fact compromises the freedom that Jenson intends to maintain as when he writes that 'The "hypostases" are Jesus and the transcendent Will he called "Father" and the Spirit of their future for us . . . What happens between Jesus and his Father and our future *happens in God* – that is the point.'[38]

But what happened to Christ's sonship here? It appears to be equated with the human Jesus in his relation to the Father. And to that extent one may either say that the human Jesus exists eternally, that is, before the Word became incarnate (in which case his human existence is compromised), or one may say that the human Jesus became the Son of God in his actions in history (in which case he did not in fact pre-exist as the eternally begotten Son of the Father). But one cannot say that Jesus as such is one of the trinitarian hypostases without blurring the distinction between God *in se* and God acting for us *ad extra*. What happens in Jenson's thinking, in my opinion, is that Jesus is actually stripped of his eternal uniqueness as Son. And this is captured in the statement that

---

[36] *CD* I/1, 420. Cf. also *CD* I/1, 416ff.
[37] *STI*, 141.
[38] Jenson, *The Triune Identity*, 106.

What the event of God happens to is, first, the triune persons. The fundamental statement of God's being is therefore: God is what happens between Jesus and his Father in their Spirit . . . [also] God is what happens to Jesus and the world. That an event happens to something does not entail that this something must be metaphysically or temporally prior to it.[39]

Here once again Jesus' antecedent existence as the eternally begotten Son of the Father is simply denied in order to advance a Hegelian notion of God's involvement with history. Part of the difficulty here is the fact that Jenson believes that '"the Son" in trinitarian use' does not 'first denote a simply divine entity. Primally, it denotes the claim Jesus makes for himself in addressing God as Father; as we will see, this Son is an eternally divine Son only in and by this relation.'[40]

Additionally, there is a problem in the way Jenson understands Barth's notion of divine *decision*. By choosing to unite himself with us in the man Jesus, God not only chooses that he *will be* the man Jesus, but since 'God *is* his act of choice . . . he *is* the man Jesus'.[41] In other words, the way Jenson conceptualizes the divine choice, it appears that God is not really free to decide to become incarnate and then carry out that primal decision in history; rather the incarnation happens in eternity as the ground of its happening in time, 'in eternity as the act of decision that God is'. Here God's choice is equated with God's nature and this seems to me to compromise God's freedom. The corrective here is the fact that Barth held that God's unity with us is something new as an act of will which 'has its basis neither in the essence of God nor in that of man, and which God does not owe either to Himself or to any other being . . . That is what we can call . . . God's free election of grace'.[42] More will be said about this shortly.

The Proper Significance of Jesus' Resurrection from the Dead: How to Understand Jesus' Glorified Body

This difficulty becomes especially evident when we are told that Christ's sonship is neither determined by his birth nor by his pre-existence but by his resurrection: 'He is Son in that he is resurrected.'[43] Or 'In that Christ's Sonship comes "from" his Resurrection, it comes from God's

---

[39] *STI*, 221.
[40] *STI*, 77.
[41] *STI*, 140.
[42] *CD* IV/1, 66.
[43] *STI*, 142.

future into which he is raised.'[44] Or again 'Jesus would not be the Word without the Resurrection.'[45] And '*fully* reliable love can *only* be the resurrected life of one who has died for the beloved ones'.[46] Finally, we are told not only that 'the way in which the triune God is eternal, is by the events of Jesus' death and resurrection' but that his 'individuality is constitutive of the true God's infinity'.[47] All of these descriptions unfortunately allow events that take place in creation (in history) to determine or define God's supposedly pre-existent being and nature. This is precisely the confusion of the immanent and economic Trinity that Barth was able to avoid by distinguishing God *in se* from God *for us.* Even Jenson's own insight that God could be the triune God without creation or incarnation is here called into question by the fact that Jesus could not have been the Word without the resurrection. Here history and Jesus' sonship are reversed. Is this not just because the function of the *logos asarkos* is rejected in his doctrine of the Trinity and in his Christology? It certainly appears that this rejection com-promises God's genuine pre-existence by making it dependent on a historical event or a series of historical events. Could this situation be otherwise, given Jenson's assertion that 'Since the Lord's self-identity is constituted in dramatic coherence, it is established not from the beginning but from the end, not at birth but at death, not in *persistence* but in *anticipation*'?[48] Furthermore, and against Jenson's best intentions, does this thinking not compromise the historicity of the resurrection itself because it ascribes to history a power that it cannot actually have, that is, the power to constitute God's eternal being and nature?

Compromising the fact that Jesus is the Son of God simply because he is (and not because of the resurrection), this thinking opens the door to the idea that salvation is conditioned. Thus, Jenson believes that 'the very existence of the Gospels as a corpus depends on the com-munity constituted by the faith that so judges',[49] whereas the existence of 'the Gospels' depends upon the work of the Holy Spirit rather than the community. And we are told that 'the occurrence of the gospel depends on the chain of witnesses who have brought the news from the first witnesses to those who now hear'.[50] Is it not the case that, while we

[44] *STI*, 143.

[45] *STI*, 171.

[46] *STI*, 199.

[47] *STI*, 219.

[48] *STI*, 66, emphasis in original. By contrast, as seen above, Barth writes, 'He who the third day rose from the dead was no less true God in the manger than on the cross' (*CD* I/2, 38).

[49] *STI*, 174.

[50] *STI*, 14.

are dependent on these witnesses, the occurrence of the gospel is not? And finally, this thinking leads to the idea that, once we have heard the gospel, our question should become 'what *shall* we now say and enact that the gospel may be spoken?'[51] Should the question instead not be whether and to what extent our actions and speech acknowledge God's freedom for us and thus allow him to speak to us through our dogmatic work?

In his book *The Triune Identity*, Jenson suggested that 'If we bend the old language a little, instead of replacing it, we may say that the resurrection is this God's [the Christian God's] *ousia*.'[52] But as we have just seen, this thinking simply eliminates a genuinely existing immanent Trinity. God's *ousia* is his triunity; it is the fact that God eternally exists as Father, Son and Holy Spirit. The problem here concerns making the resurrection the center of theology without making this important distinction between the immanent and economic Trinity. This affects what is said about the resurrection and the risen Lord himself.

Jenson very astutely rejects the idea that the resurrection could be construed as a vision or in any other reductionist way that would divest from the New Testament narrative its true meaning which is that Jesus is risen bodily from the dead.[53] With or without the empty tomb, he believes that 'Somehow there now exists a body that is the living Jesus' human body.'[54] Jenson embarks on a very interesting analysis of the meaning of heaven, and Ptolemaic and Copernican cosmology in order to stress that, if Jesus has no body after the resurrection, then we are in fact denying the resurrection itself as well as our own future with God. Also, as Thomas Aquinas believed, Christ embodied on the altar did not have to *travel* to get there (as in the Ptolemaic model), but by God's fiat the embodied Christ is simply in both places at once, that is, in heaven and on the altar. Here Jenson follows and intends to correct the shortcomings of the Swabians who relied on a radically 'Cyrillean' Christology. The question then is: 'Where is Christ's body, if it needs no spatial heaven and is not restricted in its presence by created spatial distances?'[55] Jenson's answer follows Paul and argues that the Church 'is the risen body of Christ. She is this because the bread and cup in the congregation's midst is the very same body of Christ'; accordingly

---

[51] *STI*, 16, emphasis in original.
[52] Jenson, *The Triune Identity*, 168.
[53] *STI*, 196–201.
[54] *STI*, 201.
[55] *STI*, 204.

Christ's risen body is 'whatever object it is that is Christ's availability to us as subjects'.[56] Since the bread and cup are the objects of Christ's promised presence, we might thus locate him and respond to his word there. 'Sacrament and church are *truly* Christ's body for us' because he makes himself available to us through them. We are told that Jesus 'needs no other body to be a risen man, body and soul'.[57] Jenson finally decides cautiously that he can say that the tomb was empty because, if it were not, then Jesus would have been merely a saint whose relics we are devoted to and not the living Lord.

There are at least two problems here. The first is that the New Testament appearance accounts suggest that Jesus had his own glorified body during the 40 days between the resurrection and the ascension.[58] This is important because it precludes confusion of Christ and the Church and suggests that our own hoped for resurrection is grounded in what has already happened in the life of Jesus himself. As T. F. Torrance puts it

> Far from being just a promise for the future, it [Christ's bodily resurrection] is an evangelical declaration of what had already taken place in Christ, and in him continues as a permanent triumphant reality throughout the whole course of time to its consummation, when Christ will return with glory to judge the quick and the dead, and unveil the great regeneration (παλινγενεσία) which he has accomplished for the whole creation of visible and invisible realities alike.[59]

Jenson's statement that 'God does in fact have a body, the body born of Mary and risen into the church and its sacraments',[60] compromises this distinction. It is Jesus Christ himself who is risen from the dead; he did not simply rise into the Church and its sacraments. Jenson would probably be horrified to find himself in the same company as Elizabeth Johnson with this assertion. But as noted above in Chapter One, it is Johnson's contention that 'the body of the risen Christ becomes the body of the community'.[61] Jenson's view appears to be another version of Bultmann's reduction of the Easter history to the rise of faith, albeit one that substitutes the Church and the sacraments for Jesus, true God and true man, who appeared to his disciples during the 40 days.

[56] *STI*, 205.
[57] *STI*, 206.
[58] Cf. Lk. 24:36f., Jn 20:24 and *CD* III/2, 327, 330, 448.
[59] Torrance, *The Trinitarian Faith*, 299.
[60] *STI*, 229.
[61] Johnson, *She Who Is*, 162.

The second problem is the fact that the Holy Spirit is noticeably absent here. And the result is that, while we may describe the Eucharist and the Church as Christ's body in virtue of their unity with their heavenly head who is Christ himself, that cannot mean that these can be substituted for his own glorified body in heaven or his presence to us through the Holy Spirit uniting him to us through these earthly media. Any such substitution implies that Christ needs the Church as the Church needs Christ and detaches our hope from Christ's active mediation of himself. This again calls into question our own hoped-for resurrection which is proleptically experienced here and now.

One further point needs to be mentioned. In one sense Jenson believes that one would not have perceived the uncanny phenomenon 'as the result of a resurrection unless one *recognized* it as someone one knew who had died'.[62] But this reasoning suggests that it is we (or the disciples) who can believe in the resurrection because we or they are able to make the connection between the one event and the rest of Jesus' life. Yet this places the power of comprehension in human hands and misses the important point that what the disciples experienced went 'utterly against the grain'.[63] Because God was present as the man Jesus in the 40 days, they were empowered to become believers rather than unbelievers. The risen Lord himself therefore, rather than their powers of recognition, enabled their comprehension here.

The Relation between Time and Eternity

This brings us to a consideration of God's being by exploring the relationship of time and eternity. Here Jenson notes that Greek philosophy has bequeathed to theology the false idea that God must be immune to time and that he must also be impassible and that modalism (locating God above time) and subordinationism (which makes the Father alone transcendent) preceded the Nicene solution.[64] The gospel contradicts both of these concepts and Jenson will solve this problem partially by following Thomas Aquinas and partially by following Gregory of Nyssa in order to understand eternity as 'God's temporal infinity'.

---

[62] *STI*, 199.
[63] *CD* III/2, 449.
[64] *STI*, 94ff.

Consistent with his belief that the identity of the God of the gospel is not determined antecedently but only by the gospel story itself, Jenson understands authentic belief to mean that one is unconditionally open to the future, but not just any future, as Bultmann apparently held. It is to be open to 'a future determined as fellowship with Jesus'; thus, Jesus in his full historical reality 'is the Word of God in that he is the identity of the future opened by the Word of God . . . he is not the Word of God in isolation as himself, nor is he first word and then the particular Word of God . . . Jesus would not be the Word without the Resurrection.'[65]

Jenson thus follows Gregory of Nyssa to fill out Thomas Aquinas's notion of God as 'He who is' in a trinitarian way. Accordingly, in the first instance, the one God is the 'mutual life of Father, Son, and Spirit'. God's being is 'a *going-on*, a sequentially palpable event, like a kiss or a train wreck'.[66] Second, that the Father is Father, or that the Son is Son or that the Spirit is Spirit 'is other than and prior to the fact that God is'. Third, Gregory thinks of the divine *ousia* in an anti-Greek way as the infinite. Thus what characterizes the Father, Son and Spirit is 'limitlessness'. While the Greeks could only envision an infinity using a spatial analogy and concluded that an infinite something would be nothing, Gregory's idea of God's deity is '*temporal* infinity. God is not infinite because he extends indefinitely but because no temporal activity can keep up with the activity that he is.'[67] While Aristotle's understanding of the infinite would imply that it lacked all boundaries, Gregory's idea was that the infinite would overcome all boundaries. The Arians, following Greek thinking, refused to call the Logos God because he acts and suffers. But Gregory believed that precisely this activity qualifies the Logos to be God and suggested, according to Jenson, that 'If they [the Arians] must divide eternity, let them reverse their doctrine and find the mark of deity in endless futurity . . . let them guide their thinking by what is to come and is real in hope rather than by what is past and old.' Thus, 'To be God is always to be open to and always to open a future, transgressing all past-imposed conditions.'[68] Interestingly, while Jenson appeals to Gregory's *against Eunomius*, Book I to advance this argument, the fact is that Gregory maintains that God's eternity consists both in his endlessness and in his being without beginning and so actually portrays the position that is adopted by Jenson

[65] *STI*, 171.
[66] *STI*, 214.
[67] *STI*, 215–16.
[68] *STI*, 216.

as a choice one might make if one were confused about the triune God's eternity![69]

This then is the proper view of eternity: 'A religion', according to Jenson, 'is the cultivation of some eternity'. And 'The biblical God's eternity is his temporal infinity.' Consequently, 'The true God is not eternal because he lacks time, but because he takes time.'[70] God is eternal 'because he is primally future to himself and only thereupon past and present for himself'. This is of a piece with Jenson's idea that the Spirit must liberate the Father and the Son for mutual relationship.[71] Thus, we finally have our full-blown definition of eternity: 'God is not eternal in that he adamantly remains as he began, but in that he always creatively opens to what he will be; not in that he hangs on, but in that he gives and receives, not in that he perfectly persists, but in that he perfectly anticipates.' God's eternity therefore consists in the fact that God 'is faithful to his commitments within time . . . Israel's God is eternal in that he is faithful to the death, and then yet again faithful'.[72]

Notice here that God's eternity is defined by his relationship with history instead of by his self-sufficient being as Father, Son and Spirit. Thus, Jenson actually believes that God is eternal '*because* he is triune'[73] and that God's whence (the Father) and whither (the Spirit), the origin and goal, do not fall apart because they are 'reconciled in the action and Suffering of the Son'. But if this is the case then Jenson has allowed history and suffering to define God's supposed eternal and self-sufficient being as triune. Hence he writes, 'the way in which the triune God is eternal, is by the events of Jesus' death and resurrection'.[74]

Here once again historical events that have meaning only because God *is* eternally the one who loves in freedom and who then acts freely for us within history are allowed to define God's being, eternity and nature. Hence we are told that

> Consciousness is as such infinite . . . The Ego as which the Father finds himself is the Son. But the Son exists not at all for himself and altogether for those for whom the Father intends him. Thus the Father's pre-occupation with the Son, Jesus' intrusion into the outward flight of the

[69] Cf. Gregory of Nyssa, *Against Eunomius*, Book I, §42 in *Select Writings and Letters of Gregory, Bishop of Nyssa*, trans. by William Moore and Henry Wilson, *Nicene and Post-Nicene Fathers of the Christian Church* (Grand Rapids, MI: Eerdmans, 1988), 98.

[70] *STI*, 217.

[71] Cf. *STI*, 223.

[72] *STI*, 217.

[73] *STI*, 218.

[74] *STI*, 219.

Father's consciousness, does not restrict the Father's consciousness but is rather his consciousness's opening to its universal scope.[75]

Unfortunately, the implication here is that God is not eternally self-sufficient but is becoming who he will be because of his relations *ad extra*. This understanding of eternity appears to be more a projection of our self-consciousness onto the eternal than an accurate depiction of God's pre-temporal, supra-temporal and post-temporal existence.[76] Here both time and suffering are allowed to define the divine nature. If, however, a proper distinction between the immanent and economic Trinity had been made, then we could say that God's time is uniquely his and so is above and prior to our time and that when God suffered in Jesus Christ it was indeed a miraculous condescension that cannot be explained in terms of consciousness. Thus, it disclosed the nature of God as one who can suffer on our behalf while remaining one who does not suffer by nature. As T. F. Torrance notes, if we try to understand passibility and impassibility logically, then they cancel each other out – God must either be one or the other. But if we understand them soteriologically, then we will see that God is both passible and impassible at the same time, just as he is human and divine at the same time.[77] Both of these features are compromised here because Jenson insists that we must abandon any thought of fixed perfection in God and define God by futurity instead of keeping our eyes fixed upon Christ himself who is the same yesterday, today and tomorrow.

We have seen that Robert Jenson's trinitarian theology offers a very clear illustration of the kinds of problem that arise for contemporary theologians when they do not formulate their understanding in relation to a clear doctrine of the immanent Trinity. Had Jenson been able to make a clear distinction between the immanent and economic Trinity, he would have been able to acknowledge God's freedom consistently by not suggesting that Jesus in his humanity as such is the revealer; that Jesus was not eternally incarnate but that he pre-existed the incarnation as the *logos asarkos*; that the God who humbles himself on our behalf in

---

[75] *STI*, 220.

[76] For a careful and nuanced interpretation of Barth's understanding of the relation of time and eternity which avoids the pitfalls of Hegelian and Processive thinking while showing how Barth's understanding of God's pre-temporal, supra-temporal and post-temporal existence is dictated by his understanding of the Trinity, see Hunsinger, *Disruptive Grace*, chapter 8. Hunsinger himself is critical of Jenson, noting that in his Hegelian thinking 'eternity, like time, is a flowing now . . . that not only moves along with time but also requires time for its own self-actualization' (188).

[77] Torrance, *The Trinitarian Faith*, 185.

the incarnation, cross and resurrection never was, is or will be dependent on events within history to become who he will be; that the resurrection does not in any sense constitute Jesus' eternal sonship, but rather it discloses who he was and is as the incarnate Son; that the resurrection is an event in Jesus' life on the basis of which he (the risen Lord) gives meaning to the faith of the disciples then and now; and finally that God's eternity is not defined by its relation to time but by who God the Father, Son and Spirit is in his pre-temporal, supra-temporal and post-temporal existence. We have also seen that Jenson is not alone in holding these beliefs; both Bruce McCormack and Douglas Farrow follow him in different ways with their thoroughgoing rejection of a *logos asarkos.*

In the last chapter we traced some of the difficulties in contemporary trinitarian theology to the way Karl Rahner has conceptualized the task and content of Christology, and we have briefly noted how Jenson's thinking was formulated in relation to Rahner's axiom of identity in this chapter. Since it is Rahner's axiom of identity that has shaped the landscape of much late twentieth-century trinitarian theology, it will be important to see exactly how that axiom arose and how it was employed by Rahner in the context of his own important theology of the symbol. In the next chapter, therefore, I will try to show exactly how and why I think certain irreconcilable conflicts arise in Rahner's thought with a view toward moving beyond these difficulties toward a resolution grounded in a contemporary doctrine of the immanent Trinity, which neither separates nor confuses the two.

Chapter Four

Experience and the Theology of the Trinity: How Karl Rahner's Method Affects His Understanding of Revelation, Grace and the Trinity

IN this chapter we shall discuss two questions concerning the doctrine of God in the theology of Karl Rahner that will shed light on the problems we have already seen gdevelop in the first three chapters regarding the way his trinitarian axiom functions for him and for others; these questions will illuminate some of the difficulties Rahner has bequeathed to contemporary trinitarian theology and in the end point a way toward a better understanding of the doctrine of the immanent Trinity and how it ought to function today. What is Rahner's understanding of God? On what is it based? In the process of answering these questions, we shall examine critically the relationship between the doctrine of God and Rahner's view of Christian revelation, focusing on the nature of his theological method. Analysis will proceed by comparing Rahner's method with the one advocated in this book, that is, one that allows the object of the Christian faith rather than transcendental experience to shape one's conception of divine and human freedom. It is hoped that by this comparison the problem we saw develop in relation to Rahner's Christology will be seen more clearly as it stems from his starting point for thinking about God.

In *Foundations of Christian Faith*, chapter 2, 'Man in the Presence of Absolute Mystery', *Theological Investigations*, Volume 4, 'The Concept of Mystery in Catholic Theology', and *Theological Investigations*, Volume 11, 'The Experience of God Today' Rahner develops his doctrine of God from his concept of absolute mystery, which is drawn from human experience of reality according to his transcendental method. This method itself establishes the foundation for answering the first question, as we shall see. In answering the second question it is important to examine carefully the foundation and determining element for any concept of God and of the creature's relation with God. The following issues will have to be discussed also: the nature of and need for Christian revelation, the role of faith and the kind of relation that exists between the creator God and creatures in Rahner's thought. I shall discuss how Rahner deals with the free grace of God's revelation and presence in history while fusing creaturely self-transcendent experience with grace and revelation according to his transcendental method. To the extent that such fusing perceives the reality of God according to the constructs of natural theology, it eliminates any practical need for revelation and faith in the triune God as the only true God. As noted above, this is puzzling in the light of the fact that Rahner has been very influential in renewing trinitarian theology today. What I hope to show in this chapter is that the starting point for Rahner's transcendental method (human experience) is the very factor that causes irreconcilable conflicts for a theology (like Rahner's) that claims to be based on revelation.

This chapter then will present the problems noted in Chapter Two in more detail and tie them more precisely to Rahner's understanding of God. Ultimately, the problem with Rahner's trinitarian theology is that his actual theological method does not bear the mark of his stated intentions, which were to begin thinking about the God–world relation from the economic Trinity, which *is* the immanent Trinity. In this chapter, I will not highlight Rahner's distinctive positive contributions to contemporary trinitarian theology. These have been well documented by others.[1] My intention here is to highlight the fact that his reliance

---

[1] See, e.g., John Thompson, *Modern Trinitarian Perspectives* (New York: Oxford University Press, 1994), 21–3, and, more critically, 26ff.; LaCugna, *God for Us*, 210ff.; Ted Peters, *God as Trinity: Relationality and Temporality in Divine Life* (hereafter: *Trinity*) (Louisville, KY: Westminster/John Knox Press, 1993), 96ff.; Gunton, *The Promise of Trinitarian Theology*, 10, 32f.; Thomas F. Torrance, *Trinitarian Perspectives: Toward Doctrinal Agreement* (hereafter: *Trinitarian Perspectives*) (Edinburgh: T&T Clark, 1994), 78ff.; J. A. DiNoia, OP, 'Karl Rahner', in David F. Ford (ed.), *The Modern Theologians: An Introduction to Christian Theology in the Twentieth Century*, vol. I (Oxford: Blackwell, 1989), 183–204; Stanley J. Grenz and Roger E. Olson, *20th Century Theology: God and the Word in a Transitional Age* (Carlisle: Paternoster Press, 1992), 237–54; Leo J. O'Donovan, SJ (ed.), *A World of Grace: An Introduction to the Themes and Foundations of Karl Rahner's Theology* (hereafter: *A World of Grace*) (New York: Crossroad, 1981); Dych, *Karl Rahner*, and Herbert Vorgrimler, *Understanding Karl Rahner: An Introduction to His Life and Thought* (New York: Crossroad, 1986).

on the human experience of self-transcendence as an interpretive tool and his subsequent use of symbolic theology to articulate his view of the trinitarian actions *ad intra* and *ad extra* create more problems than they solve. Later, in Chapter Six, I will try to make this difficulty more precise by comparing Rahner's understanding of God's self-communication (an expression Colin Gunton has correctly noted suggests emanationist overtones)[2] with T. F. Torrance's understanding of the same category. It will become clear that while Torrance sees Rahner's axiom as a potential path toward unity between Reformed and Roman Catholic theology, he also interprets the axiom differently just because he will not allow experience the same hermeneutical function as Rahner does. Torrance accepted Rahner's axiom of identity, but he also believed that Rahner had introduced a logical necessity into the doctrine of the Trinity.[3] By that, Torrance meant that Rahner had allowed his abstract thought rather than God's trinitarian self-revelation to shape what he had to say about the Trinity. In his latest book on the Trinity, Torrance very clearly distinguishes the immanent and the economic Trinity and seems to move further away from unqualified acceptance of Rahner's axiom.[4]

Rahner's analysis of experience is profound and has been useful for many in describing the creature's relation with the creator. *But* as long as it is thought that our self-transcending experiences provide a point of departure for knowing the true God, Christian theologians will always have difficulty actually distinguishing God from their ideas about God. This problem was discussed above in relation to the thinking of Gordon Kaufman and Sallie McFague and it was shown how their thinking has resolutely influenced the theology of Catherine LaCugna and Elizabeth Johnson. It is my contention that the point of departure for knowing the reality of God was and remains God's own *free* self-manifestation in his historical interventions within the realm of experience. As we shall see, contrary to those like Catherine LaCugna, Anne Carr and Elizabeth Johnson who use experience as a source for theology, this very point is what Rahner seeks to uphold. But his method causes him to be inconsistent. While Rahner would insist that this historical intervention is what happened in Israel, in Christ and in the Church,

---

[2] See Gunton, *The Promise of Trinitarian Theology*, second edn, xix.

[3] Torrance, *Trinitarian Perspectives*, 79ff.

[4] See Torrance, *The Christian Doctrine of God*, 108–9. Thus 'when we rightly speak of the oneness between the ontological Trinity and the economic Trinity, we may not speak of that oneness without distinguishing and delimiting it from the ontological Trinity' (109).

his method cannot allow him to hold consistently that the only point of departure for knowing the *truth* about our experiences is the Word of God revealed and active in Christ and the Spirit. We have already contrasted this aspect of Rahner's method with Barth's analysis and rejection of Ebionite and Docetic Christology with a view toward seeing how and why Barth refused to ground theology in experience, even though he knew that without experience of the Word and Spirit there could be no theology at all. For Rahner, by comparison, true knowledge of God is simultaneously ascribed to the grace of God and to our *innate* knowledge of absolute being. This claim is actually indebted to the Cartesian method and, as we shall see, it causes numerous problems for a theology like Rahner's that claims to be a theology of revelation.

Concerning Rahner's doctrine of God, then, we return to the opening questions: What is it? On what is it based? Following Rahner's own outline in *Foundations of Christian Faith* these questions can only be answered together by tracing the development of his own logic based upon the transcendental experience of our 'horizon'. Rahner's doctrine of God begins from the assumption that an experience of one's 'horizon' is an experience of God. And this assumption dictates what it is. Therefore, in Rahner's thought, these two questions cannot in fact be separated. Rahner provides no other foundation for this assumption than the idea that we humans must think and act in the light of this 'horizon'. Instead of pointing beyond the circle of human experience to show us that he has spoken about a reality that totally transcends it, he directs us back to our experiences. While Rahner knows God is totally transcendent, his method ascribes even to the philosopher a knowledge of God that would follow a recognition of God's grace revealed in Christ. So, instead of consistently allowing the unique object (Jesus Christ) encountered by theologians in their experiences of faith to be the norm of his theological ontology, Rahner holds that being as experienced within and without the Bible is 'graced'.

In this book I am arguing that a properly grounded theology begins and ends in faith. Such a theology would allow God the freedom to be the originator as well as the one who completes the process of true knowledge. This is where a consistent trinitarian theology would allow for the fact that it is in, by and through the power of the Holy Spirit that such knowledge as a human act takes place through our participation in Christ's new humanity. This would explain why theology has been described as *fides quaerens intellectum.*[5] *Faith* in the triune God would be a necessary prerequisite to philosophical reflection for this kind of theology. For Rahner it must be said that, in all three pieces under consideration, the word 'faith' rarely appears.[6] And the idea that the truth of human knowledge is determined *solely* by the object of the Christian faith, as it was for instance for Barth and for T. F. Torrance, would be unworkable in his system. In fact, in addition to the positive features of Rahner's identification of the immanent and economic Trinity, this axiom also leads him to synthesize the Christian God with the idea of God drawn from the self-transcending experiences of Christians.[7] Accordingly, what determines truth is the idea of God drawn from the experience of one's *term*, that is, absolute being.[8] Rahner's method presumes that the Christian doctrine of the Trinity confirms this experience and the knowledge derived from it. In this chapter I hope to show that, wherever this assumption is at work, a proper theology of revelation cannot be held consistently and a clear distinction between philosophy and theology cannot be attained. The obvious implication then is that a clear distinction between the immanent and economic Trinity is jeopardized as well.

God

Rahner's presupposition for knowing God precludes dependence on the *free* revelation attested in scripture at the outset. Since he is a being

---

[5] Perhaps the most renowned theologian to use this expression was Anselm. Karl Barth's book entitled *Anselm: Fides quaerens intellectum: Anselm's Proof of the Existence of God in the Context of His Theological Scheme* (Richmond, VA: John Knox Press, 1960) displays a continued interest in this expression as it relates to theological method.

[6] See, e.g., Karl Rahner, 'The Concept of Mystery in Catholic Theology', *TI* 4, 36–73, at 60. Where Rahner does mention faith, the meaning of the word is defined by his transcendental method. Thus, its biblical meaning is distorted. Since Rahner deduces the meaning of faith from the 'primordial mystery', which everyone always experiences (our term or whither or absolute being), he thinks that we must understand biblical faith too as pointing to this experience and not to something outside it. This, of course, distorts the very meaning of biblical faith, since what determines truth for Rahner is our experience of our 'whither' and faith in *it* as something that is always present. What determines truth for Paul (whom Rahner cites here) is the risen Lord *alone*. For Paul, faith is true faith when it points to him *alone*. Cf., e.g., 1 Cor. 12:3.

[7] Rahner, 'The Concept of Mystery', 70–1. For more on the dogmatic problems involved in this identification, see Paul D. Molnar, 'Can We Know God Directly? Rahner's Solution from Experience', *Theological Studies* (hereafter: *TS*) 46.2 (1985), 228–61, 230ff. and 248ff.

[8] See, e.g., Rahner, 'The Concept of Mystery', 49 where Rahner writes, 'we begin . . . with the finite spirit's transcendence, which is directed to absolute being'. Rahner calls this 'whither' of transcendence God in *TI* 4, 50. On this point, see also *TI* 11, 'The Experience of God Today', 149–65, 149–53ff.

who is 'entrusted into his own hands and always in the hands of what is beyond his control'[9] Rahner assumes that the human person is 'a being oriented towards God'.[10] Probably no one would deny that we are all in some sense in the hands of what is beyond our control. But the fact that there are always things in life we cannot control neither proves that there is a God nor that we are oriented to this God rather than opposed to him. By this assumption Rahner is compelled to describe knowledge of God as an orientation of human being according to his transcendental method. The meaning of the term God, for Rahner, is neither taken from scriptural revelation nor from dogmatics but from 'this orientation to mystery'.[11] Accordingly 'We inquire therefore into man, as the being who is orientated to the mystery as such, this orientation being a constitutive element of his being both in his natural state and in his supernatural elevation.'[12] This is why, for Rahner, 'At this point theology and anthropology necessarily become one'[13] and knowledge of God represents human explication in reflection of 'what is already present in [our] transcendentality'.[14] As noted above, Rahner works out the logic of this insight in his Christology: 'And if God himself is man and remains so for ever, if all theology is therefore eternally an anthropology . . . man is forever the articulate mystery of God.'[15] And this leads him to conclude that 'anthropology and

---

[9] *FCF*, 44. See also *TI* 4, 52 where Rahner writes, 'The Whither of transcendence is at no one's disposal'; *TI* 11, 151 expresses the same idea. By experiencing ourselves this way, we are placed into 'that mystery which reduces us to perplexity, which controls us and is not controlled by us'. For more on this, see *FCF*, 42.

[10] *FCF*, 44. See also *TI* 4, 49 and *TI* 11, 153.

[11] *FCF*, 44.

[12] *TI* 4, 49.

[13] *FCF*, 44.

[14] *FCF*, 44. This same idea is repeated frequently. See, e.g., *TI* 4, 50: 'All conceptual expressions about God, necessary though they are, always stem from the unobjectivated experience of transcendence as such: the concept from the pre-conception, the name from the experience of the nameless.' See also *TI* 4, 57 and *TI* 11, 149 where Rahner writes, 'The so-called proofs of God's existence . . . are possible . . . only as the outcome of an a posteriori process of reasoning as the conceptual objectification of what we call the experience of God, which provides the basis and origin of this process of reasoning.' Thus, for Rahner, the task is to 'reflect upon an experience which is present in every man' (*TI* 11, 150–1) and 'we can only point to this experience, seek to draw another's attention to it in such a way that he discovers within himself that which we only find if, and to the extent that we already possess it' (*TI* 11, 154). See also *FCF*, 21: 'The knowledge of God is always present unthematically and without name, and not just when we begin to speak of it. All talk about it, which necessarily goes on, always only points to this transcendental experience as such, an experience in which he whom we call "God" encounters man . . . as the term of his transcendence'. For Rahner's explanation of his method, see *FCF*, 24–39.

[15] *TI* 4, 'On The Theology of the Incarnation', 116.

Christology mutually determine each other within Christian dogmatics if they are both correctly understood'.[16]

Now, if God is truly free even in his relations with us *ad extra*, then Rahner's claim that knowledge of God is always present in our human striving for 'being as such'[17] illustrates the problem implicit in any attempt to harmonize reason and revelation according to his method. According to such presuppositions our very nature forces us continually to transcend our present experience toward something beyond. While there is no reason to doubt this experience, any claim that this is true knowledge of God compromises the freedom of the Christian God; for this God is especially free in relation to such necessary strivings. In this book I am contending that this difficulty can be solved only by revelation and that it will only be exacerbated by ascribing a solution simultaneously to reason and to revelation.

Rahner begins analyzing the term 'God' by considering human experience, and concludes, 'The mere fact that this word exists is worth thinking about.'[18] What does the word mean? 'The present form of the word reflects what the word refers to: the "ineffable one", the "nameless one" who does not enter into the world we can name as part of it . . . it expresses the whole in its unity and totality . . . It means that which really is wordless.'[19] Thus, Rahner writes 'the word "God" which no longer refers by itself to a definite, individual experience, has assumed the right form to be able to speak to us of God'.[20]

For Rahner, the term 'God' signifies the 'single whole of reality' and 'the single whole' of human existence.[21] And this is a significant insight. For it leads Rahner to conclude that 'If the word "God" really did not exist, then neither would those two things exist any more for man, the single whole of reality as such and the single whole of human existence in the mutual interpenetration of both aspects.'[22]

The word 'God' 'asks about reality as a whole and in its original ground'.[23] Rahner does not rigorously distinguish between the reality

---

[16] *TI* 9, 'Theology and Anthropology', 28.

[17] *FCF*, 35.

[18] *FCF*, 45.

[19] *FCF*, 46. For the same idea, see, e.g., *TI* 4, 50ff. and *TI* 11, 157, 160.

[20] *FCF*, 46.

[21] *FCF*, 47–8.

[22] *FCF*, 47–8.

[23] *FCF*, 49. Because Rahner believes this he identifies ontology with natural theology and natural knowledge of 'absolute being' with knowledge of God (*TI* 4, 52). For more on this point, see *TI* 1, 79–148, 'Theos in the New Testament', esp. 81–3 and 133. Compare Karl Rahner, SJ, *Hearers of the Word* (hereafter: *HW*), trans. Michael Richards (New York: Herder & Herder, 1969), 8ff. and 53–68.

of God and the word 'God', perhaps because, in his view, symbolic reality and its expression condition one another. The fact that the word exists gives it a reality all its own. 'This word *exists*, it belongs in a special and unique way to our world of language and thus to our world. It is itself a reality, and indeed one that we cannot avoid.'[24] Indeed, 'We should not think that, because the phonetic sound of the word "God" is always dependent on us, therefore the word "God" is also our creation. Rather it creates us because it makes us men.'[25] What creates us and makes us human? Apparently it is the synthetic word-reality which is 'the totality of the world and of ourselves'.[26] 'This real word confronts us with ourselves and with reality as a whole, at least as a question. This word exists. It is in our history and makes our history. It is a word.'[27] Rahner continues, 'It is our opening to the incomprehensible mystery . . . it is itself the final word before wordless and worshipful silence in the face of the ineffable mystery.'[28]

Knowledge of God

For Rahner, then, knowledge of God is really inseparable from one's transcendental experience of the world. It is a posteriori in the sense that it 'is an a posteriori knowledge from the world'.[29] This is what Rahner describes elsewhere as categorical knowledge of revelation.[30]

---

[24] *FCF*, 50 and *TI* 11, 160.

[25] *FCF*, 50. How or why a word can create us is not explained. But in another context Rahner suggests that key words have the power to create and recreate us. See *TI* 8, 219ff. Rahner believed we must seek unifying words that enable us to conjure up the truth of the original unity revealed in Christ. This original unity of course is already part of the structure of human being in accordance with assumptions concerning the original unity of knower and known. Rahner writes, 'Such key-words do exist, with their power to adjure, to epitomize and to unify' (220). He notes that the Logos was probably one of these words but that we must always search for new key words. 'But woe betide that age which no longer possesses any word imbued with a quasi-magical force of this kind to epitomize all in one!' (220). For a similar discussion that categorizes these key words as primordial words, see *TI* 3, 323ff. Rahner's intention in both contexts was to apply this thinking to the Sacred Heart. And this thinking may be a clue to what he means here.

[26] *FCF*, 50.

[27] *FCF*, 51.

[28] *FCF*, 51 and *TI* 11, 160.

[29] *FCF*, 52.

[30] See Karl Rahner and Joseph Ratzinger, *Revelation and Tradition*. Quaestiones disputatae, 17, trans. W. J. O'Hara (New York: Herder & Herder, 1966), 13–21. For a similar idea see also *HW*, 114–15. See also *FCF*, 153ff.

On this view, 'man's basic and original orientation towards absolute mystery' constitutes an experience of God.[31] And this experience is a 'permanent existential of man as a spiritual subject'.[32] Any conceptual proof for God is therefore simply a reflection on this 'orientation towards mystery'.[33] What proves the existence of God here is the fact 'that speaking of God is the reflection which points to a more original, unthematic and unreflexive knowledge of God'.[34] Of course Rahner thinks this way because, in addition to categorical revelation, he presumes the existence of what he calls transcendental revelation, which refers to our direct experience of the ontology of God himself via the incarnation and grace. For Rahner, it is God's quasi-formal self-communication to creatures that accounts for our '"entitative" divinization', that is, 'a transcendental divinization of the fundamental subjective attitude, the ultimate horizon of man's knowledge and freedom, in the perspective of which he accomplishes his life'.[35] This, for Rahner, is the human grace given supernatural existential. Thus, the *visio beatifica* is the direct apprehension of God, given by God himself. In reality it is no different from the object of our initial human dynamism of spirit which recognizes being in general; hence, Rahner describes grace as 'an inner, objectless though conscious dynamism directed to the beatific vision'.[36] And this insight leads to his explanation of the creator–creature relationship in terms of a quasi-formal alteration in the knowing subject.[37] It is Rahner's quasi-formal explanation of the creator–creature relationship that goes beyond the traditional distinction between nature and grace and ascribes true knowledge of God directly to human beings in their self-knowledge. That is why Rahner feels free to describe God's grace as a conscious dynamism of the creature whereas in fact, if one were to distinguish clearly nature and grace, one could never describe any creaturely activity as anything more than a creaturely activity. This

---

[31] *FCF*, 52 and *TI* 4, 42ff., 49ff., and *TI* 11, 155–6. Rahner appeals to the *Vorgriff* (prior apprehension) as the factor that guarantees this (*TI* 11, 155). On this point, see also *HW*, 53–68, esp. 59. See also 66–7. Cf. also Karl Rahner, *Spirit in the World* (hereafter: *SW*), trans. William Dych, SJ (New York: Herder & Herder, 1968), 142–4 and 156ff.

[32] *FCF*, 52 and *TI* 4, 49ff.

[33] *FCF*, 52 and *TI* 11, 152ff.

[34] *FCF*, 52.

[35] Rahner and Ratzinger, *Revelation and Tradition*, 16.

[36] *TI* 4, 61.

[37] See, e.g., *TI* 4, 65ff., 54, 61 and also *TI* 1, 319–46, 'Some Implications of the Scholastic Concept of Uncreated Grace', 328–31. See also *FCF*, 118ff. and chapter 5 where Rahner works out the logic of this theory of quasi-formal causality and the change in the structure of the creature, esp. 149. See also Molnar, 'Can We Know God Directly?', 240ff. for a critique of this thinking.

is a serious issue that is usually not addressed by those who defend Rahner without noticing this difficulty.

Thus, for example, Leo J. O'Donovan, SJ simply assumes that Rahner's quasi-formal explanation of the operation of God's redemptive grace preserves this distinction.[38] It does not in fact even recognize it. Of course the real problem here, which O'Donovan fails to address, is whether one can describe creation after the fall as intrinsically open to God at all without becoming Pelagian in one's doctrine of God. Also, James A. Wiseman, OSB joins Rahner in following Ignatius,[39] who believed in 'an experience of God which . . . is not identical with a verbalized, conceptual knowledge of God. In the Exercises, Ignatius wants to lead one to nothing else besides this experience'.[40] But that is precisely the problem. While knowledge of God is not reducible to concepts, it cannot be had without them. And appeals to mystical experience do not help, to the extent that such claims factually bypass the *need* for Jesus Christ and for faith in him to understand God, revelation and grace. This is Rahner's chief problem and it does indeed stem from his mystical theology.

Further, Walter Burghardt, SJ recently has suggested that, because Rahner's argument for direct knowledge of God is grounded in mysticism and because it is not comprehensive knowledge, his thinking is not in conflict with scripture and tradition which I believe clearly distinguish God and creatures in a way that Rahner does not.[41] Of course not all mysticism confuses our self-knowledge with knowledge of God. Each case would have to be evaluated individually. Unfortunately, however, Burghardt includes Gregory of Nyssa, Hildegarde of Bingen and Julian of Norwich together without regard for the fact that some of what they write may truly be problematic just because it seeks a direct knowledge of God, that is, a knowledge of God that bypasses the need for Jesus Christ and his Holy Spirit. In addition, I have shown in detail in this present chapter and will again show in Chapter Six that Rahner's assumption that God can be known (however imperfectly) as the term of our transcendental dynamisms leads him to compromise his own insistence that the God who meets us in experience

---

[38] Leo J. O'Donovan, SJ, 'A Journey into Time: The Legacy of Karl Rahner's Last Years', *TS* 46.4 (1985), 621–46, 626.

[39] James A. Wiseman, OSB, '"I Have Experienced God": Religious Experience in the Theology of Karl Rahner', *American Benedictine Review* (March 1993), 22–57.

[40] Wiseman, '"I Have Experienced God"', 52.

[41] See Walter J. Burghardt, SJ, *Long Have I Loved You: A Theologian Reflects on His Church* (New York: Orbis Books, 2000), 189ff.

is truly free. No doubt these Rahnerian insights are indebted to mysticism. But that hardly validates them. In addition, Rahner is led by his method to understand God as the nameless and, as we are seeing, it is this very idea that fosters the agnosticism that collapses the immanent into the economic Trinity and opens the door to pantheism and dualism. Finally, a comparison of Rahner and Torrance (Chapter Six) will show quite clearly that Rahner's failure to begin and end his theology with Jesus Christ himself as the One Mediator, leads him to argue that self-acceptance is acceptance of God and that our experience of hope determines the true meaning of the resurrection for us. Yet, any true Christian mysticism would have to assert that we must look away from our self-experience to Jesus himself and see our lives hidden with Christ in God precisely because the truth of the resurrection must come to us from outside the circle of our transcendental experience.

In keeping with his method then, Rahner insists that knowledge of God does not mean knowledge of something new coming from without but that 'We are oriented towards God'.[42] And because 'This original experience is always present' everyone already knows God as he or she knows himself or herself.[43]

> This unthematic and ever-present experience, *this knowledge of God which we always have* . . . is the permanent ground from out of which that thematic knowledge of God emerges . . . in philosophical reflection . . . we are only making explicit for ourselves what we already know implicitly about ourselves in the depths of our personal self-realization.[44]

Thinking in this way, Rahner assumes that revelation has its existence in one's consciousness and is indeed subject to the structures of the knowing subject.[45] And this leads directly to the idea that knowing ourselves means knowing God.[46] For Rahner, 'experience of *God* constitutes the enabling condition of, and an intrinsic element in the experience of self'. Therefore 'The experience of self is the condition which makes it possible to experience God' and 'the personal history of experience of the self is the personal history of the experience of God'.[47]

---

[42] *FCF*, 53, *TI* 4, 54, 61, 65ff., and *TI* 11, 156.

[43] *FCF*, 53. See also *TI* 11, 155, 161.

[44] *FCF*, 43, emphasis mine. Also, 21ff. and *TI* 11, 154–5.

[45] 'It [revelation] has its existence in man's own conscious thought and hence is subject to the a priori structure of human knowledge' (*TI* 11, 91, 'Reflections on Methodology in Theology').

[46] See *TI* 11, 154 and *TI* 13, 122–32, 'Experience of Self and Experience of God', esp. 124ff.

[47] *TI* 13, 125.

It is Rahner's concept of the luminosity of being which allows him to think this way.[48] Rahner writes of revelation that it is

> a modification of our transcendental consciousness produced permanently by God in grace. But such a modification is really an original and permanent element in our consciousness as the basic and original luminosity of our existence. And as an element in our transcendentality . . . it is already revelation in the proper sense.[49]

As we have seen above and will see again below, it is precisely this belief that makes it virtually impossible for Rahner to adhere to his stated goal of reflection on God from the economic trinitarian self-communication of God in Christ.[50]

At this crucial stage in the development of Rahner's doctrine of God it is clear that while Rahner believes God is *free*, his method of synthesizing natural and revealed theology causes him to believe that any proof of God's existence stems from an experience of ourselves. This methodological assumption compromises God's independence in relation to human experience and reflection. Thus, 'The meaning of all explicit knowledge of God in religion and in metaphysics . . . can really be understood only when all the words we use there point to the *unthematic experience* of our orientation towards the ineffable mystery.'[51] According to his method, this is the *foundation* for the doctrine of *God*. Everyone has an experience of a horizon that cannot be controlled which Rahner calls an experience of the reality of the transcendent God. Thus, when one is oriented toward what philosophy recognizes as mystery or

---

[48] See *HW*, 39 and 43 and *TI* 4, 49. For Rahner, there is an original unity between knowing and being. See, e.g., *FCF*, 149ff. for more on this idea of luminosity.

[49] *FCF*, 149.

[50] See also *FCF*, 132 for more on this. While Rahner insists that our experiences must be distinguished from the being of God, this thinking makes such distinction more than a little difficult.

[51] *FCF*, 53, emphasis mine. This same idea is expressed in *TI* 4 using the category of the 'whither' (50ff.) and again in *TI* 11, 149 and 150. For example, Rahner writes, 'But surely both together, the initial *experience* and the subsequent reflection, make it justifiable to speak of the "experience of God today"' (150, emphasis mine). Cf. also *TI* 11, 159, where Rahner writes; 'What is meant by God is to be understood *on the basis of this experience*' (emphasis mine). 'This experience is no mere mood, no matter of mere feeling and poetry carrying no conviction . . . For it is present irremovably, however unacknowledged and unreflected upon it may be, in every exercise of the spiritual faculties even at the most rational level in virtue of the fact that every such exercise draws its life from the prior apprehension [*Vorgriff*] of the all-transcending whole which is the mystery, one and nameless. It is possible to suppress this experience, but it remains' (*TI* 11, 159). All that Rahner has offered here as proof for God as an independent entity confronting us, is our *experience* of ourselves in relation to our innate apprehension of an all-transcending whole.

absolute being it legitimately can be assumed that one is speaking about the scriptural God. Eventually Rahner claims that this 'being' is identical with the immanent Trinity.[52]

According to this description we do not have to wait upon God to reveal himself at particular historical moments because it is assumed that this orientation to 'mystery', which orientation and mystery can be adequately described by the metaphysician, and therefore what 'we call God'[53] *is* truly the *totally other*, the God of Christianity present to us in history in the incarnation of the Son in the humanity of Christ and through the Holy Spirit.

Now, how can Rahner say that God is truly transcendent and free and that both philosophers and theologians know him in this way? In other words, the obvious question here is: If God is really transcendent in the sense discussed above, then why does he not transcend this orientation, experience and definition as well? While Rahner would say it is this particular God we know, his very method renders such a God totally unknowable.[54] Indeed Rahner's presupposition is that *no reality*

---

[52] *TI* 4, 71–2. Why? Because 'The three mysteries, the Trinity and its two processions and the two self-communications of God *ad extra* in a real formal causality corresponding to the two processions, are not "intermediate mysteries". They are not something provisional and deficient in the line of mystery which comes *between* the perspicuous truths of our natural knowledge and the absolute mystery of God, in so far as he remains incomprehensible even in the beatific vision. Nor are they as it were mysteries of the beyond . . . behind the God who is for us the holy mystery.' Obviously this is all true for Rahner because he really believes that what natural theology calls God and what Christians call God are one and the same thing. This, because of the luminosity of being. In fact, of course, the only way this could be true is if God were *not free* but subject to the a priori structures of human knowledge. See also, *TI* 4, 228. It is just this position that is exploited by Elizabeth Johnson as seen above.

[53] *FCF*, 54.

[54] Cf. *TI* 11, 159. Our *Vorgriff* would not innately correspond with it. See *SW* where Rahner maintains that if God is an 'absolutely "unknown", something "coming from without" in every respect, [he] is not knowable at all to a human subject according to Thomistic principles' (182). Such a God would not be subject to the a priori structures of the human mind since there would in fact be no original unity between knower and known. This insight would wreck Rahner's concept of luminosity as applied to God. Rahner could not hold his important insight that humanity is (via the *species impressa*) entitatively assimilated to God (*TI* 1, 327–8). His entire theory of *quasi-formal* causality is based on this insight. Rahner cannot actually maintain a real distinction between philosophy and theology because of this. So in his philosophy of religion he maintains that we cannot prejudge whether revelation has occurred (*HW*, 173–4). This view apparently affirms the freedom of God's revelation as unmerited and incalculable grace. But how do we know of this grace? Because, Rahner says, we must reckon with God's silence. And here is Rahner's problem. There cannot possibly be a *real* divine silence on this view since Rahner has already presupposed that his philosophy of religion, by which he knows this silence, is a 'condition that is itself created by God's speaking' (*HW*, 174). And the fact that this is not a real possibility for God is confirmed by Rahner's belief that if God did not speak, we humans by

at all, including God, transcends the limit of experience accessible to
the metaphysician. Such a reality, says Rahner, could never be known.[55]
Thus, in spite of Rahner's own awareness that he should not deduce
the incarnation and grace from the abstract notion of God's absolute
proximity as the holy mystery,[56] the fact is that being in general is the
limit of Rahner's doctrine of God. God's being cannot transcend this.
And of this 'being' we humans always do have a 'prior apprehension'
(*Vorgriff*) against which we interpret our experiences.

So while Rahner the theologian insists that God is *free*, Rahner the
philosopher assumes that the *true source* of our knowledge of God is
'the transcendental experience of our orientation towards the absolute
mystery'.[57] In fact, because experience of orientation is the determinant
here, Rahner's approach cannot imagine God actually existing *apart*
from human experience: 'we can speak of God and the experience of
God . . . only *together*'.[58] Thus, 'a radical distinction between a statement
about "God in himself" and "God for us" is not even legitimate'.[59]
Rahner quite properly wished to overcome separating the treatises on
the one God and on the triune God. But part of the reason for his
identifying the immanent and economic Trinity is because he cannot
conceive of the permanence of the humanity of Christ in any other
way, and because our 'experience of the incarnation and grace'[60] make
it impossible for the being of God, which we know by reflecting upon
ourselves, to be different from the being of God revealed. Had Rahner's
starting point been God's economic trinitarian self-revelation, it is
possible that he might have avoided introducing a mutually conditioned

---

nature could hear at least his silence (*HW*, 16, 172, 175). This confusion of course invalidates
any real distinction between what philosophy discovers as revelation and what the Christian
believes is God's free revelation.

[55] *FCF*, 67. Being in general is the limit of all knowledge for Rahner: 'Our proposition
about the comprehensibility of being in itself did indeed arise from the fact that in the first
question about being every possible object of cognition is already anticipated under the
aspect of being in general. There can, therefore, be no existent thing that does not
automatically and objectively fit into the context of being in general. For this very reason
every thing is comprehensible' (*HW*, 96). The same ideas are expressed in *FCF*, 24ff.

[56] *TI* 4, 72.

[57] *FCF*, 54 and *TI* 11, 159ff.

[58] *FCF*, 54. Also *TI* 11, 159 and *TI* 4, 50–1. This follows from his belief that being and
knowing form an original unity. Thus, 'The question as to the ultimate cause of the possibility
of subsisting-in-oneself is thus identical with the ultimate cause' (*HW*, 57).

[59] *FCF*, 54–5. This is why Rahner insists on identifying the immanent and economic
Trinity and vice versa (*TI* 4, 70–2). On any other view we would have a merely formal
reconciliation of natural and revealed theology, that is, of 'one and three' (*TI* 4, 71).

[60] *TI* 4, 68 and 72.

understanding of divine and human relations; it is just because he conceives the 'identity' of the immanent and economic Trinity in light of his understanding of God as 'holy mystery' based on our transcendental experience that he allows our experience within the economy to condition revelation and grace.

Since the starting point for knowledge of God is our experience of 'mystery',[61] Rahner describes a 'more original unity'[62] among (1) natural theology, (2) revealed theology and (3) knowledge of God attained from 'experience of existence', perhaps from mystical experience or visions.[63] This derives from historical experience itself. And knowledge of it 'contains *elements* which subsequent theological reflection will appeal to as *elements* of grace and revelation'.[64] Moreover, 'Everything which we say here about knowledge of God ... refers to a more original experience.'[65] Rahner says this is not 'natural philosophical knowledge of God', though in part it is.[66] His point is that this experience of mystery (God) is what he will appeal to as the validation of his doctrine of God.[67]

Revelation – Grace

To the extent that Rahner includes grace and revelation as 'elements' in our experience it is impossible to distinguish clearly between philosophy and theology, reason and revelation, and ultimately between nature and grace. Thus, for Rahner, 'There is no knowledge of God which is purely natural.'[68] This is true for Rahner because 'grace pervades the essence of man from his very roots with divine influence, and thereby gives him the possibility of acting positively for his own salvation, and so implants in him a free and active tendency towards his own consummation'.[69] It is precisely because the creature is endowed with this modality that 'the difference between "inner and outer" break down at this point. The orientation towards the self-bestowal of God as most radically different from the creature is the innermost element of all in it'.[70]

---

[61] *TI* 11, 155.
[62] *FCF*, 56.
[63] *FCF*, 55.
[64] *FCF*, 56, emphasis mine.
[65] *FCF*, 56.
[66] *FCF*, 56.
[67] *TI* 4, 53–4.
[68] *FCF*, 57.
[69] *TI* 10, 273–89, 'Immanent and Transcendent Consummation of the World', 280.
[70] *TI* 10, 281.

Thus, for Rahner's descriptions of experience, 'it is no great loss if the analysis of man as *potentia oboedientialis* is not a "chemically pure" presentation of pure nature but is mixed up with trace elements from actual nature, and hence from its state of grace'.[71] Because Rahner maintains that nothing but this 'holy mystery' by which a person always lives 'even where he is not conscious of it'[72] is the *true* God, Rahner concludes that 'Grace and the beatific vision can only be understood as the possibility and the reality respectively of the immediate presence of the holy mystery as such.'[73] 'Grace . . . makes God accessible in the form of the holy mystery and presents him thus as the incomprehensible.'[74] Hence, for Rahner, even God's grace cannot be different from the 'absolute being' we all know and experience and define as God based upon our self-experience.

Grace and glory for Rahner manifestly mean that we cannot control the horizon of our own existence. And it may well be that we cannot control our horizon. But this uncontrollability hardly means we have seen or recognized grace as an act of a God existing independently of this experience. From all this Rahner concludes that knowledge of God 'has always been familiar to us' and indeed is 'self-evident'.[75] Furthermore, 'Mystery is already there with the very essence of the natural and supernaturally elevated being of man.'[76] It is clear that, having insisted that the being of God conform to what natural theology discovers as God on the basis of experience, Rahner *must* insist that *grace*, that is, knowledge of God revealed, is present all along 'with the very essence of the natural . . . essence of man'. Thus, there is no real distinction between nature and grace at this point. Indeed, as we have already seen, Rahner finally concludes that grace is 'an inner, objectless though conscious dynamism directed to the beatific vision'.[77] And the beatific vision is a term that Rahner applies to the highest possible description of an immediate experience of God.[78] Grace then,

---

[71]   *TI* 4, 165–88, 'Nature and Grace', 187; also *TI* 9, 28ff. See also *FCF*, chapter 4.

[72]   *TI* 4, 54, 'He would not be God if he ceased to be *this* holy mystery.'

[73]   *TI* 4, 55.

[74]   *TI* 4, 56.

[75]   *TI* 4, 57; also *TI* 11, 161.

[76]   *TI* 4, 59.

[77]   *TI* 4, 61.

[78]   For more on Rahner's notions of obediential potency and supernatural existential with critical analysis, see Chapter Five below. In that chapter it is argued that it is precisely Rahner's theology of the symbol that causes the problem here.

for Rahner, is not defined *only* as the free *charis* of God revealed in Jesus,[79] but also as our *orientation* towards 'the immediacy of God'.[80] This means nothing other than our 'orientation towards absolute mystery'.[81] '*We call this orientation grace* and it is an inescapable existential of man's whole being.'[82]

This clear synthesis of nature and grace is no mere accident of Rahner's thought. It is the unavoidable consequence of his method. At one and the same time he believes he can know the scriptural God, revelation and grace and also deduce their meaning from the experience of 'not being at one's disposal'.[83] This he assumes is an experience of 'mystery' which he terms the experience of God.[84] So he thinks that when we experience our inability to control all this we are actually experiencing God.[85] 'The transcendence in which God is already known . . . may not be understood as an active mastering . . . of God himself . . . By its very nature subjectivity is always a transcendence which listens, which does not control.'[86]

Rahner then makes his distinction between nature and grace identical with the distinction between our finiteness (being grounded in mystery) and the experience that this is not at one's disposal. This is described as the 'unity between transcendence and its term'.[87] The *term* or goal of this orientation or transcendence Rahner calls God: 'God is present as the asymptotic goal, hidden in itself, of the experience of the limitless dynamic force inherent in the spirit endowed with knowledge and freedom.'[88] It could have 'a thousand other

---

[79] Cf. Ex. 33:19; Mt. 10:8; Rom. 11:5f.; Eph. 1:5f. Grace is the incomprehensible *free* gift of God's turning to the creature that we cannot merit. It implies forgiveness of sin. See also Ex. 34:9; Rom. 5:20 and Ps. 103:8f.

[80] *FCF*, 57.

[81] *FCF*, 52 and *TI* 4, 61ff.

[82] *FCF*, 57, emphasis mine, and also 25 and 34.

[83] *FCF*, 57–9, 43 and 75–6. See also *TI* 11, 156. See also *TI* 4, 52 where Rahner writes, 'The Whither of transcendence is at no one's disposal', and *TI* 4, 53, 'For the Whither . . . the nameless being which is at the disposal of none and disposes of all . . . we can call "holy" in the strict and original sense.'

[84] *TI* 4, 54. 'If man himself is therefore to be understood as the being of the holy mystery, it also follows that *God* is present to man *as* the holy mystery.'

[85] *TI* 11, 156, 160, etc.

[86] *FCF*, 58. This would have been a strange insight, especially for the Johannine community or for Paul to accept in view of the fact that the problem of sin suggests just the opposite, that is, since the fall and apart from dependence on Christ, humanity will always try to control God in various ways.

[87] *FCF*, 58. This is an exact rendering of the ontological principle of luminosity as Rahner has understood this.

[88] *TI* 11, 153; see also 156, *FCF*, 59–60, *TI* 4, 62 and *TI* 13, 123.

names'.[89] It could be ' "absolute being" or "being in an absolute sense" or the "ground of being" which establishes everything in original unity'.[90] Rahner calls it 'the holy mystery'.[91] His ultimate goal is to show that the *term* or source of our transcendence is 'identical with the word "God" . . . We must first describe the experience and the term of the experience *together* before what is experienced can be called "God" '.[92] From this series of presuppositions it is perfectly logical for Rahner to conclude that God is experienced whenever we experience our *term*, horizon or the nameless and indefinable. Rahner contends that because the horizon (the *term* of transcendence) is infinite, it is not only not at our disposal, but it cannot be given a name.[93] In this way Rahner attempts to preserve God's freedom and transcendence.

There is, however, a very serious and frequently overlooked problem with this position. If it were truly impossible to name this *term* – if it (the term) were truly transcendent and free – then it actually could not be conceptualized. Rahner, however, does name this term of experience the 'nameless'. It should be noted clearly that the idea of the 'nameless' serves a very definite function in his thought from the very beginning. It is our *experience* of our *horizon* which *is* the basis, foundation and norm of knowing God. Thus, this *term* is not really unnamable. It can indeed be categorized – but as that in human experience which is not at our disposal.

This is an extremely significant point. Because Rahner conceives creator and creatures under the dialectically necessary umbrella of an original unity between knower and known (horizon, term, nameless, mystery), his presuppositions disallow a God who is free in the scriptural sense described above, or in the sense understood by Karl Barth and Thomas F. Torrance. So when Karl Rahner describes what is wrong with pantheism and dualism in a Christian doctrine of God, he is unable to escape the pantheist dilemma. Against dualism Rahner writes,

---

[89] *FCF*, 60. At this point in his reflections, it really makes little difference to Rahner what we name him since the term God refers to an experience on the basis of which that which we all experience (the term) is what 'we call God' (*TI* 11, 159).

[90] *FCF*, 60.

[91] *FCF*, 60, *TI* 4, 53.

[92] *FCF*, 61, emphasis mine.

[93] *TI* 4, 37, 42, 53, 60. 'The name God is the nameless infinity' (*TI* 4, 6). God, for Rahner, is 'the all-transcending whole which is the mystery, one and nameless' (*TI* 11, 159). Indeed, Rahner believes that, if the term God ever were forgotten, 'we should still constantly, though silently be encompassed by this nameless mystery of our existence, judging us and endowing us with the grace of our ultimate freedom, and we would discover the ancient name for it anew' (*TI* 11, 160).

The difference between God and the world is of such a nature that God establishes and is the difference of the world from himself, and for this reason he establishes the closest unity precisely in the differentiation. For if the difference itself comes from God, and, if we can put it this way, is itself identical with God, then the difference between God and the world is to be understood quite differently than the difference between categorical realities . . . God to be sure is different from the world. But he is different in the way in which this difference is experienced in our original, transcendental experience. In this experience this peculiar and unique difference is experienced in such a way that the whole of reality is borne by this term and this source and is intelligible only within it. Consequently, it is precisely the *difference* which establishes the ultimate unity between God and the world . . .[94]

If God *alone* establishes and maintains the world in existence, then the *difference* between God and creatures must be grounded in *God alone*. But then it could not be said that 'God is the difference of the world from himself', since, as other, he alone establishes and maintains the world in its difference without ceasing to be God. Then, Rahner would have to admit, however, that we truly cannot experience our radical dependence on God simply by experiencing our horizon, since we are identical with our horizon and not with God. Thus, to experience our distinction and union with our *term* may be necessary. But it is not necessarily an experience of God. In fact, according to the scriptural view and the view I am espousing in this book, nothing in creation is identical with God. And so, in a Christian doctrine of God where the method was dictated by this fact, one would have to acknowledge a continuing difference of *essence* between creator and creatures. This would mean that faith in the creator would be necessary to perceive and to maintain a clear and sharp distinction here without falling into pantheism or dualism. Rahner makes many distinctions since he knows that the Christian God is free, but he makes no such distinction and cannot because, according to his method, he assumes that God and human beings are already *one in intellectu*. Thus, while Rahner insists that God is free to be silent, his method causes him to describe a God who is not *really* free to reveal himself or not.[95] Indeed, for Rahner,

---

[94] *FCF*, 62–3, emphasis mine.
[95] See also *TI* 6, 71–81, 'Philosophy and Theology', 75. Rahner writes that revelation 'presupposes as a condition of its own possibility the one to whom this revelation remains unowed'. Also *HW*, 168. Rahner writes, 'there would be no word of God were there no one who was at least intrinsically capable of hearing it'. See also *HW*, 92, where Rahner writes, 'In virtue of his nature as spirit, man constantly and essentially hears a revelation from God.' Since, for Rahner, revelation occurs as a transcendental necessity of the human spirit,

'God is the most radical, the most original, and in a certain sense the most self-evident reality.'[96] The important point here is that Rahner's definition of mystery is an ontological definition of our human relation with our horizon, which horizon is necessary as the condition of conceiving or experiencing anything.[97] This *term* is *mystery* because, logically enough, it is 'nameless' and 'not at our disposal'.[98] This *term* or mystery cannot be defined, even by the *Vorgriff* Rahner insists. But the conflict, which I have tried to illustrate here, is that *he has already defined it* conceptually by the terms nameless, horizon, condition of the possibility, absolute being and holy mystery. This inconsistency is traceable to Rahner's starting point for his doctrine of God as noted above, that is, one's unthematic experience of the absolute. He is unwilling to begin his transcendental method solely by acknowledging

---

which includes grace Rahner even writes, 'revelation occurs of necessity' *HW*, 93; see also (*HW*, 20, 94–6 and 147ff.). See also *FCF*, 172. While Alan Torrance, *Persons in Communion: Trinitarian Description and Human Participation* (hereafter: *Persons in Communion*) (Edinburgh, T&T Clark, 1996), believes that Rahner does not hold that 'the human being is created to be the free and creative co-condition of the event of communication' (268) the truth is that Rahner's transcendental method has built into it the principle of mutual conditioning with the result that Rahner continually sees our relation with God as one of mutual conditioning. For more on this, see Paul D. Molnar, *Karl Barth and the Theology of the Lord's Supper: A Systematic Investigation* (New York: Peter Lang, 1996), chapter 2 and below n. 105.

   [96] *FCF*, 63 and *TI* 4, 57.

   [97] For more on this, see *HW*, 66–7 where Rahner writes, 'A revelation from God is thus possible only if the subject to whom it is supposed to be addressed *in himself* presents an a priori horizon against which such a possible revelation can begin to present itself in the first place.' Thus, 'God does not for his part initiate the relationship; he is already implicit in the openness of this relationship' (*HW*, 66, n. 9). This, of course, is why Rahner maintains that we by nature can come to terms with revelation and can perceive it (*TI* 1, 83). This, because the whole of nature has always been 'imbedded' in a supernatural context (*TI* 1, 81). Obviously that is why, for Rahner, natural knowledge of God and theological knowledge based on revelation cannot contradict each other.

   [98] *FCF*, 64–5. Obviously Rahner did not just invent this idea. He got this from the fact that 'man experiences himself as being at the disposal of other things, a disposal over which he has no control' (*FCF*, 42). Now this experience can hardly be disputed. But as a proof for the reality of God who *transcends such an experience* it presupposes what is not proven and is thus inadequate. This inadequacy follows from Rahner's method. He thinks he has discovered the being of God by examining our experience of our term. Thus, he writes, 'there is and can be only *one* proof: in the whole questionable nature of man seen as a totality' (*TI* 9, 127–44, 'Observations on the Doctrine of God', 140. See also *TI* 11, 149). Of course the positive position I am espousing is that only God can prove himself and that he does so in his Word and Spirit. Recognition of this precludes identifying God as the term of our transcendental dynamisms. The difficulties involved here will become even clearer when we compare Rahner's thinking with the thinking of T. F. Torrance in Chapter Six below.

the normativity of the scriptural revelation. Instead, Rahner insists that this *term* is not only a *mystery* which can be described philosophically; but it is a 'holy' mystery which we must worship.[99] And this synthesis of the object of philosophy and of theology represents the conflict of his method once again. It becomes even clearer when Rahner's thought is compared with Kant.

Rahner and Kant

Rahner neither wishes to ignore Kant's critique of pure and practical reason nor does he wish to leave us purely on the level of ideas. So, he insists that all of this is not just something going on in the human mind *because* if this were true then we 'would lose all connection with the original experience'.[100] Does this assertion really overcome Kant and actually refer us to God (a true transcendent other independent of us who then actually exists in relation to us precisely in his otherness)? Does this assertion point to anything *beyond* a regulative idea drawn from practical reason (the human experience of self-transcendence)? I do not see how these questions are answered by this assertion. In faithfulness to his method Rahner *assumes* that the universality of the experience proves that it cannot be just an idea. 'For this term is what opens up and makes possible the process of transcendence. Transcendence is borne by this term, and this term is not its creation.'[101] Yet, on the crucial question of what *proves* that this *idea* of a *term* determining the validity of our experiences, actually corresponds with a real and true 'being', a *Ding an sich* (in the case of trinitarian theology an immanent Trinity), Rahner passes over the *question* and assumes that, because we cannot describe our experience without this idea of a term or horizon, it must be real.

So, while Kant asked metaphysicians to prove this connection between idea and reality, Rahner simply *assumes* it, and by making that assumption he never really answers him. Thus, Rahner concludes, 'The affirmation of the reality of the absolute mystery is grounded for us, who are finite spirits, *in the necessity with which the actualization of*

---

[99] *FCF*, 66. See also *TI* 4, 61 and 67. On 67 Rahner writes, 'We can therefore affirm at once with certainty that the two mysteries of incarnation and grace are simply the mysteriously radical form of the mystery which we have shown to be the primordial one, from the point of view of philosophy of religion and also of theology: God as the holy and abiding mystery'.

[100] *FCF*, 67 and *TI* 11, 159–60.

[101] *FCF*, 67 and *TI* 11, 160.

transcendence as our own act is given for us.'[102] Because the foundation for and validation of knowledge of God is a 'self-validating' experience of one's horizon, Rahner, once again, does not conceptualize any independent freedom for God.

> The basic and original knowledge of what 'being' is comes from this act of transcendence, and it is not derived from an individual existent which we know. Something real can encounter us only in knowledge, and to state that there is something real which is a priori and in principle inaccessible to knowledge is a self-contradictory statement.[103]

And according to his method that must be so. But the only way this can be true is *if* we possess *innately* knowledge of every possible reality. Yet this possession is just what Kant called into question. If God is not an individual existent that we *can* know, then there is no real knowledge of God in his uniqueness and otherness as one who loves. And indeed if he is not an *existent* that truly is *inaccessible* to human insight, then he is not a real transcendent other at all, since he is accessible necessarily and always as we must affirm him as the term of all our transcendental acts.

It should be stressed that, by assuming that knowledge of God is a universal experience of human beings as they are, Rahner has obviated any real transcendence or freedom for God *independent* of what human experience ascribes to him. Thus, while it is clear that Rahner has profoundly indicated that we cannot leave the sphere of experience and reflection to know the transcendent God, he has not shown that knowledge of God is a *free* human response of faith to God's confrontation of his creatures in Christ and the Spirit as expressed in scripture; a human response that is begun, upheld and completed through our human participation in Christ's new humanity and thus in the life of

---

[102] *FCF*, 67, emphasis mine. The foundation for all of this in Rahner's thought is what was described above as the luminosity of being. Because Rahner assumes an *original unity* of the knowable and its cognition (*HW*, 40–1) he argues that they 'must derive from a single origin' (*HW*, 41). Thus, the problem of objectivity for Rahner is solved by his assumption of this original unity between subject and object, which necessarily must be deduced from the knowing subject. It is precisely on the basis of this insight that Rahner develops his notion of the pre-concept (*Vorgriff*) (*HW*, 53–68) as part of a person's subsisting-in-himself which is self-validating. Rahner assumes it is self-validating because of his supposition of the original unity between knower and known. And if you do not have a self-validating experience then you simply cannot know what he is talking about, according to him. Hence, 'We must experience here what mystery is, or we shall never understand its true and perfect sense' (*TI* 4, 53).

[103] *FCF*, 67 and *TI* 11, 150. On 160 of *TI* 11 Rahner insists that this kind of God does not exist today.

the Trinity. Rather, 'In the act of transcendence the reality of the term is *necessarily* affirmed because in this very act and *only* in it do we experience what reality is.'[104] Here is the crux of the matter. It is here that the creature either *needs* God, grace, revelation and faith or has them as part of his or her ontology; in which case theology will never escape the appearance of redefining God, revelation, grace and faith as elements that can be seen and described without the *need* to choose between a strict philosophical and theological method. It is just this thinking that allows Rahner to apply his ontology of the symbol to the immanent and economic Trinity, with damaging results, as we shall see below in Chapter Five.

Pantheism

The hallmark compromise of the divine freedom sought by the *creatio ex nihilo* is the fact of *mutual conditioning* which determines Rahner's thought in significant ways. For Rahner there can be no God without creatures as there can be no creatures without God. This is because Rahner identifies knowledge of God with the necessity of affirming our horizon. Again, Rahner would certainly insist that God is free precisely because he is nameless. But the question I have raised here is whether the term of our experience which Rahner has described truly is nameless. For if it were, God would then be inaccessible to human insight and that would be the most that anyone could assert without explicitly relying on revelation. We would not be able to know him by experiencing ourselves. As I have suggested above, however, Rahner's method begins precisely by naming the nameless because he assumes there is an original *unity* between knower (creature) and known (God). 'We have discussed both the holy mystery, which exists absolutely and which we call by the familiar name "God", and our transcendence to this holy mystery together. In the original unity of this transcendental experience, the two are *mutually dependent* on each other for their intelligibility.'[105]

---

[104] *FCF*, 68, emphasis mine. Cf. also *TI* 11, 155–6, 159.
[105] *FCF*, 68. For an example of Rahner's statement regarding proofs for the existence of God, see *FCF*, 69, where he writes, 'That which does the grounding is itself grounded, as it were, and what is present in silence and without a name is itself given a name.' Because Rahner thinks this way he actually maintains that 'God confers on man the power to make a genuine answer to his Word, and so makes his own further Word dependent upon the way in which man does in fact freely answer' (*TI* 1, 111). This follows again from his assumption that 'In any act of cognition it is not only the object known but also the knowing subject that is involved' (*TI* 11, 87). Indeed 'It [knowledge] is dependent not only upon the object, but also upon the essential structure of the knowing subject . . . they *mutually condition* one

And indeed they are. But what has Rahner described here? According to his own presuppositions he has described our original experience of our unity with the one and all of created being. We do not have to believe in the God of scriptural revelation to describe this mutually dependent relation. Thus, this description of God does not actually result from faith in the triune God seeking understanding, but from a synthesis of faith and understanding. In order to describe the Christian God there would have to be a clear statement that his particular *freedom* precludes the idea that he can be described in revelation and grace as mutually dependent in this way. Faith in the creator means knowledge of one who *freely* acts *for us*. This implies that he is dependent on no one and nothing *to be* and to be our God *ad extra*. It is this blurring of the distinction between philosophy and theology that influences Rahner's own perception of and application of his axiom that the immanent Trinity is identical with the economic Trinity. Instead of allowing the immanent Trinity to determine the content of our experience of God in the economy, Rahner projects our experience of our *term* which takes place within history, into the immanent Trinity and in that way reunites the treatises on the one and triune God.

Rahner's identifying knowledge of God with the necessity of affirming one's horizon then prevents him from speaking of God as an individual existent confronting people at specific points in history. And yet this is exactly the kind of act that any realistic scripturally based theology grounded in grace and revelation must affirm. Otherwise the theologian would run the risk of allowing an agnosticism to lead toward pantheism and dualism. In that way, although such a theologian might strongly affirm the importance of thinking about God from the economic trinitarian actions *ad extra*, such a theologian would have in fact grounded his or her thinking in a prior idea of God. Whereas in scripture God is the Lord of Israel and the one who is revealed in the events of the cross and resurrection, for Rahner he is the 'inconceivable and incomprehensible single fullness of reality. This fullness in its *original unity* is at once the condition of the possibility both for knowledge and for the individual thing known objectively'.[106] Thus, the proofs for the existence of God express this experience of union and distinction between oneself and the ground of this experience, that is,

---

another' (*TI* 11, 87), emphasis mine. See also *TI* 4, 49 and *HW*, 39–41, 43. As noted above, this reasoning certainly calls into question Alan Torrance's belief that Rahner did not espouse such a view of co-conditioning by creatures (above n. 95).

[106] *FCF*, 69.

the *term* (horizon).[107] The metaphysical principle of causality itself comes from the same experience.[108] Hence, this principle too proves to Rahner that in his analysis of the experience of transcendence and its term he has truly described the creator–creature relationship. Yet this is possible because Rahner has actually synthesized both creator and creature under a metaphysical notion of being drawn from an experience of 'absolute being'.[109] So, all proofs of God spring from this 'same transcendental experience'.[110]

Analogy of Being

Rahner also redefines the analogy of being using the transcendental method. We do not learn about God 'from something which does not have much to do with God'.[111] Because 'transcendental experience is the condition which makes possible all categorical knowledge of individual objects, it follows from the *nature of transcendental experience* that the analogous statement signifies what is most basic and original in our knowledge'.[112] Thus, for Rahner, *analogy* cannot mean a similarity between two utterly different beings (creator and creature) which do not exist in an original ontological *unity*. It must mean 'the tension between a categorical starting point and the incomprehensibility of the holy mystery, namely, God. We ourselves, as we can put it, exist analogously in and through our being grounded in this holy mystery which always surpasses us.'[113] Here, as elsewhere, Rahner appears to maintain divine and human freedom by distinguishing our categories (human freedom) from the holy mystery which always surpasses us (divine freedom). But, inasmuch as this 'holy mystery' has already been categorized as part of the *very structure of created being and mutually determined* by our experience of it, the problem of how to envision God's freedom remains. If this holy mystery is the creator God existing utterly in himself and in whom we can only *believe*, then it cannot logically be described as the necessary *term* against which all human knowledge takes place, that is, the metaphysical idea of absolute being.

---

[107] *FCF*, 70.

[108] *FCF*, 70. Rahner insists that causality should not be interpreted as in the natural sciences but through experience of our term.

[109] *FCF*, 71.

[110] *FCF*, 71.

[111] *FCF*, 72.

[112] *FCF*, 72, emphasis mine.

[113] *FCF*, 73.

This assumption by Rahner allows him to think he can describe God as the absolute instance of a general principle of being. Thus, when Rahner defines God as person he writes, 'The statement that "God is a person" . . . is true of God only if, in asserting and understanding this statement, we open it to the ineffable darkness of the holy mystery.'[114] When asked where our philosophy receives its content Rahner would say, 'from our historical experience'.[115] Consequently, while he intends to do a theological ontology, his method leads him to make the experience of self the foundation, norm and source of understanding God, revelation and grace.[116]

This of course is the major predicament that Rahner has bequeathed to contemporary trinitarian theology, so that those theologians who have unequivocally accepted his axiom are led to shape God according to their experiences of faith rather than allowing God the freedom to determine what can and cannot be said about him. I have already illustrated how this problem has affected the thought of Catherine LaCugna and Elizabeth Johnson, and we will see in the next chapter that this thinking leads Ted Peters, in his important book on the Trinity, to ground his knowledge of the Trinity in an experience of the 'beyond and intimate' rather than in God's actions *ad extra* in Christ and the Spirit.[117] Here it is important for contemporary theologians to see that it is Rahner's transcendental method that prevents him from being faithful to his own trinitarian insights. This will become clearer in Chapter Six when I try to spell this out more precisely by comparing his understanding of God's self-communication with that of T. F. Torrance.

The rest of Rahner's doctrine of God simply works out the logic of this 'transcendental' reflection on experience. 'Man implicitly affirms absolute being as the real ground of every act of knowledge . . . and affirms it as mystery. This absolute . . . which is always the ontologically silent horizon of every intellectual and spiritual encounter with realities,

---

[114] *FCF*, 74.

[115] *FCF*, 74.

[116] *FCF*, 75. None of this is contradicted in *TI* Volume 4 or Volume 11. Both articles insist on the same point.

[117] Also see David Coffey, *Deus Trinitas: The Doctrine of the Triune God* (hereafter: *Deus Trinitas*) (New York: Oxford University Press, 1999), who uses our transcendental experiences of knowledge, love and goodness to understand the knowledge, love and goodness of the triune God. In so doing he reads a pneumatized Rahnerian theological anthropology back into the New Testament and so compromises the person and work of Christ as well. See Molnar, 'Deus Trinitas: Exploring Some Dogmatic Implications of David Coffey's Biblical Approach to the Trinity', forthcoming in the *Irish Theological Quarterly*.

is therefore always infinitely different from the knowing subject.'[118] While this may be true, I would say we cannot therefore leap to the conclusion that this absolute being is the Christian God. For in a Christian doctrine of God we speak of one who is of a completely different being and nature than the absolute being conceivable as the 'single whole of reality' and we cannot speak of the Christian God in abstraction from his Word and Spirit.

Creatio ex nihilo

At this point in his discussion in *Foundations of Christian Faith*, Rahner explains the creation 'out of nothing'.[119] It is a clear expression of the fact that for the Christian theologian creation can in no sense be seen or described as necessary to God without denying God's freedom. But the conflict between philosophical and theological presuppositions surfaces here once again. Though Rahner intends to maintain God's freedom *in se* and in revelation and though he states this eloquently, he does not realize that his method, which distinguishes us from God by distinguishing us and our *term*, cannot actually preserve the freedom he describes as a theologian. So while he writes, 'God does not become dependent on the world, but remains free vis-à-vis the world and grounded in himself',[120] his thinking does not bear that out consistently. Attempting to preserve human and divine freedom, Rahner says God does not become an object of categorical knowledge, which knowledge always involves mutual necessity between cause and effect and presumably leads to the definition of causality envisioned by natural science but which is inapplicable here.[121] Thus, Rahner is faced with the problem of explaining how we (in our categories) actually know God while maintaining his freedom. Instead of turning to the God of scriptural revelation, he answers from his method by saying that God is the '*absolutely distant term* of the transcendence within which an individual finite thing is known'.[122] And this answer demonstrates again the logical and theological problem involved in synthesizing natural and revealed theology as in the following dilemma.

Either Rahner may argue that we have no innate and reliable categorical knowledge of the triune God since he is free. This would preserve creaturely and divine freedom and point us to revelation and thus to

---

[118] *FCF*, 77 and also *TI* 4, 50.
[119] *FCF*, 78.
[120] *FCF*, 78.
[121] *FCF*, 70.
[122] *FCF*, 78, emphasis mine.

God's economic trinitarian action as that which authenticates our concepts. Our concepts would be limited and would point beyond that limited range only when God intervened to enable it. But then, of course, Rahner would have to maintain that we have *no real knowledge* of God by reflecting on ourselves apart from scriptural faith in the triune God. *Or* he may argue that knowledge of our *term* (which of course has to involve categories – the nameless being a category too) is *real knowledge* of God; in which case he has in fact denied his own description of God's freedom. But he cannot *logically* argue both that God is *free* (that we have no categories for him) *and* that we know him as the 'term' of our spiritual dynamism. What is it that leads Rahner to believe he has maintained God's freedom here? Clearly, it is the idea that God is the *horizon* we all experience necessarily as that which is 'not at our disposal'.[123] So, by conceptually making this 'term' not just remote but 'absolutely distant' Rahner believes he is maintaining the freedom of the Christian God. But the problem here is that no matter how distant this *term* may be, Rahner and any philosopher can still describe it (categorically) as the holy mystery, absolute being, the nameless or as Rahner himself stated 'by a thousand other names', and indeed as the creator God of Christianity, without ever believing in the triune God. Insofar as this is thought possible, the *freedom* of God implied by the Christian *creatio ex nihilo* recedes into the background since the transcendental method *must claim* a true knowledge of God as part of an experience of one's horizon. And whenever this assumption is the starting point of a doctrine of God, Christian revelation, which sees the scriptural word as its only norm for truth (because Christ alone is the eternally begotten Son of the Father), becomes more a conclusion than a starting point for reflection. We have already seen the christological difficulties caused by this methodology above in Chapter Two. Once this happens it is hard to see why we would *need* Christian revelation in any practical way, except perhaps as that which confirms our own self-experience.

Categorical–Transcendental Revelation

By removing knowledge of God from the realm of the categorical and placing it into the realm of experience Rahner posits an original unity between creator and creatures.[124] Thus, this cannot be understood

---

[123] See *TI* 11, 159–60.

[124] *FCF*, 79. This is the more 'primordial unity of the spirit' he presumes exists and defines in *TI* 4, 38ff.

without an experience of freedom and responsibility. At this point Rahner applies his method to the scriptural understanding of God, revelation and grace. We know God 'in a transcendental experience in which the subject . . . is experienced as being borne by an incomprehensible ground . . . the absolute mystery which is not at our disposal . . . Creatureliness, then, always means both the *grace* and the mandate to preserve and to accept that tension of analogy which the finite subject is'.[125]

The same procedure takes place in *Theological Investigations* Volume 4, 'The Concept of Mystery in Catholic Theology', and again in Volume 11, 'The Experience of God Today'. And the results reveal once again how difficult it is to describe revelation and grace as free acts of God calling for faith seeking understanding once it is assumed that experience can be a starting point equal to scripture in this matter.

The transcendental method excludes the idea that a special inconceivable act of God within experience is the sole source of truth. Thus, the key to interpreting lectures 2 and 3 of *Theological Investigations*, Volume 4, 'The Concept of Mystery . . .' is to realize that what dictates Rahner's view of incarnation, grace and glory and his identifying the immanent and economic Trinity is not a special inconceivable act of God. It is not the revelation of something previously hidden as it might be in Scholastic 'school theology'. Rather it is the fact that he believes each of these represents the radical proximity of God to creatures in their self-transcending experiences. That is why Rahner's distinction between nature and grace, reason and revelation, and philosophy and theology can be perfectly clear in one description and become quite obscure in another. Each of these 'supernatural' mysteries is understood by Rahner as a truth confirming one's unity and distinction with absolute being (mystery – term – horizon) which one always experiences. Thus, incarnation, grace and glory are not truths that reveal something totally from beyond the sphere of human experience. Rather they simply confirm that the holy mystery is *indeed* always present as the *term* of our experience is present.

Consequently, the immanent Trinity is identical with the economic Trinity and God's radically close relation with creatures can only be expressed in terms of quasi-formal causality.[126] While Rahner the theologian insists that truth is grounded in the triune God, in Christ and in grace, he is led increasingly away from a specifically Christian

---

[125] *FCF*, 80, emphasis mine.
[126] See Molnar, 'Can We Know God Directly?', 240ff., 245ff. for more on this problem.

interpretation of those concepts as he applies his method. The operative principle of his method asserts that theological and philosophical truth can be known from one's experience of and interpretation of oneself. The problem here is that the triune God, Christ and grace tend to become instances of his general transcendental principles.

> The experience of God to which we have appealed . . . is not necessarily so a-Christian as appears at first sight. On the contrary . . . it is precisely Christianity which makes real this experience of God in its most radical and purest form, and in Jesus Christ achieves a convincing manifestation of it in history . . . This experience of God . . . really constitutes the very heart and centre of Christianity itself and also the ever living source of that *conscious manifestation* which we call 'revelation.' . . . Through this experience of God Christianity itself simply achieves a more radical and clearer understanding of its own authentic nature. For in fact in its true essence it is not one particular religion among others, but rather the sheer objectivation in history of that *experience* of God which exists everywhere in virtue of God's universal will to save all men by bestowing himself upon them as grace . . .[127]

Why should Christianity and not other religions possess this objectivity? If the experience of God exists everywhere, as this statement indicates, then why should Christian experience be any more authentic than any other religious experience? Of course Rahner intends to preserve Christianity's uniqueness, but again his method explains that uniqueness as an instance of his general principle of being applied to human experience. Consequently, as a Christian theologian, Rahner maintains Christianity is the 'pure form' of an experience of God, which all religions describe. Yet, this creates more problems than it solves. For if truth is contingent on anyone's experience of God, then any statement that Christianity is the 'purest' expression of religious experience can only make it appear that Christian experience is somehow inherently better than other religious experience, which it is not.

The problem I have tried to present in this chapter and throughout this book surfaces here once more. Any attempt to explain the objective uniqueness of Christianity by pointing to our subjective experience interpreted philosophically or religiously will always describe grace and God's universal will to save as properties of creaturely being. Yet if scriptural faith and revelation are normative, then it is clear that the objective uniqueness of revelation never resides in anyone's religious experience, but in the uniqueness of the Christian God acting *ad extra*

---

[127]   *TI* 11, 164, emphasis mine.

in free revelation and free grace. Rahner's argument would have been more convincing had he held that a Christian's experience is not one among others because it is tied to Christ alone. Instead he argues that it is not one among others because it is a more radical form of what everyone experiences. This thinking opens the door not only to a form of Ebionite Christology as discussed above and to a form of degree Christology, but it gives the unfortunate impression that Christ's uniqueness itself is somehow the result of the community's projection of its own self-experience onto the man Jesus.

Thus, Rahner believes that Jesus is a 'convincing manifestation' of our self-experience in history. Yet, if this is so, it is hard to know why he was crucified and not installed as king of Israel or heralded as the solution to the philosophical problems of the Greeks.[128] If Rahner's norm here had been the Word of God revealed, he would have realized that Jesus (as truly God and truly human) brings us all what we, in our religious experiences *cannot* procure for ourselves, that is, God's inconceivable act of revelation and salvation manifested in his life, death and resurrection. The prophets and apostles were witnesses to that truth. Also, he would have realized that describing this self-sufficient revelation of a *free* God as a 'conscious' or unconscious manifestation in ourselves compromises the very objectivity he sought to maintain. Instead of presenting Christianity as the purest or most radical form of religion, he would have been more able to show that *everyone*, including Christians, depends always upon God's *free grace* for salvation and for objective verification of these truth claims. Christians cannot point to any religious experience or set of experiences as the pure or true form of religion any more than anyone from another religion can do it. This, because God's grace *alone* makes 'religion' true existentially and theoretically. Thus, Christians are those who actively live this truth, namely, their justification by faith.[129]

Rahner's conclusion really goes beyond the limits of theology to the extent that the principles of his method dictate the solution to this

---

[128] Cf., e.g., 1 Cor. 2:8.

[129] Cf. Acts 11:26. The word 'Christians' was first used at Antioch to refer to the disciples who accepted the teaching of the apostles. Rahner's difficulty here is that he assumes that God's 'universal will to save' is identical with grace as a constituent element in human experience. It really is not. And as long as grace is conceptualized in this way, there can be no clear distinction between God's will and human experience, which in fact is not structurally altered by the incarnation as Rahner thinks. Humans exist in *relation* to God's salvific act in Christ and the Spirit, not in identity with it. Barth's critique of religion (Christianity included) and his understanding of the truth of the Christian religion in *CD* I/2, 280–361 is predicated upon the freedom of grace understood in this way.

problem. And it is this predicament that causes major difficulties when he himself works out the implications of his trinitarian axiom. He writes,

> It is, therefore, a task precisely for Christianity itself to point ever anew to this basic *experience of God*, to *induce* man to discover it within himself, to accept and also to avow his allegiance to *it* in its verbal and historical objectivation; for, in its pure form and as related to Jesus Christ as its seal of authenticity, it is precisely this that we call Christianity.[130]

Is it now the task of Christians to point out to other Christians and non-Christians that they can achieve knowledge of God in this way and that their allegiance is to their experiences of 'absolute being' which being can well be explained as a universal human manifestation without *faith* in Jesus and the Spirit and thus without need of a strictly theological method that begins in faith and seeks understanding? Again, it is another question entirely whether Christianity is the 'pure form' of *this experience* at all since Christ actually points us away from any existential or conceptual self-reliance to complete dependence on him. Thus I would say that biblical revelation is at variance with Rahner's conclusion as we are told that *we cannot really achieve knowledge of the true God* in this way since we *are* dependent *only* on the One Mediator – to whom *alone* we owe allegiance.[131] Or, in other words, we must think from a center in God and not from a center in ourselves, if we are to think in accordance with the revelation of God in Jesus Christ.

Mediated Immediacy

Returning to *Foundations of Christian Faith*, Rahner assumes once again that 'grace' is embedded in the world of experience,[132] and recognizing that leads to the truth of the Christian doctrine of God. It is worth examining this final assertion by Rahner of how to find God in the world using the transcendental method.

Rahner has established two things thus far in *Foundations*: (1) 'As ineffable and incomprehensible presupposition, as ground and abyss, as ineffable mystery, God cannot be found in his world.' This is his way of insisting that God is *free*. (2) Yet all religion, including the Christian religion, 'declares phenomena existing within our experience as definite and exclusive objectifications and manifestations of God'.

---

[130] *TI* 11, 164–5, emphasis mine.
[131] See, e.g., Eduard Schweizer, *Jesus*, trans. David E. Green (Atlanta: John Knox Press, 1971), 89–90. This self-reliance is exactly what was advocated in Gnosticism.
[132] *FCF*, 81.

This is his way of insisting that we, as creatures, can know God. Examples of these phenomena Rahner suggests are the pope (as vicar of Christ) and Jesus himself; 'in this way God as it were appears within the world of our categorical experience'.[133]

In relation to this theological problem, namely, that God is the ineffable silent term of all knowledge and that religion claims a categorical knowledge of God, Rahner proposes his theory of 'mediated immediacy'.[134] This theory basically articulates the unity and distinction between ourselves and our horizon or term as discussed above. The conflict between reason and revelation is evident since at one and the same time Rahner affirms indirect knowledge of God through created symbols and experiences and *direct knowledge* of and experience of God through grace and revelation. It is, of course, this latter affirmation which I believe is excluded by God's freedom (*creatio ex nihilo*). While Rahner holds the *creatio ex nihilo* as any Christian theologian would, his philosophical and theological explanations of it categorize grace and revelation as elements within human consciousness – as existentials of human beings as they exist in the world. The reason he thinks this way is that within his system it is completely impossible to conceive of God acting in the incarnation, grace and glory, while remaining absolutely other than the creature as the naturally known efficient cause.[135]

Thus, when God acts (imparts himself) in the incarnation, grace and glory, this *must* take place via quasi-formal causality[136] because this signals the kind of entitative divinization of the transcendental subjective attitude necessary for Rahner's natural theology. Quasi-formal causality means that 'God imparts himself immediately of himself to the creature'.[137] In Rahner's mind there is a certain necessity involved here: 'God as his own very self *must* penetrate into the non-divine region of the finite.'[138] This, because the triune God can be none other than the *holy mystery* Rahner discovered as efficient cause from his philosophy of religion (natural theology).

As efficient cause, God creates another. God does not act this way in relation to creation. He is 'formal' cause acting in creation. The problem here, however, is that the creator God is not merely a naturally known efficient cause. In fact the creator God, as efficient cause, is no less than

---

[133] *FCF*, 81.
[134] *FCF*, 83ff.
[135] *TI* 4, 66–72.
[136] *FCF*, 67.
[137] *FCF*, 66.
[138] *FCF*, 67, emphasis mine.

the efficient cause acting in the form (creation). But, Rahner cannot conceive of such a God and such a transcendent divine action on and in the creature. This is because he insists that revelation of the immanent Trinity cannot contradict the fact that the absolute holy mystery (the efficient cause) is the reality of God revealed. Thus, for Rahner, there is *no triune God transcending the concept of mystery* drawn from the *experience* of one's *term*, that is, the nameless. That is why, in his trinitarian doctrine, Rahner can only conceive of God in his proper reality as the unoriginated origin, while in the incarnation, grace and glory we apparently meet something less than this, that is, the Real Symbol (Christ).[139]

As an example of Rahner's difficulty here consider this statement taken from his article 'The Concept of Mystery in Catholic Theology':

> It is simply contradictory that something should belong completely to the order of creation, by being created, and still belong to the strictly divine order, by being strictly supernatural. Supernatural reality and reality brought about by the divine self-communication of quasi-formal, not efficient type, are identical concepts.[140]

This is a clear and *necessary synthesis* of *supernatural* and *natural reality* which must follow from Rahner's *method.* Rather than thinking of God's grace as his incomprehensibly *free act on* and *in* the creature – the act of the efficient cause (the creator) – Rahner thinks of it as the quasi-formal alteration of the knowing subject, that is, the reality 'brought about' by God's immediate communication of himself to the creature in grace and glory. In fact this is a denial that the incarnation is a mystery of faith as 'Scholastic' theology saw it. Yet isn't that the very mystery of our faith, that is, that Jesus, being *true God* and *true man*, belongs to the creaturely sphere and yet is truly supernatural – *no less God* than the creator – the efficient cause? And isn't the real problem of knowing God truly solved *only* by the fact that in Jesus we have the revelation of the Father (efficient cause) *only* because God has acted and does act freely (grace) on our behalf in Jesus and the Spirit?[141]

Yet, if Christian revelation means God *freely* reveals himself in and through history without becoming dependent on history, then we really

---

[139] *FCF*, 228ff. and 237–41. More will be said about the problematic nature of Rahner's symbolic understanding of the trinitarian actions later in this chapter and again in the next chapter.

[140] *FCF*, 67.

[141] For Rahner's explanation of quasi-formal causality, see also *TI* 1, 329ff. and *FCF*, 119ff.

have no *direct* knowledge of God, and any such claim would make our experience more than human or God less than transcendent in order to explain incarnation, grace and glory. The main point of a theology that is faithful to revelation and is based on the New Testament is that we, as creatures, can know God truly when our thinking in faith points to and participates in his sovereign intervention in history (by grace). Sign and thing signified, though seen as related in faith, would not be synthesized. While Rahner continually insists on the distinction between sign and reality, he also synthesizes them to the extent that grace and revelation (what is signified) cannot transcend being in general which we experience and know from philosophy.[142] The New Testament view seems closer to the concept of mystery which Rahner rejects as Scholastic 'school theology', since he believes that this view maintains that mystery is obscured and veiled and only accessible to *faith*.[143] Rahner cannot go along with this because, for him, *ratio* is a spiritual entity of absolute transcendence and therefore is the very faculty by which the presence of *mystery* is assured.[144] That is why Rahner asserts that God (as unknown) is included essentially in every act of cognition.[145] The comprehensive concept of mystery which Rahner has in mind[146] derives from his consideration of humanity in its natural and supernaturally elevated state as 'oriented toward mystery as such'.[147] This analysis follows from his method. It asserts that we humans can have a self-validating experience of God, and in that assertion the *real need* to depend on God's special intervention into history, either in Israel, Christ or the Church or by awaiting the coming of the Holy Spirit, can no longer be stated with the same clarity and consistency as in the New

---

[142] See *TI* 4, 221–52, 'The Theology of the Symbol', 234–5, where Rahner writes, 'They [the principles of symbolic ontology] arise because the concept of being is "analogous", that it, [*sic*] it displays the various types of self-realization of each being, and being in itself, and hence also the concept and reality of the symbol are flexible. But because these are necessarily given with the general concept of beings and being – as the "unveiled" figure of the most primordial "truth" of being – the symbol shares this "*analogia entis*" with being which it symbolizes.' Rahner's explanation of God, Christ, Church and sacrament all bear the mark of this thought. For him 'the symbol is the reality, constituted by the thing symbolized as an inner moment of moment of itself, [*sic*] which reveals and proclaims the thing symbolized, and is itself *full of the thing signified*' (*TI* 4, 251, emphasis mine). This is why he thinks there is a mutual causal connection between the sacramental signs and God's grace (240). See also Karl Rahner, *The Church and the Sacraments*, Quaestiones disputatae, 9, trans. W. J. O'Hara (New York: Herder & Herder, 1968), 38.

[143] *TI* 4, 38–40.

[144] *TI* 4, 41.

[145] *TI* 4, 41ff., 49–50.

[146] *TI* 4, 48ff.

[147] *TI* 4, 49.

Testament and in the tradition. For our orientation already contains what scripture and the tradition claim we can only receive as *free gift*.

Rahner clearly recognizes the problem here and states that God could be said to play an indirect role as the 'primordial ground' of experience. Or, he says, a person might worship nature as divine or make scientific truth the answer thinking in this fashion. Nonetheless, despite the fact that 'it is very difficult to distinguish clearly here between nature and supernatural grace in their mutual relationship'[148] this can be called 'natural religion'. Here Rahner turns to Christian revelation again to explain God's transcendence and immanence. He says that categories such as sacrament, Church, revelation and scripture only point to the 'transcendental presence of God'. But how can he describe these in terms of 'mediated immediacy'? His answer is clear. If God is to remain infinite while encountering us in religion 'then this event must take place on the basis of transcendental experience as such'. This means that this presence must be a modality of this relationship. Since transcendental experience of absolute being allows for an immediacy of God, it must be true. Again Rahner is consistent in his method by holding that Christian categories do not point to specific interventions of God in history which can be seen only in faith. Rather, they point to the 'modality of this transcendental relationship'.[149]

Of course, for Rahner, this modality is our supernatural existential, which he frequently describes in terms of quasi-formal causality. And this explanation is ultimately traceable to his philosophy of the symbol, which assumes fusion and mutual dependence of sign and thing signified.[150] But, in connection with his doctrine of God, this means 'immediacy' to God 'must be embedded in this world to begin with'.[151] And this follows since he has already assumed that experience of our *term* (God – the single whole of reality – absolute being) is an innate experience of creatures. Thus, religion simply is a moment in and modality of our transcendental and 'mediated immediacy to God'. But what kind of God can be known *directly* by knowing the medium (religion) and God *embedded* in the religious medium? A God who 'as the transcendental ground of the world has from the outset embedded himself in this world as its self-communicating ground'.[152] Rahner clearly

---

[148] *FCF*, 85.
[149] *FCF*, 85.
[150] See, e.g., *TI* 4, 236 and above. Also *TI* 4, 228ff. See also Molnar, 'Can We Know God Directly?' and *Karl Barth and the Theology of the Lord's Supper* for more on this.
[151] *FCF*, 87.
[152] *FCF*, 87.

intends to say that the Christian God has been involved with the world since the very beginning. But as he explains how we interpret experience of the Christian God according to his method, he cannot really conceive of a God truly existing independently of the world (i.e. an immanent Trinity).

The significance of all this highlights the problem I have sought to clarify in this chapter and throughout this book. Because our self-experience is both starting point and norm for the question of God and his activity in the world, Rahner believes that the 'categorical presence of God' is simply the religious subject objectivating his or her religious experiences. As such they (categories-objectivations) perform a 'valuable role'. Actually 'The role indeed really belongs to those phenomena in themselves.'[153] This attempt to speak of a God who is and remains *free* in the scriptural sense or in the realistic theological sense advanced by Barth and Torrance ascribes too much to created phenomena. It assumes that all religious experience points to the reality of God insofar as it points to the horizon (*term*) of human experience. But this is the very assumption that causes Rahner to compromise the scriptural and the traditional distinctions between God (the true God) and his *free* grace and idols and existentials which might lead us away from the true God and not toward him. Rahner concludes his treatment in *Foundations* by defining God's intervention in history with an example of what validates our 'good idea' which we think corresponds with God's intervention.

> The moment I experience myself as a transcendental subject in my orientation to God and accept it, and the moment I accept this concrete world in which . . . the absolute ground of my existence unfolds historically for me and I actualize it in freedom, *then* within this subjective, transcendental relationship to God this 'good idea' [his intervention] receives objectively a quite definite and positive significance.[154]

Perceptively, Rahner asks what is to prevent me from calling *anything* an *intervention* of God arguing in this fashion? His answer is: 'Why, then, may this not be the case?'[155] How this question is actually

---

[153] *FCF*, 88. Cf. also *TI* 4, 221–52. Symbols must have this function for Rahner because being and appearance are intrinsically and essentially related, so that one cannot really exist without the other. See 230ff. All of this is true for Rahner because he believes that symbols possess an 'overplus of meaning' (225).

[154] *FCF*, 88, emphasis mine.

[155] *FCF*, 89.

answered can be a matter of no small concern both to philosophers and theologians.

Following the position for which I have argued, that is, that the God of scripture, the triune God, is truly *free* even in his involvement in human experience, we would have to say that this may not be the case because God himself is not in any way *dependent* on anyone or anything to be God in himself or God for us *ad extra*. This insight would preclude arguing, as Rahner does, that our orientation to God contributes *objectively* to the positive significance of our ideas about his intervention in history. The only way Rahner's insight could be true is if the Christian God were in fact 'embedded' in the world as a 'ground of being', recognizable by the metaphysician and the philosopher of religion as well as by the theologian, thinking within the biblical faith.

This is not to say that God cannot be conceptualized as a 'ground of being'. Obviously, insofar as we all actually depend upon God for our being he is the 'ground of being'. The question raised here is what specific object determines the truth of our metaphysical concept of God's being? If it is the immanent Trinity acting *ad extra* in Christ and the Spirit, then it is my contention that we cannot actually begin thinking about him outside of faith in the Father, Son and Spirit. This would mean that we could not begin thinking about God truly as the 'ground of being' prior to an acknowledgment of the unique being of God revealed in Christ and the Spirit. Any attempt to define God as the 'ground of being' before believing in the immanent Trinity and without allowing the economic Trinity to determine what is said, might lead directly to the conclusion of the Deists, that is, that Christ is unnecessary really to know God.[156] Interestingly, the position, which I am questioning here, is exactly what *must* be stated in a philosophy of symbolic reality.[157] But it is just this idea which obscures philosophical and theological investigation.

---

[156] Etienne Gilson, *God and Philosophy* (New Haven: Yale University Press, 1979), 104–5ff.

[157] See Molnar, 'Can We Know God Directly?', 238ff. and 251ff. See also *Karl Barth and the Theology of the Lord's Supper*, esp. chapters 2 and 4. See *TI* 4, 225ff. Rahner believes that 'in the long run everything agrees in some way or another with everything else' (225). Thus, for Rahner, symbols are related essentially with what is symbolized and the two are intrinsically and mutually dependent. All of this is true because what is symbolized 'passes over into the "otherness" of the symbol' (240). In other words, in a symbolic philosophy, signs and things signified are embedded in one another in such a way that no clear and sharp distinction between them can be made. Clearly, this cannot apply to knowledge of God who is and remains different from the creature in his encounter with creation. This symbolic thinking is exactly what leads to Rahner's insistence on a quasi-formal explanation of the creator–creature relationship once again (245ff.). The whole problem here centers on the

The philosopher can indeed bypass Christ and attempt to know God. He or she may always discover a 'supreme being', but that is the most that can be discovered thereby. The theologian of revelation cannot bypass Christ (and by implication the Old and New Testaments) and attempt to know God. Thus, he or she will know that the unity and Trinity of the Christian God would preclude any attempt to define God as a supreme being without allowing Christ and the Spirit the sole freedom to determine the truth of the concept. Then a clear and sharp distinction between the immanent and economic Trinity would be maintained since it would be very clear that the being of God revealed (the immanent Trinity) actually transcends and is different from the being of God recognized by the philosopher apart from biblical faith (supreme being recognized as the term of our experiences of self-transcendence).

Because he is faithful to his method (attempting to harmonize natural knowledge of God with revealed knowledge) Rahner is actually unable to resolve this theological problem. Thus, he must maintain that *what* is categorized, that is, 'the holy mystery', is not conceptually beyond the religious phenomena which, in themselves, are supposed to convey God's grace. On this view the theological question of how we really know that this or that 'concept' of God's intervention is *true* is left ambiguous. For Rahner, of course, the answer resides in his *assumption* that transcendental experience of one's horizon is a real experience of *God* simply because people experience themselves this way. And their experiences are self-validating. Thus, what 'we call' God and his intervention ultimately depend not on God *alone* but on God as well as the strength of our transcendental experiences. I am arguing that this mutual coordination of God's action in history with our historical self-experience compromises the unique objectivity and freedom of God envisioned by the scriptural revelation and recognized and upheld in a properly conceived doctrine of the immanent Trinity.

Furthermore, this assumption by Rahner actually subverts the real need for Christian revelation as an independent source of truth coming to us from something other than our self-experience. One does not *need* to believe in God's special presence in history in his Word and Spirit if one already possesses this truth in the experience of

---

fact that, in a Christian doctrine of God, God is and remains ontologically different from his creatures, even in the incarnation, grace and glory. There is in fact no original ontological unity between creator and creatures as there must be for a symbolic ontological explanation of absolute being in relation to finite being.

his orientation toward the absolute, which absolute may well have little or nothing to do with the eternally triune God of Christianity.[158] In Rahner's doctrine of God then we are told that we need this God. But his method ends exactly where it began, that is, with our human experience of ourselves which we 'call' God.[159]

And this leads to his theory of anonymous Christianity in which he spells out the implications of this position by maintaining that everyone can know and experience what Christians know and experience in faith simply by having these transcendental experiences.[160] Rahner's position that Christianity is present in everyone in an incipient state[161] simply confirms the fact that he is consistent in carrying through the logic of his method. If he did not say this he would have to deny that we could know God by knowing our *term* and that grace was embedded in creation. Ultimately, he would have to deny his theory of luminosity and his philosophy of symbolic reality. Because human being is already changed ontologically (obediential potency and supernatural existential) in virtue of the incarnation, Rahner believes that people do not have to hear about Christ to be Christians. Rather, in deciding for or against themselves they already decide for or against God and Christ.

The problem with anonymous Christianity is the same problem that is apparent in Rahner's doctrine of God. He never really shows us that we are believing in and knowing anything that truly transcends us and exists in reality apart from our experience and interpretation of that experience. Thus, God, grace, revelation and faith are simply qualities of human experience interpreted philosophically and theologically for Rahner. As long as that is the case we really do not need to believe in Jesus and the Spirit *before* knowing the true God. And as long as this is the case we shall never answer the theological question of whether what we 'call' God, grace, revelation and salvation are *true* as realities coming to us from a real God independent of us. For Rahner we do not really *need* the grace of God revealed in Christ to explain 'reality' to ourselves and others. God merely confirms our transcendental experiences and our interpretations of them. Thus, for Rahner, everyone is a believer

---

[158] See, e.g., Gilson, *God and Philosophy*, 105ff., and Feuerbach, *The Essence of Christianity*, 50–8. The god of the Deists (cf. Gilson) and the god of Feuerbach are not the Christian God but an apotheosis, a mythological human invention.

[159] See *FCF*, 53–4 and Rahner and Weger, *Our Christian Faith*, 13 and 25.

[160] See, e.g., *TI* 12, 161–78, 'Anonymous Christianity and the Missionary Task of the Church'. On 161 many additional references to Rahner's treatment of this topic of anonymous Christianity are given.

[161] *TI* 12, 164.

whether he or she knows it or not. This, simply because everyone has unthematic experiences of absolute being in order to continue to exist meaningfully in the world.[162]

Such thinking leads to speculation like that of the 'questioner' who poses for Rahner the assertion in *Our Christian Faith* 'that everyone who lives their world-view with determination and commitment will find that this world-view proves true'.[163] In fact the answer to the question of which 'world-view' is true cannot be answered by examining anyone's determination and commitment to it. And this is the predicament of Rahner's method; that is, he begins and ends his thought about truth with the determination and commitment of one's transcendental experiences. Rahner also insists that a person is a believer in the 'unreflected core of her existence' as long as she loves, is loyal and committed to the truth.[164] The problem with this assertion, however, is that on his presuppositions Rahner cannot tell us whose version of 'truth' is really true since we can in fact know the truth without knowledge of Christ. That is because what actually determines the truth of his doctrine of God is our reflection on this 'unreflected core of existence'. For this reason, belief in God for Rahner means belief in mystery or human existence or reality as a whole. It cannot mean belief in the Christian God who transcends humanity and confronts people who experience him in judgment and grace according to the Old and New Testaments. It is obvious that one can live and be committed in fact without acknowledging the truth of Christianity. Paul's analysis of his own position in Galatians and Romans would provide a good example of this.[165]

Though Rahner certainly wished to present a more open view of salvation in this theory, the net effect renders Christianity less rather

---

[162] On this, see *TI* 7, 211–66, 'The Eucharist and our Daily Lives', 223. Rahner writes, 'there may be many who face up to life bravely . . . yet who do not regard themselves as believers at all. But . . . in their calm acceptance of their lives they actually achieve, implicitly and in principle, what the conscious and professed believer does explicitly'.

[163] Rahner, *Our Christian Faith*, 19–20.

[164] Rahner, *Our Christian Faith*, 12–13.

[165] Cf. also *TI* 6, 231–49, 'Reflections on the Unity of the Love of Neighbour and the Love of God', 232 and 238ff. It is interesting to note that Moltmann too accepts a version of Rahner's 'anonymous Christianity': 'Are there "anonymous Christians" outside Christianity in the world? There are: they are the poor, the hungry, the thirsty, the sick and the imprisoned of Matt. 25 whom Christ declares to be his "brothers and sisters", whether they are Christians or not . . . there are also 'anonymous Christians' where deeds of mercy and justice are done to them', Jürgen Moltmann, *History and the Triune God: Contributions to Trinitarian Theology* (hereafter: *History and the Triune God*), trans. John Bowden (New York: Crossroad, 1992), 122.

than more necessary. This, because the pivotal factor that determines the truth of Christianity on this view is to have significant human experiences, beginning with the experience of our horizon. Any real dependence on Christ in the New Testament sense would demand faith and action with respect to him alone.

To sum up. We have seen *what* Rahner's doctrine of God states and we have seen that it is *based* on 'transcendental experience'. I have contended that this starting point compromises God's *freedom* and the consequent *need* to *believe* in the *triune* God *before* being able to make sense of the creator–creature relationship. Further, I have contended that this leads to Rahner's synthesis of nature and grace and to the idea that God's free grace and free revelation can be described as 'elements' or modalities within human experience by the philosopher of religion as well as the theologian.

In the context of my presentation of a contemporary doctrine of the immanent Trinity, it is extremely important that we note the ambiguity in Rahner's thought here. On the one hand Rahner has reshaped contemporary theology in a positive way by insisting that we begin thinking about God from the economic Trinity which *is* the immanent Trinity. Most contemporary theologians would certainly agree with this. On the other hand, however, Rahner's transcendental method, which begins with experience instead of with an acknowledgment of Jesus, the Word incarnate as the sole way to the Father, leads him to think about the immanent and economic Trinity in categories drawn from his philosophy of the symbol. This in fact means that it is God as defined by our self-experience that Rahner portrays instead of God uniquely revealed in Christ. This is certainly not what Rahner intended, but it is unfortunately where his method unwittingly led him. We will explore this predicament more deeply in the next chapter by showing how Rahner's method of beginning theology from self-transcending experience leads to difficulties in Christology and trinitarian theology. By comparing the way the doctrine of the immanent Trinity functions in the theology of Karl Barth with a number of prominent contemporary theologians who tend to follow Rahner's method rather than Barth's, I hope to show more clearly why a proper doctrine of the immanent Trinity could have allowed Rahner and others to take human experience seriously without making it the starting point and thus the norm for their trinitarian reflections. To this we now turn.

Chapter Five

Can a Metaphysical Principle of Relationality Be Substituted for the Relations of the Immanent Trinity? Karl Barth and the Current Discussion

I N this chapter we shall explore several factors that indicate how a number of contemporary theologians, such as Eberhard Jüngel, Catherine LaCugna, Jürgen Moltmann, Wolfhart Pannenberg, Ted Peters and Karl Rahner either fail to think through the implications of the doctrine of the immanent Trinity or, by merely paying lip-service to the doctrine, allow some principle rather than God to define the meaning of relationality. This chapter will not involve an exhaustive treatment of the thought of each theologian; instead the focus here will be on how their thinking relates both to the theology of Karl Barth and to a proper doctrine of the immanent Trinity. Here, with the help of Barth's theology, we shall explore some of the problems that result from allowing relationality rather than the triune God to dictate trinitarian thinking. I also hope to show more precisely, with particular focus on his theology of the symbol, the kinds of difficulty that Rahner has bequeathed to modern trinitarian theology. Hopefully this will lead us closer to a contemporary doctrine of the immanent Trinity.

We have already noted in Chapter One that the purpose of a doctrine of the immanent Trinity, broadly speaking, is to recognize, uphold and respect God's freedom. We also noted that Karl Barth insisted that the doctrine of the Trinity was not merely a description of salvific events but a statement about the eternal Father, Son and Spirit as the one who enables the events of salvation and redemption. Hence for Barth trinitarian doctrine or trinitarian thinking could not displace God as the foundation of true knowledge, since God's action in revelation is not a dogma, view or principle but the actual Word of God working *ad extra* as creator, reconciler and redeemer. Our position therefore has been that knowledge of God takes place from Jesus Christ through the power of his Holy Spirit and consequently it must be sought in and from a center outside us, that is, from a center in God acting for us. It must be sought and found objectively in Christ and subjectively through the Holy Spirit.

While Christian theologians agree that the doctrine of the immanent Trinity should uphold God's freedom, we have already seen that the way many today employ trinitarian categories leads from agnosticism to monism and dualism and thus compromises divine and human freedom. We have also seen that most modern theologians adopt Rahner's axiom of the identity of the immanent and economic Trinity in some form, even if only to move beyond it, to speak about God's involvement with the world. But I have suggested that this axiom, with its vice versa, tends to compromise divine and human freedom by seeing our human relationship with God as one of mutual conditioning. It is apparent that some confusion and reversal of the creator–creature relationship results both in Rahner's own thought and when Rahner's axiom is accepted along with the vice versa. We noted above that several indications of such a reversal today are: (1) the trend toward making God, in some sense, dependent upon and indistinguishable from history; (2) the lack of precision in Christology which leads to the idea that Jesus, in his humanity as such, is the revealer; (3) the failure to distinguish the Holy Spirit from the human spirit; (4) a trend, following Rahner, to begin theology with experiences of self-transcendence.[1] Up to this point we have seen the marks of one or another of these difficulties in the works of a number of prominent contemporary theologians and I have suggested that a proper doctrine of the immanent Trinity could serve to overcome these difficulties. While the doctrine is not to be constructed in order to avoid these difficulties, it is necessary as a statement of and recognition of God's freedom that does indeed lead away from them. In other words, while a proper understanding of the doctrine of the immanent Trinity acknowledges the importance of

---

[1] For an almost classic case of a contemporary theology that allows Rahner's transcendental method to define the terms of discussion in exactly the wrong way, see 'Trinitarian Theology as Participation' by Frans Josef Van Beeck, SJ in *The Trinity: An Interdisciplinary Symposium on the Trinity*, ed. Stephen T. Davis, Daniel Kendall, SJ and Gerald O'Collins, SJ (Oxford: Oxford University Press, 1999), 295–325.

God's triune relations as the free basis of his actions as creator, reconciler and redeemer, we must insist that relationality does not define God, and we cannot use either the doctrine of the immanent or of the economic Trinity to validate a general principle of relationality.

That a doctrine of the immanent Trinity should function this way is not always clearly recognized today. For instance, Colin Gunton appraises Catherine LaCugna's *God for Us* as 'a polemic against the doctrine of the immanent Trinity' and wonders whether her approach 'finally escapes the pantheism which results from any attempt to bring God and the world too close'.[2] I agree with Gunton that the doctrine upholds divine and human freedom. But I believe pantheism does not *just* follow an attempt to bring God and the world too close; it follows, as Barth clearly saw, from an attempt to see this closeness in abstraction from the immanence God has freely established by grace in Jesus Christ.

> If the freedom of divine immanence is sought and supposedly found apart from Jesus Christ, it can signify in practice only our enslavement to a false god . . . the Church must . . . see that it expects everything from *Jesus Christ* and from Jesus Christ *everything*; that He is unceasingly recognised as the way, the truth, and the life (Jn. 14.6) . . . The freedom of God must be recognised as His own freedom . . . as it consists in God and as God has exercised it. But in God it consists in His Son Jesus Christ, and it is in Him that God has exercised it . . . If we recognise and magnify it, we cannot come from any other starting point but Him or move to any other goal.[3]

For LaCugna

> Economy and theology are two aspects of *one* reality: the mystery of divine–human communion . . . There is neither an economic nor an immanent Trinity; there is only the *oikonomia* that is the concrete realization of the mystery of *theologia* in time, space, history and personality . . . [economic and immanent mislead because] *Oikonomia* is not the Trinity *ad extra* but the comprehensive plan of God reaching from creation to consummation, in which God and all creatures are destined to exist together in the mystery of love and communion . . . *theologia* is not the Trinity *in se*, but, much more modestly and simply . . . the mystery of God with us. . . . The life of God is not something

---

[2] Colin Gunton, Review of Catherine LaCugna, *God for Us*, *SJT* 47.1 (1994), 136–7. Gunton suggests greater distinction between the economic and immanent Trinity in *The Promise of Trinitarian Theology*, 137ff. Thompson, *Modern Trinitarian Perspectives*, argues with clarity and subtlety for the *unity* and *distinction* of the economic and immanent Trinity (25ff.) and opposes grounding the doctrine in philosophy or anthropology.

[3] *CD* II/1, 319–20.

that belongs to God alone. *Trinitarian life is also our life* . . . The doctrine of the Trinity is not ultimately a teaching about 'God' but a teaching about *God's life with us and our life with each other.*[4]

Unwilling and unable to distinguish God *in se* from God acting *ad extra*, this thinking invites pantheism and dualism. God is no longer the subject acting toward us and for us from within history but becomes little more than our experiences of love and communion. Clearly, the expression 'God's life with us' depicts an apotheosis unless it *first* refers to God in himself; and the way LaCugna conceives the doctrine prevents this: the mystery of God revealed is

> the mystery of persons in communion who embrace death, sin, and all forms of alienation for the sake of life [while the Spirit transforms us so] 'we become by grace what God is by nature', namely, persons in full communion with God and with every creature . . . The life of God – precisely *because* God is triune – does not belong to God alone.[5]

Here, persons in communion are substituted for Jesus Christ and the lordship of the Holy Spirit is transformed into a necessary attribute of creatures. Because God is triune he must be in communion with all creatures and his life cannot be uniquely his. Here, love in general defines God's love and displaces his freedom:

> Love by its nature is outgoing and self-giving . . . Divine self-sufficiency is exposed as a philosophical myth . . . [Thus God's love] spills over into what is other than God, giving birth to creation and history . . . we become by grace what God is already by nature, namely self-donating love for the other . . . To be God is to be the Creator of the world.[6]

Role of Experience

Why this confusion? Because LaCugna begins with experience and then interprets doctrine: 'The only option is for Christian theology to start afresh from its original basis in the *experience* of being saved by God through Christ in the power of the Holy Spirit.'[7] God's freedom can

---

[4] LaCugna, *God for Us*, 222–4 and 228.
[5] LaCugna, *God for Us*, 1. Cf. also 354.
[6] LaCugna, *God for Us*, 353–5.
[7] LaCugna, *God for Us*, 3, emphasis mine. While I freely admit that experience and doctrine must indeed be properly coordinated, it is misguided to suggest that the original basis for Christian theology is in our experience of being saved. Any genuine experience of salvation would necessarily point away from itself to its true basis in God's action *ad extra*,

no longer be conceived as autonomy and self-sufficiency but must be understood as 'the contemplation of the divine *oikonomia*'.[8] God must be seen as one who *needs* and cares for us and is thus not immune to our suffering.

But, according to Barth, the original basis of Christian theology is God himself acting objectively for us in Christ and subjectively within us by the Holy Spirit; his starting point for learning 'the lofty but simple lesson that it is by God that God is known . . . was neither an axiom of reason nor a datum of experience. In the measure that a doctrine of God draws on these sources, it betrays the fact that its subject is not really God'.[9] It is the deity of the Holy Spirit that creates faith. And despite criticism that his theology is not eschatological enough, Barth argues,

> This being of ours is thus enclosed in the act of God . . . we cannot as it were look back and try to contemplate . . . this being of ours as God's redeemed . . . To have the Holy Spirit is to let God rather than our having God be our confidence . . . it lies in the nature of the *regnum gratiae*, that having *God* and our *having* God are two very different things . . . We believe our future being. We believe in an eternal life even in the midst of the valley of death. In this way, in this futurity, we have it . . . the assurance of faith means concretely the assurance of hope . . . The man we know does not live an eternal life. This is and remains the predicate of God, of the Holy Spirit . . . Both [becoming rich in God and poor in ourselves] become our experience . . . But we do not have the divine and spiritual riches and the divine and spiritual poverty in our experience [because] God remains the Lord even and precisely when He Himself comes into our hearts . . . The deity of the Holy Spirit is thus demanded.[10]

---

that is, an action of the Father, Son and Holy Spirit in light of which our experience makes sense. With the exception of the fine chapter on the Trinity and Preaching by Maguerite Shuster, and a number of the patristic chapters, there is a tendency in *The Trinity: An Interdisciplinary Symposium on the Trinity* to see the doctrine of the Trinity as a description of experience rather than a description of the immanent Trinity, which takes place in and through experience.

   [8] LaCugna, *God for Us*, 169. Cf. also 397–8: 'The God who does not need nor care for the creature, or who is immune to our suffering, does not exist . . . person, not substance is the root (radix) of all reality . . . the idea of person as self-sufficient, self-possessing individual . . . is perhaps the ultimate male fantasy. Classical metaphysics, the effort to ascertain what something is "in itself", is perhaps the ultimate projection of masculinity.' While the errors of individualism are well-known and well-documented, this hardly means that the effort to find out what something is in itself is always a projection.

   [9] *CD* II/2, 3.

   [10] *CD* I/1, 462–5. Cf. also *CD* I/2, 249.

Recognizing God's actual freedom led Barth to direct us away from our experiences and ideas toward God himself who certainly is for us, but as the sovereign God.

> When we ask questions about God's being, we cannot in fact leave the sphere of His action and working as it is revealed to us in His Word. God is who He is in His works. He is the same even in Himself, even before and after and over His works, and without them. They are bound to Him, but He is not bound to them. They are nothing without Him. But He is who He is without them. He is not therefore, who He is only in His works. Yet in Himself He is not another than He is in His works. In light of what He is in His works it is no longer an open question what He is in Himself . . . there is no possibility of reckoning with the being of any other God, or with any other being of God, than that of the Father, the Son and the Holy Spirit as it is in God's revelation and in eternity.[11]

God is supremely and utterly independent of creation and is not subject to the limitation of created being which

> cannot affirm itself except by affirming itself against others . . . [God is also free] to be present with that which is not God, to communicate Himself and unite Himself with the other and the other with Himself, in a way which utterly surpasses all that can be effected in regard to reciprocal presence, communion and fellowship between other beings.[12]

God then is not a prisoner of his transcendence and so is for us; but he is the *only divine subject* and so he cannot become the predicate in a sentence in which the subject is relationality as defined through an ontology which comprehends both human and divine experience. Certainly the notion of a divine subject is slippery and can be understood in a Hegelian way which leads to pantheism and modalism. But Barth does not so use this concept because by it he asserts God's sovereignty and lordship in relation to the world and within the world (as just explained). And he continually bases his analysis in the antecedent being of the Father, Son and Spirit refusing to define eternity *by* time,[13] affirming that who Jesus is as Son does not arise from history but from an act of divine lordship,[14] and he opposes Schleiermacher because

---

[11]   *CD* II/1, 260–1.
[12]   *CD* II/1, 313. Cf. also *CD* II/1, 326–7.
[13]   Cf. *CD* I/1, 384–489 and *CD* II/1, 611ff.
[14]   Cf. *CD* I/1, 426–7. '"Begotten of the Father before all time" means that He did not come into being in time as such . . . That the Son of God becomes man and that He is known by other men in His humanity as the Son of God are events, even if absolutely

[He saw in Christ] the preservation 'of the receptivity implanted in human nature from the beginning and continuously evolving, a receptivity which enables it to take up into itself such an absolute potency of the God-consciousness' . . . The Word of God is not seriously regarded by him as the Subject of the redeeming act, but as one of the factors in the world-process.[15]

Jürgen Moltmann misunderstands Barth here. When Barth suggested that, to escape an eschatological onesidedness, he should let 'the doctrine of the immanent Trinity function as an expository canon for the proclamation of the lordship of Jesus Christ', Moltmann responded:

I must admit that in studying *C.D.* at these points I always lost my breath. I suspect you are right but I cannot as yet or so quickly enter into this right. Exegetical friends . . . have forced me first of all to think through eschatologically the origin, course, and future of the lordship of Christ. In so doing I thought I could so expound the economic Trinity that in the foreground, and then again in the background, it would be open to an immanent Trinity. That is, for me the Holy Spirit is first the Spirit of the raising of the dead and then as such the third person of the Trinity.[16]

But Barth was suggesting that the Holy Spirit is first the third person of the Trinity and then the Spirit of the raising of the dead; thus God's sovereignty and the certainty of our hope could never become dependent on historical events but would be disclosed in and through them.

Moltmann now abandons the conceptual framework that includes immanent and economic Trinity because such 'distinctions derive from general metaphysics, not from specifically Christian theology. They grasp the mystery of God merely exoterically, not esoterically, and are therefore at most applicable to God's relation to the world generally, but not to the inner self-distinctions in God himself.'[17] He believes that

---

distinctive events, in time . . . *But their distinction does not itself derive or come from time* . . . because the power of God's immanence is here the power of His transcendence, their subject must be understood as being before all time, as the eternal Subject', emphasis mine.

[15] *CD* I/2, 134–5 and 150ff. Barth insisted that the incarnation takes place in the freedom of the eternal Word and therefore does not rest on any inner or outer *necessity* (*CD* I/2, 136ff.). It is a miracle that, if it could be explained, would no longer be a miracle. When Barth speaks of God as person, he emphasizes that 'Precisely in His Word God is person' (*CD* I/1, 139), namely, Jesus as the Word is not a thing or an object, but a 'free subject' even 'in respect of the specific limitations connected with its individuality' (138); to be a real person then is to be a 'really free subject' (139), a 'knowing, willing, acting I' (II/1, 283ff.).

[16] *Karl Barth Letters 1961–1968*, 348.

[17] Jürgen Moltmann, *The Spirit of Life: A Universal Affirmation* (Minneapolis: Fortress Press, 1993), 343 and 290.

for Barth and Rahner 'the unity of God precedes the triunity' and that Barth left us with no immanent Trinity existing independently. Yet the very fact that Barth refused to allow God's being and act to be defined outside God's own actions in Christ and the Spirit and refused to see God's relations with us as mutually conditioned shows exactly the opposite. So while Moltmann finds the presence of the Spirit 'in God's *immanence* in human experience, and in the *transcendence* of human beings in God', he frees theologians from the need to believe in Jesus Christ through the power of the Holy Spirit. The human spirit 'is self-transcendently aligned towards God'.[18] By thus claiming for experience what Barth affirmed only God can give in ever new acts of freedom, Moltmann fails to distinguish consistently the Holy Spirit from the human spirit, misunderstands God's freedom and believes because 'God is in all things, [and] . . . all things are in God . . . Every experience of a creation of the Spirit is hence also an experience of the Spirit itself.'[19] Instead, Barth stressed that

> we have always to take in blind seriousness the basic Pauline perception of Colossians 3.3 which is that of all Scripture – that our life is our life hid with Christ in God. With Christ: never at all apart from Him, never at all independently of Him, never at all in and for itself. Man never at all exists in himself [but] in Jesus Christ and in Him alone; as he also finds God in Jesus Christ and in Him alone.[20]

As we have seen throughout this book, pantheism and dualism threaten whenever theology begins with experience. It is a mark of LaCugna's pantheism that she cannot find God in Jesus Christ except insofar as he humanly embodies 'divinization'. Thus, 'His person, as the achievement of truly divinized human nature is in this sense [that he lived, died and was raised to eternal life] eternal.'[21] The human Jesus embodies God's economic relatedness to us in the Spirit and to that extent is the Christ. She seeks to rehabilitate some form of subordinationism, arguing that Jesus finds his origin in God and that subordinationism 'is not always the same as Arianism; the monarchy of the Father necessarily entails at least an economic, if not an ontological, subordination of the Son'.[22] Rahner's axiom and method have been

---

[18] Moltmann, *The Spirit of Life*, 7.
[19] Moltmann, *The Spirit of Life*, 34–5.
[20] *CD* II/1, 149.
[21] Cf. LaCugna, *God for Us*, 317, n. 143 and 296.
[22] LaCugna, *God for Us*, 119. She misunderstands Barth's theology as modalist, claiming that he says that God was one subject existing in 'three modes of revelation, as Father, Son and Holy Spirit' (252). For Barth, revelation is threefold *ad extra* because God who *is* Father,

influential here and have led some to believe that experience is actually a source for theology.[23] Barth clearly saw the issue:

> All Subordinationism rests on the intention of making the One who reveals Himself . . . the kind of subject we ourselves are . . . Subordinationism finally means the denial of revelation, the drawing of divine subjectivity into human subjectivity, and by way of polytheism the isolation of man . . .[24]

Using Rahner's theology as a point of departure, but rejecting his Thomistic view of theology as the science of God, LaCugna welcomes Eberhard Jüngel's view that 'the economic doctrine of the Trinity deals with God's history with [humanity], and the immanent doctrine of the Trinity is *its* summarizing concept'.[25] But if the doctrine is seen this way, then the freedom of God to unite himself with creatures in a manner that surpasses communion between others who are not God (Barth's view) is compromised by the need to affirm itself against others, that is, God might only have as much freedom as our experiences allow. Agnostic modalism follows: 'An immanent trinitarian theology . . . cannot be an analysis of what is "inside" God, but a way of thinking and speaking about the structure or pattern of God's self-expression in salvation history'; and as noted in Chapter One, LaCugna argues that there *may* be distinctions in God, but not necessarily, since we have no 'transeconomic perspective' from which to know.[26] While Jüngel says

---

Son and Spirit in eternity has freely acted in revelation as God for us. Like Rahner, she equates God's original being (unity) with the unoriginate, which she equates with the Father. For a proper defense of Barth against the charge of modalism see Hunsinger, *Disruptive Grace*, 191.

[23] Cf. Anne Carr, 'Theology and Experience in the Thought of Karl Rahner', *Journal of Religion* 53 (1973), 359–76, at 359 and above, Chapter One. Ellen Leonard, 'Experience as a Source for Theology', in the Proceedings of the Annual Convention of *The Catholic Theological Society of America* (1988), Vol. 43 ed. George Kilcourse 44–61 believes that 'It is the task of theology to revision God in the light of contemporary experience', 56. Without necessarily being influenced by Rahner, Gordon D. Kaufman thinks this is the main function of theology. Cf., e.g., Gordon D. Kaufman, *God the Problem* (Cambridge, MA: Harvard University Press, 1972), 24 and Kaufman, *Method*, 8. William V. Dych, 'Theology in a New Key', believes that neither God nor scripture can be starting points for theology today but rather 'our shared human existence', in O'Donovan (ed.), *A World of Grace*, 3.

[24] *CD* I/1, 381.

[25] LaCugna, *God for Us*, 224, 211, 222. Cf. Paul D. Molnar, 'The Function of the Immanent Trinity in the Theology of Karl Barth: Implications for Today', *SJT* 42.3 (1989), 367–99 at 396 and Chapter Eight below.

[26] LaCugna, *God for Us*, 225, 227. 'The immanent Trinity is not transhistorical, transempirical, or transeconomic . . . to speak about God in immanent trinitarian terms is nothing more than to speak about God's life with us in the economy . . . an immanent theology of God is an inexact effort to say something about God *as God is revealed in the economy* . . .

nothing like this, he unintentionally opens the door to this kind of thinking by accepting Rahner's axiom without hesitation and by the way he states the function of the doctrine.[27]

Theological Agnosticism

LaCugna's agnostic view is not grounded in the incarnate Word and, as seen in Chapter One, is similar to the agnostic views of Sallie McFague and Gordon Kaufman. LaCugna asserts that history shows that to argue on the basis of a transeconomic perspective must mean that we leave the economy behind; then the doctrine has no bearing on our life or faith. Certainly we cannot leave the economy behind without such an effect, but that hardly means we *must* leave the economy if we argue on the basis of God's inner trinitarian life. With Schoonenberg, she claims that the question of whether God would be trinitarian apart from salvation history 'is purely speculative and cannot be answered on the basis of revelation'.[28]

Yet it is precisely on the basis of revelation that Barth believed we *must* answer this question or succumb to subjectivism, pantheism, panentheism (which is worse than pantheism)[29] or dualism just because of an agnostic inability to perceive that the truth of revelation hinges on the fact that God is in revelation what he is in himself. Hence

> It is not true, then that the father–son relation is itself originally and properly a creaturely reality. It is not true that in some hidden depth of His essence God is something other than Father and Son. It is not true that these names are just freely chosen and in the last analysis meaningless

---

Speculating about the immanent Trinity is a kind of discernment . . . a way to speak about the nature of God *with us* in the economy . . . Because the essence of God is permanently unknowable as it is in itself, every attempt to describe the immanent Trinity pertains to the face of God turned toward us' (229–30). Hence, LaCugna believes 'It would be better *if* the interrelationships of divine persons were located not in an intradivine sphere but in the mystery of the economy – which is where God exists anyway' (369).

[27] Cf. Eberhard Jüngel, *God as the Mystery of the World: On the Foundation of the Theology of the Crucified One in the Dispute Between Theism and Atheism*, trans. Darrell L. Guder (hereafter: *God as the Mystery of the World*) (Grand Rapids, MI: Eerdmans, 1983), 392, 316f. Cf. also Molnar, 'The Function of the Immanent Trinity', 390–8, Thompson, *Modern Trinitarian Perspectives*, 32f., 58ff. and Chapter Eight below.

[28] LaCugna, *God for Us*, 227; also, 334.

[29] *CD* II/1, 312. 'The mythology of a merely partial and . . . selected identity of God with the world, which under the name of panentheism has been regarded as a better possibility than undiluted pantheism, is really in a worse case than is that of the latter.' This, because it must mingle God with something else idealistically or materialistically and leads either to materialism or to spiritualism.

symbols, symbols whose original and proper non-symbolical content lies in that creaturely reality. On the contrary, it is in God that the father–son relation, like all creaturely relations, has its original and proper reality.[30]

Further, speaking of the fact that authority in the Church reflects the authority of God in his revelation, Barth writes, 'This is just as certain as that fatherhood is found first not on earth but in heaven, not among men but in God Himself.'[31] Nonetheless, LaCugna suggests that 'A theology of the immanent Trinity does not refer to "God as such apart from relationship to us" but to "God revealed in Christ and the Spirit".'[32] Substituting her 'relational ontology' for an 'ontology of substance' she argues that

> what makes God to be God, is to be the Unoriginate yet Originating person who by virtue of love of another brings about all that exists. Now it is impossible to say exactly and definitively what this personal *ousia* of God is, because this would entail explaining both what it means for God to be Unoriginate Origin . . . and what it means for divine persons *to be* in communion with every creature. What God *is* remains unspeakable.[33]

LaCugna's two crucial errors can be seen at work here. First, unwilling and unable to distinguish God from creatures, she argues that as originating person God is in relation to us simply because God loves another. Which other is she referring to? Is it the Father's love for the Son or is it God's love of creatures? Here a sharp distinction must be made to avoid pantheism. LaCugna fails to make such a distinction because she is not thinking of God on the basis of revelation but of God incorporated into her relational ontology that views the Trinity as a description of persons (divine and human) in communion. Second, it is precisely her agnosticism that allows her to substitute her arbitrary relational ontology for an ontology shaped by the nature and activity of God revealed in Christ through the Holy Spirit. Since she believes that we do not know what God is, she clearly does not think of God as the eternal Father, Son and Spirit. Rather, God can be described by many metaphors because of his incomprehensibility.[34] Of course this is why she, like McFague and many others, names God mother or

---

[30] *CD* I/1, 432. Cf. also *CD* II/1, 324ff., 286f., and Torrance, *The Trinitarian Faith*, 71, 133 and 246.

[31] *CD* I/2, 587.

[32] LaCugna, *God for Us*, 227.

[33] LaCugna, *God for Us*, 334.

[34] See Catherine Mowry LaCugna, 'God in Communion with Us', in LaCugna (ed.), *Freeing Theology: The Essentials of Theology in Feminist Perspective* (San Francisco: HarperSanFrancisco, 1993), chapter 4.

Godself.[35] But this view is fatal to faith and theology, not because it seeks to join our knowledge of God *in se* to God's actions for us, but because it dissolves God's aseity into his being for us and thus leaves us with no God existing *a se*. LaCugna *says* she endorses a God existing *a se*[36] but merely pays lip-service to such a God and so concludes: '*The life of God does not belong to God alone.*'[37] Indeed

> Christian orthopraxis must correspond to what we believe to be true about God: that God is personal . . . ecstatic and fecund love, that God's very nature is to exist toward and for another. The mystery of existence is the mystery of the *commingling* of persons, divine and human, in a common life, within a common household . . . Our relationship to others, which is indistinguishable from our relationship to Jesus Christ, determines whether we are or are not finally incorporated into God's household.[38]

It is just this commingling that Barth insisted Chalcedon sought to avoid. She does not simply reject a doctrine of the immanent Trinity but, as seen above in Chapter One, uncritically emulates Gordon Kaufman, who sees it as a symbol reflecting the threefold structure of Christian experience which we cannot say is internal to God because we have no access to

> this innermost essence . . . in history or revelation; and anything said about it is pure speculation. About the trinitarian structure of God's

---

[35] LaCugna, *God for Us*, 18. While she believes it is appropriate to name God Mother, she will avoid the distracting name Father and use God and Godself. Her 'agenda' is ultimately to refer merely to God with us rather than 'probing an intradivine realm ("God *in se*")' (n. 7). Yet she also believes that Mother expresses better than Father the deep physical bond between God and creation (303). Both Roland Frye and Robert Jenson have pointed out the gnostic and polytheist connotations in speaking of God as Mother or Godself. Cf. Kimel (ed.), *Speaking the Christian God*, 17ff. and 95ff.

[36] LaCugna, *God for Us*, 228, 321–2. See also the Review Symposium on *God for Us* in *Horizons* 20.1 (1993), 127–42 at 139 where LaCugna responds to criticism indicating that she thinks abandoning the language of 'economic' and 'immanent' will lead to greater precision (!) and that this does not imply that she does not 'believe in the immanent Trinity'. The problem of course with this particular belief is that she insists that her relational ontology must take the place of any notion of self-sufficiency for God. This leads directly to her confusion of God and the world. Our view of God is certainly one that is relational, but our concept of relation is dictated by God's free relations *in se* and *ad extra*. In other words, the Christian God is and remains self-sufficient even in his actions on our behalf. Unless that is true, the content of the concept of God is nothing more than a description of our necessary relations with others within the sphere of creation.

[37] LaCugna, *God for Us*, 354.

[38] LaCugna, *God for Us*, 383–4, emphasis mine. By comparison, for Barth 'Revelation remains identical with Christ and Christ remains the object of Christian faith, even though He lives in Christians and they in Him' (*CD* I/2, 118).

being-in-revelation, however, we can speak with confidence, because this is the only way to conceive what *is* given directly in Christian revelation.[39]

Any distinction between the immanent and economic Trinity is thus a 'pseudo-distinction'.

Since the symbol God represents *our* ultimate point of reference for unifying our experiences, Kaufman, as seen above in Chapter One, embraces both a naive pantheism and a form of self-justification:

> The symbol 'God' suggests a reality, an ultimate tendency or power, which is working itself out in an evolutionary process . . . The symbol 'God' enables us to hold this whole grand evolutionary-historical sweep together . . . God – this whole grand cosmic evolutionary movement – is giving birth, after many millennia, to finite freedom and self-consciousness in and through our human history, in *us* . . .[40]

This leads to a dualism that represents Jesus' eternal sonship as the product of Christian triumphalism rather than a reality which Christians acknowledge and describe. Salvation cannot come in one individual because this is not in keeping with contemporary pluralism or self-understanding which are dictated by modern biological and evolutionary theories. Moreover, according to Kaufman, belief in Jesus' eternal sonship reifies who Jesus is, instead of seeing him as a symbol of human self-sacrifice.[41] God and Christ are symbols we construct in order to create a better society; they help us relativize, humanize and liberate society; thus God's sovereignty is fundamentally irrelevant today and theology 'serves human purposes and needs, and it should be judged in terms of the adequacy with which it is fulfilling the objectives we humans set for it'.[42] Hence salvation 'comprises all the activities and processes within human affairs which are helping to overcome the violence and disruptions and alienations'.[43]

Similarly, instead of saying that Christ empowers us to live a life of love and communion with others, LaCugna believes that '*Entering into divine life therefore is impossible unless we also enter into a life of love and communion with others.*'[44] Indeed 'According to the doctrine of the Trinity, God lives as the mystery of love among persons' and we should

---

[39] Kaufman quoted in LaCugna, *God for Us*, 226.

[40] *TNA*, 43f.

[41] *TNA*, 50–6. For the christological implications of this thinking, see Chapter Two above.

[42] *TNA*, 19.

[43] *TNA*, 57.

[44] LaCugna, *God for Us*, 382, emphasis in original.

ask 'what forms of life best enable us to live as Christ lived'.[45] Yet, if this is the case, we neither need Christ nor can we distinguish nature and grace; thus we create the forms of life that correspond to the patterns of relationality we glean from scripture. Not surprisingly she thinks that 'the vocation and mission of *every* member of the church [is] to become Christ'.[46] Barth was very clear on this important issue: 'The relation between Jesus Christ and His church is, therefore, an irreversible relation. Whatever the glory and authority of the church may be, the glory and authority of Jesus Christ are always his own.'[47]

The doctrine of the immanent Trinity should be a true understanding of who the transcendent God who is immanent in Christ and the Spirit in virtue of his transcendence is. It is necessary to know, even though it can be known only through revelation and even though we do not know God as God knows himself. Without this knowledge, agnosticism, pantheism and dualism become possible and compromise our understanding of God as Father, Son and Holy Spirit. God then becomes only a conceptual construct *of* our *experiences* in the economy rather than God himself acting in the economy as one who enables our human freedom. For Barth

> The God of whom we speak is no god imagined or devised by men. The grace of the gods who are imagined or devised by men is usually a conditional grace . . . and not the true grace which gives itself freely . . . man's imagined grace is usually directly offered and accessible in some way to him and can be rather conveniently, cheaply, and easily appropriated.[48]

Thus human freedom is absolutely bound up with the fact that 'If the Son therefore shall make you free, you shall be free indeed' Jn 8:36.[49]

God and Relational Ontology

Ted Peters provides yet another perspective; and it is deeply influenced by the thought of Catherine LaCugna. In part this will explain why his theology exhibits problems similar to those of LaCugna and how his failure to understand the function of the doctrine of the immanent Trinity in the theology of Karl Barth contributed to this. Though Colin Gunton was quite critical of LaCugna's approach, he found much of

---

[45] LaCugna, *God for Us*, 378.

[46] LaCugna, *God for Us*, 402. Elaine Pagels has shown that this was a gnostic but not a Christian belief.

[47] *CD* I/2, 576.

[48] Barth, *Evangelical Theology*, 152.

[49] Cf. *CD* II/2, 589ff. Cf. also *CD* IV/1, 744–5 and IV/2, 129, 496.

Peters' presentation acceptable and only briefly complained that Ted Peters did not sufficiently ground his insights in a doctrine of the immanent Trinity;[50] this, despite the fact that Peters regards LaCugna's trinitarian theology as a 'real jewel'.[51] Since Peters believes that the point of trinitarian theology is to help us conceptualize God's work as creator and redeemer, he also believes that we need not assume that the three persons of the Trinity must be 'identical or equal in nature'. This, because 'The notion of one being in three persons is simply a conceptual device for trying to understand the drama of salvation that is taking place in Jesus Christ.'[52] With LaCugna, Peters thus advocates the chiastic model of emanation and return according to which 'There is neither an economic nor an immanent Trinity'[53] and believes (making no distinction between God's internal and external relations) that God is personal since he is necessarily one who is in relationship with other persons. He analyzes Jüngel's adaptation of Rahner's axiom to advance the question and argues that if we then ask what is the status of God's relationality, we are caught in a dilemma. Either we insist that God is *a se* and not dependent on the world or that God's relations *ad extra* make God dependent on the world. According to Peters, Jüngel resolved this by affirming that 'relationality already exists within the divine being, already within the immanent Trinity'.[54] In an important digression, Peters argues that Jüngel has difficulty reconciling his position that God's being is in becoming with Luther's concept of paradox, which asserted that God's power is revealed under its opposite which is weakness; Peters believes that Barth and Jüngel removed Luther's paradox by arguing that 'Jesus' weakness and humility are not said to be opposed to divinity. Rather, they are constitutive of divinity.' And from this Peters concludes that 'God is in the process of becoming Godself through relationship with the temporal creation.'[55]

Barth, however, argued that God was self-revealed and self-concealed (the only self-moved being); thus revelation includes our sinful secularity without implying that God was in the process of becoming who he would be through relationship with the world.[56] By the revelation of

---

[50] Colin E. Gunton, Review of Ted Peters, *God as Trinity*, *Theology Today* 51.1 (1994), 174–6.

[51] Peters, *Trinity*, 122ff. While we have shown that she never even perceived God's freedom as Barth understood it, he believes she 'extends the Barthian insight into practical spirituality' (123).

[52] Peters, *Trinity*, 70.

[53] Peters, *Trinity*, 125.

[54] Peters, *Trinity*, 91 and 143.

[55] Peters, *Trinity*, 92.

[56] Cf. *CD* II/1, 324 and *CD* IV/2, 346–7.

the glory of the Lord through Christ's humiliation, death and resurrection, God demonstrated an eternal power as Father, Son and Holy Spirit that did not accrue to him in or from his relations with the world. This was God's positive freedom.[57] Peters inaccurately claims to be following Barth's original insights when he mistakenly criticizes Jüngel for thinking that 'because God is self-related, God can be world-related'.[58] He trades upon an ambiguity in Jüngel's thought that can be avoided only by seeing God as the subject of both his external and internal relations. Barth reminds us:

> [God] does not need His own being in order to be who He is: because He already has His own being and is Himself . . . If, therefore, we say that God is *a se*, we do not say that God creates, produces or originates Himself. . . . He cannot 'need' His own being because He affirms it in being who He is . . . what can need existence, is not God Himself, or His reality, but the reality which is distinct from Himself.[59]

Indeed in God himself there is history in partnership:

> God was never solitary . . . [but is] the Father's eternal begetting of the Son, and the Son's eternal being begotten of the Father, with the common work which confirms this relationship, in which it takes place eternally that the one God is not merely the Father and the Son but also, eternally proceeding from the Father and the Son, the Holy Ghost . . . This history in partnership is the life of God before and above all creaturely life . . . His inner union is marked off from the circular course of a natural process as His own free act . . . it is not subject to any necessity. The Father and the Son are not two prisoners. They are not two mutually conditioning factors in reciprocal operation. As the common source of the Spirit, who Himself is also God, they are the Lord of this occurrence. God is the free Lord of His inner union.[60]

Free from limits, conditions or restrictions, as one who is self-grounded and self-moved from his own center, God is not even, as it were, subject to himself (though he is self-limited):

---

[57] *CD* II/1, 314ff. For Barth, 'the one God in His three modes of being corresponds to the Lord of glory. As it is of decisive importance to recognise the three modes of being, not only economically as modalism does, but, according to the seriousness of the divine presence and power in the economy of His works, as modes of being of the one eternal God Himself, so it is equally important to understand that God in Himself is not divested of His glory and perfections, that He does not assume them merely in connexion with His self-revelation to the world, but that they constitute His own eternal glory' (326–7).

[58] Peters, *Trinity*, 93ff.

[59] *CD* II/1, 306. See also *CD* I/1, 354 where Barth insists that God does not need 'a Second and then a Third in order to be One'.

[60] *CD* IV/2, 344–5.

God has the prerogative to be free without being limited by His freedom from external conditioning, free also with regard to His freedom, free not to surrender Himself to it, but to use it to give Himself to this communion and to practise this faithfulness in it, in this way being really free, free in Himself.[61]

Hence God can and will be conditioned, but as a manifestation of his inner freedom and not in abandoning this; as God remains lord of his life we must acknowledge who he is *in se* and *ad extra*.

Because Peters, following Pannenberg and Jenson here, neglects this important insight, he thinks that God is dependent on history to become who he will be. He rejects any *logos asarkos* and describes Jesus as having to attain his eternal sonship in the future.[62] These insights compromise God's self-sufficiency and tend toward dualism, partially because Peters' starting point for trinitarian reflection is experience rather than revelation. In fact he equates Christian experience in the Church with special revelation[63] and argues that

Relationality – a social-psychological concept . . . is becoming the key for unlocking newer understandings of the divine life . . . The trinitarian life is itself the history of salvation . . . the fullness of God as Trinity is a reality yet to be achieved in the eschatological consummation.[64]

Grounding his doctrine of the Trinity on 'revelation and Christian experience' allows relationality and temporality as we experience these to become the subject with God the predicate. Hence the Trinity

---

[61] *CD* II/1, 303.

[62] See, e.g., Peters, *Trinity*, 134ff. and 180. When Peters depicts Barth's understanding of God's eminent temporality as the simultaneity of past, present and future, he misses Barth's point, that is, that God's time is not subject to the limitations and sin connected with our time. Instead he says, 'Barth goes on to insist that the eternal life of God is dynamized by the temporal actuality of the world' (149). So Peters wonders 'why we need to maintain simultaneity of past, present and future' at all. Thus 'God's eternity is gained through the victory of resurrection and transformation' (175). For Barth, of course, God does not have to gain his eternity – he already has and is it in freedom. Peters believes his thinking is not captive to a metaphysical principle and that 'It is God who defines what divinity is' (145); yet if God depends on history then history defines God.

[63] Peters, *Trinity*, 214. Following Rahner, he thinks that logical or analytic explanations of scripture must 'always refer back to the origin from which they came, namely the experience of faith that assures us that the incomprehensible God is really . . . given us . . . in . . . Christ and the Spirit' (98) and thus mistakenly believes that the doctrine of the Trinity primarily refers to the experience of the 'beyond and intimate' (19). It is this experience of the beyond and intimate that becomes the norm for his trinitarian thinking. For more on this, see Molnar, 'Experience and Knowledge of the Trinity in the Theology of Ted Peters: Occasion for Clarity or Confusion?', *Irish Theological Quarterly* 64 (1999), 219–43.

[64] Peters, *Trinity*, 15–16. Cf. also 78, 82. Following Hegel he believes God is in the process of constituting himself and this includes God's saving relationship to the world.

becomes a reality yet to be achieved instead of our future hope grounded in Jesus Christ who is the same yesterday, today and tomorrow in virtue of God's constancy. It is no accident that Barth insisted that God was at peace and never in conflict with himself,[65] while Peters, following Hegel, believes God 'undergoes self-separation' and therefore needs an 'eschatological reunion'.[66]

Peters claims to find a further dilemma in Jüngel's position. Rejecting tritheism, Barth had opposed using the word person to describe Father, Son and Spirit and spoke of God's *ousia* as the person of God. If Jüngel follows Barth and affirms that God is personal in the divine substance then God would be only one person and would need the world in order to be personal; any correspondence between the immanent and economic Trinity would collapse. But if Jüngel describes Father, Son and Spirit as 'a community of terms defined by their relations',[67] he could establish a correspondence between God *in se* and *ad extra* but would risk tritheism. Yet this 'dilemma' is itself contrived, since for Barth, God is simultaneously one and three – not one and then three or three and then one;[68] and God is the subject of his own *ousia*. He does not equate person and substance as a modalist would, but uses person to express God's freedom *in se* and *ad extra*;[69] his entire theology, chiefly the divine perfections, illustrates that this is the particular freedom of the Father, Son and Holy Spirit.

> God's perfect being is the one being of the Father, the Son and the Holy Spirit. It is only as this that it has the perfection of which we have spoken . . . What makes it divine and real being is the fact that it is the being of the Father, the Son and the Holy Spirit . . . Here there is always one divine being in all three modes of being, as that which is common to them all. Here the three modes of being are always together . . . We can never have one without the others. Here one is both by the others and in

---

[65] *CD* II/1, 492–503.

[66] Peters, *Trinity*, 16, 82. Cf. also 83–4.

[67] Peters, *Trinity*, 95.

[68] Cf. *CD* I/1, 349–52. God's *ousia* 'is not only not abrogated by the threeness of the "persons" but rather that its unity consists in the threeness of the "persons"' (*CD* I/1, 349–50). Many think that for Barth God's oneness has priority over his threeness. Thus, Colin Gunton: 'As Pannenberg has written, the weakness of Barth's theology of the Trinity is that God's unity is seen as the *ground* of his threeness, rather than the *result*' ('The Triune God and the Freedom of the Creature', in *Karl Barth: Centenary Essays*, ed. S. W. Sykes [hereafter: *Karl Barth*] [Cambridge: Cambridge University Press, 1989], 60). For Barth, God is simultaneously one and three; neither threeness nor oneness comes first.

[69] Torrance, *Trinitarian Perspectives*, thinks God can be properly seen as three persons and 'the infinite and universal Person' (97f.). This would seem to correspond with what Barth means here.

the others, in a *perichoresis* which nothing can restrict or arrest, so that one mode is neither active nor knowable externally without the others.[70]

Peters says Jüngel did not initially commit himself to either position; but he later followed Barth by rejecting the philosopher's deity as 'simple, transcendent, immutable, eternal, *a se* . . . a God who is in-and-for-himself'. Thus the dilemma (pantheism or tritheism) is a pseudoproblem because the philosopher's God is not the one revealed in Jesus Christ, and so Peters' asks:

> Why not just go all the way and affirm a God whose personhood is itself being constituted through God's ongoing relation to the creation? . . . Why is it necessary that God be related to himself *ad intra* before becoming related to the world *ad extra*? Why does Jüngel feel constrained to depict God in terms of unrelated relatedness?[71]

Since God 'becomes personal through relationship with the other just as we do' Peters proposes that God's incarnate dealings with the world are part of an 'ongoing process of divine self-definition', and that by unequivocally accepting Rahner's axiom Jüngel may have abandoned his 'grip on a God of unrelated relatedness'. Hence, Peters pursues a trend found in Pannenberg, Moltmann and Jüngel as they head toward or beyond Rahner's axiom (rule),[72] claiming that 'the relationality God experiences through Christ's saving relationship to the world is constitutive of trinitarian relations proper. God's relations *ad extra* become God's relations *ad intra*.'[73]

But this conclusion illustrates that Ted Peters never actually understood the importance of the doctrine of the immanent Trinity in Barth's theology. From revelation, Barth asserted that history, including God's sovereign actions in history on our behalf and our life of faith, do not define who God is in eternity but reveal who God is precisely by

---

[70] *CD* II/1, 659–60. Regarding God's pre-temporality, supra-temporality and post-temporality, Barth argued: 'There is just as little place for . . . rivalry here as between the three persons of the Trinity, whose distinction is really . . . the basis of these three forms . . . there is in God both distinction and peace' (639).

[71] Peters, *Trinity*, 95f.

[72] Cf. esp. Peters, *Trinity*, 128–45.

[73] Peters, *Trinity*, 96. Having completely lost the distinction between God's internal and external relations, Peters uses trinitarian categories to describe the experience of the beyond and intimate and concludes that the absolute becomes related through the incarnation and that the related becomes absolute eschatologically (146ff., 182ff.). For more details on this issue, see Molnar, 'Experience and Knowledge of the Trinity in the Theology of Ted Peters'.

coming into conflict with our various philosophies. The idea that God's relations *ad extra* will become God's relations *ad intra* indicates a confusion and reversal of reason and revelation, which follows if Christ is not seen as God's grace and if faith and revelation become the products of human experience in the form of a relational ontology, rather than our human participation in God's truth by God's own self-sufficient act. For Barth, we can be certain about who God is and about our creation, reconciliation and redemption as each divine action, which includes history in a real relationship with God, is seen as grounded in God's eternal primary objectivity and not directly in the realm of secondary objectivity.

> If we wish to state who Jesus Christ is . . . we must also state or at least make clear – and inexorably so – that we are speaking of the Lord of heaven and earth [when speaking of the Word of Jn 1:14], who neither has nor did have any need of heaven or earth or man, who created them out of free love and according to His very own good pleasure, who adopts man, not according to the latter's merit, but according to His own mercy, not in virtue of the latter's capacity, but in virtue of His own miraculous power. He is the Lord who . . . never ceases in the very slightest to be God, who does not give His glory to another. In this, as Creator, Reconciler and Redeemer, He is a truly loving, serving God. He is the King of all kings just when He enters into the profoundest hiddenness in 'meekness of heart'.[74]

As seen above, Thomas F. Torrance adopts this same position by saying that we must think from a center in God and not from a center in ourselves.[75] This important insight is missing from Ted Peters' presentation; thus he believes that God's relations with us in creation, reconciliation and redemption will determine the nature of God *ad intra*. This reversal of God and the world obliterates the distinction between the immanent and economic Trinity. Thus he believes that God becomes personal through relationships as we do and ignores the *Deus non est in genere* which, for Barth, precludes a higher unity between God and us, which will explain his unique freedom and love.

> If they [creatures] belong to Him and He to them, this dual relationship does not spring from any need of His eternal being. This would remain the same even if there were no such relationship. If there is a con-nexion and relatedness between them and Him, God is who He is in

---

[74] *CD* I/2, 133.
[75] Cf., e.g., Torrance, *The Trinitarian Faith*, 52f. and 'The Christian Apprehension of God the Father', in Kimel (ed.), *Speaking the Christian God*, 123.

independence of them even in this relatedness. He does not share His being with theirs.[76]

Positively, against agnosticism (even a future oriented one), we may have firm knowledge of our relationship with God; negatively, this knowledge cannot be achieved by relying on our own knowledge and existence (experience), as in making a relational ontology the subject with God the predicate. Panentheism and pantheism require this mutual dependence just because and to the extent that they do not advert to the *Deus non est in genere*. Hence, the tendency to see God as a dependent deity misses God's essential freedom and expresses an apotheosis via agnosticism, monism and dualism; thus God will not be completely who he is becoming until salvation is complete:

> the immanent Trinity is consummated eschatologically, meaning that the whole of temporal history is factored into the inner life of God. God becomes fully God-in-relationship when the work of salvation – when the economic Trinity – is complete.[77]

Yet the critical insight which ought to be retrieved from Barth's theology is that God's freedom signifies that he is *a se* but not as defined by any philosophical principle. Ted Peters mistakenly supposes that *any* notion that God is *a se* must arise from philosophy whereas God's positive and negative freedom derive only from his own unique being and act as Father, Son and Spirit. Moltmann and Pannenberg also incorrectly criticize Barth for this. But, for Barth,

> God is . . . independent of everything that is not He. God is, whether everything else is, or is not, whether it is in this way or some other. If there is something other, it cannot precede God, it cannot place God in dependence upon itself . . .[78]

---

[76] *CD* II/1, 311. Cf. also 187, 310. Speaking of the incarnation as an act of God's free love, Barth said, 'while this event as a happening in and on the created world makes, magnifies and enhances the glory of God outwardly; inwardly it neither increases nor diminishes His glory, His divine being. For this is neither capable nor in need of increase or decrease. God did not and does not owe this happening to the world or to us any more than He did creation or the history of salvation . . . It was not the case, nor is it, that His being necessitated Him to do it' (*CD* II/1, 513–14). Jesus Christ did not surrender or curtail his divinity in his self-concealment and self-offering but was divine in it showing his freedom to be humiliated on our behalf (*CD* II/1, 516ff.). By contrast Peters believes 'God ceases to be God – or, at least, what we might assume to be God – in order to become human and die' (*Trinity*, 13); God needs history to be relational.

[77] Peters, *Trinity*, 181. Jesus is not the sole norm for Peters' understanding of the Trinity; it is also our experience of the beyond and intimate. Thus Jesus must gain his divinity and the Holy Spirit must find his divinity by accomplishing community between Father and Son and with the world (*Trinity*, 180–1).

[78] *CD* II/1, 308.

God is free in himself – before and apart from his freedom from conditioning *ad extra*: 'The fact that in every way He is independent of all other reality does not in itself constitute God's freedom but its exercise. It does not constitute His divinity, but He is divine in it.'[79] God does not need his own being but freely affirms himself in being.

This is a crucial ingredient of a doctrine of the immanent Trinity, which disallows the mutual dependence intrinsic to created being but which is inapplicable to God's living and loving; it enables us to affirm that God's pre-temporal, supra-temporal and post-temporal freedom is the foundation for a theology of creation, reconciliation and redemption which does not overemphasize the past, the present or the future in order to grasp the mystery of Christ and the Spirit. Such overemphases indicate that no clear conception of the immanent Trinity was at work in Peters thought in the first instance and that, in order to avoid these conclusions, which are tantamount to Feuerbach's reduction of theology to anthropology, we need a doctrine of the immanent Trinity which prevents this confusion and reversibility of history and eternity. I am not suggesting here that we construct a doctrine in order to prevent this reversal but that construction of such a doctrine is necessary in order to say who God is as the eternal Father, Son and Spirit. Then we may recognize that God is fully who he is without needing to submit to a metaphysical principle of relationality or temporality *ad intra* or *ad extra*. Only if we recognize this truth as the ground of salvation history may we see and preserve the freedom of God's grace, without which we have the pantheist conclusion that God will be who God is when salvation is complete. From this follows the dualist view that Jesus somehow is becoming the eternal Son (and thus is not this already – even before Easter) and that the economic Trinity is only eschato-logically the immanent Trinity. Such thinking emerges to the extent that the deity of the Holy Spirit has been displaced by the experience of faith at the outset.[80]

Christological Implications

How might the doctrine of the immanent Trinity clarify what Barth considered one of the hardest problems in Christology: does Jesus' humanity as such reveal his divinity?[81] For Barth, the incarnation was

[79] *CD* II/1, 307f.
[80] This is why Peters can actually say, 'As the Holy Spirit, God becomes so inextricably tied to our own inner self that the line between the two sometimes seems to us blurred' (*Trinity*, 19).
[81] Cf. *CD* I/1, 323.

not a principle but an act whose *terminus a quo* is 'God in Himself' and whose *terminus ad quem* is 'man in himself'; thus 'the Word of God is properly understood only as a word which has truth and glory in itself and not just spoken to us'.[82]

> Revelation as such is not relative. Revelation in fact does not differ from the person of Jesus Christ nor from the reconciliation accomplished in Him . . . we are saying something which can have only an intertrinitarian basis in the will of the Father and the sending of the Son and the Holy Spirit, in the eternal decree of the triune God, so that it can be established only as knowledge of God from God . . . [revelation] has no basis or possibility outside itself [and] can in no sense be explained in terms of man and man's situation . . . It is Jesus Christ Himself who here speaks for Himself and needs no witness apart from His Holy Spirit and the faith that rejoices in His promise received and grasped.[83]

Barth rejected the idea that Jesus' humanity *as such* disclosed his divinity because, as we have already seen several times, God's act of revelation involves both a veiling and an unveiling: 'Mystery is the concealment of God in which He meets us precisely when He unveils Himself to us, because He will not and cannot unveil Himself except by veiling Himself.' Since the form (sinful secularity) must be distinguished from the content we have a paradox, that is, 'a communication which is not only made by a . . . phenomenon, but which must be understood . . . in antithesis to what the phenomenon itself seems to be saying'. Only the Word can fulfil this paradox, while in other paradoxes, communication and form can be 'dissolved from a superior point of vantage'. Creaturely reality is an 'unsuitable medium' because 'It does not correspond to the matter but contradicts it. It does not unveil it but veils it.'[84]

Knowledge of God takes place indirectly and in faith without denying the secularity of the form of revelation. This is a miracle because what is revealed is actually concealed by the reality in which it takes place. There is neither a pure nature distinct from our fallen nature nor can human reason grasp the mystery of God apart from Christ or without Christ 'in creaturely reality'. We can neither go behind the secularity to a God in himself nor can we identify God in himself with this sphere. 'If God's Word is revealed in it, it is revealed "through it", of course, but in such a way that this "through it" means "in spite of it". The

---

[82] *CD* I/1, 171.
[83] *CD* I/1, 117–20.
[84] *CD* I/1, 163–6. Cf. also *CD* II/1, 287.

secularity proper to God's Word is not in itself and as such transparent.' God's self-communication has a twofold indirectness: creatureliness and sinfulness. God's Word has really entered our sinful secularity making it 'an authentic and inalienable attribute of the Word of God itself. Revelation means the incarnation of the Word of God.' We can neither evade this secularity nor rely on it to reveal; due to sin 'we have no organ or capacity for God'.[85]

Responding to Gogarten, Barth asks, 'What would "God for us" mean if it were not said against the background of "God in Himself"?' God's love for us is 'unmerited and free' and must always be discussed against the background of God in himself; 'what constitutes the mercy of its revelation, of its being spoken to us, is that it is spoken to us in virtue of the freedom in which God could be "God in Himself" and yet He does not will to be so and in fact is not so, but wills to be and actually is "God for us".' A sharp distinction between the immanent and economic Trinity follows: ' "God for us" does not arise as a matter of course out of the "God in Himself" . . . it is true as an act of God, as a step which God takes towards man and, by which man becomes the man that participates in His revelation.' Our human becoming is conditioned by God, but God

> is not conditioned from without, by man. For this reason – and we agree with Gogarten here – theology cannot speak of man in himself, in isolation from God. But as in the strict doctrine of the Trinity as the presupposition of Christology, it must speak of God in Himself, in isolation from man.[86]

Thus we must seek and find the immanent Trinity 'in the *humanitas Christi*' as Luther did since 'we do not see and have directly'. Identifying God in himself and God for us would allow an *analogia entis*, which neither takes seriously the incarnation nor our sinful secularity.

Barth rejected the idea that Jesus' humanity as such revealed his divinity because this idea would obliterate Jesus' pre-temporal existence as the eternal Word and so would obscure the truth of the incarnation as an act of God and God's existence within time. The Chalcedonian formulation of the two natures, unmixed and not identical, distinguished but not separated, followed from a distinction of the kind just described. Identifying the immanent and economic Trinity would give us an axiom by which we could actually avoid both the need for faith and the need to admit that

[85] *CD* I/1, 166, 168.
[86] *CD* I/1, 171–2.

God's presence is always God's decision to be present . . . God's self-unveiling remains an act of sovereign divine freedom. To one man it can be what the Word says and to another true divine concealment . . . In it God cannot be grasped by man or confiscated or put to work. To count on it is to count on God's free loving-kindness, not on a credit granted once and for all, not on an axiom to which one may have recourse once and for all, not on an experience one has had once and for all . . . [Hence] even Christ's humanity stands under the caveat of God's holiness, that is, that the power and continuity in which the man Jesus of Nazareth was in fact the revealed Word . . . consisted here too in the power and continuity of the divine action in this form and not in the continuity of this form as such. As a matter of fact even Jesus did not become revelation to all who met Him but only to a few . . . Revealing could obviously not be ascribed to His existence as such. His existence as such is indeed given up to death, and it is in this way, from death, from this frontier, since the Crucified was raised again, that He is manifested as the Son of God.[87]

Since God remained throughout the divine subject of the incarnation,[88] incarnation did not befall him, but was his own act in union with the Father and the Spirit. This detail, which is noticeably absent from contemporary Christology, especially Spirit Christologies, enabled Barth to avoid agnosticism, pantheism and dualism in his Christology and doctrine of election and elsewhere.

Barth, Pannenberg and the Meaning of Revelation

Comparing Barth and Pannenberg should clarify the issue. For Barth, Jesus Christ is the Son who reveals and reconciles us to the Father. The dogma of the Trinity adds to scripture the interpretation that Jesus can reveal and reconcile because 'He reveals Himself as the One He is.' Apart from revelation and reconciliation, Jesus Christ already was in himself the Son or Word of God. Against an agnosticism that equates God's incomprehensibility with a higher essence of God in which there is no Son or Word, in which God exists with a different name, or no name (McFague and LaCugna think God can be named mother while Rahner thinks of God as nameless and wordless), Barth argues that revelation and reconciliation have eternal validity because 'God is God the Son as He is God the Father'; the eternity and glory of God especially reflect this. This interpretation arose from the incomprehensible truth that creation and reconciliation are equally divine works based on the

---

[87] *CD* I/1, 321, 323.
[88] Cf. *CD* I/2, 131ff. Cf. esp. *CD* II/1, 516ff.

'unity of the Father and the Son . . . we have to accept the simple presupposition on which the New Testament statement rests, namely, that Jesus Christ is the Son because He is'. As already seen above in Chapter Two, all thinking about Jesus and thus about God *must* begin here. The dogma of the deity of Christ springs from this insight which can neither be proven nor questioned epistemologically; it refers to Christ's eternal 'antecedent' existence as Son or Word and is not a 'derivative statement' but a basic statement. Theology must begin with Jesus the Word just because he is, and his incarnate being in *no way* derives its meaning from anyone or anything else. As a *derivative* statement acquired from experiences of self-transcendence, which include the experience of Christ and the Spirit, the doctrine of the Trinity then explains, in varying degrees for Johnson, Kaufman, LaCugna, McFague, Moltmann, Peters, Rahner and others, the content of Christian experience instead of God *in se*. While this dogma is not found in scripture, it properly refers to the true and eternal deity of Christ seen in his work of revelation and reconciliation. 'But revelation and reconciliation do not create His deity.'[89]

Failure to acknowledge Christ's true and eternal deity compromises the truth of revelation and reconciliation. Here Barth's concept of the *logos asarkos* is important. As discussed above in Chapter Three, he believed this abstraction was necessary because God acting for us must be seen against the background of God in himself who could have existed in isolation from us but freely chose not to. He rejected a *logos asarkos* in his doctrine of creation if it implied a 'formless Christ' or 'a Christ-principle' rather than Jesus who was before the world with God as the Word; he rejected it in connection with reconciliation if it meant a retreat to an idea of God behind the God revealed in Christ; but he still insisted it had a proper role to play in the doctrine of the Trinity and in Christology. In stark contrast, as we saw above, Robert Jenson rejects such a concept, because history rather than God acting in history was determining his thinking at that point; indeed he was trying to reconcile God's freedom with Rahner's axiom as it stands (with the vice versa).[90] Ted Peters follows Jenson's thinking in this matter.

---

[89] *CD* I/1, 414–15 and *CD* II/1, 625ff.

[90] As noted above, Jenson believes such a concept prevents the procession of the Son from being the same as Jesus' mission. And indeed it does; precisely in order to prevent God's eternal freedom from being confused with his freedom for us. Again, I am not arguing here for a separation of Jesus' humanity and divinity but for the fact that, unless his mission is seen against the background of his being *in se* before the world was, then his deity will be equated with or seen as the outcome of history. We have already seen how this thinking

As discussed above in Chapter Three, Barth refused to discredit Christ's antecedent existence precisely because his deity could not be recognized without distinguishing between the Son of God in himself and in his actions for us. Without a clear acknowledgment of this distinction there could be no recognition of the freedom of grace either. While Pannenberg emphasizes the need to grasp Christ's eternal Sonship,[91] and neither opposes the importance of the dogma nor advocates detaching the 'for us' from Christ's antecedent existence, he differs from Barth regarding this distinction. Similarly, Peters and LaCugna do not overtly deny the 'antecedently in himself', insofar as they argue that this is needed to secure our understanding of salvation and redemption. *But* their thinking about Christ's eternal sonship is, in Barth's words, in the grip of an 'untheological speculative understanding of the "for us"'.[92] That is the issue. Because Christ's antecedent existence precludes an untheological understanding here, it must be acknowledged first. Several implications follow.

First, failure to hear this as the *basis* of our grasp of God's being for us turns his being for us into 'a necessary attribute of God. God's being is then essentially limited and conditioned as a being revealed, i.e., as a relation of God to man'.[93] Revelation and reconciliation are no longer seen as acts of grace since God's nature is to forgive and human nature must have a God who forgives. This is what happened to LaCugna and Peters. Instead of the triune God *freely* acting for us *within* history, we are told that 'trinitarian life is our life', that it does not belong to God alone, and that God can *only* exist for us; this is why Peters mistakenly criticized Jüngel and Rahner for asserting that God is self-related before being related to the world. These views exhibited a tendency seen in the Christologies of Pannenberg and Rahner to make God dependent on history. Pannenberg believes Barth failed to ground the doctrine of the Trinity in revelation but that Rahner made progress with his thesis of

---

leads Jenson and Peters to displace the immanent Trinity from their thinking about the historical Jesus and the Spirit and thus to argue for an immanent Trinity that will exist eschatologically. That is why Jenson substitutes Christ's resurrection for his *ousia* and that is why Pannenberg thinks Christ's resurrection constitutes his sonship.

[91] E.g. Pannenberg, *Systematic Theology 2*, 370ff.

[92] *CD* I/1, 420.

[93] *CD* I/1, 421. See Molnar, 'The Function of the Immanent Trinity' and Chapter Seven below for a discussion of how this problem manifests itself in the theology of Jürgen Moltmann. Moltmann conceives Christ's antecedent existence in terms of suffering love, which is more blessed in giving than in receiving, and so sees God's actions in history as necessary attributes of God. Peters agrees with this aspect of Moltmann's thought.

identity, although by keeping the Father transcendent, he did not go far enough; he should have seen that the Father 'has made himself *dependent* upon the course of history'.[94] Therefore, the truth that Jesus is the Son of God depends upon contingencies within history: 'The statements are true if the conditions hold.'[95] Hence, 'the Easter event is not merely the basis of the knowledge that Jesus of Nazareth even in his earthly form was the eternal Son of God, but also *decides* that he was this by giving retrospective confirmation'.[96] Pannenberg's belief that Jesus' human self-distinction from the Father is the ground of his divine sonship virtually eliminates any genuine pre-existent sonship:

> The eternal Son is first . . . an aspect of the human person . . . Hence self-distinction from the Father is constitutive for the eternal Son. [Indeed] the difference between Father and Son in God's eternal essence, *depend* upon, and take place in, the fact that God as Father is manifest in the relation of Jesus to him . . . [Furthermore] The self-distinction of the Father from the Son is not just that he begets the Son but that he hands over all things to him, so that his kingdom and *his own deity are now dependent upon the Son.*[97]

Barth's positive conception of freedom neither requires nor permits this internal and external dependency which inevitably obscures grace. According to Pannenberg, while the Father is neither begotten nor sent, 'the designation "Father" might well involve a *dependence* of the Father on the Son and *thus* be the basis of true reciprocity in the trinitarian relations'.[98] While we will stress, against Rahner, that there should indeed be true mutuality between the Father and Son within the Trinity, here *true reciprocity* does not express the *free* mutual relatedness of Father, Son and Spirit and thus cannot be a reliable basis for our human freedom. Instead, it follows the introduction of history into the Godhead in such a way that, in some sense, history determines the outcome of the Father's relation to the Son within history. God is no longer the free subject of his own internal and external relations: 'the divine essence overarches each personality' and 'love is a power which shows itself in those who love . . . Persons do not have power over love. It rises above

---

[94] Wolfhart Pannenberg, *Systematic Theology, Volume 1* (hereafter: *Systematic Theology 1*), trans. Geoffrey W. Bromiley (Grand Rapids, MI: Eerdmans, 1991), 327–9, emphasis mine; and 296.

[95] Pannenberg, *Systematic Theology 1*, 56.

[96] Pannenberg, *Systematic Theology 1*, 331, emphasis mine.

[97] Pannenberg, *Systematic Theology 1*, 310–13, 322, emphasis mine. Cf. also *Systematic Theology 2*, 391.

[98] Pannenberg, *Systematic Theology 1*, 312, emphasis mine.

them and thereby gives them their self-hood . . . This applies especially to the trinitarian life of God'.[99] Here it appears that love is the subject, God's freedom to love is the predicate and God's love for us is conditional.

Second, failure to recall that the Son of God for us is 'antecedently the Son of God in Himself' means failure to recognize that theology is knowledge of a 'divine act' (knowledge of faith); its *terminus a quo* and *terminus ad quem* is the actual stepping forth of God from his inaccessibility. This influenced Barth's doctrine of analogy, which stressed that God is by nature hidden from human insight and that there are no analogies that are true in themselves. Today, instead of seeing God stepping forth from his inaccessibility to meet us, many see God's being as somehow *inherent* in the world process so that God's eternal sonship becomes the product of certain historical events, rather than their presupposition, inner meaning, and concluding goal. Analogies are thus considered true in themselves just as Jesus, in his humanity as such, is thought to reveal God. All theologians assert God's incomprehensibility but many do not allow Jesus Christ, the incarnate Word, to govern their conception of God's incomprehensibility from *beginning* to *end*. We have been exploring this difficulty at length in this book and its significance today cannot be stressed too strongly.

Third, restricting the task of theology to understanding Christ in his revelation would mean that the criterion for this understanding would 'have to be something man himself has brought'; Jesus will be called the Son of God 'on the basis of our value judgment',[100] and Ebionite or Docetic Christology will result. The christological and trinitarian implications of this important insight were discussed above in Chapter Two. Interestingly, Pannenberg now approaches Christ's deity by not considering the divine nature 'in isolation'. This must be discovered, according to Pannenberg, 'in his human reality'. And, as seen above in Chapter Two, his eternal sonship

> precedes his historical existence on earth and must be regarded as the creative basis of his human existence. If the human history of Jesus is the revelation of his eternal sonship, we must be able to perceive the latter in the reality of the human life. The deity is not an addition to this reality. It is the reflection that the human relation of Jesus to God the Father casts on his existence, even as it also illumines the eternal being of God.[101]

---

[99] Pannenberg, *Systematic Theology 1*, 430 and 426–7.
[100] *CD* I/1, 421.
[101] Pannenberg, *Systematic Theology 2*, 325. Chapter 10 concerns the deity of Christ.

But if the human history of Jesus is the revelation, then how do we distinguish, and why must we acknowledge a pre-existent divine sonship as the creative basis for our present insights? Since Jesus' deity is 'the reflection that the human relation of Jesus to God the Father casts on his existence' there can be neither a clear distinction between an act of God coming into history in Jesus, nor a need to believe in Jesus' sonship, since it is already an aspect of his humanity; it is an insight that comes from the community as a retroactive perception based in history itself. His deity can neither be the free subject of the incarnation nor can it be equated with his eternal sonship as it *is* from eternity; his sonship is first an aspect of his humanity and then, because of the historical event of the resurrection, becomes what it was supposed to have been.

Pannenberg seems to maintain both the eternal reality of Jesus' humanity[102] and that 'the assuming of human existence by the eternal Son is not to be seen as the adding of a nature that is alien to his deity. It is the self-created medium of his extreme self-actualization in consequence of his free self-distinction from the Father, i.e., a way of fulfilling his eternal sonship.'[103] But to see the humanity this way means it cannot be distinguished from his deity as the medium in and through which God acts toward us and for us within our humanity, and we can hardly avoid concluding that the Son needed to become incarnate to actualize his eternal sonship; this obscures the incarnation as the merciful act of condescension on the part of God for us (grace).[104] It is no accident that Pannenberg frequently substitutes Jesus' message for his person. Indeed, 'In the debate about the figure of Jesus it is of decisive importance that we should not put his person at the center. The center, rather, is God, the nearness of his rule, and his fatherly love.'[105] For Barth, there is no debate about the figure of Jesus. He *is* the Son in whom we are confronted with a decision to accept him for who he is, that is, the kingdom of God which is present and future, or to seek the ground of revelation in someone or something else. For Pannenberg, Jesus' appearance in history involved a claim 'that needed divine confirmation'[106] which the community saw in his resurrection. For Barth his claim was grounded in his being as the Son who could

---

[102] Pannenberg, *Systematic Theology* 2, 367, n. 126.
[103] Pannenberg, *Systematic Theology* 2, 325.
[104] Pannenberg's thinking is echoed by many today.
[105] Pannenberg, *Systematic Theology* 2, 335. Cf. Barth, 'We cannot say that Jesus did not act in His own right, but in the name of another, namely God . . . He acts in the name of God, and therefore in His own name' (*CD* III/2, 62).
[106] Pannenberg, *Systematic Theology* 2, 337.

forgive sins; hence the power of the resurrection was not absent from Jesus' earthly life since this power is that of God's presence in his person and work.[107] This is why Barth rejected two-stage Christology[108] while Pannenberg believes 'Only the Easter event determines what the meaning was of the pre-Easter history of Jesus and who he was in his relation to God.'[109] This lack of precision implies that Jesus' identity is in some sense dependent on the community: 'Only by way of the relation of Jesus to the Father can we decide how and in what sense he himself may be understood to partake of deity, namely, as the Son of this Father.'[110] Yet this is not our decision at all; we may only accept him as he was and is. Since Jesus Christ is the power and wisdom of God

> we must really keep before our eyes God's reconciliation along with His revelation . . . it is actually to those who are called . . . that He is what He is, God's power and wisdom . . . we have to be saved and therefore to have faith if we are to recognise this δύναμις θεοῦ at the very point at which alone in all ages it can be recognised . . . We cannot gain this key ourselves. We can only receive it.[111]

Karl Rahner's Christology: Does Jesus' Humanity as such Reveal?

Let us conclude this chapter by returning now to Rahner's thought and noting some problems with Rahner's Christology, which indicate more precisely why I think his axiom cannot be given unqualified agreement. Part of the difficulty, as we shall see, is that Rahner allows his analysis of human relations to shape his understanding of God's being and action. His philosophy and theology of the symbol cause

---

[107] *CD* II/1, 605–6. 'He, the crucified One, is the power of God (1 Cor. 1:24). Note that He not only has this power but that in His existence He Himself is it. He certainly has it as well . . . the epitome and sum of all the power He enjoys as given and active in Him by God is the fact that God in His power raised Him from the dead (1 Cor. 6:14; 2 Cor. 13:4).' Following Acts 2:24 Barth says, 'He is the One for whom it was impossible that the resurrection from the dead should not take place. This was only His declaration as the Son of God, and therefore as the possessor of the power of His Father which He gained by this event, according to Rom. 1:4. He did not have to become this. He is from the very beginning the possessor of "the power of an endless life" (Heb. 7:16) . . . Jesus Christ is not merely the bearer and executive of a power of God which is given Him but which is not originally and properly His. On the contrary, Jesus Christ has the power of God because and as He Himself is it.'

[108] Cf. Barth, *Evangelical Theology*, 29–30. Cf. also *CD* I/1, 459–60.

[109] Pannenberg, *Systematic Theology* 2, 345.

[110] Pannenberg, *Systematic Theology* 2, 326.

[111] *CD* II/1, 607.

him to compromise God's freedom *in se* and *ad extra.* Formulating his axiom, Rahner considers three difficulties: (1) that the incarnation might not be a certain instance of the identity of the immanent and economic Trinity; (2) that any divine person could have become incarnate and so there would be no connection between the missions and the intratrinitarian life; and (3) how to interpret Christ's human nature (which concerns us here): 'is the humanity of the Logos merely something foreign which has been assumed or is it precisely that which comes into being when the Logos expresses himself into the non-divine?'[112] Should we start from a known human nature or one more clearly revealed by the incarnation? Should not human nature be explained through the 'self-emptying, self-utterance of the Logos himself?' On the surface, Barth and Rahner are at one affirming that true humanity and true deity can be understood only through the Logos becoming incarnate. But they are actually far apart because Rahner's thought is governed by his philosophy of symbolic expression and because he begins with transcendental experience.

Barth and Rahner and those who follow Rahner's transcendental method are in conflict over the role of experience in theology. As seen in the previous chapter, it is out of our transcendental experience of the absolute, which Rahner calls the 'mystery, one and nameless'[113] that we come to know God. Our self-knowledge is the condition for this possibility. Unthematic experience and knowledge of God are part of the very structure of our divinized subjective orientation toward mystery and 'the meaning of all explicit knowledge of God in religion and in metaphysics . . . can really be understood only when all the words we use there point to the *unthematic experience* of our orientation towards the ineffable mystery'.[114] Hence revelation (God's self-communication to creatures) is

> a modification of our transcendental consciousness produced per-
> manently by God in grace. But such a modification is really an original
> and permanent element in our consciousness as the basic and original

---

[112] Rahner, *Trinity*, 31, n. 27.

[113] *TI* 11, 159. Cf. *FCF*, 44 and *TI* 4, 50, where Rahner writes, 'All conceptual expressions about God, necessary though they are, always stem from the unobjectivated experience of transcendence as such: the concept from the pre-conception, the name from the experience of the nameless.' This thinking plays a decisive role in Rahner's view of the incarnation. Our spiritual movement helps us appropriate the ancient Christologies: 'For no under-standing is possible anywhere if what is understood remains fixed and frozen and is not launched into the movement of that *nameless mystery* which is the vehicle of all understanding' (*TI* 4, 106, emphasis mine).

[114] *FCF*, 53.

luminosity of our existence. And as an element in our transcendentality
... it is already revelation in the proper sense.[115]

Why is this the case? Because, as we have already noted in Chapter Four,

> The three mysteries, the Trinity and its two processions and the two self-communications of God *ad extra* in a real formal causality corresponding to the two processions, are not 'intermediate mysteries'. They are not something provisional and deficient in the line of mystery which comes between the perspicuous truths of our natural knowledge and the absolute mystery of God ... Nor are they as it were mysteries of the beyond ... behind the God who is for us the holy mystery.[116]

All this rests upon a supernatural existential which means 'it belongs to the very essence of concrete human nature to be called to grace, to be able to find God in the particularities of all history ... the history of salvation and revelation are coextensive with the history of the human race'.[117] Thus, 'the offer and the possibility of grace is given with human nature itself as ... historically constituted ... the supernatural existential wants to affirm something about the reality of grace, namely, that it is a constituent part of our historical human existence'.[118] But for Grenz and Olson

> the supernatural existential is a highly unstable concept. If the theologian emphasizes the universal aspect denoted by the term *existential*, the concept may easily fall into intrinsicism and become little more than another religious a priori like Schleiermacher's God-consciousness. If one puts forward the supernatural aspect, the supernatural existential may easily fall into extrinsicism and become little more than another theological assertion about the transcendence of God's self-revelation ... [supernatural existential] is highly ambiguous and of dubious value in solving the dilemma of transcendence and immanence in contemporary Christian theology.[119]

I agree. The universal aspect allows many who follow Rahner to claim that God's universal offer of salvation is given in transcendental experience rather than exclusively by God's Word and Spirit. This has affected the theological landscape today perhaps more than any of

---

[115] *FCF*, 149. Following Schoonenberg, LaCugna believes 'Revelation is the experienced self-communication of God *in* human history, which thereby becomes the history of salvation' (*God for Us*, 218).
[116] *TI* 4, 72.
[117] Dych, *Theology in a New Key*, 13.
[118] Dych, *Karl Rahner*, 36–7.
[119] Grenz and Olson, *20th Century Theology*, 246–7.

Rahner's other insights. As seen above, this thinking could lead to the feminist belief that we creatures make the symbol God function and therefore we should reconstruct the symbol in order to help achieve equality between men and women. But this thinking can also lead to the view that our love of neighbor is itself, as such, love of God and thus could undermine our genuine need for revelation by ascribing grace to our human experiences of love.[120]

In any case, Rahner contrasts his 'neo-Chalcedonianism' with a 'pure-Chalcedonianism' for which 'the human as such would not show us the Logos as such . . . he would show himself only in his formal subjectivity'. Then the human nature, as already known to us, logically and ontologically but not temporally ('that which is not trinitarian') is what is assumed in the incarnation. But then the Logos would not have 'stepped outside his intra-divine inaccessibility and shown *himself through* his humanity and *in* his humanity'. We could not say 'He who *sees* me, sees *me*. For when we glimpse the humanity of Christ as such, we would in reality have seen nothing of the subject of the Logos himself, except at most his abstract formal subjectivity.' How then do we interpret the ἀσυγχύτως (unmixed) of Chalcedon? Following his principles of symbolic ontology Rahner affirms that the subject (Logos) expresses *itself* in the humanity; thus the relation between the Logos and the assumed human nature is

> more essential and more intimate. Human nature in general is a possible object of the creative knowledge and power of God, because and insofar as the Logos is by nature the one who is 'utterable' (even into that which is not God) . . . [When the Father freely empties himself] into the non-divine . . . that precisely is born which we call human nature [which is not something] from behind which the Logos hides to act things out in the world. From the start it is the constitutive, real symbol of the Logos himself . . . [Thus] man is possible because the exteriorization of the Logos is possible . . . what Jesus is and does as man reveals the Logos himself; it is the reality of the Logos as our salvation amidst us . . . here the Logos with God and the Logos with us, the immanent and the economic Logos, are strictly the same.[121]

The humanity is posited as the Logos's own way of positing himself. While Rahner's intention is to see our humanity as created and restored in Christ and not to foster a 'lifeless identity', this statement certainly seems to suggest that Jesus' humanity is the Logos present among us.

---

[120] See Coffey, *Deus Trinitas*, for a clear example of this position.
[121] Rahner, *Trinity*, 31–3.

At least one Rahnerian actually interprets Christ's humanity as his divinity under the rubric 'theandric'.[122]

Also, confirming this reading of Rahner, Joseph H. P. Wong explains that, when Christ's humanity is thought of as the very expression of the Logos, the idea is conveyed that 'the symbol not only renders the symbolized present, but is its very reality'.[123] This makes it impossible to distinguish either Christ's divinity and humanity or the immanent and economic Trinity. Here Rahner applies his notion of quasi-formal causality and believes that the doctrine of the Trinity can be properly grasped only 'by going back to the history of salvation and of grace, to our *experience* of Jesus and the Spirit of God, who operates in us, because in them we really already possess the Trinity itself as such'.[124]

But here Rahner's symbolic ontology has caused more problems than it solves. He believes that 'all beings are by their nature symbolic, because they necessarily "express" themselves in order to attain their own nature' and that 'The symbol strictly speaking (symbolic reality) is the self-realization of a being in the other, which is constitutive of its essence.' God is the supreme instance of this. Thus 'Being *as such*, and hence *as one* (*ens* as *unum*), for the fulfillment of its being and its unity, emerges into a plurality – of which the supreme mode is the Trinity.'[125] And

> All activities, from the sheerly material to the innermost life of the Blessed Trinity, are but modulations of this one metaphysical theme, of the one meaning of being: self-possession, subjectivity. 'Self-possession,' however, is itself realized through a double phase: a flowing outwards, an exposition of its own essence from its own cause – an *emanatio*, and a withdrawing into itself of this essence . . .[126]

The 'mysterious unity of transcendence through history and of history into transcendence' has its 'roots in the Trinity, in which the

---

[122] See David Coffey, 'The Theandric Nature of Christ', *TS* 60.3 (September, 1999), 411ff. Thus he writes, 'For Rahner, human nature, though created, is potentially divine, and in the case of Christ actually so' (412). It is important to note that Coffey's belief that Christ's human nature as 'theandric', that is, 'human in a divine way, or, equally, divine in a human way' is 'inevitable once human nature is defined in terms of orientation to God' (413). Such a definition, as we have seen, is intrinsic to Rahner's transcendental method and from my point of view it necessarily confuses nature and grace and reason and revelation.

[123] Joseph H. P. Wong, *Logos-Symbol in the Christology of Karl Rahner* (Rome: Las-Roma, 1984), 193. Cf. also *TI* 4, 251 and 239. Similarly, Peters, *Trinity*, presses Rahner's axiom 'to its extreme consequence' (192); thus 'the loving relationship between the Father and the Son within the Trinity *is* the loving relationship between the Father and Jesus . . . [hence] when we look at Jesus we see the real thing [the Son]' (22).

[124] Rahner, *Trinity*, 40, emphasis mine.

[125] *TI* 4, 224, 234 and 228.

[126] *HW*, 49.

Father is the incomprehensible origin and the original unity, the "Word" his utterance into history, and the "Spirit" the opening up of history into the immediacy of its fatherly origin and end'.[127] But according to the doctrine of the Trinity, God is not first origin and original unity as Father. The unity of God is the unity of the Father, Son and Holy Spirit.

Here Rahner's metaphysics, which states that being as one emerges into a plurality for the fulfillment of its being, leads him to compromise the simple fact upon which Barth's theology stands. For Barth, there is no knowledge of God's oneness if it does not take place through and in Jesus Christ by the power of the Holy Spirit at the start. For Rahner, one knows God's oneness whenever one recognizes a supreme one transcending the many, whatever name is given to this reality.[128] This leads both toward subordinationism and to Rahner's belief that the Trinity does not reveal anything that contradicts our natural knowledge of God. In the end Rahner has no difficulty equating self-acceptance with acceptance of Christ[129] and saying that 'man is the event of God's absolute self-communication'.[130] But this 'universalism' shows that Rahner's starting point was transcendental experience as explained above, rather than God's act in Christ and the Spirit. More will be said about this in the next chapter. Here it is important to note that Rahner's idea that the Word is God's utterance into history allows no clear distinction between the Word's internal utterance and external expression. Rahner speaks of humanity in general as coming into existence when God expresses his Word into the void; as seen above in Chapter Two, he conceives the hypostatic union as Jesus' human self-transcendence into God and blurs the very fact that, for Barth, would preserve a clear distinction between nature and grace.

For Rahner a 'symbol renders present what is revealed' and is 'full of the thing symbolized'.[131] Hence Christ's human nature as such discloses the Logos.[132] Yet since this is exactly what Barth denied in order to affirm both a true humanity and a true divinity in Christ, he clearly distinguished between Christ and our need for him in a way that Rahner

[127] Rahner, *Trinity*, 47.

[128] Cf. *TI* 1, 91, *FCF*, 60, and *TI* 11, 153–6. As seen above in Chapter Four, the term God refers to an experience on the basis of which that which we all experience (the term of our transcendental orientations) is what 'we call God'.

[129] Cf. *TI* 4, 119. This leads to Rahner's anonymous Christianity and encourages the idea that love of God and neighbor are finally identical.

[130] *FCF*, 126ff.

[131] *TI* 4, 239 and 251.

[132] *TI* 4, 239ff. and Rahner, *Trinity*, 32–3.

cannot. For Rahner, Christ's human nature is the real symbol (expression) of God (the unoriginate) in the world.[133] It comes about as God expresses himself into the void. But while Rahner indeed insists that God is free and not subject here to a 'primal must', God's freedom actually is compromised. According to scripture it was by the Holy Spirit that Mary conceived Jesus and not by a symbolic expression into the void. The former suggests a miraculous act of lordship *for us*; the latter a natural process. Faithful to his symbolic ontology, Rahner concludes both that God's act of positing the Logos results in its exteriorization and that the human nature is full of the unoriginate (God). The appearance (humanity) allows God to be present while being full of the reality symbolized.[134] Conceived in this way it is difficult, if not impossible, to claim that the Son is the subject of this event: 'what happened to Jesus on earth is precisely the history of the Word of God himself, and a process which *he* underwent'.[135] From this Rahner draws two problematic conclusions: First, 'the creature is endowed, by virtue of its inmost essence and constitution, with the possibility of being assumed'. Therefore, 'the finite itself has been given an infinite depth and is no longer a contrast to the infinite'. Second,

> God's creative act always drafts the creature as the paradigm of a possible utterance of himself. And he cannot draft it otherwise . . . The immanent self-utterance of God in his eternal fullness is the condition of the self-utterance of God outside himself, and the *latter continues the former*.[136]

All of this follows from Rahner's understanding of God's love as 'the will to fill the void'.[137] Had he kept to a clear doctrine of the immanent Trinity (which he believed was important) then he could have said consistently that God loves in freedom as the Father, Son and Spirit and thus could and did create in freedom. Instead he argues that creation is the continuation of God's immanent self-utterance and presumes that there is a void which God wishes to fill by means of creation and incarnation. Yet, the doctrine of creation implies that before creation

---

[133] *TI* 4, 115.

[134] *TI* 4, 237. Cf. also 225 and 231.

[135] *TI* 4, 113.

[136] *TI* 4, 115, emphasis mine, and 117. 'God has taken on a human nature, because it is essentially ready and adoptable' (110); human nature 'when assumed by God as *his* reality, simply arrived at the point to which it always strives by virtue of its essence' (109). For Barth, 'human nature possesses no capacity for becoming the human nature of Jesus Christ' (*CD* I/2, 188). When it is assumed by God in Christ it receives a new point of departure towards which it could no longer strive by virtue of its essence which is affected by sin.

[137] *TI* 4, 115–17.

nothing but God, as Father, Son and Spirit, existed – no void existed simultaneously with God. God's freedom is so conditioned by creation that, as seen in the previous chapter, Rahner believes that grace pre-supposes nature as a condition of its own possibility.[138]

Of course Rahner insists that God's expression *ad extra* is *free*. But since, according to his symbolic ontology, 'All beings must express themselves', God can express himself outwardly only 'because God "must" "express" himself inwardly'.[139] Thus, when Rahner describes the incarnation as the continuation of God's inner symbolic movement *ad extra*, he conceptually compromises God's freedom to have existed without becoming incarnate. And he extends symbolic expression beyond Jesus to all humanity in their acts of self-transcendence just because he believes, as already noted in Chapter Four, that 'in the long run everything agrees in some way or another with everything else',[140] and that what is symbolized passes 'over into the "otherness" of the symbol'.[141] Moreover, when he describes creation as 'a continuation of the immanent constitution of "image and likeness"', he claims that an encounter with the man Jesus is not only an encounter with but knowledge of the Logos.[142]

Rahner then says what Barth insisted could never be said, that is, 'If God wills to become non-God, man comes to be . . . And if God himself is man and remains so for ever, if all theology is therefore eternally an anthropology . . . man is for ever the articulate mystery of God.'[143] There is and can be no clear distinction between Christ and us here. It is thus perfectly logical for Rahner to understand love of neighbor 'in the direction of a radical identity of the two loves' and say that 'the love of God and the love of neighbour are one and the same thing'. Thus

> wherever a genuine love of man attains its proper nature and its moral absoluteness and depth, it is in addition always so underpinned and heightened by God's saving grace that it is also love of God, whether it be explicitly considered to be such a love by the subject or not . . . this is the direction in which the understanding of the thesis of identity as it is meant here leads . . . wherever man posits a positively moral act in the

---

[138] 'Grace exists . . . by being the divinising condition [of the person], and hence pre-supposes and incorporates into itself the whole reality of this person as the condition of its own possibility' (*TI* 6, 73).

[139] *TI* 4, 236.

[140] *TI* 4, 225.

[141] *TI* 4, 240.

[142] *TI* 4, 236–9, Rahner, *Trinity*, 32–3.

[143] *TI* 4, 116.

full exercise of his free self-disposal, this act is a positive supernatural salvific act . . . wherever there is an absolutely moral commitment of a positive kind in the world . . . there takes place also a saving event, faith, hope and charity . . .[144]

Therefore, 'Christology is the end and beginning of anthropology . . . this anthropology, when most thoroughly realized in Christology, is eternally theology',[145] and 'for all eternity such an anthropology is really theology'.[146] Indeed 'anthropology and Christology mutually determine each other within Christian dogmatics if they are both correctly understood'.[147] For Barth, this reversibility of Christ's divinity and humanity and mutual conditioning compromises theology's foundation in the immanent Trinity because 'There is a way from Christology to anthropology, but there is no way from anthropology to Christology.'[148] And from what was said above, we can see that many who follow Rahner's basic insights have used this thinking to argue that there should no longer be any clear distinction between the immanent and economic Trinity. Rahner never intended to say what they say and in fact he affirmed God's sovereignty.[149] Unfortunately, however, his symbolic logic leads to what others have concluded and to inconsistencies in his own position.

Here, contemporary trinitarian theology is in turmoil because the question has ceased to be: What is God, *as God*, saying to us in the humanity of the Word and in our humanity by the Holy Spirit uniting us to this Word in faith? The questions have become: How can we make the Trinity a doctrine which is alive so that it reflects our experiences of faith and incorporates relationality and temporality into the divine life? Or how can relationality, which was given dogmatic status in the doctrine of the Trinity, enable *us* to reconceive God in order to create a society of persons existing in freedom and equality? This is the kind of self-designed irrelevance that follows an inability to speak first about God *as* God the Father, Son and Holy Spirit and then, on that basis, about our relations with God, other creatures and the world in light of revelation and faith.

Interestingly, Rahner's axiom is meant to affirm that the 'Trinity of salvation history, as it reveals itself to us by deeds, is the "immanent"

---

[144] *TI* 6, 233, 236–7, 239.
[145] *TI* 4, 117.
[146] *TI* 1, 185.
[147] *TI* 9, 28.
[148] *CD* I/1, 131 and *CD* III/2, 71.
[149] Rahner, *Trinity*, 36–7 and *TI* 4, 112.

Trinity'.¹⁵⁰ But since symbols are necessary (and thus condition the expressive reality – God) and since they are full of the reality symbolized, they have the power to render present what is revealed. And there literally cannot be any clear distinction between Christ's humanity and divinity at exactly the point where a precise analysis of one of Christology's hardest problems could clarify the meaning of revelation, reconciliation and redemption. For Rahner all of these become explicable, first in and by our transcendental experiences and then through the doctrines. Therefore, when Barth spoke eschatologically he argued:

> Let us be clear that . . . we are again speaking of the Second Coming of *Jesus Christ.* Christian Eschatology is different from all other expectations for the future, whether they be worldly or religious or religious-worldly, in that it is not primarily expectation of something, even if this something were called resurrection of the flesh and eternal life, but expectation of the *Lord.*¹⁵¹

When Rahner speaks of hope he equates our transcendental experience with grace and revelation; he does not *start and end* his thinking with Jesus' actual resurrection and second coming.

> If one has a radical hope of attaining a definitive identity and does not believe that one can steal away with one's obligations into the emptiness of non-existence, one has already grasped and accepted the resurrection in its real content . . . The absoluteness of the radical hope in which a human being apprehends his or her total existence as destined and empowered to reach definitive form can quite properly be regarded as grace, which permeates this existence always and everywhere. This grace is revelation in the strictest sense . . . this certainly is revelation, even if this is not envisaged as coming from 'outside'.¹⁵²

---

¹⁵⁰ Rahner, *Trinity,* 47.

¹⁵¹ Barth, *Credo,* 166–7. Underestimating Jesus' lordship followed from depreciating the foundation of the community in his resurrection and a failure to perceive the 'consolation of the Holy Spirit in whose work the community may find full satisfaction at every moment in its time of waiting' (*CD* III/2, 509).

¹⁵² Rahner and Weger, *Our Christian Faith,* 110–11. In *TI* 17, 16 Rahner begins his analysis of Jesus' resurrection saying, 'It is possible to enquire about Jesus' resurrection today . . . only if we take into account the whole of what philosophy and theology have to say about man. Here we must start from the assumption that the hope that a person's history of freedom will be conclusive in nature . . . already includes what we mean by the hope of "resurrection" . . . this hope must include knowledge of what is really meant by resurrection.' And for Rahner 'the knowledge of man's resurrection given with his transcendentally necessary hope is a statement of philosophical anthropology even before any real revelation in the Word' (18). By the time Rahner appeals to grace and scripture they can only describe something that everyone already knows and experiences without faith in Christ and the

Rahner's axiom 'provides us with a methodical principle for the whole treatise on the Trinity. The Trinity is a mystery whose paradoxical character is preluded in the paradoxical character of man's existence.' Rahner explores human self-transcendence assuming that we have an obediential potency for revelation and a supernatural existential which identifies revelation and grace with our transcendental dynamisms. But these very assumptions blur the distinction between nature and grace. Consequently, while Rahner is materially correct to assert that no theology can deny in principle that the doctrine of the missions is a starting point for the doctrine of the Trinity and that, without this, one cannot avoid 'the danger of wild and empty conceptual acrobatics',[153] he compromises the free basis of the missions in God's pre-temporal eternity by applying his symbolic ontology to the incarnation.

So he maintains two critical insights, which Barth's doctrine of the immanent Trinity resisted. He makes it possible to equate Jesus' humanity with the power of the Word, thus providing an explanation of Christianity that circumvents Jesus' deity and the need for faith in him *before* thinking about God and salvation.[154] And he argues that everyone has an obediential potency and a supernatural existential which can also be starting points for grasping the Trinity. This ends in the universalism that Barth consistently rejected by refraining from agnosticism, pantheism and dualism. Rahner can thus say that 'the mystery of the Trinity is the last mystery of our own reality, and that it is experienced precisely in this reality'.[155] This statement is not as far removed from the positions of LaCugna and Peters as one might at first glance assume. So when Ted Peters criticizes Rahner for still wanting to maintain an essential Trinity prior to the economy, there is a mixture of truth and error. Rahner knew quite well that without a real immanent Trinity the freedom of God would be compromised. In

---

Spirit. We shall analyze in more detail how Rahner allows this transcendental experience of hope to define his understanding of grace, revelation and the resurrection in the next chapter.

[153] Rahner, *Trinity*, 47–8.

[154] Torrance, *Trinitarian Perspectives*, reflecting the views of a 1975 Colloquium on Rahner's doctrine of the Trinity, notes this and other problems in Rahner's view (79, 82, 91), even though he also presents Rahner's positive contributions to the discussion. Interestingly, David Coffey (*Deus Trinitas*) makes this christological error (equating Jesus' divinity with his humanity) the centerpiece of his trinitarian theology. And Catherine LaCugna, 'The Trinitarian Mystery of God', in *Systematic Theology: Roman Catholic Perspectives*, ed. Francis Schüssler Fiorenza and John P. Galvin (Minneapolis: Fortress Press, 1991), 151–92, writes, 'The divinity of Christ lies in his perfect humanity, which is why he can be seen as the perfect fulfillment of our own humanity' (188).

[155] Rahner, *Trinity*, 47.

this respect his thinking certainly is in harmony with Barth, Jüngel and Torrance. But the logic of his symbolic ontology allows for no such free existence of God to be determinative. In this respect his thinking was ahead of his time, because he was already allowing history to condition God's own being and action in the ways noted above. Here then is the real basis for the difficulties that can be seen in contemporary trinitarian theology in so far as it has been shaped by Rahner's axiom. My suggestion in this book is that Barth's doctrine of the immanent Trinity could help us perceive and actually avoid these difficulties and thus present a doctrine of the Trinity that truly sees human freedom established on the basis of and not in abstraction from God's eternal sovereign freedom.

One contemporary theologian who does indeed establish human freedom on the basis of God's eternal sovereign freedom is Thomas F. Torrance. In the next chapter we shall therefore compare the thought of T. F. Torrance with Karl Rahner with a view toward seeing how exactly they agree and differ in their respective views of God's self-communication in Christ. This will show that, while Rahner's axiom of identity can provide a non-controversial way of seeing that the economic Trinity is and should be the ground of our understanding of the immanent Trinity and that the two cannot be separated, it also can lead to a serious compromise of both divine and human freedom. Such a compromise would occur if the starting point and conclusion of one's reflections were someone or something other than the One Mediator, Jesus Christ.

Chapter Six

Karl Rahner and Thomas F. Torrance: God's Self-Communication in Christ with Special Emphasis on Interpreting Christ's Resurrection

KARL Rahner and Thomas F. Torrance have made enormous contributions to twentieth-century theology. Torrance is quick to point out that Rahner's approach to trinitarian theology which begins with God's saving revelation (the economic Trinity) and pivots 'upon God's concrete and effective self-communication in the Incarnation' does indeed have the effect that Rahner intended. First, it reunites the treatises *On the One God* and *On the Triune God.* This opens the door to rapprochement between systematic and biblical theology and binds the New Testament view of Jesus closer to the Church's worship and proclamation of the triune God. Second, it opens the door to rapprochement between East and West by shifting from a more 'abstractive' Scholastic framework to one bound up with piety, worship and experience within the Church. Third, it opens the door to rapprochement between Roman Catholic theology and Evangelical theology 'especially as represented by the teaching of Karl Barth in his emphasis upon the self-revelation and self-giving of God as the root of the doctrine of the Trinity'.[1]

[1] Torrance, *Trinitarian Perspectives*, 78.

This chapter will explore how the notion of self-communication functions in the theology of Torrance and Rahner with a view toward seeing how, where and why they agree and disagree about the meaning of this important concept. There is no doubt that self-communication is a central category for each theologian. And despite the fact that it could have emanationist overtones, as noted above, the concept itself enables both Torrance and Rahner to fashion contemporary explanations of the Trinity, grace, incarnation and revelation, which are intended to function in the three ways just noted. In fact, self-communication is, in many contexts, simply another term for self-revelation.

I shall have to limit myself by addressing one key issue, namely, how consistent are Rahner and Torrance in beginning their theologies with God's economic trinitarian self-communication? In other words, how successful is each theologian in keeping the treatises *On the One God* and *On the Triune God* together without allowing some prior concept of God to determine the truth of his theological reflections? We shall concentrate on their respective methodologies by focusing on how each theologian interprets the resurrection. It is hoped that this comparison will lead to a clearer understanding of how a proper doctrine of the immanent Trinity might function today.

Several important features that structure T. F. Torrance's view of God's self-communication can be noted. First, the *homoousion* which stresses the *enousios* Logos (that the Logos is internal to God's being) is central.[2] Thus, 'Everything hinges on the reality of God's *self-communication to us in Jesus Christ . . .* so that for us to know God in Jesus Christ is really to know him as he is in himself.'[3] Second, his theological realism implies that theology must be both devout and scientific.[4] It must be devout in the sense that for Athanasius, as seen above in Chapter One, it is 'more godly and true to signify God from

---

[2] Torrance, *The Trinitarian Faith*, 72–3, 130–1 and 311. Cf. also Torrance, *The Christian Doctrine of God*, 129. See also Kang Phee Seng, 'The Epistemological Significance of ϑμοουσιον in the Theology of Thomas F. Torrance', *SJT* 45.3 (1992), 341–66, 344ff. For a brief but good biographical and theological introduction to Torrance's theology, see Alister E. McGrath, *Thomas F. Torrance: An Intellectual Biography* (Edinburgh: T&T Clark, 1999). See also Elmer M. Colyer, *How to Read T. F. Torrance: Understanding His Trinitarian and Scientific Theology* (Downers Grove, IL: InterVarsity Press, 2001) and Elmer M. Colyer (ed.), *The Promise of Trinitarian Theology: Theologians in Dialogue with T. F. Torrance* (Lanham, MD: Rowman & Littlefield, 2001).

[3] T. F. Torrance, *Reality and Evangelical Theology* (Philadelphia: Westminster Press, 1982), 23.

[4] Torrance, *The Trinitarian Faith*, 51.

the Son and call him Father, than to name God from his works alone and call him Unoriginate'.[5] It must be scientific in that 'scientific knowledge was held to result from inquiry strictly in accordance with the nature (κατα φύσιν) of the reality being investigated, that is, knowledge of it reached under the constraint of what it actually and essentially is in itself, and not according to arbitrary convention (κατα θέσιν)'.[6] This theological realism attempts to recognize truth for what it is by thinking after the truth itself. This scientific method is not unique to theology but because theology is under the compulsion of a unique object it certainly knows what cannot be known in other scientific endeavors.[7] For instance, science can neither observe the event of creation itself nor that of the resurrection because we would have to be able to get behind creaturely processes to observe them and that is impossible.[8] Still, in the overlap between natural sciences and religion, Torrance believes there is room for a new kind of natural theology as we shall see. Third, the relation between subjectivity and objectivity must neither compromise the object nor the subject. Therefore, to know God our thinking must have a point of access in God himself and in our creaturely existence. But this in no way compromises Torrance's belief that only God can reveal God. Torrance frequently opposes subjectivism and dualism while seeking a unitary theology – not a monistic or agnostic theology – but one that respects human subjectivity while finding the true meaning of human subjectivity in a center in God and not in itself. This helps him overcome a particularly thorny issue for modern theology that I have highlighted throughout this book. He argues that we cannot read back our ideas and experiences into God if we are to have a proper theology and that the controlling factor is and remains Christ's active mediation of himself through the Holy Spirit and thus through the Bible, the Church and its sacraments. Arius was the prime historical example of someone who failed to think scientifically about God precisely because he did not think from a center in God.

Therefore, for Torrance, the all-important point of his theology is that we have a point of access in God and in creaturely existence in the

---

[5] Torrance, *The Trinitarian Faith*, 49, and *The Christian Doctrine of God*, 117.

[6] Torrance, *The Trinitarian Faith*, 51. See Thomas F. Torrance, *Christian Theology and Scientific Culture* (New York: Oxford University Press, 1981), 27, 29. Cf. also *The Christian Doctrine of God*, 206.

[7] Cf. Torrance, *Christian Theology and Scientific Culture*, 8, and *Reality and Evangelical Theology*, 30–1.

[8] Cf. Thomas F. Torrance, *Space, Time and Resurrection* (Grand Rapids, MI: Eerdmans,

incarnation which is God's self-communication to us: 'Jesus Christ himself, then, is the hearing and speaking man included in the Word of God incarnate'.[9] Torrance relies upon Hilary of Poitiers for his belief that 'The very centre of a saving faith is the belief not merely in God, but in God as Father, and not merely in Christ, but in Christ as the Son of God, in him, not as a creature, but as God the Creator, born of God.'[10] Therefore, when we come to God as Father through the Son our knowledge is 'grounded in the very being of God and is determined by what he essentially is in his own nature'.[11] Since it is in Jesus Christ that we may truly know this God then we may thus know him in a way that is godly and precise. For Torrance, then, the *lex orandi* and the *lex credendi*, piety and precision, godliness and exactness belong together.[12]

Like Rahner, Torrance believes 'created intelligibility . . . by its very nature is open to God and points beyond itself to God',[13] but Torrance does not believe that an inferential argument can be developed from that created intelligibility to God's uncreated intelligibility and so he consistently opposes building a 'logical bridge' between the world and God or between our thoughts and God's being.[14] Although Torrance believes there is a role for natural theology, he grants it no independent status in relation to positive theology. Like Rahner, Torrance seeks to integrate 'so-called natural theology and so-called revealed theology' indicating that

> natural theology has its natural place in the overlap between theological and natural science where they operate within the same rational structures of space and time and have in common the basic ideas of the

1976; reissued Edinburgh: T&T Clark, 1998), 77.

[9] Torrance, *Reality and Evangelical Theology*, 88. For Torrance 'it is specifically in Jesus Christ, the incarnate Son, that God has communicated himself to us . . . Thus it is only in him who is both ὁμοούσιος with the Father and ὁμοούσιος with us, that we may really know God as he is in himself' (*The Trinitarian Faith*, 203).

[10] Hilary cited in Torrance, *The Trinitarian Faith*, 53.

[11] Torrance, *The Trinitarian Faith*, 53.

[12] Cf. Torrance, *The Trinitarian Faith*, 43.

[13] Thomas F. Torrance, *The Ground and Grammar of Theology* (Charlottesville: University Press of Virginia, 1980; reissued Edinburgh: T&T Clark, 2001), 99. See also Thomas F. Torrance, *God and Rationality* (London: Oxford University Press, 1971; reissued Edinburgh: T&T Clark, 2001), 186. Torrance gives an excellent account of how this openness is to be understood through the Holy Spirit in chapter 7.

[14] Torrance, *The Ground and Grammar of Theology*, 99 and 75ff., 79, 81, 86. Torrance regards Anselm's argument as a scientific one rather than a logical one. Within this method intelligibility and being are not separated, but created intelligibility operates under the compulsion of God's uncreated intelligibility. Cf. also *Reality and Evangelical Theology*, 24.

unitary rationality of the universe – its contingent intelligibility and contingent freedom, contributed by Christian theology to natural science . . .[15]

Torrance, however, insists upon the irreversibility of the creator–creature relation and of our knowledge and God's being and act.[16] Finally, Torrance insists that God's being and act are indeed one *ad intra* and *ad extra*; thus God can be known only out of God himself[17] and what God is toward us in Christ and the Spirit, he is eternally in himself.[18] This last point of course is where Rahner and Torrance agree about the immanent and the economic Trinity. Like Rahner, Torrance maintains that God was free to create or not.[19] He also insists that creation does not take place through an inner compulsion in God's being.[20] Further, Torrance emphasizes that the Gift and the Giver are one in Christ and the Spirit. Thus, he understands grace in a way that does not ascribe God's (onto-relational) personal actions directly to created being and in a way that does not detach God's actions in history from the being of his Word and Spirit.[21] Both theologians also agree that there should be dialogue between science and theology.

[15] Torrance, *The Ground and Grammar of Theology*, 100 and 107. While Colin Gunton agrees with Torrance that parallel rationalities may be found in the sciences of God and of created realities and that 'created and uncreated intelligibility' may be viewed together, he prefers to maintain a distinction between natural theology and 'a theology of nature' rather than speaking, with Torrance, of a transformed natural theology. See Colin E. Gunton, *A Brief Theology of Revelation* (Edinburgh: T&T Clark, 1995), 63. This makes sense since traditional natural theology is understood as a knowledge of God from nature, whereas Torrance's 'transformed natural theology' operates within the ambit of revelation and is thus a knowledge of nature from revelation based on faith and grace.

[16] Torrance, *The Ground and Grammar of Theology*, 67, *The Christian Doctrine of God*, 18ff. and 158, and *The Trinitarian Faith*, 49, 76 and 82.

[17] Cf., e.g., Torrance, *The Trinitarian Faith*, 52 and 207, *The Christian Doctrine of God*, 11, 13ff., 22 and 74, and *God and Rationality*, 72, 176.

[18] Cf., e.g., Torrance, *The Trinitarian Faith*, 71, 130, *The Christian Doctrine of God*, 8, 92, 158, 237, and *Reality and Evangelical Theology*, 14, 141. These are only a few of the many places where this insight is stressed.

[19] Torrance, *The Trinitarian Faith*, 52, 90–3, 105, and *The Christian Doctrine of God*, 207.

[20] Torrance, *The Trinitarian Faith*, 93, and *The Ground and Grammar of Theology*, 66.

[21] See Torrance, *The Trinitarian Faith*, 138, 140f., 201, 215, 222 and 297, *The Christian Doctrine of God*, 63, and *Theology in Reconciliation*, 131ff., where Torrance stresses that Christ's real presence (*self*-communication) in the Eucharist is grounded in God's real presence to himself. Cf. also Thomas F. Torrance, *Theology in Reconstruction* (London: SCM Press, 1965), 182f. For Torrance's onto-relational notion of persons (divine and human), see *The Christian Doctrine of God*, 102ff., 124, 133, 157 and 163, and *Reality and Evangelical Theology*, 42ff. The ontic relations of the three divine persons in the one God 'belong to what they essentially are in themselves in their distinctive *hypostases*'. Thus, relations among persons belong to what they are as persons.

Torrance's View of the Resurrection

A brief but not exhaustive exploration of Torrance's understanding of Christ's resurrection should allow for an interesting comparison of the two theologians and will illustrate that each of the above-mentioned factors is at work in his theology of the resurrection. Torrance begins by noting that in his last conversation with Barth the two theologians agreed (1) that natural theology had a place within positive theology, and (2) on the importance of the resurrection of the body when speaking of Christ's resurrection from the dead. Thus, for Torrance, there should be a proper natural theology, that is, one that does not create a chasm between God and the universe and then try to bridge that chasm without allowing its knowledge to be shaped by the content of Christian revelation. Such a natural theology can neither be independent nor antecedent to 'actual or empirical knowledge of God upon which it is then imposed'.[22] Torrance therefore rejects any a priori understanding of God as he has actually communicated himself to us in the economy and argues that the resurrection should be the starting point for scientific theology.

> *The raising of the Christ* is *the* act of God, whose significance is not to be compared with any event before or after. *It is the primal datum of theology, from which there can be no abstracting,* and the normative presupposition for every valid dogmatic judgment and for the meaningful construction of a Christian theology.[23]

As such it cannot be derived from empirical reflection and is 'established beyond any religious a priori'.[24] Torrance thus insists that the resurrection is *utterly unique* and therefore it, like the incarnation, conflicts with our prior knowledge and belief about God by forcing itself upon our minds as an ultimate event whose truth was and is identical with the transcendent truth of God. This is why Jesus was an offense to the Jews and folly to the Greeks. Based on prior beliefs and knowledge, Jesus' resurrection 'was deemed to be utterly incredible'.[25] While one 'may (or will be able to) observe the resurrected actuality of Jesus Christ' as a new creation within the old order, it must be known in accord with its own nature and out of itself.[26] Torrance thus argues that the order of redemption intersects with the order of creation in the

---

[22] Torrance, *Space, Time and Resurrection*, 1.
[23] Torrance, *Space, Time and Resurrection*, 74, emphasis in original.
[24] Torrance, *Space, Time and Resurrection*, 74 and 175ff.
[25] Torrance, *Space, Time and Resurrection*, 17.
[26] Torrance, *Space, Time and Resurrection*, 78.

resurrection so that 'the basic structure of what emerges in the Easter event is absolutely new: a reality which is not only entirely unknown to us but entirely unknowable in terms of what we already know or think we know, and knowable through a radical reconstruction of our prior knowledge'.[27] For Torrance, the very idea that the act of resurrection is an interruption of the laws of nature assumes that creation and resurrection can be observed a posteriori or predicted a priori and fails to recognize that it, like Jesus himself (as God and man), is *utterly unique*. It is a creative act of God within nature and cannot be grasped in the same way that we formulate natural laws, since natural laws only express connections immanent in nature. The resurrection did not arise from history and is not a natural process that can be observed as such. 'Just as in justification the law was not destroyed but established, so in the resurrection time is not annihilated but recreated, for it is taken up in Christ, sanctified in his human life and transformed in his resurrection as man.'[28] Christ's ascension refers us back to the historical Jesus as the place where we may know the immanent Trinity.[29]

Because Christ's resurrection is utterly unique, Torrance argues that the kingdom did not come by the processes of history. If it had, there would have been no need for Christ's resurrection.[30] There was nothing comparable in the Old Testament and it is dominant in the New Testament as a supernatural miraculous event that could not be explained from the human or natural side. Christ was not only raised bodily from the dead but was appointed Messiah. Indeed, Jesus' birth and resurrection are linked and his whole life is a miracle. Jesus' resurrection also has corporate implications: we receive immortality from him. Unbelievers are affected since they will be judged by Jesus. But only believers will enjoy the fruit of the resurrection. The New Testament does not first focus on individual resurrection but on God's covenant mercies and on Christ's resurrection, which can only be understood in faith because it exists in a transformed context which it brought about. Jesus appeared only to believers. Therefore one must dwell in it to grasp it. It will appear differently inside and outside of the community.[31]

Torrance opposes any non-cognitive or non-conceptual faith as a form of dualism which disjoins God from the world and permits no knowledge of God as he is in himself.

[27] Torrance, *Space, Time and Resurrection*, 175.
[28] Torrance, *Space, Time and Resurrection*, 98.
[29] Torrance, *Reality and Evangelical Theology*, 37, and *Space, Time and Resurrection*, 128ff.
[30] Torrance, *Space, Time and Resurrection*, 28.
[31] Torrance, *Space, Time and Resurrection*, 32–7.

> Even though God transcends all that we can think and say of Him, it
> still holds good that we cannot have experience of Him or believe in
> Him without conceptual forms of understanding – as Anselm used to
> say: *fides esse nequit sine conceptione*.[32]

He would thus oppose an application of the historical-critical method,
which separates the empirical and the theoretical or the dogmatic and
factual such as might happen if someone refused to accept the com-
mission of the risen Lord as part of the original tradition coming from
Jesus.[33] What Torrance rejects is the kind of source, form or redaction
criticism that operates with the assumptions of 'observationalism and
phenomenalism. Thus they assume that theoretical elements can only
have a later origin and have to be put down to the creative spirituality
of the early Christian community rather than to Jesus himself.'[34] If the
facts presented in the New Testament are taken out of their theological
contexts they are mutilated and can no longer be properly conceived.
Torrance, like Rahner, wishes to see fundamental theology and dogmatic
theology unified. But he insists that Christ must be the starting point
and that that excludes an a priori knowledge of the resurrection because
such a priori knowledge is not actually scientific. This is precisely why
he rejects Bultmann's view of the resurrection.

He argues that Bultmann's view that the objective form of incarnation, atonement, resurrection and ascension resulted from
unscientific mythologizing based on an unscientific world-view is
unacceptable because it ignores the fact that early Christians were well
aware of the *conflict* between the gospel and the prevailing world-view.
Rather, it is Bultmann's own dualist and scientifically antiquated
world-view that allowed him to mythologize the New Testament and
'then "demythologize" it in terms of his own mistaken exaltation of
self-understanding, which transfers the centre of reference away from
the action of God in the historical Jesus to some spiritual event of
"resurrection" in man's experience'.[35]

Torrance insists that his critically realist theology will avoid fundamentalism and extreme realism. It will not argue that scripture is

---

[32] Torrance, *God and Rationality*, 170.
[33] Torrance, *Space, Time and Resurrection*, 7.
[34] Torrance, *Reality and Evangelical Theology*, 80.
[35] Torrance, *Space, Time and Resurrection*, 17–18, n. 25. Cf. also *Reality and Evangelical Theology*, 82. For an interesting analysis of Bultmann, see *God and Rationality*, chapter 3, 'Cheap and Costly Grace'. Torrance writes, 'whenever we take our eyes off the centrality and uniqueness of Jesus Christ and His objective vicarious work, the Gospel disappears behind man's existentialized self-understanding, and even the Reality of God Himself is simply reduced to "what He means for me . . ."' (60).

impregnated with changeless divine truth that can be authoritatively interpreted, and it will think about realities through thoughts rather than thinking only thoughts themselves. One's thoughts therefore must be controlled by God's self-communication as Father, Son and Holy Spirit.[36] Torrance rejects neo-Protestant dualism which might lead to historicizing the scriptural material by searching for raw facts without penetrating to understand what it says out of its own dynamic processes. Torrance dismisses what he calls a kind of Q fundamentalism that supposes an earliest layer of the New Testament message from which it will think. Theology is interested in the different layers of tradition only as they are correlated and controlled by God's self-revelation. We cannot say then exactly how ideas are related to the realities we experience because it is an ontological relation that eludes formalization. Yet it is only in that relation that we can know. Theology must dwell within the semantic relations of the New Testament so that one's mind may apprehend the realities intended and be shaped by God's objective self-communication in Christ. This is why Torrance insists that the resurrection must be interpreted historically *and* theologically. A merely theological view would end in mythology and Docetism while a merely historical view would not take account of Jesus' uniqueness from the start and would be neither open-minded nor scientific.[37]

How then does Torrance understand subjective and objective realities in connection with the resurrection? Our thinking must be governed by or shaped and informed by 'the self-evidencing force and intrinsic significance of their [the biblical reports] objective content, i.e. the self-revelation and self-communication of God through Jesus Christ and in the Holy Spirit'.[38] This is different from logical inferences empty of ontological content. What makes scripture transparent then is the divine light that shines through. Torrance is very consistent arguing this position. For example, in *Reality and Evangelical Theology* he opposes fundamentalism and liberalism precisely because each approach to scripture, in its own way, fails to acknowledge that the truth of God's

---

[36] Torrance, *Space, Time and Resurrection*, 9f. See Torrance, *God and Rationality*, 170ff. Torrance believes the Holy Spirit creates our capacity for God, is not mutually correlated with us, is essentially in God as is the Son, and enables us to participate in the Father and Son without ceasing to be Lord: 'As the Spirit of Truth He is the self-communication and the self-speaking of the divine Being dwelling within us who renews our minds, articulates God's Word within our understanding, leads us into all truth, so that through the Spirit we are converted from ourselves to thinking from a centre in God and not in ourselves, and to knowing God out of God and not out of ourselves' (174).

[37] Torrance, *Space, Time and Resurrection*, 94.

[38] Torrance, *Space, Time and Resurrection*, 11.

self-communication is and remains grounded in God himself and not in the media through which God interacts with us.[39] Thus fundamentalism makes the Bible a 'self-contained corpus of divine truths in propositional form' and fails to acknowledge the identity of being between what God is toward us in Jesus Christ and what he is in himself.[40] Fundamentalism refuses to see that God's self-communication is his free continuous act which must be given and received and whose content is God himself. Liberalism stumbles at the identity of God and his revelation by denying the deity of Christ and assimilating the Spirit of Christ to the human spirit. It is thus 'thrown back upon the autonomous religious reason to provide the ground on which all that is claimed to be divine revelation is to be considered';[41] this detaches Christ from God and Christianity is then detached from Christ.

Finally, the theologian must interpret scripture within the frame of objective meaning that gave rise to the layers of the apostolic tradition. There was an integration of the self-proclamation of Christ with the apostolic proclamation of him which had an impact on the early Church and they should not be separated. Therefore, as Torrance notes, Jesus was not a Christian since a Christian is saved by him. For that reason theology is not concerned with Jesus' private religious understanding of God but with his vicarious life and activity through which we know the God and Father of Jesus Christ as redeemed sinners.

Most importantly, the context of objective meaning here for the theologian 'is bound up with the incarnation of the Son of God to be one with us in our physical human existence' so that in and through his vicarious life and passion he could 'redeem human being and creatively reground it in the very life of God himself, and therefore it is also bound up with the resurrection of Jesus Christ in body, or the physical reality of his human existence among us'.[42] In the resurrection, God's incarnate and redeeming purpose is triumphantly fulfilled. Because of this any abstraction from the incarnation, life, death and resurrection leaves scholars unable to find the unity of scripture.

Therefore, it is clear that for Torrance an *objective* self-disclosure took place which was the basis for Christianity and that the incarnation

[39] Torrance, *Reality and Evangelical Theology*, 85–8, 90.
[40] Torrance, *Reality and Evangelical Theology*, 17–18.
[41] Torrance, *Reality and Evangelical Theology*, 15.
[42] Torrance, *Space, Time and Resurrection*, 13. For Torrance, following Athenagoras, 'If there is no resurrection, human nature is no longer genuinely human' (81–2). Without this, theology collapses into moralism, existentialism and subjectivism. Unless Jesus actually rose, then the power of sin and death and non-being remain unbroken. 'Everything depends on the resurrection of the body, otherwise all we have is a Ghost for a Savior' (87).

and resurrection still force themselves in the same way on our minds today.[43] Indeed for Torrance the resurrection accounts must be accepted in their own settings in Israel, which had a non-dualistic view of reality (as against hellenic, gnostic or mystic views). Because Christians did not separate the humanity from the incarnate Son and spoke of bodily resurrection, they rejected Docetism and adoptionism. This led to a radical revision in the concept of God. Judaism in fact refused to go forward with the Church by accepting the implications of the resurrection, that is, that God himself was directly and personally present in the passion and resurrection of Jesus. The resurrection therefore destroyed the dualist view of God's relation with the world. In fact the root of the doctrine of the Trinity is formed here because resurrection of the body implies a knowledge that participates in Christ's being and life. Torrance's realist view of the resurrection then stresses that God acts within space and time; that our thinking must be faithful to the nature of the event and that we must develop radically different notions of space and time in accordance with this. In other words, the resurrection must be seen in the light of Christ's divine–human natures; indeed his own uniqueness is what makes the resurrection credible. Since the resurrection is the other side of the cross, our humanity is sanctified in *his* life of obedience; his healing and forgiving as well as his death and resurrection are bound up with who he is in relation to the Father. Important here are the notions 'enhypostasis' and 'anhypostasis'.

Christ remained passive in the sense that he did not use his divine power to avoid temptation and the cross (this corresponds to the anhypostatic element); he experienced a real death in submitting to the Father's judgment and was so powerless that he had to be raised up by God himself. This was a vicarious act of Jesus for us, and it was thus positive and creative, since the resurrection was the Father's justification of our humanity; this corresponds to the 'enhypostatic' element in the incarnation. While our humanity is indeed sanctified, it is sanctified in *his* life of free obedience. The hypostatic union implies a living and dynamic union which ran through his whole life. Therefore atonement cannot be separated from Christ, its 'Agent'.[44] The subject of the resurrection then is

> a divine-human subject, and therefore a unique happening defined by the nature of the unique Agent. Other human agents were involved in the life of Jesus . . . but because we have here a different Subject, the Son

[43] Torrance, *Space, Time and Resurrection*, 18. Cf. Torrance, *The Christian Doctrine of God*, 46f.
[44] Torrance, *Space, Time and Resurrection*, 42–55.

of God incarnate in human existence . . . we have to understand the
inner movement of his history in a way appropriate to his nature – that
applies to his birth, to the whole of his life, and to his resurrection . . .[45]

It must be accepted or rejected on its own ground. But it confronts us
with a self-communication of God which lays claim to our commitment.
This is not an act of blind faith because it is the subjective pole of
commitment to objective reality.[46] Torrance advocates what he calls
repentant thinking because it is thinking that must yield to God's self-
revelation which is clearly not to be found first within experience but
first in Jesus Christ and then in experience. There is no reason to separate
the two. But there is every reason to see that the meaning of experience
is illuminated by the *historical events* of incarnation, atonement,
resurrection and ascension: God's own self-revelation thus prevents us
from grounding our beliefs in faith. The only proper ground of faith
then is the reality to which it is correlated as its objective pole. Bultmann
clearly reduced the objective to the subjective pole by collapsing the
Easter event into the disciples' experience of faith. It is clear that this
thinking is a consistent outworking of Torrance's pivotal insight that
theology must think from a center in God and not in ourselves. Even
though Torrance explains that knowledge arises from experience and,
in his view, through intuition, he is very clear that 'evangelical experience' depends upon Christ's self-communication and ultimately upon
the Son's mutual knowing and loving relation with the Father for
intelligibility. Thus, experience is controlled from a center in God and
must be open and completed beyond itself in the Word and Spirit.[47]

[45] Torrance, *Space, Time and Resurrection*, 94. Thus both the ideas of the virgin birth and
the empty tomb were not invented but forced themselves upon the early Church against its
current beliefs (56). Because the resurrection of our human nature is the goal of the
atonement, Torrance can also say, in light of the concepts of 'perichoresis' and 'enhypostasis',
that 'the resurrection also means that the steadfastness of the Son of Man is such that it held
on its way in utter obedience to the Father in the spirit of holiness in the midst of judgment,
death and hell, and in spite of them, so that he raised himself up from the dead in perfect
Amen to the Father's Will, acquiescing in his verdict upon our sin but responding in complete
trust and love to the Father. The resurrection is the goal of the steadfast obedience of the
Son of Man in answer to the steadfast love of the Father . . . the resurrection is the complete
Amen of the Son to the Father as of the Father to the Son . . . It is with the resurrection that
the *I am* of God is fully actualized among us – the *Ego eimi* of God to man, of God in man,
and so of man in Christ to God' (67–8).

[46] Torrance, *Space, Time and Resurrection*, 18–19.

[47] See Torrance, *The Christian Doctrine of God*, 83–111. David Fergusson presents a very
helpful analysis of the relation between the resurrection and faith by showing how the
traditional view that is grounded in scripture sees the resurrection as an event in the life of
Jesus that gives meaning to faith rather than as an event that is created within or realized by
the believer. Cf. 'Interpreting the Resurrection', *SJT* 38.3 (1985), 287–305.

Here the notion of self-communication functions in the incarnation and resurrection constituting the intelligible constitutive ground of Christian faith, so that in and through these events the 'Word of truth' from God himself is communicated to us. Because Jesus Christ himself is that ground and authority there is no extraneous ground.[48] The incarnation and resurrection are ultimate and carry their own authority in themselves. As such they call for intelligent commitment and belief. In this sense theology is faith seeking understanding.[49] Because God became man in Christ, our knowledge is grounded in the internal being and reality of God. The resurrection has stripped death and evil of their force and the union between God and man established in Christ remains valid beyond death; Christ is and remains Lord of time as a man of his time. The truth of these events can be seen as all-embracing miracles. Hence they cannot be *verified* or *validated* on any other grounds than those they themselves provide. Since acts of God include nature, they can be investigated but can in fact only be explained from grounds in God. Thus, the incarnation and resurrection are not to be seen as interruptions of the natural order or infringements on its laws but as a restoration of order within nature where it had been damaged.[50]

Unless we accept the resurrection as part of God's self-revealing activity in history and as an ultimate belief, we will try to account for it in terms of ordinary experience and then it will appear as self-contradictory and meaningless.[51] For Torrance we must think through self-critically this ultimate belief in relation to others such as creation, incarnation and the love of God; we should grasp the significance of Christ's humanity for understanding the gospel and its message of salvation in relation to the ascension and second coming as well. All of this will reflect on our understanding of the resurrection. If we hold a view of the ascension in which Jesus' humanity is 'swallowed up in the Spirit or Light of the eternal God, or a concept of the eschatological future which has little more material content to it than that somehow the future is more real than the past or the present, and in which the humanity of the advent Christ is replaced by "hope"'[52] then we have a Docetic view of the resurrection. The human realism of our

---

[48] Torrance, *Space, Time and Resurrection*, 20.
[49] Cf. Torrance, *Theology in Reconstruction*, 163ff. Thus, 'There is no authority for believing in Jesus outside of Jesus himself' (121) and 'Justification by grace alone tells us that verification of our faith or knowledge on any other ground, or out of any other source, than Jesus Christ, is to be set aside' (163).
[50] Torrance, *Space, Time and Resurrection*, 22–3.
[51] Torrance, *Space, Time and Resurrection*, 25.
[52] Torrance, *Space, Time and Resurrection*, 26.

view of the resurrection, ascension and second coming then will affect our view of the historical and risen Jesus Christ himself.

The fact that the resurrection will look different to those who believe and are affected by its transforming impact does not imply that the evidence for the resurrection is only the evidence of belief. The resurrection is rather an objective event that includes those for whom it has taken place. Thus for St Paul, 'we have already been raised up before God in him: to what has objectively taken place in him there is a corresponding subjective counterpart in us which as such belongs to the whole integrated reality of the resurrection event'; but this does not mean that Christ's resurrection 'can simply be identified with or resolved into that counterpart'.[53] Anything less or other than the resurrection of Christ's body would deny that in his humanity we have an *objective* act of God in time and space. Redemption would then collapse as well. Torrance therefore regards acceptance of the empty tomb as crucial.[54] The union of God and man which began in the incarnation and occurred throughout Jesus' incarnate life was fully and finally achieved in the cross and resurrection. Our human nature is in fact restored in Christ. That was the goal of the atonement. Reconciliation becomes eternally valid because Jesus is the resurrection and the life – it is identical with his person. Our human nature is now set within the Father–Son relation.

Because Christ himself is the bridge between the reality of God and the world, we may here speak of God without having to transcend creaturely speech and thought.[55] This is why Torrance argues that theological statements direct us to what is new and beyond our language and cannot contain it; while concepts must retain their creaturely content, we cannot claim to lay hold of divine reality by them.[56] Yet they must be employed in an act of objective intention in which creaturely content is not ascribed to God as such but becomes the medium of transcendental reference to him. Thus, theological concepts are essentially open, that is, they are closed on our side but open on God's side.[57] This is why Torrance rejects a container notion of space and time; such a notion would not be able to maintain the positive

[53] Torrance, *Space, Time and Resurrection*, 38–9.
[54] Torrance, *Space, Time and Resurrection*, 66. Cf. also Torrance, *Reality and Evangelical Theology*, 37.
[55] Torrance, *Space, Time and Resurrection*, 68–71.
[56] Cf. Thomas F. Torrance, *Space, Time and Incarnation* (London: Oxford University Press, 1969; reissued Edinburgh: T&T Clark, 1997), 20f.
[57] Cf. Torrance, *God and Rationality*, 170ff., *Space, Time and Resurrection*, 131f.

point that, in Christ, God himself became man without ceasing to be God. It would inevitably suppose that, if Christ was truly human, then he could not continue to exist simultaneously as the Lord of creation, that is, the Son of God would have emptied himself into a containing vessel.[58] Grace is not contained in the sacraments and thus handed on by means of them. It is identical with Christ's own action as the incarnate, risen and ascended Lord who was and is present within space and time as the reconciler through the Holy Spirit and will return at the second coming to complete our redemption. This then is how Torrance maintains the integrity of divine and human freedom specifically in his analysis of the resurrection.

Rahner's View of the Resurrection and the Transcendental Method

Now let us see Rahner's view of the resurrection and how it relates to his theological method. In Rahner's view:

> Although we ourselves may always remain dependent on the testimony of the first disciples in order to be able to connect our experience of the spirit explicitly and by name specifically with Jesus, we may nevertheless say with confidence that wherever and whenever we experience the unshakeableness of our own hope of a final victory of our existence, there takes place, perhaps anonymously, that is, without reference to the name of Jesus, an experience that he is risen. For this power of the spirit that we experience in this way as life's victorious defiance of all forms of death is the power of the Spirit which raised Jesus from the dead and thereby displays its victorious power to the world in history.[59]

It seems clear that Rahner has made a number of important assumptions here. First, he believes with the rest of Christendom that we today are dependent on the biblical witness in order to know about Jesus' resurrection and its significance in our lives today. Second, he assumes that, wherever anyone has an unshakeable hope of some kind of life after death, then they have already had an experience that Jesus is risen through the power of the Spirit. Now this makes no sense at all, unless it is understood from within Rahner's transcendental method as described in Chapter Four above. It will be recalled that this method was and is intended to make sense of the traditional doctrines of Christianity such as Christology, the Trinity, faith and the resurrection

---

[58] Torrance, *Space, Time and Resurrection*, 123ff.
[59] Rahner and Weger, *Our Christian Faith*, 113.

(among others) to contemporary people without falling into Mono-physitism or mythology and indeed without in any way compromising the traditional doctrines or God's freedom.

But clearly there is a difference between Torrance and Rahner here. How indeed can one claim even an anonymous experience of the Holy Spirit and of Jesus' resurrection without knowing about Jesus explicitly through the witness of the apostles first? While it may be possible for someone to have such an experience without knowing exactly what it implies, it is impossible to have an experience that Jesus is risen anonymously, that is, without knowing about Jesus' own resurrection and its significance for us (without faith in the risen Lord). Here I shall analyze briefly why Rahner reaches this conclusion and its implications for his appeal to the economy to know God, revelation, faith and grace. At the end of the last chapter we already saw that Rahner attempted to explicate Christian hope first by appealing to transcendental experience and then by connecting that experience with Jesus in order to interpret doctrine. Hence, for Rahner:

> If one has a radical hope of attaining a definitive identity and does not believe that one can steal away with one's obligations into the emptiness of non-existence, one has already grasped and accepted the resurrection in its real content . . . The absoluteness of the radical hope in which a human being apprehends his or her total existence as destined and empowered to reach definitive form can quite properly be regarded as grace, which permeates this existence always and everywhere. This grace is revelation in the strictest sense . . . this certainly is revelation, even if this is not envisaged as coming from 'outside'.[60]

In these two statements Rahner has ascribed the power of the resur-rection to us in our experience of hope and has described grace and revelation as part and parcel of those same experiences. How can he possibly escape subjectivism and universalism once he has taken these positions? How can he possibly distinguish nature and grace, reason and revelation and ultimately God's self-communication from our own self-experience and/or self-acceptance? Certainly it is obvious that such an inability collapses theology into anthropology and leaves him in the very position he designed his theology to avoid.

A large part of the answer to these questions can be found in Rahner's transcendental method. We will not explore this method in detail here since that was already done in Chapter Four. Instead, we will recapitulate

---

[60] Rahner and Weger, *Our Christian Faith*, 110–11.

those aspects of his intentions and method that bear upon the present discussion. Rahner is famous for his desire to overcome a merely formal approach to theology. He wanted to incorporate fundamental theology (that area of theology that deals with the most basic introductory questions such as revelation, faith, authority, the ways of knowing God and the nature and task of theology itself)[61] into dogmatic theology so that the justification of one's belief today would not be detached from the material content of theology.[62] He wanted 'to give people confidence from the very *content* of Christian dogma itself that they can believe with intellectual honesty'.[63] Thus, Rahner sought a closer unity between fundamental theology and dogmatic theology. The concept of mystery does not hinder this because mystery does not describe something senseless and unintelligible but the 'horizon of human existence which grounds and encompasses all human knowledge'.[64] Theological science actually is 'the "science" of mystery'.[65] Hence, creatures have a positive affinity, given by grace, to the Christian mysteries of faith, which he conceptualizes as our obediential potency and supernatural existential. The former refers to our openness to being (as spirit in the world) and as such it refers to our openness to God's self-communication, at least as a possibility. 'This potency is . . . our human nature as such. If the divine self-communication did not occur, our openness toward being would still be meaningful . . . we are by nature possible recipients of God's self-communication, listeners for a possible divine word.'[66] The latter refers to

> a basic structure which permeates the whole of human existence; it is not a localized part or region of our being, but a dimension pertaining to the whole. Our being in the world, or our being with others, could serve as examples . . . this existential . . . is not given automatically with human nature, but is rather the result of a gratuitous gift of God . . . Because of the supernatural existential, grace is always a part of our actual existence.[67]

The Christian mysteries that Rahner has in mind include 'the self-communication of God in the depths of existence, called grace, and in

---

[61] Richard P. McBrien, *Catholicism Completely Revised and Updated* (San Francisco: HarperSanFrancisco, 1994), 1240.

[62] *FCF*, 11ff.

[63] *FCF*, 12.

[64] *FCF*, 12. See Karl Rahner, 'Reflections on Methodology in Theology', in *TI* 11, 101ff. and *TI* 4, 36–73.

[65] *TI* 11, 102.

[66] John P. Galvin, 'The Invitation of Grace', in O'Donovan (ed.), *A World of Grace*, 64–75, 72.

[67] Galvin, 'The Invitation of Grace', 71–3.

history, called Jesus Christ, and this already includes the mystery of the Trinity in the economy of salvation and of the immanent Trinity'.[68]

In order to bring fundamental theology and dogmatic theology closer, Rahner also wishes to avoid 'a too narrowly Christological approach'. Thus he writes, 'It is not true that one has only to preach Jesus Christ and then he has solved all problems. Today Jesus Christ is himself a problem' as 'the demythologizing theology of the post-Bultmann age' has shown. Hence, 'we cannot begin with Jesus Christ as the absolute and final datum, but we must begin further back than that'.[69] In this way Rahner lays the foundation for his transcendental method, which he then develops in order to overcome both the secular loss of God's transcendence and in order to present a view of God's immanence that will not compromise his transcendence. In fact Rahner frequently seeks to preserve both God's transcendence and human freedom by arguing that human freedom and human dependence on God 'vary in direct and not in inverse proportion'.[70] How then does Rahner get to his position on the resurrection?

First, as seen in Chapter Four, he believes that there is a relationship of mutual conditioning between subject and object in knowledge. A transcendental line of inquiry 'raises the question of the conditions in which knowledge of a specific subject is possible in the knowing subject himself'. Thus,

> In any act of cognition it is not only the object known but also the subject knowing that is involved. It is dependent not only upon the distinctive characteristics of the object, but also upon the essential structure of the knowing subject . . . The a priori transcendental subjectivity of the knower . . . and the object of knowledge . . . are related to one another in such a way that they mutually condition one another . . .[71]

And 'The philosophical question as to a particular object is necessarily the question as to the knowing subject, because *a priori* the subject must carry with it the limits of the possibility of such knowledge. Thus the "transcendental" structures of the object are already determined *a priori*.[72] Knowledge is thus not simply a posteriori. 'Man can only find and retain what he encounters in history if there is an *a priori* principle of expectation, seeking and hope in man's finding and

---

[68] *FCF*, 12.
[69] *FCF*, 13.
[70] *FCF*, 79. See also *TI* 5, 12.
[71] *TI* 11, 87.
[72] *TI* 9, 34.

retaining subjectivity.'[73] Indeed, as we have already seen, for Rahner revelation exists within the realm of human thought and is subject to the a priori structures of human knowledge since God becomes a constitutive principle of the subject who hears the word which is more than a word about God. The condition that makes this hearing possible in the human subject is God himself through his self-communication. He upholds this act as an intrinsic principle.[74] Hence,

> the transcendental experience of the expectation of one's own resurrection, an experience man can reach by his very essence, is the horizon of understanding within which and within which alone something like a resurrection of Jesus can be expected and experienced at all. These two elements of our existence, of course, the transcendental experience of the expectation of one's own resurrection, and the experience in faith of the resurrection of Jesus in salvation history, mutually condition each other.[75]

Because of this mutually conditioning relationship, it is perfectly logical for Rahner to believe that 'we do not learn something which is totally unexpected and which lies totally outside of the horizon of our experience and our possibilities of verification' when we hear the witness of the apostles regarding the resurrection.[76]

Second, using the ideas of formal and quasi-formal causality, Rahner believes that God has made himself an intrinsic principle of human transcendentality. Rahner very clearly does not want to say that God inserts himself into the chain of secondary causes 'as one cause among them' but still he argues, as we have already seen, that God's presence in time and space is 'embedded in this world to begin with'. This allows

---

[73] *TI* 17, 47.

[74] *TI* 11, 91–2.

[75] *FCF,* 273–4. Cf. also *TI* 17, 16ff. Thus, for Rahner, 'we might now formulate the proposition that the knowledge of man's resurrection given with his transcendentally necessary hope is a statement of philosophical anthropology even before any real revelation in the Word. But we should have to counter this by saying that, at least initially, the elucidation of man's basic hope as being the hope of resurrection was in actual fact made historically through the revelation of the Old and New Testaments' (18). This last statement shows that even Rahner's understanding of the scriptural view of revelation is largely determined by what is experienced in transcendental experience. Thus, in order to experience the fact that Jesus is alive 'He (the Christian) has only to accept believingly and trustingly his own transcendental hope of resurrection and, therefore, also be on the look out, implicitly or explicitly, for a specific event in his own history, on the basis of which his hope can be believed in, as something that has been realised in another person' (19). Indeed, 'the "facts" of Jesus' resurrection must simply be determined in the light of what we have to understand by our own "resurrection"' (20).

[76] *FCF,* 275.

him to identify God's immediacy to us as a 'moment in and a modality of our transcendental and at the same time historically mediated immediacy to God'.[77] His positive point is to avoid seeing grace as a thing standing between God and us and to see it as does Torrance, as God's personal trinitarian action.

> The one God communicates himself in absolute self-utterance and as absolute donation of love. Here is the absolute mystery revealed to us only by Christ: God's self-communication is truly a *self*-communication. He does not merely indirectly give his creature some share of himself *by* creating and giving us created and finite realities . . . In a *quasi-formal* causality he really and in the strictest sense of the word bestows *himself*.[78]

Like Torrance, Rahner argues that the 'giver himself is the gift'. But for Rahner 'God in his absolute being is related to the created existent in the mode of formal causality, that is, that he does not originally cause and produce something different from himself in the creature, but rather that he communicates his own divine reality and makes it a constitutive element in the fulfillment of the creature.' And indeed the basis for this assertion is 'found in the transcendental experience of the orientation of every finite existent to the absolute being and mystery of God'.[79] For Rahner then, 'The term "self-communication" is really intended to signify that God in his own most proper reality makes himself the inner-most constitutive element of man.'[80] Thus, 'God's offer of himself belongs to all men and is a characteristic of man's transcendence

---

[77] *FCF*, 86–7.

[78] Rahner, *Trinity*, 36. Cf. also *FCF*, 120ff., *TI* 1, 307, 329ff., 343ff. and *TI* 4, 175ff.

[79] *FCF*, 121. Cf. also *FCF*, 44. The same idea is frequently repeated. See, e.g., *TI* 4, 50 where Rahner writes, 'All conceptual expressions about God, necessary though they are, always stem from the unobjectivated experience of transcendence as such: the concept from the pre-conception, the name from the experience of the nameless.' See also *TI* 4, 57 and *TI* 11, 149, where Rahner writes, 'The so-called proofs of God's existence . . . are possible . . . only as the outcome of an *a posteriori* process of reasoning as the conceptual objectification of what we call the experience of God, which provides the basis and origin of this process of reasoning.' Thus, for Rahner the task of theology is to 'reflect upon an experience which is present in every man' (*TI* 11, 150–1). Since this is so, theology means 'we can only point to this experience, seek to draw another's attention to it in such a way that he discovers within himself that which we only find if, and to the extent that we already possess it' (*TI* 11, 154). See also *FCF*, 21 where Rahner writes, 'The knowledge of God is always present unthematically and without name, and not just when we begin to speak of it. All talk about it, which necessarily goes on, always only points to this transcendental experience as such, an experience in which he whom we call "God" encounters man . . . as the term of his transcendence'. For Rahner's explanation of his method, see *FCF*, 24–39. All of this was discussed at length above in Chapter Four.

[80] *FCF*, 116.

and his transcendentality . . . God's self-communication in grace, as a modification of transcendence . . . cannot by simple and individual acts of reflection . . . be differentiated from those basic structures of human transcendence'.[81] This leads Rahner to wonder:

> To put it in biblical terms: if God as he is in himself has already communicated himself in his Holy Spirit always and everywhere and to every person as the innermost center of his existence, whether he wants it or not, whether he reflects on it or not, whether he accepts it or not, and if the whole history of creation is already borne by God's self-communication in this very creation, then there does not seem to be anything else which can take place on God's part.[82]

Rahner's solution to this difficult problem is to suggest that transcendence itself has a history, 'and history is in its ultimate depths the event of this transcendence'.[83] But the obvious question that arises here is how can Rahner avoid having transcendental experience actually define what he finds within history? Rahner actually argues that 'There is never a salvific act of God on man which is not also and always a salvific act of man. There is no revelation which could take place in any other way except in the faith of the person hearing the revelation.'[84] These are indeed strange assertions because they certainly seem unable to distinguish clearly objective historical events from the subjective experiences of faith and salvation. Ultimately such an inability would lead to a blurring of the Christian message precisely by implying that salvation could be equated with our self-experience and moral behavior – two things which Rahner clearly does not want to do. But can he avoid it?

On the one hand, Rahner argues that our supernaturally elevated orientation towards immediacy and closeness to God 'must be characterized as real revelation throughout the whole history of religion and of the human spirit'. This is not merely a natural revelation. 'This transcendental knowledge, which is present always and everywhere in the actualization of the human spirit in knowledge and freedom, but present unthematically, is a moment which must be distinguished from verbal and propositional revelation as such.' On the other hand, as we have already noted in Chapter Five in connection with his Christology, he argues that

---

[81] *FCF*, 129.
[82] *FCF*, 139.
[83] *FCF*, 141.
[84] *FCF*, 142.

it deserves nevertheless to be characterized as God's self-revelation. This transcendental moment in revelation is a modification of our transcendental consciousness produced permanently by God in grace. But such a modification is really an original and permanent element in our consciousness as the basic luminosity of our existence. And as an element in our transcendentality which is constituted by God's self-communication, it is already revelation in the proper sense.[85]

Ultimately, 'God's self-revelation in the depths of the spiritual person is an a priori determination coming from grace . . . it is not something known objectively, but something within the realm of consciousness.'[86] As seen in Chapter Four, it is through his notion of quasi-formal causality that Rahner understands transcendental revelation as 'a transcendental divinization of the fundamental subjective attitude, the ultimate horizon of man's knowledge and freedom, in the perspective of which he accomplishes his life'.[87] This is our grace-given supernatural existential which itself is the beginning of the *visio beatifica* in this life. As God's self-communication to the creature then, this revelation cannot be confined to words. It must also be the giving of grace, that is, 'an inner, objectless though conscious dynamism directed to the beatific vision'.[88] The beatific vision is the direct apprehension of God, given by God, which is in reality no different from the object of our initial dynamism of spirit which discerns being in general. Hence,

> In his intellectual and transcendental dynamism, Maréchal considers man (as spirit, i.e. in his 'nature') in the inmost heart of his being as '*desiderium naturale visionis beatificae*' – to use the words of St Thomas. This desire is conditional and so there is no necessity for the actual call to the vision by grace. But it is a real longing for the absolute being and one which is present in every spiritual act as its *raison d'être* . . . it is the *a priori* condition of all knowledge where a finite object is grasped.[89]

From this insight he proceeded to describe grace as noted above (as an element in human being) and concluded that

> The experience of God to which we have appealed . . . is not necessarily so a-Christian as appears at first sight. On the contrary . . . it is precisely Christianity which makes real this experience of God in its most radical and purest form, and in Jesus Christ achieves a convincing manifestation of it in history . . . this experience of God . . . really constitutes the very

[85] *FCF*, 149.
[86] *FCF*, 172.
[87] Rahner and Ratzinger, *Revelation and Tradition*, 16.
[88] *TI* 4, 61.
[89] *TI* 4, 169.

heart and centre of Christianity itself and also the ever living source of that *conscious manifestation* which we call 'revelation' . . . through this experience of God Christianity itself simply achieves a more radical and clearer understanding of its own authentic nature. For in fact in its true essence it is not one particular religion among others, but rather the sheer objectivation in history of that *experience* of God which exists *everywhere* in virtue of God's universal will to save all men by bestowing himself upon them as grace.[90]

But, as seen in Chapter Four, the problem with this reasoning is that, once this supposition is made, creatures may then rely on their experiences, whether religious or not, to lead them to the truth that Christians believe.

Here we have recapitulated the most basic dilemma of Rahner's theology. On the one hand, he insists upon God's freedom and that in this freedom he has communicated himself and not some intermediary to creatures for their salvation. On the other hand, while he insists upon the centrality of Christ, as the unsurpassable medium of revelation and salvation, his transcendental method ascribes what is supposed to be grounded in Jesus' history to the length and breadth of human history. Thus, while Rahner insists that transcendental experience needs history and is not just self-defining, history itself has no genuine independent bearing upon transcendental experience. In other words, they mutually condition each other. This thinking leads Rahner to believe that eternity is 'imbedded in the time of freedom and responsibility' so that any radically good moral decision is an experience of the eternity promised in the resurrection.[91]

Third, as we have just seen, Rahner accepts an a priori unthematic knowledge of God, Christ, revelation, faith and hope, and it is to these that he appeals apologetically in order to speak to people within and outside the Church by connecting this experience and non-objective knowledge with the historical events of revelation and salvation. Thus, Rahner treats the theology of the death and resurrection of Jesus Christ first by establishing

the intellectual presuppositions of the core of that original experience of Jesus as the Christ, and then the core of this original experience itself. This experience is the original, indeducible and first revelation of Christology which is then articulated and interpreted more reflexively in the 'late' New Testament and in the official teaching of the church.[92]

[90] *TI* 11, 164. Some emphases mine.
[91] *FCF*, 272.
[92] *FCF*, 265.

After stating that Jesus' death and resurrection must be seen together and that Jesus' death was a death into the resurrection and that the empty tomb, although not necessarily disputed, cannot by itself testify to the resurrection, Rahner insists that Jesus' resurrection means salvation and acceptance by God. Then, attempting to avoid an idealist misunderstanding of the fact that Jesus' person and cause are one, Rahner argues that

> if the resurrection of Jesus is the permanent validity of his person and his cause, and if this person and cause together do not mean the survival of just any person and his history, but mean the *victoriousness* of his claim to be the absolute saviour, then *faith* in his resurrection is an intrinsic element of this resurrection itself. Faith is not taking cognizance of a fact which by its nature could exist just as well without being taking cognizance of.[93]

Indeed Rahner does not simply say that faith is necessary to understand or to participate in the power of the resurrection. Rather he says, 'it is only in this faith that its own [the resurrection] essential being is fully realized'. It is in this sense that Rahner asserts that

> Jesus is risen into the faith of his disciples. But this faith into which Jesus is risen is not really and directly faith in this resurrection, but is that faith which knows itself to be a divinely effected liberation from all the powers of finiteness, of guilt and of death, and knows itself to be empowered for this by the fact that this liberation has taken place in Jesus himself and has become manifest for us.[94]

By the time Rahner insists that it is primarily faith in Jesus' resurrection that gives us hope for our own resurrection, he has already connected them in such a way that Jesus' own resurrection cannot be fully what it is without our faith in our own future.

At this point Rahner turns to our transcendental experience of hope to make sense of the resurrection and argues that an act of hope in one's own resurrection takes place as a transcendental necessity either as freely accepted or rejected. Resurrection thus is not an assertion that could not be known in hope from a primordial understanding of the human, but is an expression that promises our abiding validity. It includes the whole person and not just one's body in a dualistic sense. Of course Rahner believes that we are more successful in actually objectifying our self-understanding here in the light of an experience of

[93] *FCF*, 267.
[94] *FCF*, 268.

Jesus' resurrection, since the circle between transcendental and categorical experience is operative everywhere. For Rahner 'This transcendental hope in resurrection is the horizon of understanding for experiencing the resurrection of Jesus in faith.'[95] This hope necessarily seeks historical confirmation.

The result is that Rahner appeals to the profession of faith in Gal. 1:8ff. as a 'global experience', which both Christians and non-Christians have, and believes that there should be an apologetic Christology not only for believers, but for those outside. We should presume that those outside the Christian sphere are persons of morally good will who therefore exist 'in the interior grace of God and in Christ' and that they have 'said an interior, unreflexive yes to Christ'. Therefore, in fundamental theology, Christology cannot simply construct faith in Christ (both the *fides quae* and the *fides qua*, the act and the content of faith) in a 'purely reflexive and synthetic way and by scientific retort'. It follows that a Christian must accept 'the "Christology" which he is living out in his life: in the faith of the church, in the cult of its risen Lord, in prayer in his name, and by participating in his destiny … The profession of faith in Gal. 1:8ff. is still valid *for this global experience*'.[96]

Making no clear distinction between those who have heard the gospel and those who have not, Rahner believes that Christology in fundamental theology can turn in three ways to this 'global understanding of existence which is already "Christian" because of antecedent grace', and that this would work out reflexively one part of 'transcendental Christology'. What do all three of these have in common? They have in common 'the supposition that if a person accepts his existence resolutely, he is really already living out in his existence something like a "searching Christology". These appeals do not try to do anything but clarify this anonymous Christianity somewhat.'[97] For Rahner, Jesus Christ must be the one for whom this search is being made. But there is no disguising the fact that the main function of the historical Jesus, for Rahner, is to link our prior unthematic experiences and beliefs to an event in history which then validates our transcendental experience.

---

[95] *FCF*, 269.

[96] *FCF*, 294, emphasis mine.

[97] *FCF*, 295. This is why, in addition to the traditional Christology, Rahner advocates what he calls 'existentiell Christology' and concludes that an anonymous Christian has a real and existential relation to Christ 'implicitly in obedience to his orientation in grace toward the God of absolute, historical presence and self-communication. He exercises this obedience by accepting his own existence without reservation' (306).

From here Rahner appeals to love of neighbor, to a readiness for death and to hope in the future and concludes that: (1) wherever anyone radically loves his or her neighbor, he or she is already living as a Christian; (2) wherever anyone affirms present and future reality as the ground of existence, that person already affirms a 'hoped-for death which is of such a nature that it reconciles the permanent dialectic in us between doing and enduring in powerlessness'; (3) wherever anyone hopes for a future reconciliation between what we are and what we should be or want to be, then one can rely on that hope to understand both the meaning of the incarnation and of the resurrection. This is in fact the horizon within which these events can become meaningful.[98] Finally, Rahner appeals to what he calls the searching memory that is intrinsic to all faith. Memory does not just refer to a past event; Rahner believes (following Plato and Augustine), that it can be related to something not yet found, and this coheres with the whole problematic of transcendental experience and history. Thus, we can find and retain something that encounters us in history 'only if there is present in the finding and retaining subjectivity of man an a priori principle of expectation, of searching, of hoping . . . we can call this a priori principle "memory"'.[99]

It is Rahner's transcendental method then that explains how he can appeal to our own hope as the horizon within which Jesus' resurrection can be understood as the foundation for Christian theology. Ultimately, it is because Rahner conceives of faith, grace and revelation as elements within our transcendental experience that he can appeal to universal human experience in his attempt to make Christian faith credible in a secularized world. But it is just here that he is led to believe that the resurrection is not fully realized without the disciples' faith and that Jesus is risen into the faith of the disciples and indeed into our faith insofar as the beginning of the Christian faith is identical with the unthematic knowledge of God which everyone implicitly has in each transcendental act.

Conclusions

First, it is clear that Torrance and Rahner are at one in wishing to unite fundamental and dogmatic theology and in affirming that God's self-communication in Christ and the Spirit is decisive. Second, it is clear that they both believe that knowledge of God should make sense to

---

[98] *FCF*, 294ff.
[99] *FCF*, 319.

contemporary people and that revelation and grace should be seen as God's personal presence in the historical and risen Christ and not as a thing that can be detached from God, Christ or the Spirit. Third, it is clear however, that they both disagree methodologically even though they both affirm the need to reunite knowledge of the one God and the triune God by focusing on the economy; the central issue concerns how to relate experience to the economy.

Torrance rejects building a logical bridge from experience to revelation without necessarily denying that we have the kind of experiences that Rahner describes as transcendental experiences. However, Rahner insists that such a bridge must be built for apologetic reasons. This is the very foundation for his 'searching Christology' and his appeal to the experience of the nameless. And this disagreement leads to very different notions of revelation, grace, faith and of the resurrection itself.

Rahner claims an unthematic ever-present universal knowledge of God, Christ, revelation, faith, grace and hope which is related to historical Christianity in a mutually conditioning way. He appeals to this a priori structure of the knowing subject in its intrinsic connection with history to discover the meaning of the resurrection in particular. This, because subjective and objective knowledge are intrinsically and mutually related. Thus, the resurrection cannot be its own validation, but can and must be validated from *transcendental experience* which validates all theological knowledge. This inhibits a clear distinction between nature and grace, reason and revelation, philosophy and theology, creator and creatures, the economic and immanent Trinity, Christ's bodily resurrection and our faith in him. It leads Rahner to conclude that acceptance of hope (in the form of our transcendentally necessary hope) can be equated with acceptance of Christ's resurrection, even without having heard the gospel.

It leads him to argue that the apostolic message of the resurrection is not totally unexpected but, like revelation itself, it is something people necessarily are already searching for in history itself. And it finally leads him to conclude that one can accept or reject the resurrection by accepting or rejecting one's transcendental experience of hope. Indeed he even argues, that if one were to reject the 'apostolic experience of this resurrection in Jesus', this would only incur guilt if it also involved rejecting one's transcendental experience of hope.[100] This is the corollary to his attempt to understand love of God and neighbor 'in the direction of a radical identity of the two loves' and his belief that 'the love of

[100] *FCF*, 277–8.

God and the love of neighbour are one and the same thing'. That is why, as seen in Chapter Five, Rahner concludes that

> wherever a genuine love of man attains its proper nature and its moral absoluteness and depth, it is in addition always so underpinned and heightened by God's saving grace that it is also love of God, whether it be explicitly considered to be such a love by the subject or not . . . wherever there is an absolutely moral commitment of a positive kind in the world . . . there takes place also a saving event, faith, hope and charity . . .[101]

It is no accident then that Rahner begins his Christology from below by answering the question of what is really experienced, witnessed and believed with Jesus' resurrection by asserting that 'a knowledge "in faith" of the "metaphysical" divine sonship of this Jesus may not be already presupposed.'[102]

By comparison, Thomas F. Torrance refuses to build a logical bridge from the experience of self-transcendence to the God revealed in Christ and by the Holy Spirit, and because of this he insists that revelation is and remains identical with God's actions in the historical Jesus who died, rose, ascended and is present now in the power of the Holy Spirit. He further insists that it is utterly inconceivable and indeed it stands in conflict with our prior knowledge of God and secular understanding; it calls for a constant rethinking of our theology in relation to Christ's real presence within the structures of space and time. Moreover, he insists that, according to his idea of scientific method, subject and object are not mutually conditioned even though they are inseparably related by the grace of God. Consequently, for Torrance, the resurrection is its own validation and any attempt to validate it from what Rahner describes as transcendental experience amounts to the creature using his or her own experience and language to redefine God's eternal being manifested in time and space. Therefore, Torrance could never agree that self-acceptance is acceptance of God, grace and revelation in reality. But in fact Torrance rejects this kind of thinking as unscientific, because it operates from a center in ourselves while scientific theology ought to refer us back to Christ as the center. And Torrance insists that it is Christ's uniqueness as the eternal Son of God who became man that dictates the utter uniqueness of the resurrection as the objective pole of our subjective knowledge. As it happens, then, the entire difference between Rahner and Torrance is methodological. Torrance begins and ends his

---

[101] *TI* 6, 233, 236–7, 239. Cf. *FCF*, 295.
[102] *FCF*, 279.

understanding of the resurrection and of God's self-communication with Christ as presented in the Bible. Rahner considers such a start too narrowly christological. But it is just this choice by Rahner that inhibits him from consistently turning to the economy, as he certainly intended to do, for the verification of his theology and leaves him exposed to the very subjectivism he believes he has overcome.

What then are the prospects for Reformed and Roman Catholic dialogue concerning the proper interpretation of God's self-communication in Christ? Based on what has been said in this chapter and throughout this book, the answer, I suggest, is to be found in a clearer doctrine of the immanent Trinity which will not separate Christ and creatures but also will not detach the trinitarian self-communication from Christ's active mediation of himself to us through the power of the Holy Spirit and within the historical structures of space and time. It seems clear from what has been said above that Reformed and Roman Catholic theology are already one in their desire to unite fundamental and dogmatic theology by starting theology more consistently from God's economic trinitarian actions within history.

In this regard, David Tracy offers an illuminating discussion that insists, on the one hand, that 'A Christian theological understanding of God cannot be divorced from the revelation of God in Jesus Christ.'[103] Here, as I have just indicated, Reformed and Roman Catholic theologians agree, at least formally. But, on the other hand, in accordance with his view of natural theology, Tracy proceeds to find reasons of credibility and intelligibility within human experience in order to correlate what was supposedly found in Jesus Christ with that natural knowledge. Precisely in that way he follows Rahner and compromises his own assertion that 'The Catholic theological understanding of God is, therefore, grounded in the self-revelation of God in Jesus Christ.'[104] In addition to Jesus Christ he turns to 'ontologies of relationality' supplied by process theology and feminist theology. And instead of allowing his notion of relationality to be dictated by the trinitarian relations freely revealed in the history of Christ himself, his abstract notion of human relationality conceived as love defines God's love. In the end he argues that 'A relational model of human perfection is clearly a more adequate one for understanding divine perfection than either an ancient individualist or modern autonomous one.'[105] While most

---

[103] David Tracy, 'Approaching the Christian Understanding of God', in Schüssler Fiorenza and Galvin (eds), *Systematic Theology: Roman Catholic Perspectives*, 133–48 at 133.

[104] Tracy, 'Approaching the Christian Understanding of God', 139.

[105] Tracy, 'Approaching the Christian Understanding of God', 145.

modern theologians agree in rejecting individualism and a false Cartesian autonomous view of persons, the problem here is that, instead of allowing his analogies for God to be drawn from Christ himself and thus to be understood within faith, Tracy grounds his theology of God 'in the revelation of God in Jesus Christ' *and* in 'the quest for God that *is* the ultimate meaning of all the classic limit-experiences and limit-questions of human beings'.[106] This dual grounding of theological knowledge repeats Rahner's error precisely by ascribing revelation and grace to human experience, while simultaneously insisting that Christian knowledge of God should be grounded in Christ. Such knowledge, as I have just shown in this chapter, cannot possibly be grounded in Christ because its starting point and norm is and remains our limit-experiences and what can be gleaned from those.

What has emerged then up to this point in our effort to construct a contemporary doctrine of the immanent Trinity is that any such doctrine must be grounded consistently in the economic Trinity in an irreversible way. Further, such a doctrine must respect the fact that revelation is a completely new and unexpected divine action and thus cannot be equated with any sort of transcendental experience, any aspect of transcendental experience or with what might be inferred from such transcendental experience. It is certainly not a description of our experience of faith, but instead is a description of who God is who meets us in our experience of faith. Consequently, thinking about human freedom must find its basis in God's freedom for us which was and is exercised in Christ and the Spirit. As a result of this, a clear doctrine of the immanent Trinity will reflect our need to begin and end our theological reflections with Jesus Christ himself, simply because he is our only access to the Father.

In the next chapter we shall explore the theology of Jürgen Moltmann with a view toward seeing even more precisely why it is important to perceive and maintain the irreversible noetic and ontic relation between creator and creatures disclosed in the history of Jesus Christ. Moltmann is ambiguous about the concept of experience and so he introduces a mutually conditioned view of divine and human relations that consistently compromises both God's freedom *in se* and *ad extra*. His theology provides an exceptionally clear instance of what happens when theologians are inconsistent in affirming a properly conceived doctrine of the immanent Trinity. To his theology we now turn.

---

[106] Tracy, 'Approaching the Christian Understanding of God', 146.

Chapter Seven

The Function of the Trinity in Jürgen Moltmann's Ecological Doctrine of Creation

I N this book I have accepted Barth's basic theological insight regarding the relationship between the immanent and the economic Trinity that 'a deliberate and sharp distinction between the Trinity of God as we may know it in the Word of God revealed, written and proclaimed, and God's immanent Trinity, that is, between "God in Himself" and "God for us", between the "eternal history of God and His temporal acts"' must be maintained in order to avoid confusing and reversing the role of creator in relation to creature both theoretically and practically.[1] As seen above, this insight will not allow the vice versa associated with Rahner's axiom of identity because, for Barth, theology can only take place as acknowledgment, that is,

> Jesus Christ Himself lives in the message of His witnesses . . . [thus] experience of His presence . . . does not rest on man's act of recollection but on God's making Himself present in the life of man [hence] it is acknowledgment of His presence . . . the life of man, without ceasing to be the self-determining life of this man, has now its centre, its whence, the meaning of its attitude, and the criterion whether this attitude really has the corresponding meaning -- it has all of this outside itself, in the thing or person acknowledged.[2]

We have seen that this issue of confusing and reversing the roles of creator and creature is a burning issue in contemporary theology as it was in the fourth century, when Athanasius opposed the Arian attempt

[1] *CD* I/1, 172.
[2] *CD* I/1, 208–9.

to define God by human experience. My contention is that a contemporary doctrine of the immanent Trinity will help theologians recognize and maintain both divine and human freedom by stating with clarity that God's freedom *in se* as the eternal Father, Son and Holy Spirit exists outside of and apart from our experience of faith and salvation. By recognizing that God did not and does not need to act mercifully toward us *ad extra*, even as he in fact did so and does so in his Word and Spirit, we recognize the freedom of grace. To that extent our trinitarian theology stands on the unshakeable ground that is the very presence of God in his Word and Spirit, and to that extent trinitarian theology cannot displace God's present action as its sole determining criterion.

The work of Jürgen Moltmann provides an interesting and important illustration of a prominent contemporary theologian who accepts Rahner's axiom of identity and then attempts to move beyond it in a theologically inappropriate way. It is hoped that by analyzing certain of Moltmann's key insights in relation to Barth's understanding of the union and distinction of the immanent and economic Trinity, more light will be shed on the problems and potential solutions as we work toward a contemporary doctrine of the immanent Trinity. Then it is hoped that a look at how the Trinity functions in Moltmann's ecological doctrine of creation will clarify matters even further.

As noted above, Moltmann now has moved beyond the language of immanent and economic to understand the Trinity. Nonetheless, key differences between Moltmann and Barth early on suggested that the problematic element in Moltmann's theology would be his failure to recognize and maintain God's freedom. Such failure, as we have seen, means that human freedom itself becomes threatened to the extent that it is not truly grounded in an act of God that is independent of our human experiences of suffering, love and freedom. In fact Barth was concerned that Moltmann had subsumed 'all theology in eschatology',

> To put it pointedly, does your theology of hope really differ at all from the baptized *principle* of hope of Mr. Bloch? What disturbs me is that for you theology becomes so much a matter of principle (an eschatological principle) . . . *Would it not be wise to accept the doctrine of the immanent trinity of God?*[3]

Barth hoped that Moltmann would 'outgrow' this 'onesidedness'. But Moltmann's 'panentheism', which starts from experience and reconstructs theology in process terms, cannot allow for 'an immanent

---

[3] *Karl Barth Letters*, 175, some emphases mine.

Trinity in which God is simply by himself, without the love which communicates salvation'.[4] Thus, Moltmann must 'surrender the traditional distinction between the immanent and the economic Trinity', and affirm

> Rahner's thesis that 'the economic Trinity *is* the immanent Trinity, and vice versa' . . . The thesis about the fundamental *identity* of the immanent and the economic Trinity of course remains open to misunderstanding as long as we cling to the distinction at all . . . The economic Trinity not only reveals the immanent Trinity; it also has a retroactive effect on it.[5]

As seen above and as we shall see in detail throughout this chapter, Moltmann uncritically uses the principle of mutual conditioning and eliminates any need to conceptualize a God truly independent of creatures. Any real notion of lordship applying to God's love revealed in Christ is simply reinterpreted by the experience of suffering drawing God into the vicissitudes of creation itself.[6]

To avoid any such synthesis of experience and the Word of God, Barth insisted that theology could not begin with experience and redefine God's 'antecedent' existence if the criterion for that theology were Christ.[7] As seen above, all Christian theologians claim Christ as their criterion; yet unless in Christ there is an immanent Trinity which is *recognizable* and in *no way dependent* upon anyone or anything else, and unless that truth is what is perceived and applied in faith, the whole positive point of theology is missed.[8]

Moltmann clearly begins his trinitarian theology from experience: 'God suffers with us – God suffers from us – God suffers for us: *it is this experience of God that reveals the triune God*'.[9] Methodologically his thinking invariably moves from the general to the particular and this influences his view of Christ and of the Trinity in several ways. First, Moltmann accepts natural theology as a necessary prolegomenon to theology.[10] Second, he attempts to deduce the meaning of creation not

---

[4] Moltmann, *Trinity and Kingdom*, 151.

[5] Moltmann, *Trinity and Kingdom*, 160.

[6] See above Chapter One.

[7] See, e.g., *CD* I/1, 119. See also *CD* I/1, 193 and esp. 198ff., 'The Word of God and Experience'. See also *CD* I/1, 414–15.

[8] For example, Walter Kasper, *The God of Jesus Christ*, trans. Matthew J. O'Connell (New York: Crossroad, 1986), mistakenly thinks that the views of Barth and Rahner are the same here (273–4). Compare *CD* II/1, 308–9.

[9] Moltmann, *Trinity and Kingdom*, 4, emphasis mine.

[10] See Moltmann, *Creation*, chapter 3. It is not a real immanent Trinity that defines truth here but a Trinity based on 'the saving experience of the cross' (Moltmann, *Trinity and Kingdom*, 161).

only from the traditional doctrine,[11] but from nature as well as from a *direct* knowledge of God. Third, Moltmann literally cannot distinguish creatures from the creator in any recognizable way. Thus, he argues that, although *creatio ex nihilo* means God is *free*, still God makes *room* within himself by fashioning the nothingness from which he then creates the world.[12] In the supposed existence of God before the world, God is in fact *conditioned* by this withdrawal within. While Barth maintains that God makes space for creation he insists on a doctrine of the immanent Trinity and asserts that time, experience and created space dictate nothing here, while Moltmann consistently defines God *by* the experiences creatures have of suffering, nothingness and death.[13]

While experience is important for Barth, the norm for truth is and remains revelation. Following Thomas's insight that *Deus non est in genere*[14] Barth argues that God cannot be classified with other 'supreme ideas' such as freedom and immortality and then known; this, because his *esse* really is his *act*. Therefore, 'no self-determination of the second partner [the creature] can influence the first, whereas the self-determination of the first, *while not cancelling the self-determination* of the second, is the sovereign predetermination which precedes it absolutely'.[15] The very being of the Christian God revealed thus excludes *any* pantheistic or panentheistic attempt to define his relation with creatures.

Rejecting this idea of lordship, Moltmann begins his panentheistic reconception of the Trinity from experience and insists that we *can* explain the *how* of the trinitarian self-revelation by perceiving that God *needs* to suffer in order to love.[16] This is of course in contrast to the important insight stressed in this book, namely, that for Barth and T. F. Torrance the *how* of the trinitarian self-revelation remains a mystery. Ignoring this limit that Barth and Torrance insisted upon, Moltmann argues that 'God "needs" the world and man. If God is

---

[11] Moltmann, *Creation*, 72ff.

[12] Moltmann, *Creation*, 86–94, and *Trinity and Kingdom*, 37ff. and 108ff. A God who makes nothingness in order to create and then makes this part of his being is not the Christian God. Following Irenaeus and Athanasius, T. F. Torrance astutely notes that 'creation of the universe out of nothing does not mean that God created the universe out of some "stuff" called "nothing", but that what he created was not created out of anything' (*The Trinitarian Faith*, 99). See also nn. 38 and 88 below.

[13] See, e.g., Moltmann, *Creation*, 27ff. and 97–103, and *Trinity and Kingdom*, 97 and 99ff.

[14] *Summa Theologica*, qu. 3, art. 5, and *CD* II/1, 187–90, 310 and 445–7.

[15] *CD* II/1, 312, emphasis mine.

[16] Moltmann, *Trinity and Kingdom*, 19ff., 32ff. and 197, and *Creation*, 13ff. and 108ff.

love, then he neither will nor can be without the one who is beloved.'[17] This applies to the Father's relation with the Son and to creation: 'Creation is a part of the eternal love affair between the Father and the Son.'[18] While Barth carefully excluded *any* notion of necessity from both the immanent and economic Trinity, Moltmann, as we shall see shortly in more detail, believes that the Father *necessarily* generates the Son;[19] he plays off God's nature and will which, as Barth correctly insisted,[20] is impossible in a Christian doctrine of God. Moltmann's God cannot exist without the world since 'the idea of the world is already inherent in the Father's love for the Son'.[21] For Barth, as seen above in his debate with Gogarten, 'theology cannot speak of man in himself, in isolation from God. But as in the strict doctrine of the Trinity as the presupposition of Christology, *it must speak of God in Himself in isolation from man.*'[22]

While Moltmann sees the need to maintain belief in creation from nothing and in the Trinity, it is certainly not the person and work of Christ which *alone* determines truth. Thus, he holds, contrary to Barth's view, that there are analogies that are true in themselves and that can lead to a knowledge of the trinitarian God. For this reason *perichoresis* does not describe a trinitarian *circumincessio*, which would preclude *any* natural knowledge of the Christian God, but rather is a principle by which he both separates[23] and synthesizes God's being and

---

[17] Moltmann, *Trinity and Kingdom*, 58. See Moltmann, *Creation*, where he understands human likeness to God 'as a relationship of fellowship, of mutual need and mutual interpenetration' (258).

[18] Moltmann, *Trinity and Kingdom*, 59.

[19] Moltmann, *Trinity and Kingdom*, 167. 'The generation and birth of the Son come from the Father's *nature*, not from his will. That is why we talk about the *eternal* generation and birth of the Son. The Father begets and bears the Son out of the *necessity* of his being' (emphasis mine). As we shall see, Moltmann distinguishes 'the world process and the inner-trinitarian process' by saying that in God necessity and freedom coincide (106–7). Yet, because he has confused the immanent and economic Trinity, God also needs to create and give himself away since love must move towards another. This also affects his view of time and eternity. Cf. *Creation*, 112–18.

[20] *CD* II/1, 546–7.

[21] Moltmann, *Trinity and Kingdom*, 108.

[22] *CD* I/1, 172, emphasis mine.

[23] See Moltmann, *Creation*, 16ff., 57–60 and 206ff. While Barth insisted that the oneness and threeness of God are one (*CD* I/1, 352 and 469) Moltmann's thinking tends toward tritheism (*Trinity and Kingdom*, 86). Kasper, *The God of Jesus Christ*, notes the 'danger' of tritheism in Moltmann's theology (379, n. 183). Grenz and Olson conclude that Moltmann has overemphasized God's immanence and that this 'resulted in his outright denial of monotheism and possible fall into the heresy of tritheism' (*20th Century Theology*, 184). With respect to Moltmann's belief (discussed below) that there has never been a Christian tritheist, George Hunsinger remarks, 'If this is true then one can only conclude that

act.[24] Barth rejected both tritheism and modalism just because we cannot comprehend the immanent Trinity as such by grasping the *opus Dei ad extra*.[25] By contrast, Moltmann's whole theology is dominated by the principle of mutual conditioning.[26] Thus, we have no way of distinguishing *what* is being *affected* by us in our experience. This reversal of predicates, which follows *identity*, is precisely why Barth rejected panentheism as worse than pantheism.[27]

Moltmann accepts Rahner's axiom of identity because God *must* communicate the love of salvation. While Barth maintains a sharp distinction between creation and covenant by insisting that creation is the external basis of the covenant but not the condition of its possibility (as Balthasar and Rahner assume), Moltmann confuses both with the very being of God and assumes that creation and incarnation are necessary to God as they are for the creature.[28]

Indeed, 'As the Father of Jesus Christ, he is almighty *because* he exposes himself to the experience of suffering, pain, helplessness and death. But what he *is* is not almighty power; what he *is* is love. It is passionate, passible love that is almighty, nothing else.'[29] Hence, following C. E. Rolt, 'The sole omnipotence which God possesses is the almighty power of suffering love . . . Rolt then goes on to deduce the eternal divine nature from Christ's passion. What Christ, the incarnate God, did in time, God, the heavenly Father, does and *must do* in eternity.'[30] Thus,

---

Moltmann is vying to be the first. Despite the evident scorn with which he anticipates such a charge, *The Trinity and the Kingdom* is about the closest thing to tritheism that any of us are ever likely to see', Review of Jürgen Moltmann, *The Trinity and The Kingdom*, in *The Thomist* 47 (1983), 129–39, 131.

[24] Moltmann, *Creation*, 258ff. This leads to his mistaken criticism of Barth for modalism (56ff.) and nominalism. These criticisms rest on his failure to see that the oneness and threeness of God are dictated by Christ and not by experience.

[25] Moltmann holds that there has never been a 'Christian tritheist' (*Trinity and Kingdom*, 243, n. 43). Yet Adolf von Harnack, *History of Dogma*, trans. Neil Buchanan (New York: Dover Publications, 1961), vol. 3, 90, and vol. 6, 82 and 101, cites several. Marcion was also named as a tritheist in a letter of Pope St Dionysius *c*. AD 260.

[26] See, e.g., Moltmann, *Creation*, 206. Also, 'We have understood human likeness to God in this same context of the divine perichoresis . . . as a relationship of fellowship, of *mutual need* and mutual interpenetration' (258, emphasis mine). See also 266 and *Trinity and Kingdom*, 106ff. and 148ff. For more on this, see Moltmann, *History and the Triune God*, 133, where Moltmann states that 'the mystery of creation is best grasped philosophically by panentheism'.

[27] *CD* II/1, 312–13. Karl Rahner also accepts a modified doctrine of panentheism in Karl Rahner and Herbert Vorgrimler, *Theological Dictionary*, ed. Cornelius Ernst (New York: Herder & Herder, 1965), 333–4.

[28] Moltmann, *Trinity and Kingdom*, 56ff., 99ff., 106ff., 159–61 and 167–8.

[29] Moltmann, *Trinity and Kingdom*, 197, emphasis mine.

[30] Moltmann, *Trinity and Kingdom*, 31, emphasis mine.

God *has to give himself. . . it is only in this way that he is God. He has to go through time; and it is only in this way that he is eternal . . .* He has to be man and nothing but man; and it is only in this way that he is completely God . . . 'It was necessary for God to be Man, for only so could He be truly God.'[31]

For Barth, God *freely* reaffirms himself in eternity and in time; for Moltmann, 'God must, therefore pass through time to attain his eternal being . . . In order to be completely itself, love has to suffer . . . Through openness and capacity for suffering, the divine love shows that it is life's pre-eminent organizing principle in the deadly conflicts of blind natural forces.'[32]

All of this leads Moltmann to Unamuno's panentheistic confusion of history and eternity: 'A God who cannot suffer cannot love either . . . only that which suffers is divine.'[33] This clear projection of human love and suffering into the eternal Godhead manifests the mutual conditioning associated with all human love and suffering; it cannot, however, describe the trinitarian God as free in himself or in revelation in a way which definitively overcomes suffering. This God cannot even *freely* act since 'It is not through supernatural interventions that God guides creation . . . Seen in terms of world history, the transforming power of suffering is the basis for the liberating and consummating acts of God.'[34] By this reasoning, which has identified the immanent and economic Trinity in light of the cross of Christ, God cannot overcome suffering since suffering itself is the *principle* that encompasses his very being and love.

We have seen how Moltmann's panentheistic understanding of the Trinity is in conflict with Barth's theology and how Moltmann's view that the economic Trinity has a retroactive effect on the immanent

[31] Moltmann, *Trinity and Kingdom*, 32–3, emphasis mine. Thus, for Moltmann, the incarnation means for God 'an increase of his riches and his bliss' (121).

[32] Moltmann, *Trinity and Kingdom*, 33–4. Barth specifically rejects this thinking in *CD* II/1, 304–6.

[33] Moltmann, *Trinity and Kingdom*, 38. Moltmann appears to modify his view of panentheism in *Creation* by ascribing to the creature's self-transcending movements the indwelling Creator Spirit (103). The only change, however, is that the Spirit is now the principle of infinity that 'imbues every finite thing . . . with self-transcendence' (101). Indeed the Spirit is part of the structure of creation (212). Creation is seen as evolving toward God (chapter 8) and God is necessarily related to it (207, 213). Barth consistently rejected both of these views by rejecting Pelagianism and panentheism.

[34] Moltmann, *Creation*, 211. Moltmann cites Teilhard's view as an adequate account of this. Barth correctly rejected Teilhard's gnostic pantheism several times. Cf. *Karl Barth Letters*, 116f. and 119f., and Eberhard Busch, *Karl Barth*, trans. John Bowden (Philadelphia: Fortress Press, 1976): 'Teilhard de Chardin is an almost classic case of Gnosticism' wrote Barth (487).

Trinity reflects the kind of mutual conditioning inherent in human experience, but absent from the triune God who loves in freedom. Now let us explore how Moltmann's understanding of the Trinity functions in his ecological doctrine of creation with a view toward seeing how this problem of mutual conditioning really does compromise God's freedom precisely because of Moltmann's failure to make a proper distinction between the immanent and the economic Trinity.

According to Moltmann,

> In the 1930s, the problem of the doctrine of creation was knowledge of God. Today the problem of the doctrine of God is knowledge of creation. The theological adversary then was the religious and political ideology of 'blood and soil', 'race and nation'. Today the theological adversary is the nihilism practised in our dealings with nature. Both perversions have been evoked by the unnatural will to power . . .[35]

Moltmann's ecological doctrine of creation sees God's Spirit '*in* all created beings'. In order to understand this, Moltmann has interwoven the first three articles of the Apostles' creed in a trinitarian sense in order to 'develop a pneumatological doctrine of creation. This doctrine of creation . . . takes as its starting point the indwelling divine Spirit of creation.'[36] This thinking Moltmann hopes will provide a more holistic philosophy of nature. The word ecology means 'the doctrine of the house'. And Moltmann's point is that if we see creation only as God's 'work' such a doctrine will make little sense, but 'if we understand the Creator, his creation, and the goal of that creation in a trinitarian sense, then the Creator, through his Spirit *dwells in* his creation as a whole, and in every individual created being, by virtue of his Spirit holding them together and keeping them in life'.[37] As the inner secret of creation is this indwelling of God, the purpose of Shekinah (God's indwelling) is 'to make the whole creation the house of God'.[38] To this theological

---

[35] Moltmann, *Creation*, xi.

[36] Moltmann, *Creation*, xii. Among other things this thinking eventually leads to these conclusions: first, 'The Spirit is the principle of evolution' (100); second, 'The Spirit is the holistic principle . . . he creates interactions, . . . co-operation and community [and] is the "common Spirit of creation"'; and third, 'The Spirit is the principle of individuation'. Therefore 'self-preservation and self-transcendence are two sides of the process in which life evolves. They are not mutual contradictions. They complement one another' (100). Moltmann can even say: 'Through his Spirit God is also present in the very structures of matter. Creation contains neither spirit-less matter nor non-material spirit; there is only *informed* matter' (212).

[37] Moltmann, *Creation*, xii.

[38] Moltmann, *Creation*, xiii. In connection with the notion of Shekinah (90ff.), Moltmann advocates the kabbalistic tradition of Judaism which he adopts from Isaac Luria with its divine *zimzum* (God's self-limitation); the essential problem with this doctrine is that its

side of the doctrine of creation there corresponds an anthropological side, that is, existence can become a home only if the stresses and strains between human beings and nature are overcome in a viable 'symbiosis'.

Moltmann sees his 'ecological doctrine of creation' as corresponding to his social doctrine of the Trinity presented in *The Trinity and the Kingdom*. In that work, as we have just seen, Moltmann attempted to reconceive the Trinity pantheistically in terms of 'relationships and communities' and 'out of the doctrine of the Trinity'.[39]

> By taking up pantheistic ideas from the Jewish and the Christian traditions, we shall try to think *ecologically* about God, man and the world in their relationships and indwellings. In this way it is not merely the Christian *doctrine* of the Trinity that we are trying to work out anew; our aim is to develop and practise trinitarian *thinking* as well.[40]

Such thinking avoids Kant's view that 'nothing whatever can be gained for practical purposes, even if one comprehended it [the doctrine of the Trinity]';[41] it also avoids starting from a general concept of one divine substance because then 'natural theology's definition . . . becomes a prison for the statements made by the theology of revelation'.[42] Such a doctrine of the Trinity would disintegrate into 'abstract monotheism'. Moltmann compares this to what he believes is Aquinas's idea that when we abstract from the trinitarian Persons 'what remains for thought is the one divine nature. It is this . . . which is in general to be called "God" not the three Persons, or only one of them.'[43] Finally, Moltmann hopes to avoid Hegel's idea of God as absolute subject, that is, one subject, three modes of being; here the trinitarian concept of person is replaced by mode of being and in Moltmann's view this leads to modalism, that is, 'to the reduction of the doctrine of the trinity to monotheism'.[44] Neither a 'return to the earlier Trinity of substance' nor adopting a more modern 'subject' Trinity are viable options; instead

---

pantheistic and emanationist understanding of creation obliterates the traditional distinction between God and the world by making nothing the condition of the possibility of God's action *ad extra* (cf. *Trinity and Kingdom*, 109ff. and above n. 12). Thus, e.g., Moltmann writes, 'God withdraws into himself in order to go out of himself. He "creates" the preconditions for the existence of his creation by withdrawing his presence and his power . . . Nothingness emerges' (*Creation*, 87). For Moltmann 'The doctrine of the Shekinah is the logical result of making God's pathos the starting point' (*Trinity and Kingdom*, 30).

[39] Moltmann, *Trinity and Kingdom*, 19.
[40] Moltmann, *Trinity and Kingdom*, 19–20.
[41] Moltmann, *Trinity and Kingdom*, 6.
[42] Moltmann, *Trinity and Kingdom*, 17.
[43] Moltmann, *Trinity and Kingdom*, 16.
[44] Moltmann, *Trinity and Kingdom*, 18.

he suggests that we refrain from beginning with God's unity, as he notes has been the custom in the West, and commence 'with the trinity of the Persons and . . . then go on to ask about the unity'. What then emerges is 'a concept of the divine unity as the union of the tri-unity'.[45] In his doctrine of creation he is presenting 'the corresponding ecological doctrine of creation'.[46] In both works Moltmann suggests that we 'cease to understand God monotheistically as the one, absolute subject, but instead see him in a trinitarian sense as the *unity* of the Father, the Son and the Spirit'.[47]

In the rest of this chapter I hope to show how this thinking leads Moltmann to reinterpret the doctrines of the Trinity and of creation. In addition I hope to show that the choice between monotheism and trinitarianism as Moltmann conceives it is neither required nor possible when the triune God is recognized as the one God who does not surrender his deity in his actions *ad extra.* Indeed, I believe that one can say that it is as the one absolute subject that God creates and maintains the world in existence through the Son and the Spirit without being a Hegelian, as long as there is a clear distinction drawn between the immanent and the economic Trinity. Since God remains God, therefore it would have to be God alone who is and remains the *only* divine subject in the encounter with creatures. His actions would never become dependent upon those of his creatures, since such a view is workable only if divine and human being are confused and one falls directly into the Feuerbachian dilemma. Here I intend to explore Moltmann's method and conclusions regarding the God–world relation with a view toward assessing whether and to what extent his revision of the traditional doctrines clarifies or obscures the being of God the creator, the Lord and Giver of life of the familiar Nicene Creed. This should lead to a clearer vision of the function of the immanent Trinity today. We have already seen that Moltmann reacted against the way the doctrine of the immanent Trinity functioned for Karl Barth. Now we will see Moltmann's alternative in more detail and evaluate it in the context of our discussions developed so far in this book.

Method and Problem

Moltmann contends that traditional theology has emphasized duality, that is, creation *and* redemption, creation *and* covenant, necessity *and*

---

[45] Moltmann, *Trinity and Kingdom,* 19.
[46] Moltmann, *Creation,* 2.
[47] Moltmann, *Creation,* 2; *Trinity and Kingdom,* chapter 1.

freedom, nature *and* grace. Accordingly, in his view, grace presupposes and perfects nature but does not destroy it. Moltmann says this is captured by Rahner's phraseology 'that anthropology is "deficient christology" and christology is "realized anthropology"'.[48] He believes that the second part of the proposition fails to distinguish 'grace and glory, history and new creation, being a Christian and being perfected' and has led to 'triumphalism', that is, 'the glory which perfects nature is supposed already inherent in the grace'.[49] While I agree with Moltmann that triumphalism must be avoided, I shall suggest here, against his view, that 'triumphalism' would follow only if the *glory*, which perfects nature, is supposed to be somehow inherent in nature or some synthesis of nature and grace. In other words, there would be a problem with this position only if nature and grace were not clearly distinguished and then united.

Moltmann recommends that we say that grace does not perfect nature, but prepares nature for eternal glory. Thus, as Christ's resurrection is the beginning of the new creation of the world we must speak of nature and grace in a 'forward perspective' in light of the 'coming glory, which will complete *both nature and grace*'.[50] The dualities will no longer be defined over against one another; rather 'they will be determined in all their complex interconnections in relation to a third, common to them both'.[51] That third is conceived by Moltmann as the *process* common to both, and when this is seen then, he believes, we will have a reconciliation of opposites such as freedom and necessity, grace and nature and finally covenant and creation. It is of course this common process that I believe identifies God with creation and thus fails to distinguish the above mentioned dualities in the long run. Among many problems that result from this thinking is the idea that Christ's lordship is provisional; it will be complete only in the kingdom of glory when the Son transfers the, as yet, incomplete kingdom to the Father.

> With this transfer the lordship of the Son ends . . . it means the consummation of his sonship . . . all Jesus' titles of sovereignty – Christ, kyrios, prophet . . . – are *provisional* titles, which express Jesus' significance for salvation in time. But the name of Son remains to all eternity.[52]

Moltmann also contends that

---

[48] Moltmann, *Creation*, 7.
[49] Moltmann, *Creation*, 7.
[50] Moltmann, *Creation*, 8, emphasis mine.
[51] Moltmann, *Creation*, 8.
[52] Moltmann, *Trinity and Kingdom*, 92.

Without the difference between Creator and creature, creation cannot be conceived at all; *but this difference is embraced and comprehended by the greater truth* which is what the creation narrative really comes down to, because it is the truth from which it springs: *the truth that God is all in all.* This does not imply a pantheistic dissolution of creation in God; it means the final form which creation is to find in God.[53]

The problem, however, is that if the difference is embraced in this way then one could argue, as Moltmann does, that, since God and creatures mutually co-exist, therefore the kingdom of glory arises from the history of suffering which, according to the kabbalistic doctrine of creation, God makes part of himself in order to create and in order to redeem; it follows that redemption then cannot be viewed as a free new act of God in creating a new heaven and a new earth. Thus, 'It is from the apotheosis of the Lamb that the kingdom of glory comes into being.'[54] This differs from John's Gospel which traces the origin of Jesus' glory to his relation with the Father as one who was full of grace and truth as the Word who was God (Jn 1:1, 14–18). Believers in the Word incarnate would see God's glory, while those who refused to believe did so because they 'look to each other for glory and are not concerned with the glory that comes from the one God' (Jn 5:43). The kingdom of glory in Moltmann's view comes into existence from within history and cannot be identical with God's self-sufficient glory revealed in the cross and resurrection. He argues that 'God and the world are then involved in a common redemptive process.' God participates in the world's pain; thus 'we need God's compassion and God needs ours'. And finally, 'God himself becomes free in the process . . . even God himself will only be free when our souls are free.'[55] While Moltmann says God does not act out of deficiency of being,[56] it is precisely here that God's being is indeed deficient by virtue of his need for redemption, glory and freedom. This thinking results from Moltmann's conviction that 'The trinitarian concept of creation integrates the elements of truth in monotheism and pantheism' by enabling us to 'find an integrating view of God and nature which will draw them both *into the same vista.* It is only this that can exert a liberating influence on nature and human beings.'[57]

---

[53] Moltmann, *Creation*, 89, emphasis mine.

[54] Moltmann, *Creation*, 90.

[55] Moltmann, *Trinity and Kingdom*, 39. Moltmann asks, 'Does God really not need those whom in the suffering of his love he loves unendingly?' (53). For the same idea, see *Creation*, 82ff.

[56] Moltmann, *Creation*, 23.

[57] Moltmann, *Creation*, 98, emphasis mine.

The question that is being raised here then is whether there can be a process common to both nature and grace, freedom and necessity, and so on, which encompasses them and determines their present and future meaning without obliterating the distinction between God and the world. For Moltmann this process is both possible and necessary because his theological starting point is a version of panentheism which maintains that we cannot cling to any distinction between the immanent and the economic Trinity. Thus, 'The economic Trinity not only reveals the immanent Trinity; it also has a retroactive effect on it'[58] principally because, in the words of Unamuno, as seen above, 'A God who cannot suffer cannot love either . . . only that which suffers is divine.'[59] Hence,

> *Christian panentheism* . . . started from the divine essence: Creation is a fruit of God's longing for 'his Other' and for that Other's free response to the divine love. That is why the idea of the world is inherent in the nature of God himself from eternity. For it is impossible to conceive of a God who is not a creative God. A non-creative God would be imperfect . . . if God's eternal being is love, then divine love is also more blessed in giving than in receiving. *God cannot find bliss in eternal self-love if selflessness is part of love's very nature.*[60]

Moltmann rejects identifying the world process with God as he believes this took place in the speculative theology of the nineteenth century, arguing that 'In order to understand the history of mankind as a history *in* God, the distinction between the world process and the inner-trinitarian process must be maintained and emphasized.'[61]

Yet, given the fact that it is impossible to conceive of a God who is not creative and who cannot find bliss in his eternal self-love, the question arises as to whether, in this reasoning, there can be an inner-trinitarian process distinct from that trinitarian thinking which defines

---

[58] Moltmann, *Trinity and Kingdom*, 160.

[59] Moltmann, *Trinity and Kingdom*, 38.

[60] Moltmann, *Trinity and Kingdom*, 106, emphasis mine.

[61] Moltmann, *Trinity and Kingdom*, 106–7. See also *Creation*, 103, where Moltmann explains that the German Romantics such as Goethe have turned people into indifferentists with their pantheism. He believes he has overcome this by saying 'everything is not God; but God is everything'. But all he actually has done is rejected a simple pantheistic identification of God's Spirit with matter and identified this instead with 'the overriding harmony of the relations' which he finds at work in history and nature (*Creation*, 103). We have here a more complex 'relational' identity, which can discern 'future transcendence, evolution and intentionality', but it is still an identity and not a relationship between essentially distinct beings, that is, creator and creatures. It is interesting to note that later Moltmann presents a somewhat different view of Goethe by espousing what he calls the 'true pan-entheism' that he finds in Giordano Bruno and Goethe (*History and the Triune God*, 164).

God's love as selflessness and which then insists that God cannot have existed without being the creator. The problem here is captured succinctly by Etienne Gilson in his analysis of Descartes' natural theology: 'Now it is quite true that a creator is an eminently Christian God, but a God whose very essence is to be a creator is not a Christian God at all. The essence of the true Christian God is not to create but to be. "He who is" can also create, if he chooses; but he does not exist because he creates . . . he can create because he supremely is.'[62] According to Gilson, Descartes' 'stillborn God' was 'the God of Christianity reduced to the condition of a philosophical principle' and that 'The most striking characteristic of such a God was that his creative function had integrally absorbed his essence.'[63] Despite the fact that objections could be raised to Gilson about how the nature of 'He who is' is to be conceived (i.e. Does God supremely exist merely as an act of existence whose essence is to be, or as the triune God who knows and loves himself in the freedom of transcendence which is his alone?), the question he raises here is decisive.[64] It concerns the fact that God is free and does not need to create in order to be God. It concerns the distinction between the eternal being of God and his free, but real, relations with the world.

Necessity and Freedom

Moltmann certainly recognizes and actually seeks to avoid this problem when he writes,

> The later theological interpretation of creation as *creatio ex nihilo* is therefore unquestionably an apt paraphrase of what the Bible means by 'creation'. Wherever and whatever God creates is without any pre-conditions. *There is no external necessity which occasions his creativity, and no inner compulsion which could determine it.* Nor is there any primordial matter whose potentiality is pre-given to his creative activity, and which would set him material limits.[65]

But his panentheism causes him to ascribe an inner compulsion to God's nature which he himself recognizes the *creatio ex nihilo* intended

---

[62] Gilson, *God and Philosophy*, 88.

[63] Gilson, *God and Philosophy*, 89.

[64] This is the gist of Moltmann's objection to Aquinas's view of the Trinity as 'one divine substance'; he calls this abstract monotheism as we saw above.

[65] Moltmann, *Creation*, 74, some emphases mine. See also 75, 'The world was created neither out of pre-existent matter nor out of the divine Being itself.' This is why he rejects Tillich's understanding of creation (80). Moltmann thinks Tillich's abolition of the divine self-differentiation from creation is the monism and pantheism Christians must reject (84).

to exclude. Hence in answering this question Moltmann writes, 'If we lift the concept of necessity out of the context of compulsive necessity and determination by something external, then in God *necessity* and *freedom* coincide; they are what is for him axiomatic, self-evident. For God it is axiomatic to love, for he cannot deny himself. For God it is axiomatic to love freely, for he is God.'[66] Therefore, God is not 'his own prisoner' and remains true to himself.

The only problem with this reasoning is that it constrains Moltmann to suppose that in loving the world God is 'entirely himself'.[67] And this means that, since he cannot but will the good, he has no choice in 'communicating himself' to his creation. Thus, God's own self-determination is 'an essential *emanation* of his goodness'.[68] This view follows Moltmann's hermeneutical presupposition which is that 'the eternal origin of God's creative and suffering love' must include 'God's free self-determination, and *at the same time* the overflowing of his goodness, which belongs to his essential nature'.[69] And this synthesis of God's act (of will) and being resulted from Moltmann's belief that the gnostic and Neoplatonic doctrine of emanation contained 'elements of truth which are indispensable for a full understanding of God's creation'.[70] In

---

[66] Moltmann, *Trinity and Kingdom*, 107.

[67] Moltmann, *Trinity and Kingdom*, 55. See also *Creation*, 83. This supposition follows from his method and it is worth noting the striking similarity between his conclusion and the view of the incarnation offered by Ludwig Feuerbach, that is, 'there is nothing more in the nature of God than in the incarnate manifestation of God . . . The Incarnation . . . is therefore no mysterious composition of contraries' (Feuerbach, *The Essence of Christianity*, 56). And 'The love of God to man is an essential condition of the Divine Being: God is a God who loves me – who loves man in general' (57).

[68] *Trinity and Kingdom*, 54, emphasis mine.

[69] *Trinity and Kingdom*, 54, emphasis mine. It is this 'at the same time' that is the heartbeat of all pantheism. For instance, Meister Eckhart proposed that 'at the same time and once and for all, when God existed and when He generated His Son, God coeternal, and coequal to Himself in all things, He also created the world' in John F. Clarkson SJ, et al. (trans. and ed.), *The Church Teaches: Documents of the Church in English Translation* (hereafter: *The Church Teaches*) (London: Herder, 1955), 147. This pantheistic viewpoint was rejected in 1329 based on the *creatio ex nihilo*, which excluded the idea that both creation and creator were eternal. It is not particularly surprising that Moltmann cites Meister Eckhart in support of his panentheism (which, as noted above, is really worse than pantheism): 'only if we have a concept of God with a trinitarian differentiation . . . can we say with Meister Eckhart that all is "from God", all is "through God", all is "in God" . . . [indeed] It seems to me that Giordano Bruno is returning at the end of this age as the herald of a new "paradigm" for a world in which human beings can survive in organic harmony with the Spirit of the universe' (*History and the Triune God*, 164). Curiously, David Tracy thinks that Meister Eckhart's thinking might prove useful for contemporary trinitarian theology; see 'Trinitarian Speculation and the Forms of Divine Disclosure', in Davis, Kendall, SJ, and O'Collins, SJ (eds), *The Trinity: An Interdisciplinary Symposium on the Trinity*, 290f.

[70] Moltmann, *Creation*, 83.

his resolute unwillingness to exclude emanationism and pantheism decisively Moltmann is led to believe that he can reconcile freedom and necessity in relation to the Trinity and creation without compromising the traditional doctrines. Perhaps he would be horrified to find himself in the company of Augustine in this predicament. Appropriately perceiving the need for a clear decision at this point Gilson put the matter this way

> In short, as soon as Augustine read the *Enneads*, he found there the three essentially Christian notions of God the Father, of God the Word, and of the creation. That Augustine found them there is an incontrovertible fact. *That they were not there is a hardly more controvertible fact.* To go at once to the fundamental reason why they could not possibly be there, let us say *that the world of Plotinos and the world of Christianity are strictly incomparable; no single point in the one can be matched with any single point in the other one*, for the fundamental reason that their metaphysical structure is essentially different.[71]

In his trinitarian doctrine, as noted above, Moltmann concludes that

> From eternity God has desired not only himself but the world too . . . That is why the idea of the world is already inherent in the Father's love for the Son . . . The *Logos* through whom the Father has created everything, and without whom nothing has been made that was made is only *the other side of the Son.* The Son is *the Logos* in relation to the world. The Logos is *the Son* in relation to the Father.[72]

In connection with this problem, Aquinas clearly insisted that

> There are two reasons why the knowledge of the divine persons was necessary for us. It was necessary for the right idea of creation . . . *saying that God made all things by His Word excludes the error of those who say that God produced things by necessity.* When we say that in Him there is a procession of love, we say God produced creatures not because he needed them, . . . *[and] that we may think rightly concerning the salvation of the human race, accomplished by the Incarnate Son, and by the gift of the Holy Ghost.*[73]

---

[71] Gilson, *God and Philosophy*, 48–9, emphases mine.

[72] Moltmann, *Trinity and Kingdom*, 108, emphasis in original.

[73] *Summa Theologica*, part 1, qu. 32, art. 1, emphasis mine. In this idea Thomas is in accord with Athanasius who, as we have noted in Chapter One, argued correctly and powerfully that 'it would be more pious and true to indicate God from the Son and to call him Father than to name him from his works alone and to say that he is unoriginated'. Not indicating God from the Son leads, among other things, to a false idea of creation. It led Arius to think of Christ as a work of the Father.

By contrast, in Moltmann's thought, it certainly appears that if God is not his own prisoner he is certainly the prisoner of love which by its very nature *must* freely create another in order to be true to its own nature. For Moltmann, selflessness is the essence of love, and that selflessness must apply to God's free love as well as creaturely love.[74] Consequently, God is not free to create or not but must, in his very essence, be described as creative love. Here and in Moltmann's often repeated idea that for God 'not to reveal himself and to be contented with his untouched glory would be a contradiction of himself',[75] as well as in this passage just cited, there can be no distinction between God's eternal self-sufficient love as Father, Son and Spirit and his free will to create a world distinct from himself. Rather he writes, 'The generation and birth of the Son come from the Father's *nature*, not from his will. That is why we talk about the *eternal* generation and birth of the Son. The Father begets and bears the Son out of the *necessity* of his being.'[76] Thus, for Moltmann, there can be no distinction between God's eternal self-sufficient love as Father, Son and Spirit, and his free will *ad intra* and *ad extra* in his act of creating a world distinct from himself. This is significantly different from the kind of careful distinction mentioned by Athanasius. Rejecting Patripassianism and Sabellianism it was held that

> those who irreverently say that the Son has been generated not by choice or will, thus encompassing God with a necessity which excludes choice and purpose, so that He begat the Son unwillingly, we account as most irreligious and alien to the Church; in that they have dared to define such things concerning God, beside the common notions concerning Him, nay, beside the purport of divinely inspired Scripture. For we, knowing that God is absolute and sovereign over Himself, have a religious judgment that He generated the Son voluntarily and freely; yet . . . we

---

[74] Moltmann, *Trinity and Kingdom*, 28; this idea is essential to the doctrine of the Shekinah. Since Moltmann cannot conceive of creation as an expression of God's omnipotence – God had to empty himself of this to create (*Creation*, 88) – he argues that it is God's nature to will the good, and since he cannot deny this, therefore in loving the world 'he is entirely himself'. Consequently, it is implied that it would be evil for God not to create since creation means 'communicating himself' and freedom is not freedom to choose but simple 'undivided joy in the good'. Hence, 'Love is a self-evident, unquestionable "overflowing of goodness" which is therefore *never open to choice at any time*' (*Trinity and Kingdom*, 55, emphasis mine). If God could 'choose' not to create it would in fact be an evil choice, since overflowing goodness has no 'free choice'; this for Moltmann would imply arbitrariness or the possibility of a different God than the one he has described.

[75] Moltmann, *Trinity and Kingdom*, 53.

[76] Moltmann, *Trinity and Kingdom*, 167.

do not understand Him to have been originated like the creatures or works which through Him came to be.[77]

And the eleventh Council of Toledo (675) formulated the matter carefully as follows: 'He is the Son of God by nature not by adoption; and we must believe that God the Father begot him not through his will and not of necessity, for there is no necessity in God nor does the will precede wisdom.'[78] Following this tradition, Karl Barth argued that 'The eternal generation of the Son by the Father tells us first and supremely that God is not at all lonely even without the world and us.'[79]

The consequences of this reasoning cause Moltmann to argue that God's freedom cannot mean that he is without obligation to creation since 'the self-communication of his goodness in love to his creation is not a matter of his free will'.[80] Moltmann dissolves God's will to act into what he describes as his essential nature arguing that 'his will *is* his essential activity'. Thus, 'God is not entirely free when he can do and leave undone what he likes; he is entirely free when he is entirely himself. In his creative activity he is *entirely* himself. He loves the world in the surrender of his Son with the very same love which he *is*, from eternity to eternity'.[81] Moltmann's failure to distinguish the immanent and economic Trinity then leads him to be unable to distinguish between God's being and act, nature and will, as well as creation and redemption at this crucial point.[82]

If, as Moltmann believes, the idea of creation is already inherent in the Father's necessary love of the Son, where is the distinction between God's free love and the necessary creation of a reality distinct from him to be drawn? If the Son is the Logos in relation to the world, as Moltmann says, then is he not the Logos apart from the world in

---

[77] Athanasius, *Select Works and Letters* in *A Select Library of Nicene and Post-Nicene Fathers*, trans. and ed. Philip Schaff and Henry Wace, vol. 4 (New York: Charles Scribner's Sons, 1903), *Epistle of Athanasius Concerning the Arian Bipartite Council held at Ariminum and Seleucia*, 463, part 2, no. 26.

[78] Clarkson et al. (trans. and ed.), *The Church Teaches*, 128.

[79] *CD* I/1, 139.

[80] Moltmann, *Creation*, 82–3.

[81] Moltmann, *Creation*, 82–3.

[82] Thus, instead of seeing creation and redemption as two distinct actions of the one God, for Moltmann redemption refers to a future when 'God's creation and his revelation will be one' (*Creation*, 287–8). And 'The goal of this history [of consummation] is not a return to the paradisal primordial condition. Its goal is the revelation of the glory of God ... this ... represents the fulfillment of the real promise implanted in creation itself' (*Creation*, 207). Obviously a redemption that is implanted in creation (even as a promise) cannot be conceived as a free, new action of the triune God.

himself? Are we dealing with two different Logoi here: one who exists as God the Son and another who exists as the soul of the created world? Has Moltmann here not introduced the world into the Godhead as the other side of the Son just because he has already introduced suffering into the Godhead as part of God's loving nature when he wrote, in accordance with the doctrine of the Shekinah, that creation is traced to a dichotomy in God so that there is a 'rift which runs through the divine life and activity until redemption'?[83] Moltmann is led to argue not only that God '"needs" the world and man', but that the relation between the Father and Son 'is necessary love, not free love'.[84]

In his concept of the Son as the Logos in relation to the world, Moltmann is unable to maintain what the traditional doctrine of the Trinity intended to assert, that is, that God's eternal Word is *identical* with God himself and thus the only begotten Son of the Father is identical with the Word through whom God creates.[85] But if this is the case then it is impossible to conclude that the Father bears the Son out of necessity, for his love is only necessary insofar as it is his free self-affirmation in which he is subject to no necessary determinations from within or without as Moltmann himself believes the doctrine of *creatio ex nihilo* proposed. Any such necessity would make the love of God subject to a higher law encompassing his actual free love. That higher law of course would be accessible as a philosophical principle to which God himself was subject.

Here we reach the heart of the matter. For if the immanent Trinity is the norm for the truth of our concepts of God as it should be, then the trinitarian actions *ad extra* would remain normative for any interpretation of present and future meaning; these could not be deduced from a panentheistic principle of suffering love discovered in a relational metaphysics and then applied to revelation.[86] Rather we would have

---

[83] Moltmann, *Trinity and Kingdom*, 30.

[84] Moltmann, *Trinity and Kingdom*, 58.

[85] Athanasius wrote, 'For since the Word is the Son of God by nature proper to His essence, and is from Him, and in Him, as He said Himself, the creatures could not have come to be, except through Him . . . He is the Father's Will' (Athanasius, *Against the Arians, Discourse II*, 18, 364). And Aquinas, following Augustine, wrote that 'Word and Son express the same' in order to avoid any idea that either term merely referred to a property of his which might lead to the idea that we were dealing with a being that was not fully divine (*Summa Theologica* part 1, qu. 32, art. 2). Following this tradition, Karl Barth wrote, 'In the vocabulary of Trinitarian doctrine God's Son cannot be differentiated from God's Word' (*CD* I/1, 137).

[86] Thus Moltmann argues against a Cartesian 'subject' metaphysics and an Aristotelian 'metaphysics of substance' saying, 'Both can only be done away with by means of a relational metaphysics, based on the mutual relativity of human beings and the world' (*Creation*, 50). The norm for his thinking is a relational metaphysics dictated by the relativity of people and

to acknowledge, as Aquinas himself did following Augustine, that 'by faith we arrive at knowledge, and not conversely'.[87] A Christian doctrine of the Trinity therefore would derive its meaning from God *in se* acting *ad extra* and not from the realm of history accessible to the philosopher as such. It is my belief that, because Moltmann attempts to conceive God's nature and suffering in creation in a single perspective in which both are on their way toward redemption, he incorporates need, nothingness, suffering and death directly into the nature of God.[88] In this way he compromises his own understanding of the *creatio ex nihilo* and is led to redefine the immanent Trinity by the history of the economic Trinity. In the remainder of this chapter I will restrict myself to indicating the reason why I think this happens to Moltmann and why it leads him both into the modalism he criticizes in Rahner and Barth and into tritheism.

Method and the Freedom of God

Since his understanding of the Trinity does not come only from the triune God acting *ad extra* but from a synthesis of human and divine

---

the world and not the freedom of God revealed in his Word and Spirit and acknowledged in the *creatio ex nihilo*. Hence, Moltmann's hermeneutical presupposition is that he can 'find a new interpretation of the Christian doctrine of creation in light of the knowledge of nature made accessible to us by evolutionary theories' (*Creation*, 205). Thus, his norm is not revelation but revelation interpreted from the perspective of mutual indwellings and developments he believes he has discovered in nature and history.

[87] *Summa Theologica*, part 1, qu. 32, art. 1.

[88] Thus he is led to argue as noted above that 'It is not through supernatural interventions that God guides creation. . . . Seen in terms of world history, the transforming power of suffering is the basis for the liberating and consummating acts of God' (*Creation*, 211). Creation traditionally was distinguished from salvation with the idea that creation was good but went wrong. Salvation was a free new action of God by which God negated the spheres of sin and evil that arose in opposition to his good will and were to be destroyed ultimately in the death and resurrection of Jesus Christ (*Athanasius's Orations Against the Arians*, in *The Trinitarian Controversy, Sources of Early Christian Thought*, trans. and ed. William G. Rusch [Philadelphia: Fortress Press, 1980], Book 1, 41, 104–5). By contrast, Moltmann contends that *nihil* is a 'partial negation of the divine Being, inasmuch as God is not yet creator. The space which comes into being and is set free by God's self-limitation is a literally God-forsaken space. The *nihil* in which God creates his creation is God-forsakenness, hell, absolute death' (*Creation*, 87). The result of making the *nihil* something, rather than the symbol that God is truly free in relation to all that is distinct from him and dependent upon him, is the incorporation of *nihil* itself directly into the Godhead. We have here the dualism Moltmann himself intends to reject. God-forsakenness, hell and absolute death are part of God before creation. Ultimately Moltmann can conceive of creation only as an emanation of the divine being because according to the doctrine of the *zimzum*, creation refers to a shrinkage process in God himself and then to his 'issuing' outside himself (*Creation*, 87, and *Trinity and Kingdom*, 109–10).

experience, Moltmann does not distinguish clearly between human experience of the created realm and God's being and action in his Word and Spirit. Thus, he argues against Schleiermacher that

> If one were only to relate the experience of God to the experience of the self, then the self would become the constant and 'God' the variable. It is only when the self is perceived in the experience which God has with that self that an undistorted perception of the history of one's own self with God and in God emerges.[89]

Accordingly, Moltmann assumes that Schleiermacher actually has described God by speaking of our feeling of absolute dependence and concludes that experience does not merely refer to our experience of God but to 'God's experience with us'.[90] In neither case, however, has he shown that he is speaking of the Christian God who factually transcends all of our experiences even as he makes himself known; Moltmann merely assumes that Schleiermacher's reduction of the Trinity to abstract monotheism can be overcome with the counter question, 'how does God experience me'?[91] But the fact remains that neither Schleiermacher nor Moltmann have shown that they are speaking of the Christian God whose being and action cannot be grounded in experience at all without compromising the distinction between God and the world. This has serious methodological consequences for the relationship between philosophy and theology.

Having blurred the distinction between human experience and God's experience at the outset, Moltmann argues that the more we come to understand God's experience, the closer we come to the perception that

> the history of the world is the history of God's suffering. At the moments of God's profoundest revelation there is always suffering: the cry of the captives in Egypt; Jesus' death cry on the cross; the sighing of the whole enslaved creation for liberty. *If a person once feels the infinite passion of God's love which finds expression here, then he understands the mystery of the triune God.* God suffers with us – God suffers from us – God suffers for us: *it is this experience of God that reveals the triune God* . . . Consequently fundamental theology's discussion about access to the doctrine of the Trinity is carried on today in the context of the question about God's capacity or incapacity for suffering.[92]

[89] Moltmann, *Trinity and Kingdom*, 4.
[90] Moltmann, *Trinity and Kingdom*, 4.
[91] Moltmann, *Trinity and Kingdom*, 3.
[92] Moltmann, *Trinity and Kingdom*, 4–5, emphasis mine.

Here, where we return to where this chapter began, Moltmann leaps to the assumption that an experience of suffering is not only an experience of God but also knowledge of the Trinity. This doctrinal foundation leads him to redefine both the immanent and economic Trinity by the experiences of suffering love which he discovers both in God and creatures. We have already seen that, on the one hand, this procedure compromises God's freedom with the emanationism that Moltmann himself rejects, and on the other hand, it compromises the freedom of grace with the claim that creatures have the inherent capacity for the divine and that both nature and grace are in need of completion in the kingdom of glory. He ignores the crucial point that, unless God's glory is already inherent in his grace (i.e. his free creation and subsequent intervention in history in Israel, in Christ and in the Church), then it can no longer be seen as the glory of God who is and remains factually self-sufficient because he does not create, reconcile and redeem out of need but out of his free love.

Following this logic Moltmann argues that it is not enough to say that God allows Christ to suffer or that in Christ we see the 'sufferings of God who cannot suffer'.[93] To understand correctly the suffering of the passionate God, Moltmann believes that we should start 'from the axiom of God's passion'[94] rather than the traditional view which asserts God's apathy. Moltmann therefore reinterprets the apathetic axiom to say 'God is not subjected to suffering in the same way as transient, created beings'. Since 'God does not suffer out of deficiency of being, like created beings' he remains 'apathetic'; yet 'he suffers from the love which is the superabundance and overflowing of his being. In so far he is "pathetic"'.[95] It is this same reasoning which later leads Moltmann to explain that

> God and the world are related to one another through the relationship of their mutual indwelling and participation: God's indwelling in the world is divine in kind; the world's indwelling in God is worldly in kind. There is no other way of conceiving the continual communication between God and the world.[96]

But the crucial question that remains unanswered in this reasoning is whether the divine indwelling is *essentially* other than that of the world? Or are they mutually dependent and therefore identical?

---

[93] Moltmann, *Trinity and Kingdom*, 22.
[94] Moltmann, *Trinity and Kingdom*, 22.
[95] Moltmann, *Trinity and Kingdom*, 23.
[96] Moltmann, *Creation*, 150.

Here Moltmann turns to Origen who asks, 'And the Father Himself ... does he not suffer in a certain way? ... Even the Father is not incapable of suffering'[97] and concludes that 'The suffering of love does not only affect the redeeming acts of God outwards; it also affects the trinitarian fellowship of God in himself.'[98] Moltmann classifies apathetic theology with monotheism declaring that we can only talk of 'God's suffering in trinitarian terms' by starting from God's passion *rather than* from his apathy; he seeks to develop a doctrine of *theopathy* by appealing to those rare theologians who started from 'God's passion and not from his apathy'.[99] His sources are the doctrine of Shekinah, Spanish mysticism, Russian Orthodox philosophy of religion and the Anglican idea of sacrificial love. And what does he discover?

1. According to Moltmann (following Abraham Heschel) it is the divine passion (not his apathy) which 'is God's freedom. It is the free relationship of passionate participation.'[100] Here we may note that in this definition of divine freedom God's apathy, which Moltmann said it was necessary to affirm, is immaterial for this definition of freedom. This is no accident, because, as we saw above, there is a common term that determines the nature of both freedom and necessity in such a way that God cannot really be free *as* he loves but must be free in accordance with the superior concept of fellowship or self-humiliation which is intrinsic to all selfless and suffering love, that is, pathetic love.

2. Here Moltmann adopts the doctrine of the Shekinah and grounds this in Jewish mysticism. Ultimately, he is led by this analysis to define love according to the explanation offered by the Spanish mystic Unamuno as noted above. And this becomes the foundation for his redefinition of trinitarian fellowship and of God's sabbath relationship with creation. Indeed Moltmann argues that if Shekinah is viewed 'as God in person, then it is necessary to assume a profound self-differentiation in God himself'.[101] Whereas the traditional doctrine of the Trinity was a development of thought corresponding to a differentiation between the Father and the Son which took place before creation in time, in Moltmann's thinking the differentiation arises from and is seen as necessary in the light of the Jewish mystical assertion that

---

[97] Moltmann, *Trinity and Kingdom*, 24. Even Origen does not seem to have gone as far as Moltmann, for he also stated that God the Father 'suffers ... becoming something which because of the greatness of his nature He cannot be, and endures human suffering for our sakes' (24).

[98] Moltmann, *Trinity and Kingdom*, 24.

[99] Moltmann, *Trinity and Kingdom*, 25.

[100] Moltmann, *Trinity and Kingdom*, 25.

[101] Moltmann, *Trinity and Kingdom*, 28.

God must have, before all worlds, included nothingness as well as creation in his very being. In part, this idea leads Moltmann to the dualism he theoretically rejects.

3. This thinking guides Moltmann to Franz Rosenzweig's mystical interpretation of creation and redemption. Here it becomes clear that, while Moltmann explicitly and consistently rejects pantheism and emanationism, he is compelled by the logic implied in this thinking to maintain the essential insights of both pantheism and of emanationism in his doctrines of the Trinity and of creation. And in order to overcome pantheism and emanationism Moltmann simply says that his panentheism is compatible with these Christian doctrines without being able to show how. He argues here that mysticism bridges the gap between '"the God of our fathers" and "the remnant of Israel with the help of the doctrine of the Shekinah"'.[102] First, God's descent to his people and his dwelling among them 'is thought of as a divorce which takes place in God himself. God himself cuts himself off from himself, he gives himself away . . . he suffers with their sufferings.'[103] Second, 'God . . . by suffering [Israel's] fate with her, makes himself in need of redemption. In this way, in this suffering, the relationship between God and the remnant points beyond itself.'[104] Third, God's unity is defined as a 'Becoming Unity. And this Becoming is laid on the soul of man and in his hands.'[105] In this analysis we begin to glimpse what Moltmann means by the kingdom of glory. As God himself now *needs* redemption from the division in his own being, so the kingdom of glory is that oneness which is becoming in the soul of the person who experienced suffering in the exile and experiences suffering even now, but who is looking forward to the time when God will be 'all in all' in an age of future harmony which has already begun in the form of his own acts of goodness here and now.

4. We have seen that Moltmann's basic methodological presupposition is that there is a common element beyond any antithesis between nature and grace and freedom and necessity, which, when understood, will resolve our unnatural will to power and enable us to see that we are all really in God and that God is in us. Appealing to the Anglican idea of eucharistic sacrifice he writes:

> One basic concept runs through the whole literature on the subject: the necessity of seeing the eucharistic sacrifice, the cross on Golgotha and

[102] Moltmann, *Trinity and Kingdom*, 29.
[103] Moltmann, *Trinity and Kingdom*, 29.
[104] Moltmann, *Trinity and Kingdom*, 29.
[105] Moltmann, *Trinity and Kingdom*, 29.

the heart of the triune God together, *in a single perspective*. The immediate occasion for developing the power of God's suffering theologically was the apologetic necessity for providing a reply to Darwin's theory of evolution. In what sense are we to understand God's almighty power?[106]

The key point here is that Moltmann honestly believes that the historical event of the cross and the heart of the triune God can be understood together in a single perspective. If they can, then there is no distinction between the immanent and economic Trinity. And there is no God independent of the world; there is only a God who can be seen from within the world's perspective as one who is subject to suffering love. The perspective (whether conceived relationally or not) would dictate the nature of God's love and freedom and to that extent would become that which is truly 'almighty'. Here, God can no longer be free in the traditional sense, that is, in the sense that he does not exist as one who stands in need.

The Cross

Thinking this way, Moltmann turns to C. E. Rolt, as noted above, in order to redefine God's almighty power in the light of the cross and several key points that correspond exactly with the kabbalistic understanding of creation emerge.[107]

1. 'The sole omnipotence which God possesses is the almighty power of suffering love . . . This is the essence of divine sovereignty.'[108] Here, suffering love (pathos) is that which is almighty; thus any idea that God could love in a way that does not involve suffering is eliminated at the outset. This affects everything that Moltmann says in his doctrine of the Trinity and of creation; it leads him finally to argue that the Holy Spirit's suffering is identical with the world's suffering.

> The Spirit . . . is God himself. If God commits himself to his limited creation, and if he himself dwells in it as 'the giver of life', this presupposes a self-limitation, a self-humiliation and a self-surrender of the Spirit. The history of suffering creation, which is subject to transience, then brings with it a history of suffering by the Spirit who dwells in creation.[109]

---

[106] Moltmann, *Trinity and Kingdom*, 31, emphasis mine.
[107] Moltmann, *Creation*, 86ff.
[108] Moltmann, *Trinity and Kingdom*, 31. Hence, Moltmann goes so far as to say 'God, the Father God of Love, is everywhere in history, but nowhere is He Almighty' (35).
[109] Moltmann, *Creation*, 102.

Moltmann also believes that God's Spirit is identical with the cosmic spirit; thus he writes, 'If the cosmic Spirit is the Spirit of God, the universe cannot be viewed as a closed system. It has to be understood as a system that is open – open for God and for his future.'[110] With these conclusions it seems clear that Moltmann's presuppositions cause him to ignore the problem of sin and to blur the distinction that the traditional doctrines correctly sought to maintain. Athanasius, for instance, deliberately rejected the idea that the cosmic spirit could be equated with God's Spirit in this way.[111] While Moltmann seeks to avoid Stoic pantheism as did Calvin and Barth,[112] he is led by his method to say what neither Calvin nor Barth would say, that is, that the cosmic spirit is the Holy Spirit and that, after the fall, creation is inherently open to God.

2. When Moltmann follows Rolt and attempts to deduce the eternal divine nature from Christ's passion, he asserts, as noted above, that 'What Christ, the incarnate God, did in time, God, the heavenly Father, does and must do in eternity.'[113] Here we have a specific avowal of modalism which cannot distinguish the Father and the Son in eternity and so concludes that as Christ suffered in time so the heavenly Father does and *must* do this in eternity.

---

[110] Moltmann, *Creation*, 102. Thus, he believes that 'The freedom towards God of the human being . . . is as unbounded as God's capacity for passion and patience' (*Trinity and Kingdom*, 30). And he holds that 'As God's image, men and women are beings who correspond to God, beings who can give the seeking love of God the sought-for response, and who are intended to do just that' (*Creation*, 77). Where is the need for repentance, grace and the Holy Spirit here?

[111] Torrance, *The Trinitarian Faith*, 201ff. presents the matter with great clarity especially as it relates to Athanasius's theology. Athanasius, e.g., 'would have nothing to do with any attempt to reach an understanding of the Spirit beginning from manifestations or operations of the Spirit in creaturely existence, in man or in the world' (201). Athanasius also 'turned sharply away from any conception of the Logos as a cosmological principle (or of *logoi spermatikoi*, "seminal reasons", immanent in the universe) occupying an intermediate status between God and creation' (201). 'Athanasius developed the doctrine of the Spirit from his essential relation to the one God and his undivided co-activity with the Father and the Son, and specifically from his inherence in the being of the eternal Son' (201). In this way Athanasius preserved the unity of the Trinity by arguing that 'The Father does all things through the Word and in the Holy Spirit' (202). In addition, 'The Holy Spirit does not bring to us any independent knowledge of God, or add any new content to God's self-revelation' (203). 'Thus, knowledge of the Spirit as well as of the Father is taken from and is controlled by knowledge of the Son' (203). From the outset of Moltmann's doctrine of creation this cannot be done because he actually equates God's Spirit, which is supposed to be *ex se*, with the cosmic spirit arguing that *this cosmic spirit* acts in us; this follows his refusal to distinguish the immanent and economic Trinity.

[112] Moltmann, *Creation*, 12.

[113] Moltmann, *Trinity and Kingdom*, 31.

Whereas the tradition rejected Patripassianism in order to stress the *eternal* distinction between the Father and Son (independent of creation), so that we might perceive the freedom of God's action in Christ, Moltmann, following Rolt, collapses the actions of the economic Trinity into the being of the Father in eternity by arguing that

> the surrender of the Son for us on the cross has a retroactive effect on the Father and causes infinite pain . . . God's relationship to the world has a retroactive effect on his relationship to himself – even though the divine relationship to the world is primarily determined by that inner relationship. The growth of knowledge of the immanent Trinity from the saving experience of the cross of Christ makes this necessary. *The pain of the cross determines the inner life of the triune God from eternity to eternity.*[114]

The trinitarian doctrine of the Church does not admit that the Father suffers from eternity to eternity simply because the Father almighty sends his Son for the purpose of salvation as a free gift of grace. Here the distinction between the Father and Son is an eternal one which is not defined by the historical events that took place in time. Still, the Father is not remote from the suffering of the Son on the cross since there is a *perichoresis* between the Father and the Son. Nonetheless, the events in time receive their meaning from God's free will actualized in those occurrences. Moltmann cannot say this because his method insists that Christ's suffering and the love of the immanent Trinity can be understood in a 'single perspective' which encompasses them both. It is an interesting fact, that while Moltmann charges both Rahner and Barth with modalism, they explicitly reject the modalist idea that the Father suffers.[115] Both Rahner and Barth recognized that to make suffering part of the nature of the eternal God (who existed before all worlds) would be to make God powerless to act as our savior (in history). Thus, for example, replying to a question indicating that Balthasar and others had criticized him for not having a sufficient *theologia crucis* Rahner states:

> In Moltmann and others I sense a theology of absolute paradox, of Patripassianism, perhaps even of a Schelling-like projection into God of division, conflict, godlessness and death. To put it crudely, it does not help me to escape from my mess and mix-up and despair if God is in the

---

[114] Moltmann, *Trinity and Kingdom*, 160–1, emphasis mine.
[115] *CD* I/1, 397. Other references in Moltmann's *Trinity and Kingdom* to the Father suffering are 31, 35, 59, 81 and 83. Moltmann's criticisms of Barth and Rahner can be seen in *Trinity and Kingdom*, 143ff.

same predicament . . . the classical teaching on the Incarnation and the theology of the hypostatic union . . . must include, even while avoiding Patripassianism (a suffering and dying of God the Father), a meaningful and serious statement to the effect that *God* died. . . [but] it is for me a source of consolation to realize that God, when and insofar as he entered into this history as into his own, did it in a different way than I did. From the beginning I am locked into its horribleness while God – if this word continues to have any meaning at all – is in a true and authentic and consoling sense the God *who does not suffer*, the immutable God, and so on.[116]

And in his doctrine of the Trinity Barth explained that

one can say very definitely that any systematising of the one-sidedness [of the trinitarian relations] such as is found in part in ancient Modalism (e.g., in the form of Patripassianism) is absolutely forbidden, since it would mean the dissolution of the triunity in a neutral fourth. The eternity of the fatherhood of God does not mean only the eternity of the fellowship of the Father with the Son and the Spirit. It also protects the Father against fusion with the Son and Spirit . . . [this] would also be incompatible with any serious acceptance of the biblical witness which makes the Father and the Son one in their distinction.[117]

And Barth also captured the positive point regarding God's action *ad extra* mentioned by Rahner indicating that

It is not at all the case that God has no part in the suffering of Jesus Christ even in His mode of being as the Father. No, there is a *particula veri* in the teaching of the Patripassians. This is that primarily it is God the Father who suffers in the offering and sending of His Son, in His abasement. The suffering is not His own, but the alien suffering of the creature, of man, which He takes to Himself in Him. But He does suffer it in the humiliation of His Son with a depth with which it never was or will be suffered by any man – apart from the One who is His Son . . . This fatherly fellow-suffering of God is the mystery, the basis, of the humiliation of His Son; the truth of that which takes place historically in His crucifixion . . .[118]

---

[116] *Karl Rahner in Dialogue: Conversations and Interviews 1965–1982*, ed. Paul Imhof and Hubert Biallowons, trans. Harvey D. Egan (New York: Crossroad, 1986), 126–7, some emphases mine. Moltmann attempts an answer to Rahner's objection in *History and the Triune God*, 123–4. It is evident from Moltmann's reply that while he asserts that God enters our suffering in a divine way, his explanation of this completely discounts any impassibility on the part of God and to that extent misses the point that Rahner was trying to make, that is, that God is both passible and impassible and that we do not have to choose one over the other.

[117] *CD* I/1, 397–8.

[118] *CD* IV/2, 357.

In this analysis there remains a clear distinction between the Father and the Son and between the Father's suffering as a mystery grounded in the immanent Trinity and the creature's suffering which, while not part of God's nature, is experienced by God for the salvation of creatures.

3. After indicating that the sacrifice of love on the cross was neither simply a reaction to sin nor a *free decision* of God's will, Moltmann argues that it is part of love's nature to be capable of suffering. 'Self-sacrifice is God's very nature and essence.'[119] This insight later leads Moltmann to what he considers the following harmonious balance between the Reformed doctrine of decrees and Tillich's emanationism: God's 'divine life flows into his resolve, and from that resolve overflows to his creatures'.[120] And this ultimately persuades Moltmann to argue that creation itself becomes part of God's nature in his sabbath rest.[121]

Openness to the World

Rolt's thinking leads to a view of the Trinity which is 'open' toward the world and, as noted at the beginning of this chapter, this means that

> Love *has* to give, for it is only in the act of giving that it truly possesses, and finds bliss. That is why God *has to give himself*. . . and it is only in this way that he is God. *He has to go through time*; and it is *only* in this way that he is eternal. . . *He has to be man and nothing but man*; and it is only in this way that he is completely God . . . 'It was necessary for God to be Man, for only so could He be truly God.' . . . In order to be completely itself, love has to suffer.[122]

In his creation doctrine this leads Moltmann to conclude that God's descent to human being and his dwelling among them is to be conceived as a 'division which takes place in God himself. God cuts himself off from himself. He gives himself away to his people. He suffers with their sufferings'.[123] Thus,

---

[119] Moltmann, *Trinity and Kingdom*, 32.

[120] Moltmann, *Creation*, 85.

[121] Moltmann, *Creation*, 278ff. Thus, he asserts that God's sabbath 'does not spring from God's activity; it springs from his rest. It does not come from God's acts; it comes from his present Being' (282). Consequently, 'The human sabbath' becomes 'the rhythm of eternity in time' (287). While the tradition held that God's Being and Act are one in order to preserve God's freedom, Moltmann argues that God is directly present in his sabbath and can be equated with the evolution of history itself as it transcends itself (205).

[122] Moltmann, *Trinity and Kingdom*, 33, emphasis mine.

[123] Moltmann, *Creation*, 15 and 86ff.

> God the Spirit is also the Spirit of the universe, its total cohesion, its structure, its information, its energy. The Spirit of the universe is the Spirit who proceeds from the Father and shines forth in the Son. *The evolutions and the catastrophes of the universe are also the movements and experiences of the Spirit of creation.*[124]

And Moltmann writes that it is 'one sided to view creation only as the work of "God's hands" . . . something . . . to be distinguished from God himself. *Creation is also the differentiated presence of God the Spirit,* the presence of the One *in* the many.'[125] Consequently, 'men and women correspond to the Creator in their very essence' and 'God enters into the creatures whom he has designated to be his image.'[126] In this thinking, where is the distinction between the Holy Spirit and the spirit of the universe to be found? Where is the distinction between Christ as the image of the unseen God and sinful creatures who *need* reconciliation to be found? And if it cannot be found, how is our unnatural will to power to be overcome?

Moltmann's analysis explicitly negates God's freedom in the interest of stressing the fact that suffering (the historical suffering of Christ) defines the nature of both God's freedom and love. Clearly, there is and can be no distinction here between time and eternity[127] or between God's eternal begetting of his Son in the unity of the Holy Spirit and his free (gratuitous) actions *ad extra*. Rather, God's creative and salvific functions have integrally absorbed his essence. We have here a prototypical compromise of God's freedom as expressed in the Bible and in the tradition. It is no longer the case that the one God is the single transcendent subject of his actions in his Son and Spirit. Rather, his transcendent being and action is defined by his need to be man, his need to suffer and his need for another outside himself. Moltmann's own explanation of God's freedom leaves him in a logical and theological dilemma. Either he may argue that God really is subject to no internal or external necessities. Then he would have to reject his own panentheist interpretation of the Trinity and of creation because the Christian God who loves is intrinsically free both in nature and will. Or he may argue that God is subject both to internal and to external necessities. Then he would have to reject the biblical and traditional view of creation and of the Trinity. But he cannot logically hold both positions at once. Yet

---

[124] Moltmann, *Creation*, 16, emphasis mine.
[125] Moltmann, *Creation*, 14, some emphases mine.
[126] Moltmann, *Creation*, 77–8.
[127] Moltmann, *Creation*, 287.

that is exactly what he attempts to do, because it is of the very nature of panentheism to conceive of the God–world relation from within a process common to both God and creatures, nature and grace, freedom and necessity, and into which these opposites are resolved by becoming an original perichoretic unity.

Panentheism cannot admit that God could have existed without a world but freely chose not to, that nature is not in itself open for grace but needs grace in order to become open, and that God's freedom excludes the idea that he exists because of any internal or external necessity. It would not be inaccurate to say that in Moltmann's theology, as in so many others that we have already explored, relationality is the subject and God is the predicate instead of the other way around. Thus, he argues that the doctrine of the two natures does not refer to 'two metaphysically different "natures". It is an expression of his exclusive *relationship* to the Father, by reason of his origin, and his inclusive *relationship* of fellowship to his many brothers and sisters. His *relationship* to God is the relation of God's own Son to his Father. His *relationship* to the world is the relationship of the eldest to his brethren.'[128] The fact is that the doctrine of the two natures does refer to two metaphysically distinct natures or it does not convey the same meaning as Chalcedon at all. For the man Jesus was both truly God and truly human as the One Mediator. But since Moltmann conceives the incarnation as the cessation of God's omnipotence,[129] he is forced to substitute for the reality of Jesus, *vere Deus* and *vere homo*, the perichoretic relationship inherent in suffering love itself. This thinking causes the difficulties in both the doctrines of the Trinity and of creation that we have been exploring in this chapter.

Tritheism

Since God cannot be a single subject of his actions *ad extra*, Moltmann at times is actually led to describe three subjects: 'we interpreted salvation

---

[128] Moltmann, *Trinity and Kingdom*, 120, emphasis mine. In connection with the Spirit, Moltmann attempts to overcome pantheism and to improve panentheism arguing that 'It is not the elementary particles that are basic . . . but the overriding *harmony of the relations* and of the self-transcending movements, in which the longing of the Spirit for a still unattained consummation finds expression. If the cosmic Spirit is the Spirit of God, the universe cannot be viewed as a closed system' (*Creation*, 103, emphasis mine). Here, Moltmann's concept of relationality leads to the confusion of the Holy Spirit with the movements of creation once again.

[129] Moltmann, *Trinity and Kingdom*, 118–19, and *Creation*, 88. Consequently 'God becomes omnipresent' (*Creation*, 91).

history as "the history of the Son" of God, Jesus Christ. We understood this history as the trinitarian history of God in the concurrent and joint workings of the three subjects, Father, Son and Spirit'.[130] And in considering the meaning of revelation in relation to Gal. 1:15 Moltmann contends that 'God reveals his Son . . . God does not reveal "himself". He reveals "his Son". The Son is not identical with *God's self.* He is a subject of his own.'[131] In his creation doctrine Moltmann claims that 'The Spirit also acts as an independent subject . . . each subject of the Trinity possesses his own unique personality'.[132] Also, in the kingdom of glory Moltmann believes that 'The kingdom of God is therefore transferred from one divine subject to the other; and its form is changed in the process. *So God's triunity precedes the divine lordship.*'[133] Finally, Moltmann argues that 'On the cross the Father and the Son are so deeply separated that their relationship breaks off.'[134]

Here his modalism returns to haunt him. For God's lordship is the lordship of the God who is simultaneously one and three. Previously, Moltmann argued that God's unity is the unity of his tri-unity and that he would investigate God's threeness and then proceed to ask about his unity; from this it follows that

> the unity of the Trinity cannot be a monadic unity. The unity of the divine tri-unity lies in the *union* of the Father, the Son and the Spirit, not in their numerical unity. It lies in their *fellowship, not in the identity of a single subject.*[135]

Moltmann thus logically concludes that the kingdom of glory can be incomplete and changes when transferred from one subject to another. Among other things such a change would mean that Jesus is not always Lord but becomes and ceases to be Lord in time and as time reaches its fulfillment. This is why Moltmann explicitly redefines the meaning of lordship arguing that, since Christ's lordship is purely economic, the trinitarian formulas are baptismal and that this must be the case because 'the history of the Son . . . is not a completed history'.[136] As 'Christ

---

[130] Moltmann, *Trinity and Kingdom*, 156.

[131] Moltmann, *Trinity and Kingdom*, 86–7.

[132] Moltmann, *Creation*, 97.

[133] Moltmann, *Trinity and Kingdom*, 93, emphasis mine. Moltmann also writes of the divine persons that 'They have the divine nature in common; but their particular *individual nature* is determined in their relationship to one another . . . The three divine Persons exist in their particular, unique natures as Father, Son and Spirit in their relationships to one another, and are determined through these relationships' (172, emphasis mine).

[134] Moltmann, *Trinity and Kingdom*, 82.

[135] Moltmann, *Trinity and Kingdom*, 95, some emphases mine.

[136] Moltmann, *Trinity and Kingdom*, 90.

himself is not . . . as yet complete' Moltmann believes that 1 Cor. 15:28 means that 'The divine rule was given by the Father to the Son through Christ's resurrection' and that 'In the final consummation it will be transferred from the Son to the Father. "The kingdom of the Son" will then become the kingdom of glory . . . in which God will be all in all.'[137] These assertions of course are precisely what led to the charges of tritheism noted above. Intimately connected with this are the problems of adoptionism and subordinationism.[138]

The result of this reasoning is that Moltmann cannot describe God as free to choose to relate with us; rather the Father generates the Son by necessity[139] and 'the love of the Father which brings forth the Son in eternity *becomes* creative love . . . Creation proceeds from the Father's love for the eternal Son.'[140] This reasoning leads Moltmann actually to change the creed which speaks of the Father begetting the Son in eternity in an utterly unique way. He argues that the Father not only begets the Son; this would make him 'a father in the male sense'; the procession of the Son from the Father 'has to be conceived of both as a begetting and as a birth'.[141] Thus, 'He is a motherly father too.' Moltmann's panentheism here overcomes both a 'patriarchal' monotheism of power and lordship and what he calls matriarchal pantheism with this 'bisexual' understanding of the Trinity. This, he believes, is the radical rejection of monotheism.[142] But the fact is that by *adding* the notion of birth to the notion of begetting Moltmann compounds the problem by incorporating bisexual images into the Godhead whereas there ought to be none at all.[143]

---

[137] Moltmann, *Trinity and Kingdom*, 92.

[138] This is why Moltmann argues that for Paul the title Son is not a christological title of sovereignty (*Trinity and Kingdom*, 87–8), while the *New Jerusalem Bible* (New York: Doubleday, 1986) states correctly that for Paul the title Son (as in Rom. 9:5d) implied a strictly divine significance (60, n.d). Moltmann actually believes he has avoided all subordinationism and yet makes the conspicuous subordinationist assertion that 'Through the incarnation of the Son the Father acquires a twofold counterpart for his love: his Son and his image . . . This means an increase of his riches and bliss' (*Trinity and Kingdom*, 121. See also n. 31 above). For a specific discussion of Moltmann's Christology, see Paul D. Molnar, 'Moltmann's Post-Modern Messianic Christology: A Review Discussion', *The Thomist* 56 (1992), 669–93.

[139] Moltmann, *Trinity and Kingdom*, 167. Cf. also 58.

[140] Moltmann, *Trinity and Kingdom*, 168.

[141] Moltmann, *Trinity and Kingdom*, 164

[142] Moltmann, *Trinity and Kingdom*, 165.

[143] Cf., e.g., *Athanasius's Orations against the Arians*, in Rusch (ed.), *The Trinitarian Controversy*, Book 1, 21, 84: 'if God is not as man (for he is not), it is not necessary to attribute to him the characteristics of man', also 86, 'God begets not as men beget but as God begets. God does not copy man. Rather, we men, because God rightfully and alone truly is the Father of his Son, have been named fathers of our own children.' That is, God

Moltmann makes the same mistake in his doctrine of creation, arguing that, while *creatio ex nihilo* means a calling something into existence without precondition, creation is also determined by God's withdrawal within. Thus the doctrine must mean that God creates 'by letting-be, by making room, and by withdrawing himself. The creative making is expressed in masculine metaphors. But the creative letting-be is better brought out through motherly categories.'[144] The problem here is that the use of masculine or motherly categories is irrelevant to the issue of whether, in the trinitarian and creation doctrines, the Bible intended to present us with the idea that creation ought to be understood as emanation or as the incomprehensible work which could be properly understood through faith in the Son. Then it could not be explained at all by arguing that God's love means incorporation of nothingness into the inner being of the Trinity and subsequently arguing that creation results from that negation. That is precisely the mythology that the *creatio ex nihilo* was originally designed to protect against. Even more important, however, is the fact that Moltmann distorts the fact that references to God the Father in the Bible and in the tradition were not references to maleness or femaleness as they were in pagan and gnostic religions.[145] Moltmann's suggestion that we correct our unnatural will for power by including feminine characteristics within the Godhead therefore amounts to a redefinition of God's immanent Trinity using bisexual imagery drawn from human experience. As seen above in Chapter One, Christians rejected this kind of thinking not because they were trying to impose patriarchal power models on others, but in the knowledge that God is not as we are, that is, creatures who are sexually limited.

Because Moltmann compromises God's freedom to choose, he argues that 'Freedom arrives at its divine truth through love. Love is a self-evident, unquestionable "overflowing of goodness" which is therefore *never open to choice at any time.* We have to understand true freedom as being the self-communication of the good.'[146] In Moltmann's synthesis of freedom and love we find the necessary emanation of the divine

---

the Father's unique begetting of his only Son transcends *any* such attempt to define his essence in terms of male or female sexuality. Cf. also Roland M. Frye, 'Language for God and Feminist Language: Problems and Principles', *SJT*, esp. 444ff. and the discussion of this issue above in Chapter One.

[144] Moltmann, *Creation*, 88.

[145] Cf. Frye, 'Language for God and Feminist Language', *SJT* 444 and Chapter One above.

[146] Moltmann, *Trinity and Kingdom*, 55.

goodness which the traditional doctrines intended to protect against. This then is clearly the pantheistic emanationism that was necessary to Moltmann's understanding of God's love from the outset; here there is and can be no actual distinction between the Father begetting the Son and the act of creation *ad extra* resulting from a new decision and act on the part of God. It is this thinking that leads quite logically to the idea that 'the Son's sacrifice . . . on Golgotha is from eternity already included in the essential exchange of the essential, the consubstantial love which *constitutes* the divine life of the Trinity'.[147] This leads Moltmann to believe that God's love is

> literally ecstatic love: it leads him to go out of himself and to create something which is different from himself but which none the less corresponds to him. The delight with which the Creator celebrates the feast of creation – the sabbath – makes it unequivocally plain that creation was called into being out of the inner love which the eternal God himself *is*.[148]

This emanationist interpretation of creation envisions God's mysterious and miraculous act of *creatio ex nihilo* not as an *act* of God's free *will* and decision expressing his being as the one who loves, but as a coming into being out of the inner love that God is as one who suffers.

We have returned to where we began. Can we understand and maintain God's freedom as implied in the doctrines of creation and of the Trinity if we believe that the traditional dualities can be transcended in a common being which they are said to share now or in the future? Since God is and remains distinct from creatures, even as he suffers for them in the cross of Christ, I have argued that Moltmann's belief that God needs creatures is an idea necessary to his panentheist re-interpretation of freedom but excluded from the perception of faith. Moltmann cannot maintain the freedom of God because he believes that 'The so-called "sovereignty" of the triune God . . . proves to be his sustaining fellowship with his creation and his people.'[149]

> Here the social analogy applies to the divine fellowship which is formed through the mutual indwelling of the Father in the Son, and of the Son in the Father through the Spirit. Here it does not mean the Fatherhood or the Sonship; it means the community within the Trinity. It is the *relations* in the Trinity which are the levels represented on earth through the *imago Trinitatis*, not the levels of the trinitarian *constitution*.[150]

[147] Moltmann, *Trinity and Kingdom*, 168, emphasis mine.
[148] Moltmann, *Creation*, 76.
[149] Moltmann, *Creation*, 241.

The problem with this reasoning is that Moltmann believes he can speak about the trinitarian relations *without* speaking about the essential constitution of the Trinity *as* Father, Son and Spirit by which we know of these relations. The only way this can be done is if the unity of the Trinity is conceived modalistically as a neutral fourth (fellowship/relationship) which can be appropriated apart from any specific reference to the Father, Son or Spirit acting *ad extra*.[151] The purpose of this chapter has been to indicate why I think this cannot be done.

As seen in Chapter Five, Ted Peters adopted the views of Catherine LaCugna in order to present his relational understanding of the Trinity. Ted Peters mistakenly believes that Moltmann is not guilty of tritheism because 'tritheism has never been a genuine temptation for Christian faith'.[152] Still, he believes that 'The essence of Moltmann's position is that when it comes to divine action we have three subjects, or *loci*, of activity, not one.'[153] Thus, Peters believes that Moltmann's 'social doctrine of the Trinity' that 'begins with the plurality and only then asks about the unity'[154] actually avoids tritheism although, in the end, Peters thinks that Moltmann may end up with a 'divine nominalism' that consists of a 'single infinite Godhead composed of three finite gods'.[155] In the end, however, Peters believes that Moltmann has drawn out 'some of the implications of the seriousness with which Karl Barth viewed God's interaction with world history . . . Echoing Hegel, he says the Trinity achieves its integrative unity principally by uniting itself with the history of the world . . . God's unity is not simply an original unity.'[156]

But of course that is exactly the problem I have highlighted throughout this book. A proper trinitarian theology must begin thinking from a center in God as this has been manifested in Jesus Christ and through the Holy Spirit. Such a starting point will immediately lead one to acknowledge that we begin neither with plurality *nor* with unity, but with the triune God who is simultaneously one and three. Therefore,

---

[150] Moltmann, *Creation*, 241.

[151] This faulty thinking results from Moltmann's rejection of the traditional doctrine of appropriation. 'Contrary to the Augustinian tradition, it is not that the work of creation is only "*appropriated*" to the Father, though being actually the work of the whole Trinity. On the contrary, creation is actually a product of the Father's love and is ascribed to the whole Trinity' (*Trinity and Kingdom*, 112). We have seen what Moltmann means by this.

[152] Peters, *Trinity*, 103. We have noted above that Harnack cites several tritheists and that George Hunsinger thinks Moltmann is as close to a tritheist as one could get.

[153] Peters, *Trinity*, 104.

[154] Peters, *Trinity*, 104.

[155] Peters, *Trinity*, 109.

it will be evident that in a Christian doctrine of God we are dealing with one divine subject precisely because God is one. But that one divine subject is the eternal Father, Son and Spirit and therefore God's unity can neither be perceived nor known apart from faith in his Son, and without the operation of the Holy Spirit. Father, Son and Spirit are not three subjects, just because God is essentially one and three and never is one first or three first. While Peters acknowledges that Moltmann comes close to eliminating the need for the immanent Trinity, he nevertheless believes that he does not 'totally conflate the two' and concludes that 'for Moltmann there finally can be only one Trinity, the economic Trinity . . . the immanent Trinity is the product of pious imagination'.[156] Having said this, Peters reveals once again his own basic failure to understand Barth's theology and his inability to comprehend the practical significance of acknowledging God's freedom as the basis of human freedom. He claims that Moltmann carries through on Barth's attempt to allow history in some sense to dictate God's unity. But as we saw above, nothing could be further from the truth. Because Barth's thinking was shaped by an actual acknowledgment of the freedom of the immanent Trinity disclosed in the economic Trinity, he consistently refused to allow history to dictate the divine unity. He certainly did not think that the immanent Trinity was the projection of our imagination.

In the next chapter we shall explore the work of two important theologians who also claim to be indebted to Barth, while moving beyond what they perceive to be Barth's modalist tendencies and other limitations believed to be associated with Barth's *analogia fidei*. Unlike Jürgen Moltmann, Ted Peters and Catherine LaCugna, these theologians not only do not ignore or deny the need for a proper doctrine of the immanent Trinity, but actually insist upon it. How then can the work of Alan Torrance and Eberhard Jüngel help us toward a positive understanding of divine and human freedom that takes seriously our inclusion by grace in God's own internal relations? What are the strengths and weaknesses of their critiques of Barth's theology? These are the questions that will be considered in the next chapter.

---

[156] Peters, *Trinity*, 110.
[157] Peters, *Trinity*, 107–8.

Chapter Eight

Persons in Communion and God as the Mystery of the World: Alan Torrance, Eberhard Jüngel and the Doctrine of the Immanent Trinity

I HAVE argued that a clear and sharp distinction between the immanent and economic Trinity will be necessary in order to stress that creation, reconciliation and redemption are not necessities grounded either in transcendental experience, suffering or love or some principle of relationality or of communion. Positively stated, the practical acknowledgment of God's internal freedom means that human freedom must continually find its basis and meaning outside itself and in God himself, that is, in God's external freedom exercised in his Word and Spirit on our behalf. Karl Barth's theology is helpful here because his theological thinking always left room for the fact that only God himself could be the proof that is necessary for theology to succeed.[1] Thus, when Barth spoke of faith he said,

> Not, then as experience is faith faith, i.e., real experience, even though it is certainly experience. Or, the act of acknowledgment is not as such acknowledgment of the Word of God. Nor is it this in virtue of any

---

[1] See, e.g., *CD* I/1, 264 where Barth speaks of the fact that the Bible must speak and we must hear saying, 'If it is asked with what right we say this, we answer: By no right that we have and claim for ourselves, but by the right that proves itself to be such in the event of faith when it occurs.'

perfection with which it is performed. It is the Word, Christ, to whom faith refers because He presents himself to it as its object, that makes faith faith, real experience.[2]

When he spoke of analogy he said,

> If there is a real analogy between God and man – an analogy which is a true analogy of being on both sides, an analogy in and with which the knowledge of God will in fact be given – what other analogy can it be than the analogy of being which is posited and created by the work and action of God Himself, the analogy which has its actuality from God and from God alone, and therefore in faith and in faith alone?[3]

And when he rejected the doctrine of the *vestigia* in connection with his denial that there could be a second root of the doctrine of the Trinity, he wrote, 'Revelation would not be revelation if any man were in a position to advance and to establish against others the claim that he specifically speaks of and from revelation. If we know what revelation is, even in deliberately speaking about it we shall be content to let revelation speak for itself.'[4] For Barth, then, 'what God says to us specifically remains His secret which will be disclosed in the event of His actual speaking'.[5] All of this thinking illustrates that for Barth our knowledge of God is 'an event enclosed in the mystery of the divine Trinity'.[6]

And it is important to note that for Barth knowledge was not merely a matter of viewing and conceiving God correctly, or obediently. Even though such knowledge involves correct knowledge of God, which takes place only through God himself, it includes the determination of our entire being without compromising our human self-determination.[7] This is why Barth insists that we are taken up into the life of the immanent Trinity and that anything we say about knowledge of God 'consists in the fact that we speak also and first of this event [that takes place in the mystery of the Trinity on high]. But we are now speaking of the revelation of this event on high and therefore of our participation in it.'[8] As seen above in Chapter Two, Barth insisted that the starting point and conclusion of theological reflection must be Jesus Christ

---

[2] *CD* I/1, 230.
[3] *CD* II/1, 83.
[4] *CD* I/1, 346–7.
[5] *CD* I/1, 143.
[6] *CD* II/1, 181.
[7] See *CD* I/1, 207–8 and 246f.
[8] *CD* II/1, 181.

himself and no one and nothing else. This starting point clearly separates Barth from Rahner and, as we shall see, it is Alan Torrance's failure to see the depths of this difference that leads him to think that Rahner made explicit the problems that were implicit in Barth's theology, because their theologies were so similar.

This chapter will not be an exhaustive treatment of the theology of Alan Torrance and Eberhard Jüngel. It will focus instead on some of their positive contributions toward a contemporary doctrine of the immanent Trinity; just as in the next chapter we shall explore the thought of Colin Gunton toward that same end. But in both chapters I will also call attention to several important aspects of Barth's theology that figure less prominently in their theologies and could, if properly employed, help to strengthen their arguments for a suitably conceived doctrine of the immanent Trinity. I have chosen to explore the thinking of these important theologians because each of them sees the significance of a doctrine of the immanent Trinity in a way that many of those discussed above do not. Each of these theologians is critical of Barth's theology in different ways, even though each supports Barth's basic recognition of God's freedom. It is hoped that by critically exploring the nature of some of their key criticisms and some of their proposed solutions a clearer understanding of the nature and function of a doctrine of the immanent Trinity will emerge.

Alan Torrance, *Persons in Communion*

The most important positive point to be gained from Alan Torrance's book, *Persons in Communion*, is that a proper understanding of the immanent Trinity will lead to a perception that humanity is included in a relationship with God by grace in such a way that our human participation within the Trinity excludes any Pelagianism or extrinsicism. The strength of this position is that, since our inclusion in God's trinitarian life is grounded in God's own freedom exercised for us in Jesus' own life, death, resurrection, and ongoing high-priestly mediation, it is certainly not something that remains external to us on the one hand, and on the other hand, it has an unshakeable and unassailable foundation – a foundation that is not at all dependent on our sinful human action to be beneficial to us. According to Torrance's doxological or worship model we participate in the priesthood of Christ through worship. This model directs us

> to that event of triune communion which is conceived not as a 'mode of being' to be appropriated or taken on by the human subject, but as the

gift of sharing in the life of the Second Adam . . . living out of *his* life lived in place of ours (his worthship), *his* continuing and vicarious priesthood (his worship) and in *his* union and communion with the Father in the Spirit.[9]

And this is not to be seen as a task (as Moltmann mistakenly appears to do with Pelagian results) but as a gift: 'our worship is the *gift of participating, through the Spirit, in what Christ has done and is doing for us in his intercessions and communion with the Father*'.[10]

By contrast, according to Torrance, Moltmann sees worship as a task that we must perform and this compromises the freedom of grace with the result that the emphasis in worship falls on our activity rather than on the fact that our activity has been and is included by God in Christ's activity on our behalf. Torrance believes that Moltmann's 'Pelagian interpretation of worship results from a near collapse of the "immanent" Trinity into the economic Trinity' which is brought about in part by his 'adoption of a form of panentheism that fails adequately to distinguish between God's time and created temporality'.[11] Thus, in Torrance's view, Moltmann undermines a proper emphasis on God's transcendence in the event of doxological participation and in the end historicizes God by

> 'cementing' God into the process of the human struggle . . . Moltmann fails to appreciate the extent to which participation in God's intra-divine glory requires to be described as a participation on the part of the human person in the transcendent triune Life. Doxological participation is an event of *grace* – a concept which barely features in Moltmann's theology – and not, therefore, of any natural human response or innate capacity.[12]

Part of Torrance's argument here is aimed at countering Rahner's notion of a supernatural existential as well. But Torrance's positive interest is to assert that worship is an 'event of "theopoietic" *koinonia*, which is both "in Christ" and "through the Spirit", and one, therefore, in which the Kingdom of God is "in a manner" actually and freely *present* – and not merely future, as Moltmann seems to suggest'.[13] God's unconditional grace requires human worship, but human worship is a gift of participating in Christ's high priesthood because he alone offers the required

[9] Torrance, *Persons in Communion*, 324.
[10] Torrance, *Persons in Communion*, 311, emphasis in original.
[11] Torrance, *Persons in Communion*, 311–12.
[12] Torrance, *Persons in Communion*, 313.
[13] Torrance, *Persons in Communion*, 313.

worship on our behalf. This act of worship, which Torrance calls 'worthship' 'denotes the form of communion with God required by God's grace' and it includes 'epistemic truthfulness'. Accordingly, theological epistemology is grounded in doxological participation rather than the other way around.

Torrance clarifies his positive point further by analyzing and criticizing LaCugna's position. Like Moltmann, she 'falls into a Pelagian tendency in her conception of salvation'[14] and because she fails to appreciate the importance of the Nicene *homoousion* 'she is led to what tends to be a synergistic conception of human fellowship with the Trinity'.[15] In short, like Moltmann, there is little room in LaCugna's analysis for what God has done and is doing. The emphasis falls on what we do. While Torrance believes that Moltmann and LaCugna were correct to tie the doctrine of the Trinity to worship, he believes that neither of them allowed the object of worship, that is, Christ himself to determine what they had to say. Hence in Torrance's mind, 'the primary end of the sacraments [is] the discovery of our righteousness as it is "included" by grace within the righteousness of God in Christ, and the liberation to live in the light of the fact that we have been made righteous in and through the vicarious faithfulness of Christ'.[16] According to Torrance, LaCugna misunderstands both *orthodoxy* and *orthopraxis* because she failed to understand the 'dynamic of grace'.

What then is the positive dynamic of grace that Torrance espouses? For Torrance, 'The event of grace does not stop where the free human response begins; it includes precisely that human response to the extent that the human response is completed on our behalf in Christ. Grace relates not only to the anhypostatic movement, but to the enhypostatic movement as well.'[17] For Torrance even the desire to do God's will is given us in Christ 'as we are brought to participate in *his* human life and live "out of" the vicarious worship (as this includes the totality of human "worthship") provided in him by the Spirit *on our behalf* – and where we are thereby recreated to live *out of* this event of grace in all its *objectivity*'.[18]

This is the ultimate positive point that Torrance wishes to convey in his book, namely, that we are drawn by grace into the communion of

---

[14] Torrance, *Persons in Communion*, 316.
[15] Torrance, *Persons in Communion*, 317.
[16] Torrance, *Persons in Communion*, 318.
[17] Torrance, *Persons in Communion*, 318–19.
[18] Torrance, *Persons in Communion*, 319.

the trinitarian relations by the Spirit and so we are recreated, with the result that it is Christ living in us who enables our thinking and action in such a way that our thinking and action are not obliterated or confused with the divine action (as in the thought of Moltmann and LaCugna) but upheld and brought to completion in Christ. In Torrance's words: 'we are brought to live "out of" Christ by the Spirit in such a way that "we are no longer under the supervision of the law"'.[19] This means that it is not our ethical behavior that establishes or maintains communion with God, but God himself. We are made righteous through Christ's faithfulness and it is this righteousness that is given in Christ. The true dynamics of grace then involve our human movement toward God that is

> realised in and through the Son and which constitutes, through a parallel movement of the Spirit, the ground of our communion in the divine life. This means that the trinitarian relations *ad intra* are to be conceived as open to us as creatures. It is this free and dynamic opening to humanity of the divine communion that constitutes worship as the transforming possibility for humanity – where worship is conceived as the gift of participating in the human priesthood of the Son through the presence of the Spirit.[20]

Except for the fact that worship tends to displace Christ's present action as Lord in relation to us, Torrance's thinking here is important. He clearly achieves what Rahner himself intended with his axiom of identity, namely, a proper integration of our human activity, especially in worship with the Father, Son and Holy Spirit. And he does so in such a way that grace is recognizable as grace and is therefore not confused with some universal aspect of our transcendental experience. In fact, as we shall see, Torrance is properly critical of just this aspect of Rahner's thought. In opposition to those who would assume that transcendental theology is the only possible way to understand the significance of the Trinity today, Alan Torrance shows quite plainly that a trinitarian theology that is actually grounded in God's freedom for us must continually look away from itself and toward Christ as its objective ground. And subjectively such a theology will be actualized in and through the Holy Spirit uniting us to Christ's own worship and faithfulness. This thinking is surely in accord with Thomas F. Torrance's crucial insight that we must think from a center in God rather than from a center in ourselves, if our thinking about God and humanity is

---

[19] Torrance, *Persons in Communion*, 320.
[20] Torrance, *Persons in Communion*, 323.

to be accurate and true. This simple Athanasian insight, with its profound implications, is the theme of this book. A trinitarian theology that does not in fact think from a center in God (a center that can only be given by God in Christ and through the Spirit) is bound to end in some form of agnosticism. Such a theology will then find it necessary to fill the void in knowing God with its own fabrications. As documented above, this will inevitably lead both toward monism (pantheism) and toward dualism (the separation of God from Christ with Pelagian or extrinsicist results).

Barth, Torrance and the Limits of Trinitarian Thinking: 'Revelation Model' or 'Communion Model'?

While Torrance's positive position is exactly where a theology that is properly cognizant of the doctrine of the immanent Trinity should lead, the road he takes to get to this conclusion is not completely without its potholes. Torrance is very critical of Barth for choosing 'modes of being' rather than person to describe the 'members' of the Trinity and because he believes that Barth's so-called 'revelation model' obscures the fact that communion is intrinsic to our knowledge of God and our relation with God. Still, he sees himself only modifying Barth's theology and not rejecting it. Let us discuss these important issues briefly.

We have just noted that for Barth our knowledge of God is 'an event enclosed in the mystery of the divine Trinity'. By this Barth meant to assert that

> Knowledge of God . . . as the knowledge of God which is objectively and subjectively established and led to its goal by God Himself, the knowledge of God whose subject and object is God the Father and the Son through the Holy Spirit, is the basis – and indeed the only basis – of the love of God which comes to us and the praise of God which is expected of us.[21]

Hence, 'even as an action undertaken and performed by man, knowledge of God is objectively and subjectively both instituted by God Himself and led to its end by Him; because God the Father and the Son by the Holy Spirit is its primary and proper subject and object'.[22] Barth asserts that God gives 'us a part in this event in the grace of His revelation'.[23] For this reason we may proceed with assurance and without

---

[21] *CD* II/1, 180.
[22] *CD* II/1, 204.
[23] *CD* II/1, 204.

skepticism. But we must remember that God is hidden. Still, God is an object of our cognition because he chooses to make himself so and for that reason Barth again insists that 'Knowledge of God is then an event enclosed in the bosom of the divine Trinity.'[24] Reinterpreting the doctrine of appropriation Barth insists that knowledge of the unity of God's essence and work

> will not lead us beyond revelation and faith, but into revelation and faith, to their correct understanding . . . In no sense does God's unity mean the dissolution of His triunity . . . the unity of their work [i.e. that of the Father, Son and Holy Spirit] is to be understood as the communion of the three modes of being along the lines of the doctrine of 'perichoresis'. . . according to which all three, without forfeiture or mutual dissolution of independence, reciprocally interpenetrate each other and inexist in one another . . .[25]

Because of this, in Barth's mind, 'the Triune is the subject of the *opus ad extra indivisum*'.[26]

Barth's belief that our knowledge of God is an event enclosed within the Trinity is significant, because it seems to me to discredit Alan Torrance's most important criticism of Barth's theology, that is, that his 'revelation model' obscures the importance of our communion with God. Barth himself would have been unhappy with the whole idea of models because, in his view, one does not choose a 'revelation model' or a 'communion model' or a 'doxological model' in order to explicate the meaning of the doctrine of the Trinity. Rather, for Barth, such knowledge was and must remain based on the knowledge of God revealed in and by Christ himself, as the Word incarnate. We are, as Barth noted, led into revelation and faith by the knowledge of the triune God and not beyond revelation and faith. As seen above, this obviated any opening toward Ebionite or Docetic interpretations of revelation. That is exactly why Barth understood our knowledge of God as an event enclosed in the mystery of the Trinity. Such knowledge could only take place in acknowledgment precisely because God is the one who initiates, sustains and completes our knowledge of him. This is especially true in Christology where Barth insisted that Jesus was not the revealer in his humanity as such. For Barth then, revelation was not just informational. Revelation was and is identical with Jesus Christ,

---

[24] *CD* II/1, 205.
[25] *CD* I/1, 396.
[26] *CD* I/1, 396.

and as such revelation meant and means that we are included in God's own self-knowledge, love and fellowship by grace.[27]

Here I agree with George Hunsinger who observes that Alan Torrance 'fails to appreciate the inseparability Barth establishes between "knowledge" (*Erkenntnis*) and "fellowship" or "communion" (*Gemeinschaft*) throughout his theology, not only centrally in II/1 but as early as I/1'.[28] Hunsinger cites an important text in *CD* I/1 that bears repeating here. For Barth the intra-divine fellowship of the Holy Spirit is the basis of the fact that

> there is in revelation a fellowship in which not only is God there for man but in very truth – this is the *donum Spiritus sancti* – man is also there for God . . . in this fellowship in revelation which is created between God and man by the Holy Spirit there may be discerned the fellowship in God Himself, the eternal love of God: discerned as the mystery, surpassing all understanding, of the possibility of this reality of revelation; discerned as the one God in the mode of being of the Holy Spirit.[29]

Again, this is part of what Barth meant when he insisted that knowledge of God is an event enclosed within the mystery of the Trinity. In contrast to the widespread agnosticism discussed above, Barth insisted that God reveals his innermost essence to us by revealing his name (as Father, Son and Spirit). And because God's being and act are one and God's eternal essence is 'His act as Father, Son and Holy Spirit'[30] Barth argues that

> God is He who, without having to do so, seeks and creates fellowship between Himself and us. He does not have to do it, because in Himself without us . . . He has that which He seeks and creates between Himself and us . . . He wills to be ours, and He wills that we should be His. He wills to belong to us and He wills that we should belong to Him . . . He does not exist in solitude but in fellowship. Therefore what He seeks and creates between Himself and us is in fact nothing else but what He wills

---

[27] For Barth 'Jesus *is* the revelation of the Father and the revelation of the Father *is* Jesus. And precisely in virtue of this "is" He is the Son or Word of the Father.' Barth insists that the apostolic thinking about Jesus 'always ended with the knowledge of Christ's deity because it had already begun there' (*CD* I/1, 412). But none of this is under our control: 'The knowability of the Word of God stands or falls, then, with the act of its real knowledge, which is not under our control' (*CD* I/1, 224). Real knowledge of God must find its assurance not in itself but in the Word of God so that 'His assurance is his own assurance, but it has its seat outside him in the Word of God . . .' (*CD* I/1, 224–5).

[28] Hunsinger, *Disruptive Grace*, 144, n. 20.

[29] *CD* I/1, 480.

[30] *CD* II/1, 273.

and completes and therefore is in Himself. It therefore follows that as He receives us through His Son into His fellowship with Himself, this is the one necessity, salvation and blessing for us, than which there is no greater blessing – no greater . . .[31]

Everything here turns on the perception of grace. Barth's insistence that theology must begin and end with Jesus Christ himself reflected his belief that grace is God's unmerited and free act of mercy on our behalf. Hence, even in the context of the ethical question, Barth refused to relegate theology to a separate sphere and then allow for an independent ethics. He was thus led to ask of those who sought to separate theological and philosophical ethics:

Outside and alongside the kingdom of Jesus Christ are there other respectable kingdoms? Can and should theology of all things be content to speak not with universal validity, but only esoterically? . . . as if Jesus Christ had not died and risen again; as if we could *salute the grace of God*, as it were, and then go our own way . . .[32]

And by this Barth meant to stress that God both veils himself and unveils himself in revelation without surrendering his prerogative. This meant that our inclusion in revelation was not demanded by God's essence or by ours; yet we could ignore it only at our peril. It has its free basis in the fact that God really is for us specifically in Christ and by the Spirit. For Barth

Hearing man, as the object of the purpose of the speaking God, is thus included in the concept of the Word of God as a factual necessity, but he is not essential to it. He is not, as I most astonishingly stated on p. 111 of the first edition, 'co-posited' in it the way Schleiermacher's God is in the feeling of absolute dependence. If he is co-posited in it with factual necessity, this is God's free grace.[33]

This is why it is important to realize that, when Barth puzzled over the term person and finally chose mode of being instead of person, he was not arguing on the basis of an agnostic position as Torrance seems to think.[34] Rather he was stressing that no word can make conceivable to us what only God can reveal according to his promise fulfilled in Christ. Thus, in *CD* II/1, Barth emphasizes that we do indeed know God's inner nature as Father, Son, and Spirit – as the One who loves in

[31] *CD* II/1, 273–5.
[32] *CD* II/2, 526, emphasis mine.
[33] *CD* I/1, 140.
[34] Torrance, *Persons in Communion*, 229f.

freedom. Importantly, Barth uses the word 'person' to stress that God is a 'knowing, willing, acting subject' in relation to us.[35] Barth rejects the word 'person' only in the sense that it connotes the idea that three subjects might be acting in relation to us.[36] In fact, Barth did not 'want to outlaw the concept of person or to put it out of circulation'.[37] Instead, he argued that those who want to use it can do so only because they do not have a better concept to replace it with. In effect, Barth uses the word 'person' to denote God's personal essence as the one divine subject, while speaking of his acts as Father, Son and Spirit as modes of being. Alan Torrance himself admits that God is both one person and three persons: 'Theologically speaking, *koinonia* . . . allows us to speak simultaneously of the person (singular) of God and the persons (plural) of the Trinity.'[38] And Torrance says that the term 'person' is not absolutely necessary: 'there is no "absolute" need to use the term "person" with respect to the members of the Trinity'.[39] But the point here is simply this: Torrance's choice of the term 'person' led him to find the continuity of revelation in communion and then in revelation. Barth's choice led him to allow his notion of communion to be dictated by Christ himself and so argued that human inclusion in revelation is not integral to revelation, but is a factual inclusion that cannot imply priority of one over the other because God, who seeks and creates fellowship with us, is already God who is complete in himself. And it may also be noted that Barth continually insisted that it is God the Father, the Son and the Holy Spirit who defines trinitarian thinking. Hence, his thought about the 'members' of the Trinity was rigorously dictated by the *act* of God denoted in scripture, namely, the actions of the Father, Son and Spirit as the One who loves in freedom. Torrance's criticism that 'modes of being do not love at all. Hence they cannot love each other'[40] is easily answered since for Barth modes of being were not abstractly defined, but were identified with the personal activities of the God who *is* one *as* the Father, Son and Holy Spirit. For this reason there is in God a unique knowledge, love and mutuality, and God loves creatures by freely creating, saving and redeeming them in and through his Word and Spirit. What Barth is clearly able to maintain is the identity of God's essence in his act of being Father, Son

---

[35] See *CD* II/1, 284ff.
[36] *CD* II/1, 297.
[37] *CD* I/1, 359.
[38] Torrance, *Persons in Communion*, 256–7.
[39] Torrance, *Persons in Communion*, 335.
[40] Torrance, *Persons in Communion*, 116.

and Holy Spirit. What Barth is clearly seeking to avoid is any attempt to find the root of the doctrine in anyone or anything other than revelation, namely, God's Word and Spirit.

Still, in order to accentuate his point that we cannot comprehend the divine essence, even when we know God in accordance with his revelation, Barth insists that we cannot explain the *how* of revelation; this, because when we know it, such knowledge itself is a miracle – it is an act begun, upheld and completed by God alone and hence can only be accepted and not explained. A miracle that could be explained, in Barth's estimation, would not be a miracle. Thus, 'the knowledge of God's Word is no other than the reality of the grace of God coming to man, whose How as a reality is as hidden from us as God Himself is'.[41] For Barth, then, it is because the incarnation itself is grounded in God's inner being and act that we can neither explain *how* God can be and remain totally transcendent and free and yet simultaneously become man,[42] nor *how* God can be revealed yet hidden, nor *how* God can be triune.[43] Indeed for Barth the purpose of Chalcedon and the two natures doctrine was not to control this mystery of Christ but to state it. Thus, our knowledge of the immanent Trinity (God *in se*) is indirect knowledge; it takes place only in acknowledging the supremacy of God's action *ad extra* in Christ. This respects Gregory of Nyssa's insistence that the *how* of the two natures is beyond our understanding; nevertheless 'Its being an event (its *gegenesthai*) is beyond question for us.'[44]

> What it [the Church] sees directly is only the little child in His humanity; it sees the Father only in the light that falls upon the Son, and the Son only in this light from the Father. This is the way, in fact, that the Church believes in and recognizes God in Christ . . . to all visual appearance He is literally nothing but a human being . . . This is the place of Christology. It faces the mystery. It does not stand within the mystery.[45]

Because God is really veiled in his revelation we do not stand within the mystery of revelation.

Here there is a fundamental disagreement over the limits of language. For Alan Torrance 'the communion event . . . constitutes revelation'.[46]

---

[41] *CD* I/1, 227.
[42] *CD* I/1, 476–7. This applies also to election (*CD* II/2, 20ff.) and to knowledge of God's hiddenness and wisdom (*CD* II/1, 184 and 510ff.).
[43] *CD* I/1, 367.
[44] *CD* I/2, 126.
[45] *CD* I/2, 125.
[46] Torrance, *Persons in Communion*, 230.

But, with communion as the subject, there is very little room in Alan Torrance's analysis for God to think, decide and act in relation to us. Rather we are said to participate in a 'communion event'. In fact for Torrance

> it is indeed appropriate to speak of a *vestigium creaturae in trinitate* with respect to the trinitarian event of Self-revelation. God's Self-identification in Christ, within the created order, commits us to, indeed *demands* of us, the affirmation that the created order, to the extent that it is integral to this event, is indeed taken into the event of the triune Being of God with us.[47]

For Torrance this implies that our speech about God can take place because God creates and sustains

> by the Spirit, an essential *continuity* here in such a way that our affirmation of the personhood of Christ becomes at one and the same time the affirmation of the second person of the Triunity ... What is implied here is what one might term a *creative continuity* which involves a semantic continuity grounded in a divine dynamic which takes the form of the redemptive commandeering of our terms and grammar to the extent that in Christ's 'becoming' our language or semantic thought forms 'become' integral to the reconciling and atoning dimension of the Christ event.[48]

In what sense is the created order integral to the event of revelation if it is included factually by grace? Where does Torrance find that continuity? He clearly wishes to find it in Christ. But it would appear, that because he thinks our 'adoption in Christ and participation through the Spirit must be essential elements of an interpretation of revelation',[49] he goes beyond the limit recognized by Barth. For Torrance we are brought by the Spirit 'epistemically and semantically to *indwell* the triune life as created human beings and, thereby, to participate in created ways in the Son's eternal communion with the Father. As this happens the fully human semantic means of this indwelling are *interiorised* within us, becoming constitutive of our personhood'.[50] Can one really say that the semantic means of Christ's indwelling become constitutive of our personhood? What would happen to our *need* for a present action of God to constitute our personhood if this is thought to be true? Barth

---

[47] Torrance, *Persons in Communion*, 209, emphasis in original.
[48] Torrance, *Persons in Communion*, 210, emphasis in original.
[49] Torrance, *Persons in Communion*, 104.
[50] Torrance, *Persons in Communion*, 354, emphasis in original.

argued that no theological construction had the wherewithal to effect knowledge of God. Torrance says the same thing, that is, 'Semantic atonement is realized in Christ alone and is not a property of our language.'[51] But it is not always clear that this remains true precisely because Torrance finds the continuity between God and creatures in semantic thought forms that he believes have become integral to the Christ event. As we shall see shortly, similar difficulties arise when Torrance relies on Jüngel to speak of God's overflow and of the fact that love heightens and expands God's own being in great self-relatedness and still more selflessness;[52] we will have to ask whether or not he has tried to explain what really remains a mystery even when it is revealed. Can God be 'more selfless'?

All this leads Torrance to find a continuity between our language and Christ's act that no longer must seek its veracity in a present act of God's Word and Spirit. Instead, the continuity is sought and found, following John Zizioulas, in his 'establishing the primacy of communion over revelation'.[53] Accordingly, 'his [Zizioulas's] discussion offers support for interpreting revelation in the context of a proper appreciation of the divine communion and human participation . . . rather than the other way round'.[54] But this conclusion leads exactly to a compromise of the freedom of grace from within Barth's theology because, for Barth, revelation is precisely our inclusion in the event of fellowship that is internal to God made possible by God's free action *ad extra* in the history of Jesus Christ and through the Holy Spirit. In Barth's thinking one could never claim that communion has priority over revelation, precisely because it is only in and through revelation that we know of and participate in the eternal communion of his only begotten Son through the Holy Spirit in the first place. Because God's being and act are one, revelation and communion are equally important for us. To allow divine communion *and* human participation to become the subject of the predicate, revelation would mean a failure to recognize grace as grace.

This difficulty is compounded by the fact that Torrance adopts LaCugna's rather imprecise assertion that '"God by nature is self-expressive, God seeks to reveal and give Godself . . ." and that "This is consistent with the biblical images of a God who is alive, who is ineluctably oriented 'otherward', who is plenitude of love, grace and

[51] Torrance, *Persons in Communion*, 369.
[52] Torrance, *Persons in Communion*, 281.
[53] Torrance, *Persons in Communion*, 304.
[54] Torrance, *Persons in Communion*, 305.

mercy overflowing.'"[55] Where is the necessary distinction between the immanent self-expression of God in freedom and his free action *ad extra* here? Both are clearly blended together in the thought of LaCugna, so that the overflowing nature of God coalesces with creation, incarnation and redemption. The freedom of grace is thus lost. While Torrance properly rejects LaCugna's understanding of grace, he nevertheless says that

> the grammar of this *other-ward* orientation is realised in a dynamic of communion that, by the Spirit, completes the other-ward or anhypostatic dynamic in a *consequent* 'in-ward' dynamic . . . it corresponds to the enhypostatic dynamic in the incarnation whereby the '*ex-pressive*' nature and giving of God is completed in a bringing of humanity to participate in the life of God . . .[56]

Here, LaCugna's failure to distinguish the immanent and economic Trinity marks Torrance's belief that God's expressive nature *needs* to be completed in bringing humanity to participate in the life of God.

But here Barth had the better idea. He insisted that God's expressive nature needed no completion, even though God willed and wills not to be without us. This specific recognition of God's freedom is the difference between acknowledging grace and saluting it in this context. In Barth's words:

> In the inner life of God, as the eternal essence of Father, Son and Holy Ghost, the divine essence does not, of course, need any actualisation. On the contrary, it is the creative ground of all other, that is, all creaturely actualisations. Even as the divine essence of the Son it did not need His incarnation, His existence as man and His action in unity with the man Jesus of Nazareth, to become actual. As the divine essence of the Son it is the predicate of the one God. And as the predicate of this Subject it is not in any sense merely potential but in every sense actual.[57]

Perhaps the entire difficulty here stems from the fact that communion, with the idea that person is more fundamental than being itself, is allowed to define both divine and human nature, and, to that extent, it is allowed to supplant revelation. Instead of respecting the fact that the *how* of God's triunity cannot be explained, Torrance seems to have explained this mystery *as* communion, even though he is aware that there can be no second root for the doctrine of the Trinity. Thus, 'The

[55] Torrance, *Persons in Communion*, 108.
[56] Torrance, *Persons in Communion*, 108, emphasis in original.
[57] *CD* IV/2, 112.

communion of the Trinity as such constitutes the *arche* and *telos* of all that is. It provides the hermeneutical criterion of all that has existence'.[58] But is it not the Trinity as such, God himself who constitutes this *arche* and *telos*? If so, then while communion is an important factor, as Torrance rightly believes, it cannot be substituted for God himself as an acting subject in his relations with us. Torrance objects to Barth's view of God as a single subject asserting that such a notion is not required for Christian monotheism.[59] But the fact is that, unless God is seen as the only acting divine subject in relation to us, there is the continual danger of confusion and reversal of divine and human predicates. While Torrance accepts Barth's view that *Non sermoni res, sed rei sermo subiectus*,[60] he also follows Jüngel, Wittgenstein and the Hintikkas's to argue that 'the realities of human existence, the social semantics of divine communication and the integration of language and thought are such that the *res* and *sermo* actually participate in each other in the revelation event in such a way that the language of God-talk ceases to be extrinsic to the revelation event itself'.[61]

This thinking could suggest just the kind of mixture of medium and reality that Barth tried to avoid, since only God could effect true human speech about God and God is not dependent upon or mixed with the media he uses to accomplish this communication and fellowship. This is precisely why Barth refused to think of Christ's humanity *as such* as revelation and rejected any sort of *direct* knowledge of God. God did not hand over his free act of revelation as a veiling and an unveiling to the form of revelation; and Barth decisively rejected dualism:

> There is no place for a dualistic thinking which divides the divine and the human, but only for a historical, which at every point, in and with the humiliation and exaltation of the one Son of God and Son of Man . . . is ready to accompany the event of the union of His divine and human essence . . . In the work of the one Jesus Christ everything is at one and the same time, but distinctly, both divine and human . . . it never becomes indistinguishable . . . there is no place for monistic thinking which confuses or reverses the divine and the human . . . in their common working they [the divine and human] are not inter-changeable. The divine is still above and the human below. Their relationship is one of genuine action.[62]

[58] Torrance, *Persons in Communion*, 258.
[59] Torrance, *Persons in Communion*, 220.
[60] *CD* I/1, 354.
[61] Torrance, *Persons in Communion*, 261.
[62] *CD* IV/2, 115–16.

So the ultimate question that arises here is whether or not the 'continuity' that Torrance seeks and finds in the notion of communion (relying on Zizioulas and the fact that God 'commandeers' human language) allows the notion of communion to displace God's miraculous (and thus incomprehensible) action in the present as the *sole* support upon which theology takes its stand. Does trinitarian *thinking* grounded in communion supplant God's own *act* here?

Torrance argues for a reconstructed *analogia entis* that would allow God creatively to commandeer human language – 'a commandeering grounded in a continuity established by God which is, therefore, *from* the divine *to* the human and which is to be found in that divine communion present with us in and through the human Jesus as the one who grounds, sustains and constitutes the Body of Christ'.[63] Further, Torrance says, 'Revelation, or what I would prefer to term "epistemic atonement", is thus an event of provisional, participatory communion within the intra-divine communion.'[64] While Barth is here accused of offering a too literalistic interpretation of metaphors, it is interesting to observe that Alan Torrance has here failed to distinguish revelation as God's act in Christ and the Spirit from our epistemic participation in this event. With respect to the Holy Spirit, Barth insisted correctly that 'statements about the operations of the Holy Spirit are statements whose subject is God and not man, and in no circumstances can they be transformed into statements about man'.[65] By contrast, it appears that communion, rather than God's miraculous *act*, establishes revelation in Torrance's thinking, with the result that revelation itself is subordinated to communion. While Torrance here argues that the human Jesus grounds, sustains and constitutes the Body of Christ, Barth more accurately saw that 'in itself and as such the humanity of Jesus Christ is a predicate without a subject'.[66] By stressing that the Word or Son is or remains subject of the events of incarnation, reconciliation and redemption in his actions *ad extra*, Barth had clear, consistent and accurate insights on these matters which have unfortunately become blurred in contemporary theology, because it is thought that in some sense Christ is the revealer in his humanity as such. Thus, Barth rejects the idea that

---

[63] Torrance, *Persons in Communion*, 229. See also 364, where Torrance says, 'revelation is an event of "communication-within-communion", where the impetus and semantically generative "control" in this event is the human Jesus as he mediates (enhypostatically) our participation in the triune life of God'.

[64] Torrance, *Persons in Communion*, 223–4.

[65] *CD* I/1, 462.

[66] *CD* IV/2, 102.

'omnipotence and therefore divinity accrue to the human essence of this man as such . . . rather . . . in the existence of this man we have to reckon with the identity of His action as a true man with the action of the true God. The grace which comes to human essence is the event of this action.'[67]

One Divine Subject

Before focusing on Torrance's view of the identity of the immanent and economic Trinity, let us discuss briefly how Barth's understanding of God as the one divine subject relates with Torrance's view of the matter. Together with Moltmann, Torrance, as already noted, sees Barth's use of this expression as a problem: 'Moltmann has argued that Barth "uses a non-trinitarian concept of the unity of the one God – that is to say, the concept of the identical subject".'[68] Pannenberg makes a similar criticism: 'Barth subordinated his doctrine of the Trinity to a pre-Trinitarian concept of the unity of God and his subjectivity in revelation.'[69] Torrance of course accepts this criticism since he believes that Barth's thinking has a modalist tinge and operates with a logically derived idea of God's unity as Lord (in a Hegelian manner) rather than with a concept that derives from communion.

Yet, as just stated, the truth is that for Barth the one divine subject that he envisions throughout the *CD is* the Father, Son and Holy Spirit, that is, the one who is three and loves in freedom: 'We are speaking of the knowledge of God whose subject is God the Father and God the Son through the Holy Spirit.'[70] In virtue of the eternal *perichoresis* of the Father, Son and Spirit, there is neither knowledge of God's oneness nor participation in that oneness unless it takes place in and through

---

[67] *CD* IV/2, 99.

[68] Torrance, *Persons in Communion*, 216.

[69] Pannenberg, *Systematic Theology I*, 299. Importantly, Pannenberg corrects Cremer's idea of God's love with the idea of the true infinite and concludes that 'God himself is characterized by a vital movement which causes him to invade what is different from himself' (400). Here Pannenberg compromises God's freedom, since the God who actually loves in freedom is not caused by anything to create, reconcile and redeem the world; he is the free *divine subject* of these events. Furthermore, this thinking leads directly to the modalism Pannenberg theoretically rejects: 'the divine essence overarches each personality' (430) and 'love is a power which shows itself in those who love . . . Persons do not have power over love. It rises above them and thereby gives them their self-hood . . . This applies especially to the trinitarian life of God' (426f.). Barth could avoid these ambiguities because he consistently saw God the Father, Son and Holy Spirit as the sole acting divine subject in relation to us.

[70] *CD* II/1, 181.

Christ by the action of the Holy Spirit. So Barth's concept of the one divine subject is clearly derived from and subordinate to God's actions in his Word and Spirit – God's actions in relation to us, even his condescension to act as our reconciler and redeemer, remain acts of God in virtue of the fact that all the works of the Trinity *ad extra* are indivisible.

Curiously, Torrance relies once more on LaCugna here who says, '"theological reflection on the nature of God is inseparable from [the] theology of grace, theological anthropology, christology, pneumatology, and ecclesiology"'.[71] Here, however, I think that Torrance is led astray by LaCugna's own inability to see that, while trinitarian theology arises from an encounter with God in the economy, it cannot be reduced to a theology *of* the economy as she clearly does. And while soteriology is important for understanding the Christian God, the doctrine of the Trinity cannot be reduced to a hermeneutical device for comprehending salvation. Yet, as we have seen, that is exactly how LaCugna and Peters construe the doctrine. Hence on the very page cited by Alan Torrance, LaCugna says that 'the referent for the immanent Trinity is not "God *in se*", or "God's essence as it is in itself"'.[72] When LaCugna and Peters say that reflection on God's nature is inseparable from reflection on grace and theological anthropology they clearly confuse God with the economy. It is one thing to say that our understanding of God has a bearing on these other aspects of theology. But it is quite another to say they are inseparable and that therefore the continuity of revelation prohibits any genuine recognition of God *in se*. Alan Torrance certainly does not accept this aspect of LaCugna's thought. But, given the fact that she completely fails to recognize grace as grace and therefore fails to recognize the true freedom of God that sustains Barth's theology, why then would Torrance think she can offer a valid critique of Barth's theology? Alan Torrance's goal was to provide a more integrated theology than he found in Barth. But did he not, at least in part, surrender God's subjectivity to a notion of divine communion and human participation in the process?

Barth is criticized by Torrance for focusing on revelation at the expense of focusing on worship and communion. Yet Barth insisted in *CD* I/1, and throughout the *CD*, that prayer was an essential ingredient in proper theological reflection. For him theology that takes place in faith cannot judge itself and cannot finally decide 'what is or is not true

---

[71] Torrance, *Persons in Communion*, 216.
[72] LaCugna, *God for Us*, 231.

in dogmatics' even though it is the task of dogmatics to critically examine its thought and speech about God. This, because this decision is

> always a matter of the divine election of grace. In this respect the fear of the Lord must always be the beginning of wisdom . . . The act of faith, which means, however, its basis in the divine predestination, the free act of God on man and his work, is always the condition by which dogmatic work is made possible but by which it is also called in question with final seriousness . . . Humanly speaking, there is no way to overcome this fundamental difficulty . . . We simply confess the mystery which underlies it, and we merely repeat the statement that dogmatics is possible only as an act of faith, when we point to *prayer* as the attitude without which there can be no dogmatic work.[73]

Torrance is certainly correct to call attention to the fact that, in his sacramental theology, Barth failed to emphasize Christ's high-priestly mediation and our human inclusion in God's triune life.[74] But I think Torrance is mistaken to trace that error to an Apollinarian tendency that can be discerned in *CD* volume I.[75] Instead, I think this is an inconsistency that could be corrected by retrieving Barth's repeated emphasis on the fact that theology must begin and end its reflections in faith by acknowledging that Jesus Christ is its only possible starting point. It is just this starting point that is obscured when it is thought that 'the prayer life of Jesus "as observed by the disciples and the early church, is a suitable empirical basis for the apostolic discernment of triunity"'.[76] It is not Jesus' prayer life as observed by the early Church

---

[73] *CD* I/1, 21–3, emphasis mine. Barth carries through on this insight consistently. See, e.g., *CD* I/1, 227, 231f. Barth insists that 'It is precisely ἐν πνεύματι that we shall be ready . . . to turn from ourselves to God and to pray to Him, not to contemplate God and manipulate Him . . . only the man who seeks everything in God prays to Him . . . only the man who seeks nothing in himself seeks everything in God' (*CD* I/1, 465). See also *CD* II/1, 512 where Barth insists that prayer is essential for faith.

[74] Yet, see John Webster, *Barth's Ethics of Reconciliation* (Cambridge: Cambridge University Press, 1995), who believes that T. F. Torrance's criticism of Barth's later baptismal theology is an example of misplaced anxiety about Barth's 'sacramental dualism' and that Torrance's own emphasis on Christ's vicarious humanity is similar to what Barth often says. Further, Webster believes the real divergence here concerns the fact that Torrance obscures the covenantal character of God's relation with humanity 'by his exclusive stress upon the vicarious character of Jesus' being and activity in relation to humanity. In Torrance's account of the matter, Jesus' humanity threatens to absorb that of others; in Barth's account, Jesus' humanity graciously evokes corresponding patterns of being and doing on the part of those whom it constitutes' (171). The reason I mention this here is because Alan Torrance follows the line of T. F. Torrance's critique of Barth on this issue. Still, Webster himself notes that 'Barth's separation of Spirit-baptism from water-baptism may still be made unnecessarily sharply' (172).

[75] Torrance, *Persons in Communion*, 193.

[76] Torrance, *Persons in Communion*, 360.

that is the starting point for the apostolic preaching, but Jesus himself who is the Lord, the Word of God incarnate – he alone and precisely now as the risen and ascended Lord is the suitable empirical basis for the apostolic discernment. And the moment the weight of emphasis shifts away from him, as seen above, the danger of Ebionite and Docetic Christology becomes real.

Alan Torrance then believes that Barth's theology rests 'on a prior *concept of divine freedom*' and that, to that extent, his thinking displays an internal inconsistency.[77] Yet we have seen above that Barth's thinking consistently allows for the fact that the truth of dogmatics can and must be received continually by an act of the triune God. And Barth consistently recognizes the miraculous nature of our knowledge of God as an event enclosed within the mystery of the Trinity by refusing to explain the *how* of our knowledge of God, the *how* of revelation or the *how* of the trinitarian relations. While Barth can be seen as internally inconsistent with respect to the sacrament, I do not think he was internally inconsistent with respect to knowledge of God and human participation in the life of the Trinity.

Rahner's Axiom of Identity and Participation in the Life of the Trinity

Alan Torrance's view of Rahner's axiom of identity is instructive in this regard. In a positive sense Torrance sees Rahner's axiom as reuniting the treatises on the One God and on the Trinity and as leading to a concept of grace that is more personal and directly tied to the trinitarian actions *ad extra*. But in another more negative sense Torrance notes that it is puzzling that Rahner thought he could integrate these insights with his 'transcendental anthropology'. This attempted integration and Rahner's Kantian presuppositions lead Torrance to say, 'both seem to be arguably incompatible and, at the very least, made superfluous by the implications of his identification of the immanent and economic Trinities!'[78] According to Torrance, 'There is a great deal in Rahner's discussion that echoes similar themes in Barth's discussion.'[79] In fact Torrance believes that Moltmann was right to assert that Rahner's exposition of the doctrine of the Trinity was quite similar to Barth's.[80] And he unfortunately accepts LaCugna's erroneous judgment that Barth

---

[77] Torrance, *Persons in Communion*, 48.
[78] Torrance, *Persons in Communion*, 265.
[79] Torrance, *Persons in Communion*, 267.
[80] Torrance, *Persons in Communion*, 245.

and Rahner could not break away from a Cartesian starting point because God was understood as a single divine subject.[81] As just noted, for example, the single subject that Barth has in mind is not a solitary Cartesian subject, but the unique subject who *is* Father, Son and Holy Spirit and who can only be known in faith by acknowledging the deity of Christ himself through the Holy Spirit. This subject is therefore also the object of our thought – that object cannot then be the human subject. That is why Barth insists that

> The impregnable basis of faith, the assurance of faith by God's revelation, depends on whether this basis, not just at the beginning but in the middle and at the end too, is sought in God alone, and not anywhere else, not in ourselves. Grace is the Holy Spirit received, but we ourselves are sinners. This is true. If we say anything else we do not know the deity of the Holy Spirit in God's revelation.[82]

Therefore I believe the similarities are mainly formal. But, as noted above in Chapters Four and Five, Rahner's axiom arose and took shape in the context of his philosophy and theology of the symbol. And this has a bearing on the fact that, for all their formal similarities, Barth and Rahner are not really close at all in their trinitarian theologies.

As seen above, Rahner interprets anthropology and Christology as mutually conditioned; Rahner thinks our natural knowledge of God and revealed knowledge mutually condition each other; Rahner starts his theology with transcendental experience and defines God as the nameless; Rahner understands the trinitarian self-expression in terms of symbolic necessity; for Rahner, God's self-communication is part of human experience in the form of a supernatural existential. In spite of their formal similarities, then, these views are completely antithetical to Barth's thinking.

For Barth, of course, we cannot begin theology with experience without falling into Ebionite or Docetic Christology and thus failing to understand the mystery of revelation; for Barth, natural theology must be conditioned by revealed theology and not vice versa; for Barth, there is no way from anthropology to Christology and no way from us to God, except in Jesus Christ, and this fact is recognized through

---

[81] Torrance, *Persons in Communion*, 240. In fact Barth opposed Cartesian thinking throughout the *CD*. See esp. *CD* I/1, 41, 172ff., 195ff., 214ff., *CD* I/2, 286 and *CD* III/1, 356–65. Barth thought of God as one divine subject in accordance with God's antecedent triune existence as it encounters us in revelation. Because LaCugna obliterates the distinction between the immanent and economic Trinity she mistakenly believes that Barth thought of God's triunity only as arising in connection with revelation.

[82] *CD* I/1, 466.

revelation itself; for Barth, God is not nameless but has revealed his name as Father, Son and Holy Spirit and there is no knowledge of God's oneness unless it takes place through the Son and in the Spirit; for Barth, theology must begin and end its reflections in faith – faith which is itself grounded in and created by God himself – even though it is itself a fully human act of self-determination; for Barth, as for T. F. Torrance, God's self-communication is identical with Jesus Christ himself and therefore cannot be detached from him and located in transcendental experience without compromising grace itself – Jesus Christ's divinity therefore cannot be circumvented by a method that would bypass him in any way; and finally for Barth, God's self-communication cannot be understood in terms of symbolic necessities because God is not subject to any sort of metaphysical necessities (including the necessity of relationality or communion) – God is the free subject of his inner life and of his expressions *ad extra*.[83] Perhaps Alan Torrance's assessment and criticism of Rahner's theology would have been stronger had he discussed the decisive implications of Rahner's supernatural existential and his symbolic ontology for his understanding of the Trinity. In my opinion he could have avoided implying that communion is the subject and God the predicate by insisting both that God is the sole divine subject and that God includes us in his own divine communion by grace, faith and revelation.

One final point needs to be discussed here. This concerns Torrance's understanding of Rahner's axiom of identity. According to Torrance, Rahner's denial of mutuality within the Trinity raises the question of how committed he really is to 'the two-way identification of the immanent and economic Trinities and what the hypostatic union specifically involves with respect to the unique *hypostasis* of the Son'.[84] Following Thomas F. Torrance, Alan Torrance clearly believes that Rahner has introduced a logical necessity of thought and so disjoins the immanent and economic Trinity, and that is why he mistakenly disallows true mutuality within the immanent Trinity. For T. F. Torrance that mutuality is most clearly expressed in Mt. 11:27 and parallel passages.[85] Alan Torrance traces Rahner's erroneous view to

---

[83] That is why, as seen in Chapter Five above, Barth insisted that 'The Father and the Son are not two prisoners. They are not two mutually conditioning factors in reciprocal operation. As the common source of the Spirit, who Himself is also God, they are the Lord of this occurrence. God is the free Lord of His inner union' (*CD* IV/2, 345).

[84] Torrance, *Persons in Communion*, 276.

[85] See, e.g., Torrance, *The Trinitarian Faith*, 58f., *The Christian Doctrine of God*, 57ff., 61f., 77f. and *Trinitarian Perspectives*, 91f.

what he calls a linear view of revelation as communication. But, as seen above, Rahner's error is due to his failure to allow Christ himself to be the starting point and conclusion of his theological reflections. While it may very well be true that Rahner's individualistically conceived notion of self-expression on the part of God leads him to deny mutuality within the immanent Trinity, that notion itself is thoroughly determined by his philosophy and theology of the symbol. So, the real problem in Rahner's analysis, from my perspective, is the fact that he refused to begin thinking about God, revelation, grace and faith from Jesus Christ himself and instead began with the human experiences of faith and hope in the form of our experiences of self-transcendence.

In Torrance's view, Rahner's identification of the immanent and economic Trinity becomes a mere formalism of the type he sought to avoid because Rahner 'fails to work out the implications for his two-way identification of the immanent and economic Trinities of the distinction between the *Deus ad intra* and *Deus ad extra*, and vice versa'.[86] What is needed, accordingly, is 'A more radical identification of the immanent and economic Trinities'.[87] Torrance is unhappy with the term immanent because it suggests a 'static' concept of God in himself. He prefers the expression *Deus ad intra* because he believes this is more dynamic and it leads to the kind of distinction that allows for reference to the divine economy as applied both to the *Deus ad intra* and the *Deus ad extra*. Hence, for Torrance

> the apotheosis of the divine *telos* requires to be defined with respect to the economic Trinity *ad intra*. This is not an *identification*, as it only takes place in the light of the divine freedom and, therefore, presupposes both an ontologically prior (and, indeed, from the human perspective historically prior) movement *ad extra* and also a radical distinction – though not disjunction – between the divine and the human.[88]

But that is one of the key questions being considered in this book. How can one argue for a more radical identification of the immanent and economic Trinity if, in fact, they must be distinguished because our encounter with the immanent Trinity takes place in and through the economy by grace, through faith and revelation? Isn't it precisely Rahner's vice versa in his trinitarian axiom that has been the bane of contemporary theology? It must be remembered that in Rahner's thought the symbol (Christ's humanity) is full of the thing symbolized

---

[86] Torrance, *Persons in Communion*, 278.
[87] Torrance, *Persons in Communion*, 278.
[88] Torrance, *Persons in Communion*, 279–80.

(Christ's being as the Logos) and the symbol renders present the thing symbolized because there is a mutually causal relation between the two. As we have seen repeatedly, it is this conceptual scheme that makes it factually impossible for Rahner to recognize and to maintain the priority of faith, grace and revelation in the sense that Barth insisted was necessary. That is why his identification of the immanent and economic Trinity actually led him to compromise God's freedom in the ways discussed above. Those contemporary theologians who have adopted his axiom and gone beyond it by making it more radical have compromised the divine freedom even more than Rahner, by obliterating our relation to a real immanent Trinity. They have in fact made the immanent Trinity nothing more than a description of our own experiences within the economy of salvation.

Alan Torrance considers it a flaw in Barth's theology that he failed to affirm 'the identity of the immanent and economic Trinities'.[89] Yet Barth would agree completely with Alan Torrance's main thesis which is also the thesis of T. F. Torrance, that is, that *'what God is eternally and antecedently in himself he is toward us* and *what God is toward us he is eternally and antecedently in himself'*.[90] But for this sentence to make any sense it would have to be made in the context of a clear and sharp distinction between the immanent and economic Trinity – one for which Alan Torrance himself argues, in spite of his suggestion that what is needed is a more radical identification. In my view, what is really meant here is that the more consistently one begins and ends one's reflections with the economic trinitarian self-revelation (Christ himself) as this is opened to us in and by the Holy Spirit, then the more clearly will it be realized that we are indeed drawn into the life of the immanent Trinity, because of God's special new direct and unforeseen actions in our favor. Or to put it another way, God neither remains remote from us in Christ and the Spirit (dualism) nor does

---

[89] Torrance, *Persons in Communion*, 222.

[90] Torrance, *Persons in Communion*, 222, emphasis in original. Interestingly, Bruce L. McCormack, *Karl Barth's Critically Realistic Dialectical Theology: Its Genesis and Development 1909–1936* (Oxford: Clarendon Press, 1995), notes, in connection with Barth's *The Göttingen Dogmatics*, that for Barth 'there can be no distinction in content between the immanent Trinity and the economic Trinity' (352). McCormack also notes, correctly, that because God is the subject, object and content of revelation, 'Barth was rejecting any view which would seek to establish a continuity between revelation and human thinking and feeling' (353). Finally, in McCormack's view, 'However true it may be that the immanent Trinity and the economic Trinity are identical in content, the distinction between them is nevertheless valid and necessary . . . Barth's identification of the economic and immanent Trinities has strictly anti-metaphysical significance. He was seeking to show that it is possible to speak of the being of God *in se* on the basis of revelation alone' (357–8).

God become dependent upon us by virtue of his free actions of creation, reconciliation and redemption (monism). As T. F. Torrance notes, 'God is at once the Subject and the Object of revelation, and never the Object without also being the Subject. This interlocking of the Being and the Act of God in his revelation excludes the possibility of there being any other revelation'.[91] Hence, God who is and remains free in himself, can for that very reason, in the pure overflow of love and goodness, which is not subject to any law of love or goodness, relate with us as Barth once indicated:

> His presence in the life and being of the world is His personal and therefore actual presence expressed in continually new forms according to His sovereign decisions . . . God is free to be and operate in the created world either as unconditioned or as conditioned. God is free to perform His work either within the framework of what we call the laws of nature or outside it in the shape of miracle . . . He is free to maintain as God His distance from the creature and equally free to enter into partnership with it, indeed, to lift the creature itself, in the most vigorous sense, into unity with His own divine being, with Himself. God is free to rule over the world in supreme majesty and likewise to serve in the world as the humblest and meanest of servants, free even to be despised in the world, and rejected by the world . . . This is how He meets us in Jesus Christ.[92]

Alan Torrance turns to Eberhard Jüngel for his understanding of God's love and mutuality.[93] But, as noted above, to the extent that Jüngel departed from Barth's insistence that we can only know God's love from the love of God revealed in Christ, there is a certain ambiguity in Jüngel's thinking that replicates itself in the thinking of Alan Torrance. Jüngel sees the immanent Trinity as a summary concept for the dealings of the economic Trinity with us. But if this is the case then Barth's insistence that human experience cannot set the paradigm for what can and cannot be said about God *in se* and *ad extra* is compromised. With this in mind let us briefly compare Jüngel and Barth on this specific point. I will make no attempt to present an exhaustive analysis of Jüngel's complex, imaginative and subtle thought here. I will restrict myself to analyzing how Rahner's axiom affects his theology and how that relates to the need to formulate a contemporary doctrine of the immanent Trinity. It is important to note that I completely

---

[91] Torrance, *The Christian Doctrine of God*, 22.
[92] *CD* II/1, 314–15.
[93] See Torrance, *Persons in Communion*, 274, 281f.

agree with him against Ted Peters that God must be understood as relational and loving prior to and apart from his actions in relation to us or what is thus understood will not be the Christian God at all. Here, however, I would like to explore one fine point of a difference in methodology that will illuminate some of the difference between Barth and other contemporary theologians over the function of the immanent Trinity; a difference that could be resolved with a clearer articulation of a doctrine of the immanent Trinity that avoids reducing our understanding of God *in se* to God in his actions *ad extra*.

Eberhard Jüngel

While Karl Barth approved Eberhard Jüngel's work, he noted that Grover Foley had questions about his doctrine of analogy.[94] Despite some criticisms of Rahner, Jüngel's belief that his thesis that 'The "economic" Trinity is the "immanent" Trinity and the "immanent" Trinity is the "economic" Trinity'[95] 'should be given unqualified agreement'[96] affects his theology, as we shall see. For Rahner, as seen above, 'the immanent Trinity is strictly identical with the economic Trinity and vice versa'.[97] As we have already seen, his transcendental method explains dogmatics from our experience of the 'nameless' which 'we call' God;[98] thus any real *freedom* for God in his immanent divine life is excluded.[99] As we have also seen, while Alan Torrance would agree that Rahner has not taken proper account of God's inner freedom, he does not trace this predicament to the foundations of Rahner's method as I have. Among the problems discussed above, this thinking can also reduce the church to a cultural institution using Christian categories to arrange its own existence. While Moltmann, LaCugna and many others have certainly fallen prey to this kind of thinking, and Jüngel largely escapes it, Karl Barth actually wrote to Rahner about this in March 1968:

---

[94] *Karl Barth Letters*, 71.

[95] See, Rahner, *The Trinity*, 22. See Molnar, 'Can We Know God Directly?', and Chapters Four, Five and Six above for how this thesis affects his thought.

[96] Jüngel, *God as the Mystery of the World*, 369–70.

[97] Karl Rahner, 'Theology and Anthropology', *TI* 9, 28–45, 32. See also *TI* 9, 127–44, 'Observations on the Doctrine of God in Catholic Dogmatics', 130.

[98] See, e.g., Karl Rahner, 'The Concept of Mystery in Catholic Theology', *TI* 4, 36–73 at 50ff., 'Reflections on Methodology in Theology', *TI* 11, 68–114, and *FCF*, chapters 1 and 2. For a critique, see Paul D. Molnar, 'Is God Essentially Different from his Creatures? Rahner's Explanation from Revelation', *The Thomist* 51 (1987), 575–631, and Chapter Four above.

[99] See Molnar, 'Can We Know God Directly?', 254ff.

Last Sunday I heard you on radio Beromünster, at first with pleasure . . .
In the end and on the whole, however, I was completely stunned. You
spoke much and very well about the 'little flock,' but I did not hear a
single 'Baa' which was in fact authentically and dominatingly of the
little sheep of this flock, let alone could I hear the voice of the shepherd
of this flock. *Instead, the basic note was that of religious sociology and
the other favorite songs of what is supposed to be the world of modern
culture.* In the way you are speaking now, so some fifty years ago Troeltsch
was speaking of the future of the church and theology . . . our
Neo-Protestants were and are in their own way pious and even churchly
people . . .'[100]

Barth's criticism of Neo-Protestantism and of modern method was
neither arbitrary nor uncritical,[101] but rests, as I have argued in this
book, on his clear and sharp *distinction* of the immanent and economic
Trinity as it was necessitated by the being of God revealed in Christ.
We have already seen how Barth's theology illustrates this distinction
and how Rahner's axiom, with its vice versa compromises this important
distinction. Let us see how Rahner's axiom, which is given unqualified
agreement by Eberhard Jüngel, affects Jüngel's understanding of God's
love.

More than Moltmann and Pannenberg, Eberhard Jüngel struggles
with the implications of Barth's method. Jüngel clearly accepts Barth's
method[102] but modifies Barth's view that what people experience as
love *is* actually contradicted by the love of God revealed in Christ,[103]
with the idea that God's love 'may not contradict *what people experience
as love*'.[104] For Barth there could be no compromise here because, while
humans *need* others to love, God does not; any other view might ascribe
either undue independence to creatures (who live by grace) or assume
that God *necessarily* creates and loves us.[105] While Jüngel intends to say
that human experiences of love cannot be equated with experiences of
hatred and isolation, he changes Barth's method here.

Since all understanding must be perceived in 'contexts',[106] Jüngel
understands God not just from revelation, but from the linguistic

---

[100] *Karl Barth Letters*, 287–8, emphasis mine.

[101] See Bruce L. McCormack, 'Divine Revelation and Human Imagination: Must We
Choose Between the Two?', *SJT* 37.4 (1984), 431–55, for a fine analysis of Gordon Kaufman's
misplaced criticisms.

[102] Jüngel, *God as the Mystery of the World*, 163ff., 317, 376–7.

[103] See esp. *CD* II/1, 272–85.

[104] Jüngel, *God as the Mystery of the World*, 315, emphasis mine.

[105] *CD* II/1, 282.

[106] Jüngel, *God as the Mystery of the World*, e.g., 14, 17, 32–3, 165 and 317.

and existential *contexts* of philosophical and theological assertions. Here experience seems to set the conditions; thus, where there is a genuine experience of gratitude there is an experience of the God who is 'more than necessary'[107] and therefore 'the invisibility of God is rather to be interpreted on the basis of the experience of acquaintance with God. Within the context of that experience, the truth that no one has ever seen God gains its ultimate precision.'[108] But once again, a crucial question posed above arises here: Does truth come from the miraculous intervention of God into our experience or from experience and understanding of the context? While Jüngel appears to adopt Barth's method – 'Obviously the being of the triune God is not to be deduced from the logic of the essence of love' – he cannot hold this position consistently and so he also says that 'even the understanding of the trinitarian history as the history of love presupposes a pre-understanding of love. This pre-understanding may well be corrected or made more precise if the task is to identify God and love'.[109]

Instead of allowing Christ *alone* to dictate the meaning of God's love in 1 Jn 4, Jüngel agrees with Barth that God's act must clarify its meaning. But, thinking within a 'christological context',[110] he believes he can provide a 'better understanding, when we first ask generally what love is'.[111] Here revelation can only change the meaning of our

---

[107] Jüngel, *God as the Mystery of the World*, 33. This is a 'miraculous experience' apparently because it cannot be deduced or induced from other experiences. It results from an event called 'the revelation of God'. Both his definition of miracle and of revelation, however, are quite different from Barth's. Against Pannenberg, Jüngel wrote: 'God, then, is first encountered where he allows himself to be experienced as the one who gives. That is precisely what I call revelation' (17, n. 6).

[108] Jüngel, *God as the Mystery of the World*, 376–7. Similar statements are made in Eberhard Jüngel, *The Doctrine of the Trinity: God's Being Is in Becoming*, trans. Horton Harris (hereafter: *The Doctrine of the Trinity*) (London: Scottish Academic Press, 1976), 52–60, 82ff. and 104.

[109] Jüngel, *God as the Mystery of the World*, 316–17.

[110] Jüngel, *God as the Mystery of the World*, 317.

[111] Jüngel, *God as the Mystery of the World*, 317. While Barth does say 'love is God' (*CD* IV/2, 756), this is no authorization for moving from the general to the particular. In fact he states that love and God may be equated 'presupposing that the content of the terms remains the same' (756) and insists, in a way that Jüngel does not, that God would still be perfect love without loving us (755) and that his love is grounded only in God and 'not at all in man' (771). He still insisted on giving precedence to divine over human love by not moving from the general to the particular (cf. 755, 777–8). By love, Barth means the inconceivable action *ad extra* of God in the Son and Spirit which can only be acknowledged (760). 'Only His act can be the basis of ours . . . We have thus to gain a full and clear picture of the act of His love before we can speak meaningfully of the act of ours' (760). See also *CD* I/2, 136, 162, *CD* II/1, 275, 308–9, and *CD* IV/2, 64 and 68.

pre-understanding of what love is; it is presumed that we know the truth and that revelation completes that knowledge.[112] This leads to the mutual conditioning that Barth rejected:

> Our consideration of the essence of love brings us back to our insight that God is love. On the basis of this consideration, we have gained a pre-understanding of the identification of God and love . . . *Now it is our task to think through this identification of God and love in such a way that the subject and predicate in the statement 'God is love' interpret each other.*[113]

And so while Jüngel can perceive a 'dialectic of being and nonbeing . . . which belongs to the essence of love',[114] Barth emphatically rejects any idea that nonbeing belongs to the essence of God[115] and refuses to ascribe darkness and nothingness any existence in the light of Christ.

While Jüngel, like Alan Torrance, is closer to Barth's method in intention than Moltmann, Pannenberg or Peters, he gives a status to experience which is clearly at variance with Barth's method.[116] As he makes experience co-extensive with God himself (God's love cannot contradict our experiences of love), he is led to give a reality to 'nothingness' which it does not actually have.[117] And instead of beginning his theology exclusively from the certainty that the reality of Jesus himself, true God and true man, is the norm for truth he begins as follows:

> From the material and dogmatic perspective, talk about God which is oriented to the crucified man Jesus must understand God's deity *on the basis of his humanity revealed in Jesus.* Thus, we must deal with problems which emerge in the *context* of the questions of God's thinkability, God's speakability, and God's humanity.[118]

Why doesn't he say that talk about God must understand the truth of his deity from the deity revealed in the history of the cross? Certainly the truth about humanity is revealed in Jesus. But Jüngel implies that humanity itself is part of God in such a way that it, in itself has the power of the Godhead. Thus, in spite of his valid criticisms of

---

[112] Jüngel, *God as the Mystery of the World*, 317.
[113] Jüngel, *God as the Mystery of the World*, 326, emphasis mine.
[114] Jüngel, *God as the Mystery of the World*, 325.
[115] Cf. esp. *CD* IV/4, 146–7.
[116] Indeed, according to Jüngel's own presentation of Barth's theology in *The Doctrine of the Trinity*, esp. 25ff., this very compromise is excluded.
[117] Jüngel, *God as the Mystery of the World*, 216–25.
[118] Jüngel, *God as the Mystery of the World*, 14, emphasis mine. God's humanity is now the context for understanding God, revelation, Christ and love.

Pannenberg[119] and Rahner,[120] Jüngel's own criterion leaves him with difficulties similar to Rahner's.[121]

In contrast to Barth's *analogia fidei*, Jüngel believes that the danger of drawing 'God, world, and man, or creator, creation, and creature . . . together into a structure of being which then makes it possible to understand God on the basis of the ordering of the created world under him,'[122] is polemically overstressed. Thus, Jüngel partially adopts Przywara's doctrine of analogy seeking to clarify it in light of the gospel.[123] Believing that Przywara *intended* the same thing as Protestant critics of the *analogia entis*,[124] that is, to maintain that God is wholly other and yet factually involved in creaturely being,[125] Jüngel holds, with Balthasar that 'There is no trace of the phantom of the analogia entis, which Karl Barth makes it out to be, to be found in him (Przywara).'[126] For Jüngel, Przywara 'protects the holy grail of mystery', that is, God's transcendence, even though he falsely concludes that God will always remain 'something unknown';[127] and instead of drawing God into the world (as Protestant polemics would have it) Przywara's doctrine leaves God free (transcendent). Jüngel believes the 'later' Barth recognized that the *analogia entis* was not really a 'grasping after God'.[128] But doesn't Przywara's doctrine draw God, world and humanity together into a concept of similarity and difference precisely by introducing us to God's mystery through a general concept of mystery? While the later Barth may have been concerned that the *analogia entis* would overlook God's nearness more than his otherness,[129]

---

[119] Jüngel, *God as the Mystery of the World*, 17, n. 6.

[120] Jüngel, *God as the Mystery of the World*, e.g., 222, n. 67, 251, n. 11 and 262, n. 1.

[121] Jüngel, *God as the Mystery of the World*, 220ff. 'Thus, "in the beginning the 'word' is with God, belongs to God as the word of love in that he expresses himself in order to address others"' (222).

[122] Jüngel, *God as the Mystery of the World*, 282.

[123] Jüngel, *God as the Mystery of the World*, 261, that is, 'as an "introduction to mystery" (introductio in mysterium)'. Also 262, n. 1.

[124] Jüngel, *God as the Mystery of the World*, 283ff.

[125] Jüngel, *God as the Mystery of the World*, 284ff.

[126] Jüngel, *God as the Mystery of the World*, 282.

[127] Jüngel, *God as the Mystery of the World*, 284–5. Thus, there is never a conclusion. The Augustinian 'unrest for God' arrives at no end. There is always that greater dissimilarity even in the midst of the similarity.

[128] Jüngel, *God as the Mystery of the World*, 282. Cf. Grover Foley, 'The Catholic Critics of Karl Barth in Outline and Analysis', *SJT* 14 (1961), 136–55, 149, where he notes that Barth, in reply to Brunner and to Balthasar 'cautions against all speculations on a "new Barth"'. Could this be why Jüngel thinks that Barth discovered the 'analogy of faith as the precondition for . . . proper talk about God'? (*God as the Mystery of the World*, 282). For Barth even the analogy of faith could not be a precondition for grasping the meaning of revelation.

[129] Jüngel, *God as the Mystery of the World*, 282.

he still held that we could not know it as God's nearness unless we *first* perceived his otherness. Thus, Barth's objection was primarily to the *method* of the *analogia entis* (including the method of Przywara, Balthasar and Rahner), that is, to the idea that theology could proceed from a general understanding of love or mystery toward an accurate understanding of God's particular love and God's bëing as mystery.

As Jüngel's doctrine of analogy compromises this method, it is inconsistent. On the one hand he maintains, with Barth, that

> God by no means first becomes his goal when he aims toward man. He is adequate to himself . . . A strict distinction must be maintained between the eternal derivation of God from God and the temporal derivation of man from God in order to recognize the factual relationship which obtains between the two . . .[130]

On the other hand, he asserts that

> In this creative being of God the Son as the aim of God the Father, God is aiming at man. In that God the Father loves the Son, in the event of this divine self-love, God is aiming selflessly at his creation.[131]

The absence of a distinction here between God eternally begetting the Son and *freely* deciding to create through the Son leads Jüngel to conclude that

> In the event of love, man corresponds to the God who has come to the world in both the most intensive and most extensive ways. For this God is love. In the event of love man is at his most mysterious . . . *In the event of love, God and man share the same mystery.*[132]

Our *human* acts of love may correspond with God's free love revealed in Christ but they do not share the *same mystery*.[133] The mystery of God precedes and the human mystery may follow but they do not arise out

---

[130] Jüngel, *God as the Mystery of the World*, 384.

[131] Jüngel, *God as the Mystery of the World*, 384.

[132] Jüngel, *God as the Mystery of the World*, 392, emphasis mine. The same point is repeated on 395 in connection with faith, love and hope as described in 1 Cor. 13:13. Compare the 'later' Barth, 'the divine love and the human love are always two different things and cannot be confused' (*CD* IV/2, 778).

[133] This conclusion illustrates the problem inherent in the way LaCugna exploited Jüngel's unfortunate characterization of the doctrine of the immanent Trinity as a summary concept for our experience of God within the economy. As seen above, LaCugna concludes that trinitarian life is our life. Such thinking confuses human and divine being and action and in the long run undermines a proper understanding of theological anthropology and love. The corrective here would be a doctrine of the immanent Trinity that would point to the constant need to distinguish God's free love from our experiences of love which are marked by sin and limited in their dependence upon God.

of some mysteriousness that they have in common. As Jüngel thinks that it is no longer a problem to classify God and the world together, he is led to a Docetic view, which he clearly did not intend: 'In the event of love, the believer has the decisive criterion to judge whether humanity's ways to itself are humane ways . . . What serves love is human . . . But what hinders love is inhuman.'[134] But if the essence of love is selflessness[135] and if God's love cannot contradict a human experience of selflessness, then one could argue, against Barth's view,[136] that, as long as we are selfless, love cannot mean obedience to Christ alone with a specific form of moral behavior corresponding to the divine command. And this is no small issue today, since a number of theologians now attempt to justify behavior that is clearly excluded on the basis of the biblical revelation by abstractly arguing that, as long as people are selfless and faithful, then that makes what had been previously regarded as immoral behavior acceptable. Apparently the problem of the creature grasping and controlling revelation in a general definition of love and freedom persists today and cannot be solved by choosing the language of parables[137] over the language of Scholastic theology.

How does Rahner's axiom affect Jüngel's Christology? While Jüngel perceives the affirmation of certain 'vestiges of the Trinity' as 'a dogmatic problem of the first rank',[138] his solution exhibits the same ambivalence, which led Rahner to redefine the immanent trinitarian relations in the light of history. Jüngel correctly stresses that 'Revelation cannot first gain worldly speech through interpretation'; yet he also believes an 'objection to Barth's thesis is unavoidable' because 'Revelation has as such world speech as part of itself – else it could not reveal. The world must be conceived within the concept of revelation.'[139] However, everything depends on how this secularity is perceived. What exactly is the basis for this inclusion of the world in the concept of revelation? Where is the distinction between God's Word and the humanity of Jesus to be drawn? Jüngel answers:

> The concept of revelation is a *special* human history . . . but not in and of itself. It is so by the power of a process of becoming which is not founded in its own historicity. *Such* a history speaks then, by virtue of

---

[134] Jüngel, *God as the Mystery of the World*, 392.
[135] Jüngel, *God as the Mystery of the World*, 298.
[136] E.g., *CD* IV/2, 776ff.
[137] Jüngel, *God as the Mystery of the World*, 282ff. It would appear at times that Jüngel ascribes to parables a power that Barth held came only from Holy Spirit!
[138] Jüngel, *God as the Mystery of the World*, 348.
[139] Jüngel, *God as the Mystery of the World*, 348–9.

the revelation taking place within it, of the God who reveals himself. And then it is necessary to say of that history that it is the trace of the triune God, the 'vestige of the Trinity.'[140]

But it is at this very point that a kind of mutual conditioning that compromises the freedom of revelation enters. The immanent Trinity does not refer to a being existing independently of history even while in closest union with it in Christ. Indeed, 'If God were only the one who loves himself eternally, then the differentiation between God and God would be pointless, and God would actually not love at all in his absolute identity.'[141] Thus, for Jüngel the only permissible distinction between the immanent and economic Trinity occurs 'when the economic doctrine of the Trinity deals with God's history with man, and the immanent doctrine of the Trinity is *its* summarizing concept'.[142] But as long as this is the case, the immanent Trinity cannot possibly be the indispensable premise of the economic Trinity (Barth's view) in an *irreversible* sequence that invariably dictates a certain form of knowledge and practice in dogmatics and ethics, that is, one that moves from above to below.[143] Rather, the immanent Trinity can only have as much independence as we are willing to give it on the basis of our experiences of faith in the crucified Jesus.[144] Thus, for Jüngel, the *man* Jesus is a 'vestige of the Trinity'.[145] From here Jüngel presents a type of Christology

---

[140] Jüngel, *God as the Mystery of the World*, 349. Moltmann's view is quite similar (*The Trinity*, 161).

[141] Jüngel, *God as the Mystery of the World*, 329. We are a long way from Barth's constant insistence in *CD* Vols 1–4, that as Father, Son and Spirit, God does not need anyone or anything in order to be fully one who loves. He could have remained God without us and would have suffered no lack. Barth avoided this difficulty by insisting that 'It is not . . . to satisfy a law of love, nor because love is a reality even God must obey, that He must be the Father of the Son . . . Love is God, the supreme law and ultimate reality, because God is love and not vice versa' (*CD* I/1, 483). Thus, Barth argued that 'The eternal generation of the Son by the Father tells us first and supremely that God is not at all lonely even without the world and us. His love has its object in Himself. And so one cannot say that our existence as that of the recipients of God's Word is constitutive for the concept of the Word' (*CD* I/1, 139–40). This perception of God's freedom is enabled by a clear doctrine of the immanent Trinity and, as seen throughout this book, even those who claim to follow Barth most closely, tend to blur this particular but crucial point.

[142] Jüngel, *God as the Mystery of the World*, 346, emphasis in original.

[143] *CD* I/1, 242. 'We have to think of man in the event of real faith as, so to speak, opened up from above. From above, not from below!' Also, 'We had Pentecost in view when we called revelation an event that from man's standpoint has dropped down vertically from heaven' (*CD* I/1, 331).

[144] Jüngel, *God as the Mystery of the World*, 376–7. While Jüngel correctly rejects the ideas that God is unknown in principle or a being who can be understood as possessing being (Rahner), he gives to experience a place Barth did not give it and this I believe opens the door to the problems we have been considering.

[145] Jüngel, *God as the Mystery of the World*, 349.

from below which culminates in Pannenberg's most dubious assertion noted above in Chapter Five: 'What is true in God's eternity is decided with retroactive validity only from the perspective of what occurs temporally with the importance of the ultimate . . . thus the truth of the incarnation – is also decided only retroactively from the perspective of Jesus' resurrection'.[146] We have seen the inadequacy of this view above.

Jüngel concludes that 'It would appear then, based on the theology of the Crucified One, that God who is love is better understood as the absolutely selfless essence.'[147] Thus,

> A 'still greater selflessness in the midst of a very great, and justifiably great self-relatedness' is nothing other than a self-relationship which in freedom goes beyond itself, overflows itself, and gives itself away. It is pure overflow, overflowing being for the sake of another and only then for the *sake of itself.* That is love. And that is the God who is love: the one who always heightens and expands his own being in such great self-relatedness still more selfless and *thus* overflowing. Based on that insight, Karl Rahner's thesis should be given unqualified agreement: '*The economic Trinity is the immanent Trinity and the immanent Trinity is the economic Trinity*' . . . The thesis that the 'economic' Trinity is the 'immanent' Trinity, and vice versa opens up the possibility of a new foundation for the doctrine of the Trinity . . .[148]

Have we not here explained the *how* of the trinitarian relations and of Christology? And are we not now standing within the mystery rather than recognizing it in faith? Are we not back to Barth's original question of whether there can be any foundation for the doctrine of the Trinity other than the scriptural revelation itself? The foundation here obviously can be derived from and corroborated by *experience* within history. While Barth certainly would say that the immanent trinitarian actions *ad extra* include us with all our experiences in a real relationship with God through faith, grace and revelation, he would never introduce the notion of mutual conditioning into the Godhead precisely because it is a relation with God and not an apotheosis. As we have seen throughout this book, he would never accept the vice versa of Rahner's axiom without the careful qualifications that are required by an actual perception of God's internal and external freedom. That is why I have consistently argued that it is not advisable to give Rahner's axiom unqualified agreement.

---

[146] Jüngel, *God as the Mystery of the World,* 363, n. 39.
[147] Jüngel, *God as the Mystery of the World,* 369.
[148] Jüngel, *God as the Mystery of the World,* 369–70. Some emphases mine.

Before concluding this chapter, it is worth noting that Alan E. Lewis alleges that Barth 'illogically' drove a wedge between the economic and immanent Trinity when he maintained that God could have remained satisfied with his own eternal glory, but chose not to[149] and he was puzzled by my criticism of Jüngel for attempting to understand God's love by first seeking a general definition of love.[150] In this book I am arguing that Barth did not separate or collapse the immanent into the economic Trinity but distinguished and united them in accordance with the fact that creation, reconciliation and redemption were factual necessities grounded only in God's free grace. Barth did not allow God's being and act to be defined by his relations *ad extra*. But Lewis compromises the freedom of grace envisioned by Barth by contending that God needs the world,[151] that his nature needs perfecting,[152] and that God could not have done other than he did in Christ.[153] Lewis makes love the subject and God the predicate saying 'The ineffable love which takes God down that path is free and sovereign, even if there is no possibility for God to be or act otherwise'.[154] But love does not take God down the path of creation and redemption. The triune God who loves chooses to go down that path in full loving freedom.

Lewis rightly stresses that Jüngel has done much to establish God's priority. But when Jüngel argues that (1) a pre-understanding of love is necessary to grasp God's love for us in Christ, (2) what serves love is human, (3) God and humanity share the same mystery and (4) nothingness is part of God's being, he is clearly inconsistent with his own belief in God's freedom by introducing the mutual conditioning associated with the vice versa of Rahner's axiom which he unfortunately adopts without hesitation. Jüngel and Lewis allow selflessness, abstractly considered, to define God's free selfless love for us exercised in Christ and the Spirit.

The most important lessons to be learned then from Jüngel's analysis are that (1) contemporary theology must continue to stress, with Barth, that the inclusion of history in revelation is and always remains the result of God's free grace – it is a miracle whose *how* cannot ultimately be explained, but one that must be accepted in faith; (2) contemporary

---

[149] Alan E. Lewis, *Between Cross and Resurrection: A Theology of Holy Saturday* (hereafter: *Between Cross and Resurrection*) (Grand Rapids, MI: Eerdmans, 2001), 208ff.

[150] Lewis, *Between Cross and Resurrection*, 253.

[151] Lewis, *Between Cross and Resurrection*, 210.

[152] Lewis, *Between Cross and Resurrection*, see 212–14 and 218ff. where Lewis follows Moltmann with occasional reservations.

[153] Lewis, *Between Cross and Resurrection*, 209ff.

[154] Lewis, *Between Cross and Resurrection*, 211.

theology cannot ignore the problem of sin when it comes to constructing theological analogies; (3) contemporary theology must stick rigorously to its proper starting point which is the love of God revealed in Jesus Christ and therefore it must not allow retrospective views of history or experience to determine the free love of the immanent Trinity – when this happens then God's free love, which is the basis of human freedom itself, is compromised by the fact that it becomes indistinguishable from our human love, which is unfortunately marred by sin and in need of reconciliation; (4) finally, contemporary theology must be clear that the immanent Trinity is and remains the indispensable presupposition for the economic trinitarian actions within history. Such an acknowledgment of God's freedom will lead theologians specifically and conceptually to distinguish their trinitarian thinking from the actions of God within the economy with the result that it will be seen with clarity that, when we truly know God, it is an event that takes place within the mystery of the divine Trinity.

In the next chapter it will be helpful to analyze the thought of one more important contemporary theologian who is more sympathetic to Barth than Moltmann and Pannenberg, but who nevertheless is also critical of Barth in ways somewhat similar to Alan Torrance. This will not be an exhaustive discussion of Colin Gunton's important trinitarian theology; rather it will be a discussion which focuses on a number of key issues that relate to the need for a contemporary doctrine of the immanent Trinity, that is, one which recognizes that human freedom is supported by divine freedom and that Christ is and must remain the starting point and conclusion of Christian theological reflection. Important among our considerations will be the connection between atonement and the Trinity.

Chapter Nine

The Promise of Trinitarian Theology: Colin Gunton, Karl Barth and the Doctrine of the Immanent Trinity

A MONG contemporary theologians, Colin Gunton sees the positive meaning of a proper doctrine of the immanent Trinity with clarity and consistency. After noting the importance of the revival of trinitarian theology in recent years, Gunton observes that with this revival certain dangers have also arisen. 'The first set of dangers derives from a mistaken attempt to remain concretely relevant by casting doubt on the necessity of an immanent, or, better, ontological Trinity'.[1] According to Gunton, Robert Jenson's tendency to focus exclusively on the economic Trinity has been reinforced by the work of Ted Peters and Catherine LaCugna, who both explicitly contest the importance of a doctrine of the immanent Trinity. Gunton rightly notes that Peters makes God's internal constitution dependent upon his relations with creation, while LaCugna follows Harnack's view that when the early Church went beyond a simple description of God's action within history, to reflect upon an ontology of the divine being, it made a mistake.

> It follows that any doctrine of an immanent Trinity, even one derived from an understanding of the economy, is to be rejected . . . From the outset it is made clear that we must not 'reify the idea of communion by positing an intradivine "community" or society of persons that exists alongside, or above, the human community.'[2]

[1] Gunton, *The Promise of Trinitarian Theology*, second edn, xvii.
[2] Gunton, *The Promise of Trinitarian Theology*, second edn, xviii.

273

As seen above in Chapters One and Five, LaCugna's idea that a doctrine of the immanent Trinity reflects our reifying certain thinking is deeply indebted to the thought of Gordon Kaufman, who is quite unable to allow any ontological otherness to God's existence. This is important, because it opens the door to the kind of agnosticism that places the lever in our hands for defining God, grace, revelation, faith and salvation. We have also seen the problems associated with Ted Peters' attempt to understand the Trinity as a description of our experience of the beyond and intimate; the chief problem of course was his inability to recognize and maintain either divine or human freedom.

In response to both of these misguided views, Gunton correctly insists that it is precisely the doctrine of the immanent Trinity that is necessary 'as a foundation for the relative independence and so integrity of worldly reality . . . and thus for human freedom'.[3] As seen above, Gunton rightly asserts that the problem with these views is that they do not in fact escape the pantheist position that effectively undermines both divine and human freedom. Gunton notes that it is neither just a matter of an abstract assertion of the divine freedom nor is it a matter of asserting any sort of arbitrary Deistic view of divine freedom. Rather, it is a matter of seeing and acknowledging God's actual freedom for us that is grounded in his freedom *in se*. Like Barth, however, Gunton urges that God's freedom is self-grounded and not at all dependent on history for its reality. Consequently, God really can have an intimate involvement in and with his creation in what Gunton, following Irenaeus, calls the two hands of God, that is, his Word and Spirit.

But there is another set of dangers that Gunton perceives and seeks to avoid, namely, any attempt to use the doctrine of the immanent Trinity as a weapon in a battle for certain social or ethical causes espoused by particular theologians. While the promise of trinitarian theology certainly consists in the fact that 'everything looks – and, indeed, is – different in the light of the Trinity',[4] Gunton quite rightly wishes to avoid the idea that this doctrine or any other can be wielded as a principle used by us in idealist or projectionist ways. The primary defect in this second set of dangers is 'that they turn Christ into a world principle at the expense of Jesus of Nazareth, and treat his cross as a focus for the suffering of God rather than as the centre of that history in which God overcomes sin and evil'.[5] In other words, Gunton

---

[3] Gunton, *The Promise of Trinitarian Theology*, second edn, xviii.
[4] Gunton, *The Promise of Trinitarian Theology*, 4.
[5] Gunton, *The Promise of Trinitarian Theology*, 2nd edn, xx. See also chapter 10.

appropriately wishes to stress that if the doctrine of the Trinity is detached from the doctrine of the atonement it ceases to be a description of the Christian God but instead becomes 'an uncritical validation of modern culture – or whatever – and so effectively Christianity's opposite'.[6] Interestingly, Gunton opposes any idea that trinitarian theology is only edifying to those within the Christian community and instead insists that the theology of the Trinity 'could be the centre of Christianity's appeal to the unbeliever, as the good news of a God who enters into free relations of creation and redemption with his world. In the light of the theology of the Trinity, everything looks different.'[7] What he specifically and rightly opposes is any attempt to employ a non-trinitarian apologetic based on some sort of monotheistic natural theology. This would have disastrous consequences for Christian theology not only because it would lead to a failure to respect the particularities of Christian revelation, but because it would, in effect, allow a human conception of unity to define God's unity with the result that the *homoousion* of the Father, Son and Spirit would be denied or compromised as well. With Barth, Gunton appropriately believes that there is 'an asymmetrical relationship between knowing and being, and we are not obliged to accept the apparent view of Rahner that the thesis "the Economic Trinity is the Immanent Trinity" is also true "reciprocally"'.[8]

What then is the importance of the doctrine of the immanent Trinity for Colin Gunton? The doctrine asserts that, because God is already a being-in-relation, before the creation of the world, he does not need the world. Those who believe that God must be either an 'unfeeling monarch' or one who needs the world, therefore, confuse two points: (1) the proper objection to a God who is immutable, unfeeling and distant does not necessarily imply that 'for God to enter into relation with the world he must need it in some way';[9] (2) trinitarian theology does not teach that God is unrelated to the world but that he is indeed involved 'in creation, reconciliation and redemption. But what it also enables us to say is that far from being dependent upon the world God is free to create a world which can be itself, that is to say, free according to its own order of being'.[10] Any sort of pantheism compromises both

---

[6] Gunton, *The Promise of Trinitarian Theology*, 2nd edn, xx.

[7] Gunton, *The Promise of Trinitarian Theology*, 7.

[8] Colin E. Gunton, *Theology through the Theologians: Selected Essays 1972–1995* (Edinburgh: T&T Clark, 1996), 123.

[9] Gunton, *The Promise of Trinitarian Theology*, second edn, 142.

[10] Gunton, *The Promise of Trinitarian Theology*, second edn, 142–3.

God's freedom to create, reconcile and redeem the world and the very existence and independence of the world. A doctrine of the immanent Trinity that is formulated from the economic trinitarian actions *ad extra* will see and maintain with clarity that God's involvement with the world is free and thus can indeed enable the world to be truly itself in relation to God in his otherness. This would be the kind of contemporary doctrine of the immanent Trinity that we are in search of because it formulates its view of the immanent Trinity only from God's economic trinitarian actions within history and not from some other existential or idealistic source.

Interestingly, Gunton prefers to speak of otherness and relation instead of transcendence and immanence because he believes that transcendence can easily be understood quantitatively or as the opposite of immanence with the false idea that transcendence and immanence are opposites. This is one of the reasons that he argues for 'a stronger distinction between economic and immanent Trinity, between God in eternity and God in time . . . the distinction between economic and immanent Trinity achieves more than a concept of God's freedom. It is, as we have seen, a matter of human freedom as well'.[11] Gunton thus prefers the terms otherness and relation. These latter terms are better alternatives because they are not 'contraries . . . but correlatives which require and interpret each other. Only that which is other than something else can be related to it. Otherness and relation can therefore be conceived as correlatives rather than rivals.'[12] Gunton's positive point is to stress, against monism and pantheism, that 'because God has otherness – personal freedom and "space" – within the dynamics of his being, he is able to grant to the world space to be itself'.[13]

Otherness and relation are not only important terms for a proper understanding of God's relation with the world but they shed light on relations within creation. Hence, our relation to the non-human world becomes confused if the otherness between the two is not recognized and respected. That is, if the world is personalized or if it is made the object of worship (as in some forms of creation spirituality), its very nature is misunderstood and so also is our true responsibility for the world. Also, in terms of inter-personal relations, Gunton correctly insists that monistic or totalitarian societies actually violate both the unique and distinctive being of each person and the privacy of each person.

---

[11] Gunton, *The Promise of Trinitarian Theology*, second edn, 134–5.
[12] Gunton, *The Promise of Trinitarian Theology*, second edn, 202.
[13] Gunton, *The Promise of Trinitarian Theology*, second edn, 202.

'To relate rightly to other people is to intend them in their otherness and particularity, to allow them room to be themselves.'[14] Importantly, this view of the immanent Trinity does not lead Gunton to separate God from the world. Rather, 'The doctrine of creation, trinitarianly conceived, enables us to understand the world as other than God, but as the product of a free act of creation and of a continuing free relatedness.'[15] In other words when God's otherness is properly acknowledged it will be seen that God's otherness includes his own internal relations as well as his free external relations with us.

Gunton and Barth

While Gunton agrees with Barth that because of human finitude and sin we need God's revelation in order to know him in truth and that 'such knowledge cannot be merely a human achievement, but rather must, as a human achievement, also be the gift of the Holy Spirit',[16] he also believes that we should go further than Barth and make links between the theological implications of revelation and other intellectual, moral and aesthetic concerns: 'Revelation speaks to and constitutes human reason, but in such a way as to liberate the energies that are inherent in created rationality.'[17] Here we have what appears to be only a minor linguistic distinction between Barth and Gunton that has major theological implications. Would Barth agree that revelation liberates energies inherent in created rationality or might he not insist that created rationality needs to be placed on an entirely new footing in order to operate properly?[18] In other words, from Barth's point of view, Gunton's analysis in this context underplays the seriousness of sin and the fact that revelation is offensive to us – it does not just release something inherent in created being – but rather completely transforms human reason in a way that goes against what we would consider reasonable apart from grace, faith and revelation. This is why, as seen above in Chapter Two, Barth insisted that revelation causes offense. It is hidden apart from faith and goes against what we would consider reasonable. Perhaps it is not an accident that the word faith rarely appears in Gunton's theology of the Trinity.

[14] Gunton, *The Promise of Trinitarian Theology*, second edn, 203.
[15] Gunton, *The Promise of Trinitarian Theology*, second edn, 203.
[16] Colin E. Gunton, *The One, the Three and the Many: God, Creation and the Culture of Modernity* (hereafter: *The One, the Three and the Many*) (Cambridge: Cambridge University Press, 1993), 211.
[17] Gunton, *The One, the Three and the Many*, 212.
[18] See, e.g., *CD* II/1, § 26, 'The Knowability of God', 63–178.

This difference between Barth and Gunton is important. For Barth 'The form of God's Word . . . is in fact the form of the cosmos which stands in contradiction to God. It has as little ability to reveal God to us as we have to see God in it.'[19] For Gunton, 'As finite and temporal, yet created in the image of God, human beings *have* spirit because they are open to God, each other and the world in the peculiar although limited way that characterizes personal beings.'[20] Barth is quite consistent in taking sin seriously as understood in the light of God's revelation in Christ: for him we are not in fact open to God but can only become open through the mystery and miracle of faith given by the Holy Spirit and determined by its object, that is, Christ himself the incarnate Word. Barth will not equate the Holy Spirit with the human spirit of personal beings. Interestingly, Gunton argues that the 'main difference between the human and the divine is expressed in the claim that God *is* spirit, while finite persons *have* spirit . . . God *is* spirit by virtue of the un-qualified openness of the triune persons to each other and his free and unnecessitated movement outwards'.[21] By contrast T. F. Torrance understands the Spirit absolutely and relatively:

> Absolutely considered the Spirit is God of God . . . the Being of the Spirit is the Being . . . of the Godhead. 'God is Spirit', as Jesus said to the woman of Samaria. In this absolute sense 'Spirit' refers to Deity, without distinction of Persons, and is equally applicable to the Father, the Son and the Holy Spirit. Considered relatively, however, the Spirit is Person . . . who in distinction from and together with the Persons of the Father and the Son belongs with them to the one Being of God. The Holy Spirit is, then, like the Father and the Son, both *ousia* and *hypostasis*, and with the Persons of the Father and the Son is eternally in God and inseparable from him who is *one Being, three Persons.*[22]

Torrance does not try to explain *how* God is Spirit by saying it is by virtue of the openness of the persons to each other and by virtue of an unnecessitated movement outwards. These inward and outward actions disclose the fact that God is Spirit in his unique way but it is not by virtue of these actions that he *is* Spirit – he *is* Spirit simply because he is. Torrance thus simply states the objective fact that God is Spirit because he is – and he is Spirit as the eternal Father, Son and Holy Spirit who objectively indwells us.

---

[19] *CD* I/1, 166.
[20] Gunton, *The One, the Three and the Many*, 188.
[21] Gunton, *The One, the Three and the Many*, 188.
[22] Torrance, *The Christian Doctrine of God*, 147–8. This issue will be discussed further in the Appendix.

Our receiving of the Spirit is objectively grounded in and derives from Christ who as the incarnate Son was anointed by the Spirit in his humanity and endowed with the Spirit without measure, not for his own sake (for he was eternally one in being with the Spirit in God) but for our sakes, and who then mediates the Spirit to us through himself . . . Our receiving of the Spirit, therefore, is not independent of or different from the vicarious receiving of the Spirit by Christ himself but is a sharing in it.[23]

Here Torrance makes an important distinction between Christ receiving the Spirit while yet eternally being one in being with the Spirit. This is a distinction that hardly figures in Gunton's analysis.

This apparent minor linguistic difference between Barth and Gunton can be seen in their different emphasis on Christ's humanity. It is precisely because Barth insisted that Christ's humanity *as such* could not be the starting point for Christology that he also insisted that there is *no* analogy which is true in itself.[24] By contrast, Gunton's search for transcendentals appears to operate at least in part on the assumption that there are certain concepts (analogies) that are inherently true.[25] It is because Barth acknowledged the continuing priority of the Word in the incarnation, reconciliation and redemption, that he also insisted on the priority of faith by stressing that there could be no exclusive interest in Christ's humanity and that his humanity should not become the determinative element in Christology or dogmatics. Thus, for Barth, faith recognizes that the Word is indeed the determinative element in

[23] Torrance, *The Christian Doctrine of God*, 148.

[24] Cf. *CD* II/1, 194, 226 and 358. See *CD* IV/3, 509 for how Barth carries through this insight in connection with his understanding of vocation by defining illumination as 'a seeing of which man was previously incapable but of which he is now capable. It is thus his advancement to knowledge . . . not with new and special organs . . . not in virtue of his own capacity to use them, but in virtue of the missing capacity which he is now given by God's revelation. "Jesus, give me sound and serviceable eyes; touch Thou mine eyes." It is as He does this that they become serviceable . . . It is all a process which like others really implies knowledge in man. But it is all an original creation of the One who enables him to know.'

[25] See, e.g., Gunton, *The One, the Three and the Many*, 141ff. Unlike Robert Jenson, Gunton does not want to jettison the concept of analogy altogether. But one of the marks of Gunton's view is that he believes that there are concepts 'that enable us to *think* our world . . . inherent within certain words there lies the possibility of *conceiving* things as they are' (*The Promise of Trinitarian Theology*, second edn, 138). For Barth, of course, this possibility of conceiving things as they are must continually come from God himself through the Holy Spirit and so is not a possibility inherent in certain concepts. See, e.g, *CD* II/1, 194 and 226. As the object of faith determines our knowledge of God, so too the object of faith determines our knowledge of the world for Barth. That is why he argued that the covenant was the internal basis of creation. The ultimate problem here is that Gunton conceives creation as open to God and Barth correctly insists that creation is not open to God but continually must become open through God.

the incarnation since the Word alone gives Jesus' humanity its true meaning. Because the priority of the creator over creature is not blurred but clarified in Christ, Barth insists on the positive and negative aspects of the divine freedom by emphasizing the irreversibility of analogous concepts in his doctrine of God.[26] And in connection with Christology, Barth stressed both the *enhypostasis* (God actually became flesh for us) and the *anhypostasis* (Christ's humanity draws its meaning from the immanent Trinity and not from history). Barth preferred the ancient to the modern Christologies because they grappled with the problem of Christology, namely, Jesus Christ as *vere Deus vere homo* in his unique self-sufficient existence,[27] and not an apotheosis;[28] meaning was found *only* in him.

As seen above, Barth understood revelation as the unveiling of what is veiled because he took seriously the miraculous nature of human knowledge of God.[29] That God unveils himself implies a real knowledge of the immanent Trinity and of his will for us. But because Christ alone is the norm, human interpretation and the fact of Christ can never be reversed.[30] This then is the thinking that eventually led Barth to argue that any view of Christ that saw God's revealing activity wholly as a property of the man Jesus has allowed 'man to set himself on the same platform as God, to grasp Him there and thus to become His master'.[31] The error of mysticism,[32] of Schleiermacher,[33] of Hegel[34] and

---

[26] See *CD* II/1, 301ff. See Barth's illuminating discussion of this issue in *The Göttingen Dogmatics*, 156ff. Barth insisted that, while our knowledge of the Son takes place through the incarnate, in Jesus, 'he is also the Logos of God beyond his union with humanity, just as the Trinity is more than the incarnation. As the Father is not just the Creator, so the Logos is what he is even apart from Jesus Christ' (156). Because for Barth the man Jesus never existed apart from the Logos, he rejected any notion that the Logos was 'enclosed in the human nature' (158). While he believed that the Logos indwells Christ's human nature, he rejected the idea that the divine freedom from limitation applied to the flesh just as it did to the Logos because 'We may not say that the Logos subsists only in the human nature of Christ' (158). He thus rejected the idea that Jesus was revealer in his humanity as such.

[27] Cf. *CD* I/2, 23 and *CD* IV/1, 179ff.

[28] *CD* I/2, 129.

[29] See *CD* I/1, 168. While human freedom is not set aside or weakened by an encounter with God (*CD* I/1, 246ff.), 'it cannot in any sense be regarded as its [human freedom] product, as the result of an intuition' *CD* I/1, 247.

[30] See *CD* I/2, 6ff.

[31] *CD* I/1, 323. In *CD* IV/3, 504 Barth insisted that vocation could not be controlled by us for the same reason, that is, because the emphasis even here must be on 'the concrete person of Jesus Christ who as the Son of God calls him by the Holy Spirit'.

[32] *CD* II/1, 409 and Karl Barth, *Protestant Theology in the Nineteenth Century: Its Background and History* (hereafter: *Protestant Theology in the Nineteenth Century*) (Valley Forge, PA: Judson Press, 1973), 468 and 471ff.

[33] Barth, *Protestant Theology in the Nineteenth Century*, 468 and 471ff.

[34] Barth, *Protestant Theology in the Nineteenth Century*, 412ff., esp. 418–20.

in general of nineteenth-century theology consists in their uncritical presumption of *identity* here.[35] They failed to note God's holiness, that is, his right to make himself known as he chooses, while at the same time 'He still inhabits and asserts the sphere which is proper to Him and to Him alone . . . the Godhead is not so immanent in Christ's humanity that it does not also remain transcendent to it, that its immanence ceases to be an event in the Old Testament sense, always a new thing, something that God brings into being in specific circumstances.'[36] This is why Barth insists that God cannot be classified with other 'supreme ideas' such as freedom and immortality and then known; this, because his *esse* really is his *act*. Therefore, 'no self-determination of the second partner [the creature] can influence the first, whereas the self-determination of the first, *while not cancelling the self-determination* of the second, is the sovereign predetermination which precedes it absolutely'.[37] The very being of the Christian God revealed not only excludes *any* pantheistic or panentheistic attempt to define his relation with creatures, but it excludes any attempt to ascribe meaning directly to human concepts or experiences; it excludes the attempt to correlate otherness and transcendence following such a procedure.

By contrast, Colin Gunton, in partial reliance on John Zizioulas and in connection with ecclesiology, criticizes Barth's doctrine of election because it has been taken to imply universal salvation. 'The moment of truth in the contention is that if election is ordered christologically, and with greater emphasis on the divine Christ than on the human Jesus of Nazareth, the fate of us all appears to have been pre-determined in eternity.'[38] Gunton notes that an ecclesiology that is then ordered to a 'monophysite or docetically tending christology has even more disastrous effects',[39] which he detects in the documents of Vatican II. What is Gunton's remedy? He suggests

> a greater stress on the fact that the ecclesiological significance of Jesus derives equally from the humanity of the incarnate . . . that Jesus is without sin does not imply that he is omniscient, or even infallible . . . It

[35] *CD* II/1, 291ff.

[36] *CD* I/1, 322–3. This is why Barth rejects any sort of divinization of Christ's human nature (*CD* IV/1, 132) and why he insists that in becoming a man Christ did not change himself into a man so that his divinity in some sense ceased (*CD* IV/2, 401ff., see also *CD* II/1, 360ff.).

[37] *CD* II/1, 312, emphasis mine.

[38] Gunton, *The Promise of Trinitarian Theology*, 67. Additional criticisms along these lines may be seen in C. E. Gunton, *Christ and Creation* (Grand Rapids, MI: Eerdmans, 1992), 94ff.

[39] Gunton, *The Promise of Trinitarian Theology*, 67.

is part of the being of a human person to be contingent and fallible (though not, of course, to be sinful) ... In view of the temptations and the trial in Gethsemane, may we claim even indefectibility of Jesus? He did, indeed, escape defection. But how? Not through some inbuilt divine programming, though that is the way it has often been made to appear, but by virtue of his free acceptance of the Spirit's guidance.[40]

Some crucial difficulties arise in connection with this analysis. Unlike Barth, Gunton does not consistently maintain the dialectical unity and distinction within the priority of the action of the Word in what George Hunsinger has called the Chalcedonian pattern. Instead, he emphasizes the Holy Spirit in such a way that it becomes virtually impossible to maintain two insights that are crucial to Barth's theology and are important in preserving both divine and human freedom: (1) he argues that Jesus' significance derives equally from his humanity; and (2) he argues that the Spirit rather than the Word is the source of Jesus' authentic humanity. While Jesus' humanity is crucial because what is not assumed is not saved, and while it is important to stress, as both Gunton and Barth do indeed stress, that the Word assumed our sinful humanity and not some idealized humanity, Gunton's emphasis on Jesus' humanity sometimes appears to eliminate the significance of his being the Word incarnate and at times actually tends to separate the actions of the Word and Spirit instead of seeing these actions in their *perichoretic* unity.

Thus, for instance, in the passage just cited he argues that Jesus is not omniscient or infallible and that his indefectibility is traceable to his free acceptance of the Spirit's guidance. But why is Jesus' indefectibility traceable *only* to the Spirit's guidance and Jesus' free human acceptance of that guidance? Is it not the case that the incarnation refers to a mystery and miracle involving the Word who, in Barth's theology, never ceases to be the subject of the events of incarnation, reconciliation and redemption? Isn't the mystery of Jesus Christ identical with the fact that, while not ceasing to be divine and thus omniscient, he became a man who did indeed share our ignorance and limitations in order to overcome them on our behalf? And when Barth speaks of the Spirit's activity within history, he always links that activity to the activity of the Word with the result that he never plays off the Word and Spirit against each other. By contrast, Gunton, who follows the thought of Edward Irving argues that 'The Spirit ... is the source of Jesus' authentic

---

[40] Gunton, *The Promise of Trinitarian Theology*, 67–8.

humanity'.[41] Accordingly, Gunton intends to correct what he sees as Barth's tendency to universalize election for christological reasons with Irving's approach which limits that universality to redemption for pneumatological reasons. Thus, 'Election has to do . . . with the mysterious activity of the Spirit, communicating the benefits of redemption to particular people at particular times.'[42] But what are those benefits and how can they be discerned without faith in Christ himself as the giver of those benefits? Here it seems Gunton leaves out the action of the Word which takes place in and through the action of the Holy Spirit.

A closer look at some of Gunton's criticisms of Barth in relation to Barth's own position might help bring to light a point that I would like to emphasize here, that is, the continuing need to acknowledge the importance of Barth's insight that the Word is and remains the subject of the event of the incarnation and the one who, even now, speaks his Word to us through the words of scripture in the power of the Holy Spirit. While Gunton is quite right to stress, in line with the eastern tradition, the fact that when the Holy Spirit is properly acknowledged and emphasized, then Jesus' full humanity and ours, together with the eschatological nature of our redemption, will come more clearly into view, it is equally important that we do not fail to acknowledge and emphasize the inseparability of the Spirit and the Word. It is also important to make room for the fact that in the Holy Spirit God continues to speak his Word to us here and now in and through the historical witness of scripture. One of the ways that Barth stresses the historicity of revelation is by showing how scripture, as a human document, is also God's Word.

In this connection we will compare Barth and Gunton on five episodes in Jesus' life: (1) the relation of the virgin birth to the beginning of Jesus' life, (2) Jesus' baptism and the temptations, (3) Jesus' death on the cross, (4) Jesus' resurrection and (5) Jesus' ascension. Gunton contends that the western tradition, beginning with Augustine and 'culminating in Barth',[43] failed to do justice to Jesus' humanity because of its failure to give proper emphasis to the Holy Spirit.

The Virgin Birth

Gunton maintains that the virgin birth has been used to screen Jesus from the pressures of human existence or to express his total involvement

---

[41] Sykes, *Karl Barth*, 63.
[42] Sykes, *Karl Barth*, 64.
[43] Gunton, *Christ and Creation*, 50.

in our humanity. He notes that the doctrine of the immaculate conception completely shields Jesus from participating in our sinful flesh, while Barth's understanding of the virgin birth has a similar outcome with the opposite intent. Because Barth's concern is to say that at the beginning and end of Jesus' earthly life there was a miracle, 'a new divine initiative, a mystery of revelation',[44] he pays less attention to the divine action *within* creation and instead focuses on God's action *towards* creation. Thus when Barth speaks of God acting solely through God and that 'God can be known solely through God' this indicates that he is unable 'to specify an action of the Spirit except in terms of "God Himself in His freedom exercised in revelation to be present to His creature"'.[45] The problem with Barth, accordingly, is not with what he says but with what he does not say. Barth misses the point that the Holy Spirit is 'the one enabling the creation truly to be itself'.[46]

Gunton wishes to avoid tritheism while relying on Edward Irving to offset this apparent one-sidedness in Barth's thought, and so he stresses that, when the function of the Holy Spirit is properly emphasized, then it is seen that Jesus

> is indeed part of the network of creation, in all its fallenness. By forming a body for the Word in the womb of Mary, the Spirit shows that the being of the human Jesus is not merely the passive object of the eternal Son's determination: it is also flesh of our flesh . . . That is the point of denying that Jesus bore the flesh of unfallen Adam. If he did, what is his *saving* relation to us in our lostness?[47]

In this context then the virgin birth should be seen as a statement about Christ's humanity, which is that of fallen creatures, but is led to perfection by the Holy Spirit. Hence 'the doctrine of the virgin birth is not to "prove" the divinity of Christ, but to link together divine initiative and true humanity. Jesus is within the world as human, and yet as new act of creation by God.'[48] While it must be admitted that Barth does not say that the Holy Spirit is the 'perfecting cause of creation' in the sense described by Gunton, though he is aware of this, he does say a number of things that are underplayed or missing from Gunton's account.

First, Barth insists that the incarnation is an action of the Word, that is, the Word or Son of God is and remains the subject of the event of incarnation. Thus,

44 Gunton, *Christ and Creation*, 51.
45 Gunton, *Christ and Creation*, 51.
46 Gunton, *Christ and Creation*, 51.
47 Gunton, *Christ and Creation*, 52.
48 Gunton, *Christ and Creation*, 53.

As the Son of God made His own this one specific possibility of human essence and existence and made it a reality, this Man came into being, and He, the Son of God, became this Man . . . Thus the reality of Jesus Christ is that God Himself in person is actively present in the flesh. God Himself in person is the Subject of a real human being and acting. And just because God is the Subject of it, this being and acting are real. They are genuinely and truly human being and acting. Jesus Christ is not a demigod. He is not an angel. Nor is He an ideal man. He is a man as we are, equal to us as a creature . . . equal to us in the state and condition into which our disobedience has brought us.[49]

Barth therefore insists that in the incarnation

the Word is the Subject. Nothing befalls him; but in the becoming asserted of Him He acts. The becoming asserted of Him is not, therefore, to be regarded as an element in the world process as such . . . God's Word becoming a creature must be regarded as a new creation . . . it is a sovereign divine act, and it is an act of lordship different from creation.[50]

This is why Barth regards the equation 'very God very man' as irreversible. If Jesus is to be seen not only as God who is man but as man who is God, then 'it is so because it has pleased very God to be very man'.[51] Jesus is indeed the incarnate Word, but it is the Word who speaks, acts, reveals and reconciles us. It is 'the Word and not the flesh. The Word is what He is even before and apart from His being flesh. Even as incarnate He derives His being to all eternity from the Father and from Himself, and not from the flesh.'[52] While it is important to stress the action of the Holy Spirit as Gunton does, it is also important to see that the Word and Spirit are both active in the incarnation and therefore emphasis on the Spirit does not have to imply, as it seems to imply for Gunton, that the Word's activity must be restricted. Nor should it imply that Jesus' human actions are pre-programmed. Gunton wants to say that Jesus' free human actions are enabled by the Spirit *rather than* determined by the Word. But why can we not say that Jesus' free human actions, as the actions of the Word, are indeed enabled by the Spirit in such a way that we cannot ultimately explain *how* this can be so? Rather we must simply confess the fact that it is so. In one sense, as T. F. Torrance says, the Word restricts his activity so as to submit obediently to the Father's will on

49 *CD* I/2, 150–1.
50 *CD* I/2, 134.
51 *CD* I/2, 136.
52 *CD* I/2, 136.

the cross out of love for us.[53] Still, he does not cease being divine in the incarnation, but acts as God become man.[54]

Gunton, who follows John Owen, makes an unfortunate separation of God's Word and Spirit acting *ad extra*. Thus, 'Owen *limits* the direct operation of the Word . . . Owen holds that "The only singular immediate act of the person of the Son on the human nature was the *assumption* of it into subsistence with himself". . . the humanity [of Jesus] is not subverted by the immanently operating Word.'[55] Where then does the human Jesus receive the capacity to do God's work? For Owen 'The Holy Ghost . . . is the *immediate, peculiar, efficient* cause of all the external divine operations: for God worketh by his Spirit, or in him immediately applies the power and efficacy of the divine excellencies unto their operation'.[56] But, as we have just seen, for Barth and for T. F. Torrance, the direct operation of the Word is not limited to only one aspect of the incarnation and is not simply equated with the action of the Son 'on the human nature'. For Barth it is the action of the Son as man within human history that counts. Still, as we have just seen, he does not cease being divine in the incarnation but acts as God become man. Owen's view would be tantamount to saying that in the incarnation God ceased to be divine when he became man. But Barth also did not envisage Jesus' activity as 'determined' by the Word as subject in the sense that his actions were less than free human actions of obedience on Jesus' part under the guidance of the Holy Spirit.

Second, contrary to Gunton's assertion, Barth indeed insists upon the fact that Jesus' humanity is the humanity of sinful creatures: 'The Word is not only the eternal Word of God but "flesh" as well, that is, all that we are and exactly like us even in our opposition to Him. It is because of this that He makes contact with us and is accessible to us.'[57]

---

[53]   Thus, Torrance believes 'Jesus Christ came among us sharing to the full the poverty of our ignorance, without ceasing to embody in himself all the riches of the wisdom of God, in order that we might be redeemed from our ignorance through sharing in his wisdom' (*The Trinitarian Faith*, 187). Christ's ignorance, however, was 'an economic and vicarious ignorance . . . by way of a deliberate restraint on his divine knowledge throughout a life of continuous *kenosis* in which he refused to transgress the limits of the creaturely and earthly conditions of human nature' (187).

[54]   Thus, Torrance also insists that 'The self-humiliation of God in Jesus Christ, his *kenosis* or *tapeinosis*, does not mean the self-limitation of God or the curtailment of his power, but the staggering exercise of his power within the limitations of our contingent existence in space and time . . . God is revealed to have the inconceivable power of becoming little and contingent, while remaining what he eternally and almightily is' (*The Christian Doctrine of God*, 214–15).

[55]   Gunton, *The Promise of Trinitarian Theology*, 70.

[56]   Gunton, *The Promise of Trinitarian Theology*, 70.

[57]   *CD* I/2, 151.

Barth notes that, while Jesus himself did not commit sin, he nonetheless shared our sinful flesh and thus experienced God's judgment in our stead. 'He bore innocently what Adam and all of us in Adam have been guilty of. Freely He entered into solidarity and necessary association with our lost existence. Only in this way "could" God's revelation to us, our reconciliation with Him, manifestly become an event in Him and by Him.'[58]

Third, in speaking of the *natus ex Maria virgine* Barth stresses that we are dealing with a mystery and miracle. But Barth does not think of the miracle at the beginning of Jesus' human life and the miracle at the end of his life (the resurrection) as indications that he is not fully human, as Gunton seems to suggest. Rather, Barth insists that Jesus was born as no one else was born and that we must acknowledge the unique object in question. Still, according to Barth, Jesus was not born because of male conception but because of 'female conception'.[59] The *conceptus de Spiritu sancto*, which according to Barth is the more important creedal clause, states positively the 'coming of His Word into human existence' and asserts that this is not just any mystery but that here

> God's reality becomes one with human reality. By its *natus ex Maria* it states that the person of Jesus Christ is the real son of a real mother, the son born of the body, flesh and blood of his mother, both of them as real as all the other sons of other mothers. It is thus that Jesus Christ is born and not otherwise. In this complete sense, He, too, is a man . . . He is man in a different way from the other sons of other mothers. But the difference . . . is so great, so fundamental and comprehensive, that it does not impair the completeness and genuineness of His humanity.[60]

For all its mystery and miraculous nature, Christmas is an event that concerns creatures – not in any monistic sense but in the sense that the Lord makes it so: 'It is not an event in the loneliness of God, but an event between God and man. Man is not there only in a supplementary capacity . . . he participates in the event as one of the principals . . . as the real man he is. The Word became flesh.'[61] But the fact of this participation is the result and embodiment of God's grace and judgment:

---

[58] *CD* I/2, 152.

[59] *CD* I/2, 185.

[60] *CD* I/2, 185. Importantly Barth notes that this miracle had already acquired the practical importance of 'a protection against gnostic and docetic ideas like those of Valentinus, according to whom Christ had received nothing from His human mother' (*CD* I/2, 185).

[61] *CD* I/2, 186.

> In that grace is imparted to him he is given not simply to be the spectator
> of an unusual event, but to participate in an event which contradicts and
> withstands him. Something decisive befalls him . . . something . . . which
> he can affirm and appreciate only in faith and not otherwise. Of course,
> in the judgment in which he is placed grace is concealed.[62]

Judgment here is signified by the fact that: (1) 'human nature possesses
no capacity for becoming the human nature of Jesus Christ . . . It cannot
be the work-mate of God.' It becomes this 'by the divine Word'. Mary's
virginity is not the denial of humanity in God's presence but 'of any
power, attribute or capacity in [us] for God'. This power comes to
Mary from God and in that sense it cannot be explained, but can only
be acknowledged. It is clear then that Barth does not ignore the
humanity of Christ but stresses that humanity in such a way that he
respects the fact that the *how* of this event cannot be explained but can
only be accepted. (2) Barth insists that the creature whose flesh the
Word assumes has lost 'his pure creatureliness' because 'he became
disobedient to his Creator'.[63] This nature, which is marked by sin, must
be judged (opposed and negated) so that we can humanly act as God's
fellow-workers. For flesh to be united with God is a mystery that must
be wrought, and that is what is signified by the *natus ex virgine*. Barth
insists that it was not the miracle that made possible God's becoming
man in Christ and the new beginning that took place there. Barth
insists that

> we can as little say that as we can say on Mk. 2.1–12 that the truth and
> reality of the fact that the Son of man has power on earth to forgive sins
> was made possible and effected by the healing of the paralytic. The
> forgiveness of sins is manifestly the thing signified, while the healing is
> the sign, quite inseparable from, but very significantly related to, this
> thing signified, yet neither identical with it nor a condition of it . . .[64]

This is why Barth insists that knowledge of what is here revealed is
knowledge of faith.

How then does Barth understand the action of the Holy Spirit in all
of this? When Barth speaks of the Holy Spirit he says that when the
Church depicts the Holy Spirit it refers to God in the strictest and
fullest sense, the Lord (that is, what Gunton portrays as God's
transcendence). This means that humanity relies on God 'upon whose
grace he is utterly thrown, and in whose promise alone his future

---

[62] *CD* I/2, 187–8.
[63] *CD* I/2, 188.
[64] *CD* I/2, 189.

consists'.[65] Jesus' human nature is conceived by the Holy Spirit. If we are clear about this then we will realize that there is no parallel between God the Holy Spirit and other deities which are the product of human mythology. The 'mythical miracles' associated with the gods invented by us are not real miracles, that is, 'signs of God, the Lord of the world'.[66] If God himself, God the Holy Spirit, is the author of this sign (the virgin birth), as he indeed is, then it cannot be understood as a natural possibility. It must be acknowledged as 'a pure divine beginning' and thus we cannot inquire 'as to whether or how this reality can be anything else but a pure divine beginning'.[67] It is the divinity of the Holy Spirit as the author of Christ's human nature together with the miraculous nature of the virgin birth that makes the virgin birth 'a sign of the mystery of Christmas'.[68] But why, Barth asks, is the Holy Spirit in particular named here? As Gunton remarks in a somewhat disparaging way, Barth says (with nuances left out of Gunton's reference): 'The Holy Spirit is God Himself in His freedom exercised in revelation to be present to His creature, even to dwell in him personally, and thereby to achieve his meeting with Himself in His Word and by this achievement to make it possible.'[69] The Holy Spirit enables us to believe, to be free for God and his work and to be an object of God's reconciliation. The Holy Spirit guarantees that human beings can participate in revelation and reconciliation.

It must be remembered that by revelation Barth aims to describe all that God does as Emmanuel or God with us. It is not noetic in place of emphasizing Jesus' saving significance as Gunton says.[70] But, as we have seen, for Barth, that which is noetic includes all aspects of human freedom.[71] Hence, God acts for us as our creator, reconciler and redeemer and thus includes us in Christ in a genuine participation in his own inner knowledge, love and freedom. Barth, however, insists upon the fact that the virgin birth indicates to us that, since God the Holy Spirit creates for us the possibility of being his free children in the

---

[65] *CD* I/2, 197.
[66] *CD* I/2, 197.
[67] *CD* I/2, 198.
[68] *CD* I/2, 198.
[69] *CD* I/2, 198.
[70] Gunton, *The Promise of Trinitarian Theology*, 20.
[71] See John Webster, *Barth's Moral Theology: Human Action in Barth's Thought* (T&T Clark: Edinburgh and Grand Rapids, MI: Eerdmans, 1998), 108, for his response to Gunton's criticism of Barth for underplaying the role of the Holy Spirit. It is precisely Barth's view of the Holy Spirit that enables him to give proper weight to human self-determination (freedom).

Church, the whence and whither of the Christian life remain a mystery grounded in an act that can be effected only by God in the unity of his Spirit and Word. Hence, Barth also insists that the virgin birth 'eliminates the last surviving possibility of understanding the *vere Deus vere homo* intellectually, as an idea or an arbitrary interpretation in the sense of docetic or ebionite Christology. It leaves only the spiritual understanding . . . in which God's own work is seen in God's own light'.[72]

Several other important points are made by Barth which show that he is much more aware than Gunton allows of the function of the Holy Spirit in relation to Christ's humanity and ours. Indeed, I would say that Barth's trinitarian understanding of the matter is clearer than Gunton's in the sense that he does not relegate the action of the Word into a corner and leave the rest to the Spirit. Rather, he sees the Spirit acting together with the Word: 'The very possibility of human nature's being adopted into unity with the Son of God is the Holy Ghost. Here, then at this fontal point in revelation, the Word of God is not without the Spirit of God . . . there is the togetherness of Spirit and Word.'[73] Further, Barth insists that human freedom takes place in and through the Holy Spirit; that God claims us for himself in the Spirit; that in virtue of the Holy Spirit there is 'a Church in which God's Word can be ministered, because it has the language for it . . . The freedom which the Holy Spirit gives us in this understanding and in this sphere . . . so far as it is . . . nothing else and no less than Himself – is the freedom of the Church, the children of God.'[74] This freedom is involved in the assumption of human nature by the Son of God: 'Through the Spirit flesh, human nature, is assumed into unity with the Son of God . . . this Man can be God's Son and at the same time the Second Adam and as such . . . the prototype of all who are set free for His sake and through faith in Him.'[75] Barth even insists that 'The sign of the baptism in Jordan, like the sign of the Virgin birth, points back to the mystery of this Man's being which was real in itself apart from this sign . . . [it] means that the Holy Spirit is the mystery of this being.'[76] And the mystery to which Barth refers is the fact that when the Spirit descended on Jesus (cf. Jn 1:32f.) he descended upon Jesus who 'actually is the beloved Son of God', and this could not mean that

[72] *CD* I/2, 177.
[73] *CD* I/2, 199.
[74] *CD* I/2, 198.
[75] *CD* I/2, 199.
[76] *CD* I/2, 199.

Jesus became the Son of God because of the Spirit's descent. In sum, for Barth the Spirit is important because, first, 'it refers back the mystery of the human existence of Jesus Christ to the mystery of God Himself ... that God Himself creates a possibility, a power, a capacity, and assigns it to man, where otherwise there would be sheer impossibility'.[77] And second, it refers back to the 'connexion which exists between our reconciliation and the existence of the Reconciler, to the primary realisation of the work of the Spirit'.[78]

One final point: while we saw above that adoptionist thinking threatens much contemporary Christology, with trinitarian implications, Barth is straightforward about the matter precisely because of his view of the Holy Spirit: 'The man Jesus of Nazareth is not the true Son of God because He was conceived by the Holy Spirit and born of the Virgin Mary ... He is the true Son of God and because this is an inconceivable mystery intended to be acknowledged as such, therefore He is conceived by the Holy Spirit and born of the Virgin Mary.'[79] For this reason he must be acknowledged as the one he is: 'The mystery does not rest upon the miracle. The miracle rests upon the mystery.'[80]

Jesus' Baptism and the Temptations

Because the tradition has neglected the importance of these two events, Gunton believes the charges of Docetism leveled at orthodox Christology are justified. Indeed he links Barth with this tradition since he argues that there is 'a fundamental flaw in his [Barth's] doctrine of God ... because he is weaker in handling the detail of that [Christ's] humanity, his theology can take on a Docetic air'.[81] For the tradition, the baptism has been taken to reveal the Trinity: 'The Father acknowledges the Son and sends the Spirit.'[82] But Gunton wants to consider 'those relationships that concern him [Jesus] as a human being, abstracting them, so far as is possible without distortion, from the ways in which, as the eternal Son, he is related to the Father and to the world'.[83] It will be remembered that for Barth we can never for a moment consider Jesus' humanity or his human relationships in abstraction from faith in the mystery of his being as the Word or Son incarnate – the very idea

---

[77] *CD* I/2, 199.
[78] *CD* I/2, 200.
[79] *CD* I/2, 202. See also *CD* IV/1, 207.
[80] *CD* I/2, 202.
[81] Sykes, *Karl Barth*, 60.
[82] Gunton, *Christ and Creation*, 53.
[83] Gunton, *Christ and Creation*, 47.

that this is possible consists in a separation of that which cannot be separated, that is, Jesus' divinity and humanity. That is why Barth rejected abstract Jesus worship. Barth was adamant about this point in his Christology, and Gunton's unwillingness to accept the limitation that Barth held was imposed by revelation itself is the key to their different epistemologies as we shall see shortly.

In any case Gunton argues that in order to focus on the *human* savior we must see that the Spirit directs Jesus' human life as the prophet, priest and king of Israel. In this context the general human relevance of the temptation stories becomes clear: 'If Jesus did not share our human trials, he is as irrelevant to our needs as if he had not borne the same flesh.'[84] Gunton rightly opposes any Docetic account of the temptations which might suggest that Jesus did not experience conflict here. In this regard he cites Edward Irving against Schleiermacher to say: 'Jesus was enabled to resist temptation not by some immanent conditioning, but by virtue of his obedience to the guidance of the Spirit.'[85] Barth is here criticized once again for not incorporating Jesus' free obedience into his theology at this point: 'his freedom is that he accepts it as a gift from the Father's sending of the Spirit. Freedom is . . . something exercised in relation to other persons . . . it is the gift of the Spirit who is God *over against us*, God in personal otherness enabling us to be free.'[86] Thus, for Gunton, in remaining true to his call to be the Messiah of Israel Jesus 'establishes his freedom'.[87] Gunton wants to stress, with Irving, that Jesus' relation to the Spirit changes because of his glorification: only after his resurrection could Jesus pour out the Spirit that led him during his life. Jesus' human actions as priest, prophet and king illustrate that (1) Jesus' humanity is 'perfected by the Spirit'; (2) 'In the perfect offering of himself to the Father through the eternal Spirit we witness one sample – and Irving can even speak of this as a *random* sample – of the creation in its integrity.'[88] Because creation has fallen into sin and disruption it has therefore lost its directedness to God. This is what is restored in Jesus' free obedience in a way that respects his and our freedom.

Interestingly, Karl Barth insisted that 'The Son of God exists with man and as man in this fallen and perishing state. We should be explaining the incarnation docetically and therefore explaining it away

---

[84] Gunton, *Christ and Creation*, 53.
[85] Gunton, *Christ and Creation*, 54.
[86] Gunton, *Christ and Creation*, 55.
[87] Gunton, *Christ and Creation*, 55.
[88] Gunton, *Christ and Creation*, 57.

if we did not put it like this, if we tried to limit in any way the solidarity with the cosmos which God accepted in Jesus Christ.'[89] Hence, Barth insisted that God did not evade our fallen state but 'exposed Himself to and withstood the temptation which man suffers and in which he becomes a sinner and the enemy of God'.[90] Jesus' sinlessness consists in the fact that he 'was obedient in that He willed to take our place as sinners and did, in fact, take our place. [His sinlessness] did not consist in an abstract and absolute purity, goodness and virtue. It consisted in His actual freedom from sin itself, from the basis of all sins.'[91] But this freedom is not pre-programmed for Barth any more than it was in the Gospels. This freedom consists in the fact that, unlike Adam, Jesus did not try to become his own judge but acknowledged that God was the only righteous judge. Jesus

> was a man as we are. His condition was no different from ours. He took our flesh, the nature of man as he comes from the fall. In this nature He is exposed every moment to the temptation to a renewal of sin – the temptation of impenitent being and thinking and speaking and action. His sinlessness was not therefore His condition. It was the act of His being in which He defeated temptation in His condition which is ours, in the flesh.[92]

At his baptism in the Jordan Jesus entered his way as the Judge who was then judged in our place on the cross. This has significance precisely because this man was and is the Son of God incarnate. This is the mystery of Jesus Christ and his sinlessness manifests the miracle of the grace of reconciliation. Barth analyzes the temptation stories indicating that Jesus was led by the same Spirit that the Baptist had seen descending on him in the Jordan into the wilderness in order to be tempted. And Barth insists that, while others should refrain from temptation, Jesus was willing to expose himself to it. And what was Jesus' temptation? It consisted in the fact that Jesus might not have been true to his calling by choosing to avoid the cross. This would have meant, however, that without his obedience the enmity of the world against God would have continued. Barth does a masterful job analyzing the temptation stories in the Gospels, and he shows clearly an awareness of Jesus' human experience and even identification with our fallen condition. But he does so in full awareness that the mystery of Jesus' existence is that as

---

[89] *CD* IV/1, 215.
[90] *CD* IV/1, 215.
[91] *CD* IV/1, 258.
[92] *CD* IV/1, 258–9.

man he was also the eternal Son who could forgive sins and judge us as well as experience judgment in our place and on our behalf. Barth's analysis of Jesus in Gethsemane takes full account of Jesus' human struggle and of his prayer that if it was in accordance with God's will his suffering might not have to be experienced. Nevertheless he was obedient. Yet it was not his obedience that caused our freedom from sin. His obedience was a sign of the fact that he could and did overcome sin: 'In the power of this prayer [in Gethsemane] Jesus received, that is, He renewed, confirmed and put into effect, His freedom to finish His work, to execute the divine judgment by undergoing it Himself.'[93] Experiencing this burden on behalf of all others, Jesus once for all liberated the human race from sin. In his prayer 'there took place quite simply the completion of the penitence and obedience which He had begun to render at Jordan and which He had maintained in the wilderness'.[94]

Unlike Gunton, Barth is able to do justice to the fact that what took place in the human life of Jesus was in fact the act of God the Son in the unity of his divine and human natures and under the direction of the Spirit. The mystery of Jesus' suffering and death cannot for a moment be separated from his being as the eternal Son of the eternal Father and assigned in that way to his free obedience. His free obedience was every bit a human action but it was at the same time the action of the Son of God. This did not make it any less free. Rather this mystery gives it its true meaning. It is important to acknowledge the working of the Spirit as Gunton insists. But Barth's theology offers an important additional feature without which the action of the Spirit is in danger of being separated from the Word once again. Barth insists that Jesus' human actions are never merely the actions of a human being who was not also the eternal Son of God. In that regard Jesus himself is the reconciler and the subject of the events of incarnation and reconciliation. That is the mystery of the Christian faith.

In spite of the important contributions Gunton has made to our understanding of the proper relation between the immanent and economic Trinity, there remains a problem with his theological epistemology. Instead of arguing with Barth that our knowledge of God is an event enclosed in the mystery of the Trinity, Gunton at times appears to imply that relationality is the subject while God's act becomes the predicate. Thus, he argues 'to a theology of being from

---

[93]   *CD* IV/1, 271.
[94]   *CD* IV/1, 272.

structures of relations. Who we are is made known to us through the relations in which we stand . . . Those relations reveal different ranges of mutuality and reciprocity, but they all . . . provide us with mirrors in which we may see ourselves as we are.'[95] And Gunton rejects Barth's view of God as one in three modes of being, not because it is modalist, but because 'it fails to reclaim the relational view of the person from the ravages of modern individualism. To be personal . . . is not to be an individual centre of consciousness or something like that . . . but to be one whose being consists in relations of mutual constitution with other persons.'[96] Hence, for Gunton, 'That is one of the glories of trinitarian thinking, for it enables unique and fruitful insight into the nature of being – all being – in relation.'[97] Here, once again, however, we must ask whether it is trinitarian thinking grounded in our experience of relations that can accomplish all this; is it not the case that even our trinitarian thinking cannot displace God's own act of unveiling which is here necessary for a proper understanding of divine and human relations? Do the relations in which we stand make known who we are, or is it God himself in his Word and Spirit who does this in and through our faith as we read scripture and live the Christian life? This important difference, in my view, stems from a failure to distinguish the immanent and economic Trinity precisely by separating God's Word and Spirit at the point where Barth refused to do so.

Jesus' Death

In connection with Jesus' death Gunton stresses the action of the Spirit in order to illuminate two features of Jesus' humanity: (1) the involvement of the incarnate Son in the network of the fallen creation and (2) his obedience to the Father's will that took place in the temptations and ministry.

> The relation of the human Jesus to the creation is therefore describable as a saving one. What he achieves, freely because through the enabling of the Spirit, is a matter of redemption because he offers to God the Father, through the Spirit, a renewed and cleansed sample of the life in the flesh in which human being consists.[98]

Therefore, contrary to Barth's view, Gunton insists that Jesus' miraculous birth 'belongs dogmatically more with the temptation and

---

[95] Gunton, *Christ and Creation*, 72.
[96] Gunton, *The Promise of Trinitarian Theology*, second edn, 195.
[97] Gunton, *The Promise of Trinitarian Theology*, second edn, 195–6.
[98] Gunton, *Christ and Creation*, 58–9.

cross than with the resurrection'.[99] This, because it indicates the beginning of Jesus' human story that moves toward the cross. As the Father's new creation was initiated through Jesus' birth, so the cross is where Jesus, through the Spirit 'perfected the obedience that he had learned through his temptation and ministry' [100] Hence, 'his obedience is salvific because here we have a representative sample of fallen flesh purified and presented to God the Father'.[101]

The question that must be asked of this analysis from the perspective of Barth's theology, however, is what happened to the particularity of the Son as an actor in all of this? Is it because of Jesus' free obedience, even as enabled by the Spirit, that redemption is achieved? Or is it because the offering he made to the Father was an offering made by the Son of God himself in the flesh? As T. F. Torrance has put it,

> After all, it was not the *death* of Jesus that constituted atonement, but Jesus Christ the Son of God offering Himself in sacrifice for us. Everything depends on *who* He was, for the significance of His acts in life and death depends on the nature of His Person . . . we must allow the Person of Christ to determine for us the nature of His saving work, rather than the other way round.[102]

Gunton's stress on the Spirit and on the humanity of Jesus is important. But by transferring the emphasis away from the person and work of Christ himself as the savior, his thinking underplays the mysterious and miraculous nature of Jesus' entire earthly life, including his death and resurrection. This man Jesus was God acting among us forgiving sins, healing and restoring us from death (sin) to new life. As Barth rightly insisted: 'This Son [of John's Gospel] is in no sense a being devoid of will . . . there are texts which imply the exercise of a very energetic will on the part of Jesus . . . there can be no question of supposing that Jesus is a sort of vacuum, the mere place where God lives and does His work as another and a stranger.'[103]

Barth also takes the problem of sin far more seriously than Gunton in that he believes our old sinful lives are doomed to death – they are not merely perfected, but brought from death to new life. These are problems that Barth consistently attempted to counter by his insistence that there never was a time when Jesus' humanity could or should be

[99] Gunton, *Christ and Creation*, 59.
[100] Gunton, *Christ and Creation*, 59.
[101] Gunton, *Christ and Creation*, 59.
[102] Torrance, *God and Rationality*, 64.
[103] *CD* III/2, 64.

considered in itself apart from the fact that it is the humanity of the eternal Son or Word of God. If Jesus' human life is solely the work of the Spirit, then does that not raise the question of whether or not the significance of the Word is left out of both the immanent and the economic Trinity? There is in fact, as Barth stressed, no way to God the Father, except through the Son. Barth astutely saw the problem here when he wrote:

> Jesus does . . . the work of the Saviour. But He really does it. It is not merely His fate to execute it. It does not simply happen in Him. 'No one taketh my life from me, but I lay it down of myself . . . and I have power to take it again.' And this laying down of His life is the fulfilment of the commandments which He has received [Jn] (10.18).[104]

This is what Barth meant when he wrote that 'God acts as Jesus acts'.[105] He had in mind Jn 9:33 where the man born blind observed, 'If this man were not of God he could do nothing.' Importantly, 'He acts in the name of God, and therefore in His own name . . . In what spirit but the Holy Spirit could the will to do so be born?'[106] Consequently, for Barth

> it is not merely the eternal but the incarnate Logos and therefore the man Jesus who is included in this circle [of the inner life of the Godhead]. He did not give up His eternal divinity when He concealed it to become man. He is still in the bosom of the Father . . . even in His coming to this world. Only on this assumption does Johannine Christology make sense.[107]

It is precisely at this point in his theological anthropology that Barth appeals to the doctrine of perichoresis to insist that the doctrine of the Trinity helps us understand the unity and trinity of God disclosed by Jesus in his relation with the Father. Indeed, Barth insists that it is precisely the inner life of the Trinity that is the very foundation of Jesus' human life among us. 'The Johannine Jesus, too, proclaims Himself unequivocally to be man. His history, too, is plainly a human history . . . the particular concern of the Fourth Gospel [in opposition to Docetism] . . . was a desire to show that the eternal divine Logos was this man Jesus'.[108]

[104] *CD* III/2, 64–5.
[105] *CD* III/2, 62.
[106] *CD* III/2, 62.
[107] *CD* III/2, 65.
[108] *CD* III/2, 66.

Unlike Gunton, however, Barth insists that Jesus' laying down his life for his friends is the same thing as God's so loving the world that he gave his only begotten Son.

> The giving of the Son by the Father indicates a mystery, a hidden movement in the inner life of the Godhead. But in the self-sacrifice of the man Jesus for His friends this intra-divine movement is no longer hidden but revealed. For what the man Jesus does by this action is to lay bare this mystery, to actualise the human and therefore the visible . . . aspect of this portion of the divine history of this primal moment of divine volition and execution.[109]

In his haste to emphasize the human story of Jesus in abstraction from his action as the Word or Son, Gunton has, to a certain extent, made Jesus a passive object who does little more than illustrate for us certain human features that are attributed to the action of the Spirit rather than the Word. For Barth, in virtue of the eternal perichoresis of the Father, Son and Spirit, we have an active disclosure of the love of God in Jesus' human action because he is included in and expressive of the eternal love of the immanent Trinity.

Gunton believes that in Barth election is conceived binitarianly with the result that the kenotic dimensions of Christ's life are underplayed and Barth loses a sense of eschatology; in addition it is said that Barth's focus on our human relations with God leads him to neglect creation itself.[110] In response to this, one might ask whether Mt. 11:27 is also too binitarian? Further, while Gunton wishes to see Jesus' human actions as enabled by the Spirit so as to avoid any idea that they are programmed or '*determined* by the (immanent) Word',[111] Barth actually insisted that election should be understood as the continual choice of a living subject, that is, Christ himself as electing God and elected man. If election is seen this way, then the Word would also be seen as active in a non-determinative way in the history of Jesus and precisely by his positing a truly limited humanity in that Jesus was a man of his time. Rather than making Jesus a timeless metaphysical idea, Barth insisted that all theological reflection had to begin and end with him as he was and is, namely, as electing God who was elected man. Gunton believes that Barth 'centered his development [of his treatise on the Trinity] on a conception of Jesus Christ as revelation'.[112] Alan Torrance makes a

---

[109] *CD* III/2, 66.
[110] Gunton, *Christ and Creation*, 95.
[111] Gunton, *The Promise of Trinitarian Theology*, 70.
[112] Gunton, *The Promise of Trinitarian Theology*, 20.

similar criticism by arguing that the root of the doctrine of the Trinity for Barth was 'the biblical concept of revelation'.[113] This thinking, which is of course indebted to Wolfhart Pannenberg, is not exactly accurate.

While Barth does say his concept of revelation is decisive, he also makes it very clear that it is revelation itself, that is, Jesus himself who is the root of the doctrine. Hence, Barth writes,

> What we do in fact gather from the doctrine of the Trinity is who the God is who reveals Himself, and this is why we present the doctrine here as an interpretation of revelation. We are not saying, then, that revelation is the basis of the Trinity, as though God were the triune God only in His revelation . . . What we are saying is that revelation is the basis of the doctrine of the Trinity . . . We arrive at the doctrine of the Trinity by no other way than that of an analysis of the concept of revelation.[114]

It is obvious from the context here that Barth's concept of revelation is determined by revelation itself, which he twice cites as the basis for the doctrine. This is extremely important, because if Jesus Christ is the starting point, then Barth's concepts of revelation and of the Trinity stand or fall by the extent to which they faithfully describe the reality of God present and active in the history of Jesus himself.

Jesus' Resurrection

According to Colin Gunton, the resurrection of Jesus extends his 'relations with the chosen people of God . . . universally'.[115] Here, Gunton is willing to speak of a retroactive force in that the resurrection 'brings it about that this man is not just for and against Israel, the mediator of her salvation and judgment, but that his eschatological rule is universal'.[116] Gunton rejects all subjectivist and Bultmannian views of the resurrection because he believes that creation's promised perfection is here realized by the Spirit. Like Robert Jenson before him, Gunton asks 'who it was [who] raised Jesus from the dead'.[117] In one sense Gunton notes that it is indeed an action of the triune God. But in virtue of the fact that scripture appropriates certain actions to certain

---

[113] Torrance, *Persons in Communion*, 239.

[114] *CD* I/1, 312. See also *CD* I/1, 346, where Barth insists that 'the root of the doctrine of the Trinity lies in revelation'.

[115] Gunton, *Christ and Creation*, 61.

[116] Gunton, *Christ and Creation*, 61. Astutely aware of the problems with theories like Rahner's anonymous Christianity, Gunton insists, 'To proclaim the universality of Jesus is not to condemn to hell all those who do not respond to him. It is to leave to the mercy of God the means of the final realisation of the kingdom' (61).

[117] Gunton, *Christ and Creation*, 62.

persons of the Trinity, Gunton also stresses that 'Incarnation and salvation must be understood as peculiarly the work of the Son' and argues that Jesus' resurrection should also be interpreted 'trinitarianly'. Here he objects to T. F. Torrance's understanding of Jesus' resurrection as the completion of his active obedience as the incarnate Son, asserting that, unless 'this is balanced by a firm assertion of the passivity of the Son, the link, made so firmly in Paul between Jesus' resurrection, as the first fruits, and ours is likely to be difficult to maintain'.[118]

Here again Gunton wishes to emphasize pneumatology. The Spirit should here be seen as the one who perfects creation and who is the agent of the eschatological act of resurrection. It is therefore as the first fruits of the transformation of the whole of creation that Jesus is the future for the world. 'If the resurrection is to be more than a revelation of the meaning of Christ and the will of the Father; if, that is to say, it is to *do* as well as simply *show* something . . . then it is as the beginnings of an eschatological redemption that we must see it . . . The resurrection brings it about that the particular humanity of Jesus becomes the basis of universal redemption.'[119]

Gunton thus stresses two key points. First,

> the resurrection establishes the representative status of Christ, because, as 'the first-born among many . . .', Rom. 8:29, he becomes the means whereby, through the Spirit, other created reality becomes perfected. It is . . . a matter of relationality: of how the relations to God of this human life become through the agency of the Spirit, the means of restoring to right relation those who had sought their own way and thus gone astray.[120]

Second, 'the churchly dimension of the matter is shown by the fact that the Spirit, by relating his people to the Father through the crucified and risen Jesus, moves towards perfection those first created in the image and likeness of their maker'.[121]

Again, what is completely missing from this analysis is any recognition of the active mediation of Jesus, recognized in faith, as the Word or Son of God not only revealing himself, but revealing the work of salvation that he himself had accomplished on our behalf. This does not take place without the Spirit but in the Spirit. But when Gunton observes that the Holy Spirit brings it about 'that the particular

---

[118] Gunton, *Christ and Creation*, 62–3.
[119] Gunton, *Christ and Creation*, 63–4.
[120] Gunton, *Christ and Creation*, 64.
[121] Gunton, *Christ and Creation*, 64–5.

humanity of Jesus becomes the basis of universal redemption' this implies a practical separation of Jesus' humanity and divinity and indeed suggests that it is Jesus' humanity as such that is a kind of passive focal point for the redemption of humanity. This needs to be balanced by the fact that Jesus' resurrection was only seen and understood by those with faith in him – faith given and received by the Holy Spirit. As T. F. Torrance notes: 'The Spirit is said to speak . . . what he has received from the Son.'[122] Hence, the mystery and miracle of this event must be respected. And it must be acknowledged that the power of the resurrection is the very power of God creating new life out of death, a power that was not absent from Jesus' person and work even before the resurrection. The resurrection is not merely the perfecting of human life, it is the restoration of human life from the brink of extinction. This is why Barth insisted that the resurrection could not be described as 'an operation proper to the *humanitas Christi* but rather as something done to it, as a being raised from the dead by God . . . the Godhead is not so immanent in Christ's humanity that it does not also remain transcendent to it'.[123] Hence for Barth

the power and continuity in which the man Jesus of Nazareth was in fact the revealed Word . . . consisted here too in the power and continuity of the divine action in this form [the man Jesus] and not in the continuity of this form as such . . . Revealing could obviously not be ascribed to His existence as such. His existence as such is indeed given up to death, and it is in this way, from death, from this frontier, since the Crucified was raised again, that He is manifested as the Son of God.[124]

Barth could speak powerfully about the resurrection in a way that Gunton does not:

The Church exists among Jews and Gentiles because Jesus in His resurrection does not shatter the power of death in vain but with immediate effect; because as the witness to eternal life He cannot remain alone but at once awakens, gathers and sends forth recipients, partners and co-witnesses of this life . . . Man elected by God is man made participant by God in eternal salvation. It is this man whom God's community in its perfect, its Church form can reveal. It reveals that even death is surrounded by life, even hell (in all its terrible reality) by the kingdom of the beloved Son of God.[125]

[122] Torrance, *The Trinitarian Faith*, 248.
[123] *CD* I/1, 323.
[124] *CD* I/1, 323.
[125] *CD* II/2, 264–5.

Here a proper understanding of the power of the resurrection is tied to a proper understanding of predestination. For Barth, as is well known, predestination or election is unequivocally linked with Jesus Christ himself as electing God and elected man. But for Barth election, which is indeed the sum of the gospel, is a living action on the part of the living God. It is not, as Gunton and Jenson assume, identical with a timeless and static past action of God: 'It is not the case, then that God did will but that now He no longer wills, or wills only the effects of His willing . . . God is never an echo. He is and continues to be and always will be an independent note or sound. The predestination of God is unchanged and unchangeably God's activity.'[126] Here Barth strongly opposes the idea that God could in any sense become 'His own prisoner'. Barth thus insisted that

> Only as concrete decree, only as an act of divine life in the Spirit, is it the law which precedes all creaturely life. In virtue of its character and content this decree can never be rigid and fixed. It can never belong only to the past . . . it is an act of divine life in the Spirit . . . it is the presupposition of all the movement of creaturely life . . . [it is] an act which occurs in the very midst of time no less than in that far distant pre-temporal eternity. It is the present secret, and in the history of salvation the revealed secret, of the whole history, encounter and decision between God and man . . . If it is true that the predestinating God not only is free but remains free, that He does not cease to make use of His freedom but continues to decide, then in the course of God's eternal deciding we have constantly to reckon with new decisions in time . . . developments and alterations . . . are always possible and do in fact take place.[127]

For Barth then 'The Word of the divine steadfastness is the resurrection of Jesus from the dead, His exaltation, His session at the right hand of the Father. By these events God confirms the fact that the Elect is the only-begotten Son of God who can suffer death but cannot be holden of death, who by His death must destroy death.'[128] That is why Barth insists that 'To believe in Jesus means to have His resurrection and prayer both in the mind and in the heart.'[129] In Barth's theology then, the mystery of faith consists in the fact that the man Jesus, as Son of God, not only died for our sins out of love for us, but rose again from the dead and in this very power of the resurrection he continues to

---

[126] *CD* II/2, 183.
[127] *CD* II/2, 184–7.
[128] *CD* II/2, 125.
[129] *CD* II/2, 127.

interact with us now in the power of his Holy Spirit. He speaks his Word which can be heard and obeyed in faith. The Spirit unites us to him and thus enables the transformation of our humanity. It goes without saying that, like Gunton, Barth's theology of the resurrection, with special clarity in *CD* III/2, stresses its objective facticity against any subjectivist or Bultmannian interpretation.

Jesus' Ascension

For Gunton the ascension is a historical event in the sense that it happened within history. It is 'the final closure of Jesus' earthly career' and involves 'the taking up of his humanity into God'.[130] Gunton correctly rejects the idea that there has always been a humanity of God and insists, against Barth, that the ascension is not merely revelation but event, that is, 'something which brings about a new state of affairs. History is decisive.'[131] Here, Gunton makes a clear distinction between the immanent and economic Trinity to argue that Jesus is humanly taken into the eternity of God and lives as the mediator. This does not, he says, imply a change in the inner being of God.

Gunton does not wish to see the resurrection as a retroactive force in Pannenberg's sense, which implies that Jesus' oneness with God was realized in the resurrection and thus that 'he was not uniquely one with the Father [before the resurrection], but that after it he is made to have been one with him all along'.[132] In Gunton's view, Pannenberg's thinking also underplays the fact that the Holy Spirit is 'the one by whom we understand Jesus to have been from the beginning one with the Father'.[133] Gunton wants to give the Spirit structural significance in Jesus' human life which he finds missing from both Pannenberg and Barth. Gunton is therefore critical of the fact that the ascension has often been treated as an appendix to the resurrection 'as for example in Barth's treatment of the virgin birth and resurrection as miracles to mark the beginning and end of Jesus' earthly life'.[134] By contrast, Gunton argues that it is the ascension 'that establishes Jesus as the eternal mediator between heaven and earth, by virtue of that which he did and suffered as man'. Ascension thus completes 'the earthwards movement of the Son, the opening of heaven to earth'.[135]

---

[130] Gunton, *Christ and Creation*, 65.
[131] Gunton, *Christ and Creation*, 65–6.
[132] Gunton, *Christ and Creation*, 66.
[133] Gunton, *Christ and Creation*, 66.
[134] Gunton, *Christ and Creation*, 66–7.
[135] Gunton, *Christ and Creation*, 67.

Interestingly, many of Gunton's criticisms of Barth are echoed by Douglas Farrow in his recent book on the ascension. Farrow also accuses Barth of a kind of Christomonism and Docetism. He also believes that a residue of natural theology caused Barth to define eternity by time and that Barth's doctrine of election 'seals the historical Jesus in eternity'. But, like Gunton, Farrow tends to separate God's actions in his Word and Spirit, as, for example, when he criticizes T. F. Torrance saying, 'To look beyond Jesus' humanity to the operation of his divinity in order to explain his "towering authority" over the world is a move that runs counter to everything we have been saying. We must look instead to the Spirit'.[136] Why should we look to the Spirit *instead* of the Word? Should we not instead look to the Spirit to be enlightened by the Word through sharing in his new humanity, as T. F. Torrance rightly held?[137] In Farrow's view, 'it is only by means of the Spirit . . . that this human work of filling and fulfilling, satisfying and perfecting, is achieved'.[138] Why *only* by the Spirit? Can we separate the Spirit from the Word at this important point without falling into some form of Docetism or adoptionism? It is no accident that Farrow totally rejects any idea of a *logos asarkos* while, as we have seen above, Barth insisted that such an idea was essential to enable us to see the free basis that God's actions *ad extra* have in the inner being of God.

This thinking leads to the odd conclusion that Jesus' *human* pre-existence is what is being referred to in the Gospel of John, a view that Gunton himself rightly criticizes. Even more puzzlingly, as seen above in Chapter Three, Farrow contends '*That* he [Jesus] goes [ascends] makes him the way [to the Father].'[139] This is reminiscent of Gunton's observation that the ascension 'establishes Jesus as the eternal mediator . . . by virtue of that which he did and suffered as man'. But is it really by virtue of his human actions that Jesus *becomes* the mediator and the way to the Father? Or is it not the case that, mysteriously and miraculously from the very beginning of his earthly way, Jesus was the way to the Father and the eternal mediator, just because he was the Word incarnate? In his important and illuminating book, Farrow insists

---

[136] Farrow, *Ascension and Ecclesia*, 266.

[137] See, e.g., *The Trinitarian Faith*, 248ff. Following Athanasius, Torrance writes, 'It is because the Word and the Spirit mutually inhere in one another that the Holy Spirit is not dumb but eloquent of Christ the incarnate Word' (249, see also 267ff.). For Torrance, Jesus 'makes our humanity in him partake of the Holy Spirit with which he has been anointed and sanctified *as man* for our sakes, and thereby unites it through himself with the Godhead' (267).

[138] Farrow, *Ascension and Ecclesia*, 267.

[139] Farrow, *Ascension and Ecclesia*, 36.

that 'Jesus-history' rather than Jesus the incarnate Word as the living subject of these events, is his theological criterion. But in my view it is precisely his understanding of Jesus-history, which, as we have already seen, is defined as 'the sanctification of our humanity through the life and passion and heavenly intercession of Jesus',[140] that leaves out the most important ingredient in Christology that Barth's theology supplies: namely, the fact that it is precisely because this man was God himself active among us that leads to the sanctification of our humanity in his, through the activity of the Holy Spirit. Importantly, Farrow believes that people today stumble more over Jesus' humanity than his divinity. Yet his very analysis shows that the greatest problem today is the same as it always has been: the attempt to construct a Christology that bypasses Jesus' actual uniqueness as truly divine and human without separation or confusion.

In fact, Barth's theology never loses its emphasis on the unity of the Word and Spirit acting *ad extra* because Barth insisted that Father, Son and Spirit were also one *ad intra* and indeed he insisted that our sanctification is traceable to the action of God incarnate and not to Jesus' human action as such. This is why Barth continually stresses that true theological knowledge takes place in faith as a work of God in and through our human activity without mixture and confusion of divine and human action.[141] As noted above, Farrow's thinking leads him to search for a 'eucharistic world-view',[142] while Barth clearly and correctly recognized that *all* world-views represent human attempts to avoid the lordship of Jesus Christ.[143] In Barth's thinking any such search betrays its Docetic tendency at the outset by allowing a world-view rather than the living Christ to be its criterion of theological truth. Beyond that, the very idea that Jesus humanly pre-existed his birth on earth[144] – even if it is understood retroactively in Farrow's sense – suggests a Docetic understanding of humanity just because it cannot admit that Jesus' humanity is just as fully limited as ours, in the sense that it came into being at a particular point in time. It is just here that a proper understanding of the *logos asarkos* would have allowed Farrow to make a distinction made by Barth. He could have said that, while God's eternal decree is to be God for us, and that while this decree indicates God's eternal attitude toward the world (with Jesus Christ as the

---

[140] Farrow, *Ascension and Ecclesia*, 6.
[141] See, e.g., *CD* II/1, 55f.
[142] Farrow, *Ascension and Ecclesia*, 73, 78.
[143] See, e.g., *CD* IV/3, 254ff. and Chapter Three above.
[144] Farrow, *Ascension and Ecclesia*, 297.

beginning of all God's ways and works *ad extra*), still God is and remains the free Lord of both his inner life and his works *ad extra*. Therefore one cannot collapse God's pre-temporal, supra-temporal and post-temporal existence manifested in the history of Jesus into 'Jesus-history' without calling into question God's freedom *in se* which is the basis, meaning and goal of all created freedom. In my opinion this is indeed what finally happens to Farrow when he concludes, 'here, in this man, we encounter an expression of the love of God that has eternal validity'.[145] Why does he not say that here, in this man, we encounter God himself; not just *an* expression of God's love, but God himself in the flesh as the subject of this event in his unity with the Holy Spirit?

With respect to Barth's view of Christ's ascension, he argues that the resurrection and ascension add 'only the new fact that in this event He was to be seen and was actually seen as the One He was and is. He did not become different in this event.'[146] What did Barth mean by this? He meant that 'The being of Jesus Christ was and is perfect and complete in itself in His history as the true Son of God and Son of Man.'[147] Thus, the risen and ascended Jesus Christ does not need new qualities or further developments. Rather, the covenant was indeed fulfilled in him with the reconciliation of the world.

> His being as such (if we may be permitted this abstraction for a moment) was and is the end of the old and the beginning of the new form of this world even without His resurrection and ascension. He did not and does not lack anything in Himself. What was lacking was only the men to see and hear it as the work and Word of God – the praise and thanksgiving and obedience of their thoughts and words and works.[148]

Does this mean that the historical events of resurrection and ascension then were unnecessary or meaningless? No. What Barth intends to say is that the power of the resurrection was not absent from the life of Jesus even before the actual occurrences and that the actual occurrences mean the disclosure of his glory and the exaltation of humanity in him.

In fact Barth's understanding of this matter is anti-Docetic:

> Like all men, the man Jesus has His lifetime . . . a fixed span with a particular duration . . . the eternal content of his life must not cause us to miss or to forget or to depreciate this form . . . as though we could see

---

[145] Farrow, *Ascension and Ecclesia*, 293.
[146] *CD* IV/2, 133.
[147] *CD* IV/2, 132.
[148] *CD* IV/2, 132–3.

and have the content without it . . . It is as a man of His time, and not otherwise that He is the Lord of time.'[149]

For Barth, 'At bottom Docetism is "the failure to respect the historically unique character of the redemptive deed of Christ".'[150] In this context Barth insists upon the historical nature of the resurrection because as a man of his time Jesus appeared among the apostles as 'the Resurrected'. It was by their specific historical memory of the 40 days and not by some timeless idea that the apostles and churches they founded lived in relation to Jesus.

In his physical resurrection from the dead Jesus is the 'Revealer of His hidden glory as God's eternal Word incarnate.'[151] But this has significance for us because, as Jn 20:21 says, 'These [signs] are recorded so that you may believe that Jesus is the Christ, the Son of God, and that believing this you may have life through his name.' Barth also insists that the ascension, together with the empty tomb, are indispensable for understanding the Easter message. They 'mark the limits of the Easter period'.[152] Both are indicated rather than described because for Barth the content of the New Testament witness was neither the empty tomb nor the fact that the disciples saw Jesus 'go up to heaven',[153] but 'that when they had lost Him through death they were sought and found by Him as the Resurrected'.[154] The empty tomb and ascension therefore are signs of Easter as the virgin birth is the sign of the nativity.

For Barth the ascension serves a positive function by pointing forward and upward. As the empty tomb marks the beginning of Easter history, so the ascension marks its end. Still, for Barth 'the ascension – Jesus' disappearance into heaven – is the sign of the Resurrected, not the Resurrected Himself'.[155] For Barth the point of the ascension then is that when Jesus left the disciples 'He entered the side of the created world which was provisionally inaccessible and incomprehensible . . . This does not mean . . . that he ceased to be a creature.'[156] He was a creature who lived and acted as God incarnate and now had been taken up into heaven and would come again. He would be

---

[149] *CD* III/2, 440.
[150] *CD* III/2, 441.
[151] *CD* III/2, 451.
[152] *CD* III/2, 452.
[153] *CD* III/2, 453.
[154] *CD* III/2, 453.
[155] *CD* III/2, 453.
[156] *CD* III/2, 454.

with them always even to the end of the world (Mt. 28:20). This is an important text that Barth often repeats in order to stress that it is the living Jesus Christ who is risen and ascended and that it is indeed this same glorified Jesus Christ who is the object of faith and hope and who will come again to complete for the rest of history what was a completed event for us in his history. For Barth, 'The ascension is the proleptic sign of the *parousia*, pointing to the Son of Man who will finally and visibly emerge from the concealment of His heavenly existence and come on the clouds of heaven (Mt. 24:30).'[157] The ascension is thus indispensable as a sign of the fact that at the conclusion of the Easter history Jesus is not to be sought in any kind of hiddenness but in the hiddenness of God, a hiddenness that 'burgeons with the conclusive revelation still awaited in the future'.[158]

While Barth might agree with Gunton that Jesus' ascension completes the earthward movement of the Son, his thinking certainly calls into question Gunton's belief that Jesus is established as the mediator by virtue of that which he did and suffered as man. For Barth the mystery and miracle that Jesus Christ was and is means that what he did and suffered as man disclosed who he was and what he actually accomplished by virtue of who he was. From the beginning, that is, from his conception, Jesus was already the mediator in a mysterious and miraculous way because he was the Word incarnate. This activity obviously did not take place without the action of the Holy Spirit. This was indeed the power of the resurrection that was hidden from the disciples and revealed in the Easter history. Jesus himself was and is actively the mediator as the only man who was God. Thus when T. F. Torrance finds Jesus' 'towering authority' in his divinity, this insight is not opposed to the fact that the Spirit enables Jesus' free human activity; rather this insight complements the fact that Jesus could reconcile the world and could forgive sins because he was uniquely the Son of God in the flesh. That is why theological knowledge is the knowledge of faith: it begins by, in and through the Holy Spirit who unites us to Christ as the one who speaks his Word as a revelation of the Father. According to Barth, Jesus' resurrection revealed that he was and is 'the bearer of all power in heaven and earth'.[159] In this sense the ascension is the concluding form of the Risen Christ's appearances by which he created faith and created the Church. Barth also stresses Calvin's view that the ascension is

[157] *CD* III/2, 454.
[158] *CD* III/2, 454.
[159] Barth, *Credo*, 113.

the *end* of these appearances of the Risen One . . . God's revelation having taken place once and for all in Christ, the Ascension makes a separation, a distance between Him and His disciples, between Him and the world generally. Ended is the time of His direct, His 'worldly' presence in the world, to which the 40 days unmistakably belonged. There dawns – one could also say, there returns, the time of the *Church*.[160]

In the time between the resurrection and ascension and his second coming Jesus is present indirectly and in faith as God and man and through the Holy Spirit so that reconciliation may be acknowledged and lived as free grace: 'It is no longer and not yet the time for the "beholding of His glory" (Jn i. 14; cf. 2 Cor. v. 7).'[161]

The difference between Barth and Farrow and Gunton then concerns the fact that for Barth the ascension shows the kind of power Jesus exercised in his earthly life and in his risen and ascended life. Farrow and Gunton insist that something new happened in history to Jesus and that history is determinative here. Barth insists that something new happened to Jesus in history too, but that it is the power of the Word incarnate that is determinative here. Thus, for Barth we must acknowledge that Christ's history was a completed event while at the same time we must acknowledge that he is coming again to complete the redemption that is a reality in his risen and ascended existence, as the hope of our future. Here once again a clear distinction between the immanent and economic Trinity allows Barth to steer clear of any suggestion that history rather than God acting within history determines past, present and future meaning.

Conclusion

More than any other modern theologian, besides Thomas F. Torrance, Colin E. Gunton sees the importance of a contemporary doctrine of the immanent Trinity. Gunton clearly wishes to avoid any sort of illegitimate agnosticism and the pantheism and dualism that follow. He vigorously opposes any sort of projectionism. Further, he certainly avoids grounding theology in transcendental experience and sees that everything looks different in the light of the Trinity. He wishes to maintain Christ's uniqueness and particularity and makes every effort to avoid any sort of modalism or idealism.

But in recent years especially, Gunton has become more and more critical of Barth's theology because he believes that Barth paid less

---

[160] Barth, *Credo*, 113–14.
[161] Barth, *Credo*, 114.

attention to Jesus' humanity and to ours. This critique is based on Gunton's belief that Barth's doctrine of the Spirit is inadequate. I have contrasted Gunton and Barth on key theological issues that Gunton himself suggests might allow for greater emphasis on history and humanity to show that Barth's doctrine of the Spirit insists, in a way that Gunton's does not, that there can be no separation of the Spirit and Word without falling into the dangers of Ebionite and Docetic Christology. Ultimately, the difficulty here concerns the fact that Gunton is willing to abstract from Jesus' being as the Word in areas of his reflection and then search for transcendentals or analogies grounded in a concept of relationality that is not always dictated by the immanent Trinity.

Chapter Ten

Conclusion

THERE is a thread that runs through this book. And that thread suggests that there is a tendency today among theologians to allow experience rather than the Word of God revealed to dictate the meaning of theological categories. A contemporary doctrine of the immanent Trinity should recognize that, while the doctrine of the Trinity begins with an experience of God in the economy, it nonetheless directs us away from our experiences and toward God's Word and Spirit as the source of theological knowledge. To be sure, God meets us in our experiences of faith and hope; but the object of trinitarian reflection is and remains God and never becomes our experiences of faith and hope. In this sense the doctrine of the immanent Trinity is a description of who God is who meets us in and through our experiences and not simply a description of salvation history or of our experiences of faith and hope. We have seen repeatedly that, whenever and wherever theologians think the doctrine is simply a way of describing the Christian experiences of faith, hope or salvation, such thinking invariably substitutes some form of trinitarian thinking for the trinitarian God acting *ad extra*.

It has been my contention that there are at least four indicators that suggest that much trinitarian theology today has failed to recognize the need for a suitable doctrine of the immanent Trinity. As we have seen, these indicators are (1) the trend toward making God, in some sense, dependent upon and indistinguishable from history; (2) the lack of precision in Christology which leads to the idea that Jesus, in his humanity as such, is the revealer; (3) the failure to distinguish the Holy

Spirit from the human spirit; (4) a trend to begin theology with experiences of self-transcendence, thus allowing experience rather than the object of faith to determine the truth of theology.

I have argued that a proper doctrine of the immanent Trinity is one that recognizes, respects and upholds God's freedom *in se* and *ad extra*; a doctrine that realizes that human freedom is grounded in God's freedom for us exercised in his Word and Spirit. I have stressed that such a doctrine will not become embroiled in what Rahner called wild conceptual acrobatics by speculating about God's inner nature in abstraction from God's own self-communication in the economic Trinity. I have argued that a proper doctrine of the immanent Trinity will acknowledge that our relation with God is an irreversible one, so that while we can and must say that we meet the immanent Trinity in our encounter with the economic Trinity, still we cannot simply assert that the economic Trinity *is* the immanent Trinity and vice versa. Instead, a clear and sharp distinction must be drawn; one that allows for the fact of God's free grace.

I have stressed, therefore, that theologians should neither separate nor confuse the immanent and economic Trinity and that, because theology really is faith (in the triune God) seeking understanding and not understanding seeking faith, we must adhere to the economic Trinity for our information about the immanent Trinity. This is crucial, because even some theologians who do not deny the relevance of the immanent Trinity altogether tend to allow some principle of relationality or temporality or transcendence and immanence to be defined first from a general ontology based upon some form of transcendental experience. Only then do they turn to the economy to see how the doctrine of the Trinity may enrich that ontology. I have tried to show that a contemporary doctrine of the immanent Trinity would prevent any such thinking simply because it would lead to the positive recognition that God has in fact exercised his transcendent freedom to be for us specifically in Christ and the Spirit. These are not just concepts describing Christian experience; they are not concepts that we invest with meaning according to our own social, psychological or political goals and ideals. Jesus Christ and the Holy Spirit cannot be ignored or bypassed even for a moment because in fact there is no other way to God the Father than through the Son. This is not an imperialistic projection of Christian self-consciousness, but a humble acceptance of God's actual judgment and grace. I have agreed with Karl Barth, who believed the content of the doctrine of the Trinity is that God is the eternal Father, Son and Holy Spirit and that God's internal relations could not be reduced to God's relations with us as creator, mediator and redeemer. This fact itself, which is in accord with T. F. Torrance's view that what God is toward us he is eternally in himself, is indeed the surest of facts, beyond which there can be no other which can serve as the root of the doctrine of the Trinity today. There is no escaping Athanasius's observation that 'It is more pious and more accurate to signify God from the Son and call him Father, than to name him from his works and call him Unoriginate.' The central difficulty surrounding contemporary trinitarian theology is precisely the failure to stick to this particular approach to God. From this Athanasian insight it follows that God can only be known with certainty and clarity from God himself as he includes us in his own eternal knowing and loving through faith and by grace. Every attempt to understand the Christian God that bypasses the Son of God incarnate amounts to a human attempt to construct the image of God without God himself and even against God himself.

This very limitation then is what is disregarded most in recent trinitarian theology. Karl Rahner, who is considered one of the pre-eminent theologians of the twentieth century, and who is famous for having restored the doctrine to the center of Christian faith and practice, will not allow Jesus Christ to be his exclusive starting point, and so in that very way he bypasses the sure foundation for trinitarian theology and, as we have seen, he allowed his thinking about the Trinity to be shaped by his philosophy and theology of the symbol. The result was a kind of universalism that claimed that we can experience Christ and Christ's resurrection without knowing about him specifically and by simply thematizing our own transcendental experiences. I have addressed his work extensively because his methodology has affected so many other modern theologians, whose work is a logical outworking of his faulty premises.

This is a form of self-justifying theology that I have shown to be excluded from a trinitarian theology that begins and ends its reflections with Jesus Christ himself, who is the Son of God incarnate simply because he is – without any need for proof or verification from Christian experience or ideology. His existence in history for us simply calls for acknowledgment, not verification – only he can verify who he is in and through the power of his Holy Spirit. One of the key functions of a proper doctrine of the immanent Trinity is to allow for the fact that God sets the terms for theological insight; not the Church and certainly not humanity with its questions and insights, however important they may be, humanly speaking.

I have discussed Karl Barth's deliberate and consistent rejection of Ebionite and Docetic Christology because it reflected his constant attempt to begin his trinitarian theology with Jesus Christ himself and not with some idea of divinity or some experience of Jesus' importance for the community. This led him to a clear distinction (but not a separation) of the immanent and economic Trinity. We have seen that this is not the dominant view today. And we have also seen that much modern theology of the Trinity tends to assume that Jesus is in some sense the revealer in his humanity as such. This lack of precision in Christology leads to an emphasis on Jesus' humanity that tends to ignore the all-important fact that this man was God, and it thus also underplays the consequent need for faith. Even the most sophisticated contemporary trinitarian theologies seem to allow an emphasis on the Holy Spirit to displace the action of the Word in union with the Holy Spirit. For some, there is a tendency to confuse the Holy Spirit with the human spirit. For others, there is the tendency toward adoptionism and thus toward the separation of the Word and Spirit. Yet if T. F. Torrance and Karl Barth are right in stressing that the very center of Christian theology concerns the fact that Jesus really was God, then any adoptionist overtones simply reflect the fact that contemporary theology finds it difficult, perhaps even a little embarrassing, that it must begin at this particular place and this place alone, namely, with Jesus who is the eternally begotten Son of the Father who came down from heaven for us and for our salvation.

A proper doctrine of the immanent Trinity that made a clear and sharp distinction between the immanent and economic Trinity would continually return to Jesus Christ himself, prompted by his Holy Spirit to understand divine and human freedom. Because such a doctrine speaks of the eternal Father, Son and Spirit as the foundation for human freedom and for the relative independence of the created world in general, proper theological thinking can never be agnostic. Agnostic thinking, as we have seen, speaks of a divine incomprehensibility as of a void left for us to fill with as many images of transcendence (and/or immanence) as we can muster. But we have seen that a proper doctrine of the immanent Trinity sees at once the danger and irrelevance of such thinking. God's being and act are God's very definite acts as creator, Lord, reconciler and redeemer. While God is and remains incomprehensible even in his revelation, he nevertheless is known and knowable as a very definite object in faith and by grace. Here is the true mystery of the triune God that is at once both veiled and unveiled by God's own act. God is not an object we can control existentially either in thought or in prayer; but the Christian God is still Emmanuel – God with us. Yet this God is and remains the only divine subject in the encounter and the roles may never be reversed. A sound doctrine of the immanent Trinity recognizes this freedom of God as the basis of our own human freedom; it recognizes what Barth referred to as the antecedent existence of the Father, Son and Spirit.

It is unfortunate but true that, wherever this false kind of agnosticism is allowed to function, that is, in theologies that do not keep to God's economic trinitarian self-revelation, God becomes dependent upon creation and humanity in some way, shape or form. This dependence, we have seen, dominates the thinking of those who explicitly reject, ignore or pay lip-service to a doctrine of the immanent Trinity. It also affects the thinking of those who accept the doctrine but see it mainly as a description of the events of salvation or the experience of salvation. Any such dependence, however, whether it is blatantly untheological or apparently profoundly theological, represents a failure to respect the fact that God alone reveals God. God alone establishes and maintains fellowship between himself and creatures. Consequently, pantheism is one of the chief threats to contemporary trinitarian theology. If God cannot in fact be distinguished from our own experiences and thoughts about ourselves and the world we live in, as he certainly cannot in a pantheistic or panentheistic view, then trinitarian theology, for all its attempts to reinvigorate the Christian life, actually makes Christianity more irrelevant than ever. What could be more irrelevant than a theology that really believes trinitarian life is our life? Our life is doomed to death and in need of a reconciler and redeemer. Our new life is hidden with Christ in God. Pantheism, which makes the truth dependent upon one's point of view, never even sees the need for another outside itself because, from the very outset, pantheism identifies God with creation and sees them as in some sense mutually dependent. It is precisely such thinking that places the key to salvation in the hands of Christians as they attempt to live the Christian life. But it is just such a form of self-reliance that has been rendered illusory by what has happened on our behalf in the history of Jesus Christ himself and his ongoing history, through the Spirit and in the Church and world today. A proper doctrine of the immanent Trinity would recognize God's freedom in such a way that our constant need for Jesus' active lordship would lead us away from any sort of self-reliance and toward Jesus Christ coming again. He is the only one who is and remains the way, the truth and the life; neither an idea of him nor an experience of him and not a doctrine about him, but Jesus the risen and ascended Lord himself, who guides us now in truth through his Holy Spirit.

We therefore end where we began, that is, with a recognition of God's freedom to be and to have been the eternal Father, Son and Spirit who existed prior to and apart from creation; we also recognize that God is not limited by his freedom *in se* so that he is also free to be for us in a way that surpasses all forms of created communion. This freedom for us, which includes both judgment and grace, is the surest of facts upon which a theology of the Trinity can indeed build. But it is a fact that will only be clearly seen and understood where and when a clear doctrine of the immanent Trinity is expressed. Such a doctrine, as we have seen, necessarily maintains a clear and sharp distinction between the immanent and the economic Trinity in each of its theological reflections.

Appendix

S INCE I have relied on the thinking of Thomas F. Torrance throughout
this book, I think it would be instructive to explore Colin Gunton's
criticisms of Torrance's trinitarian theology which appear in a recent
volume on the theology of T. F. Torrance entitled *The Promise of
Trinitarian Theology: Theologians in Dialogue with T. F. Torrance.* My
goal here is to clarify a number of important issues that have emerged
in our attempt to construct a proper doctrine of the immanent Trinity. In
addition, I would like to explore, however briefly, the problem of
the *filioque* which has not yet been discussed.

We begin with four critical issues that Gunton considers in relation
to the doctrine of the immanent Trinity. The first concerns the
justification for a theological move from the economic to the immanent
Trinity, and in this regard Gunton believes Torrance's method is
generally the same as Barth's, that is, God is toward us what he is in
himself. The second question concerns the function of the doctrine.
Here Gunton insists that Torrance properly opted for a distinction
between the immanent and economic Trinity in order to reject any
idealist attempt to confuse the two by confusing the order of knowing
with the order of being, as Rahner apparently had done. Again, Torrance
is perceived to be similar to Barth here. It is in connection with the
third and fourth points that Gunton's criticisms of T. F. Torrance
emerge.

Let us consider these briefly as they relate especially to a doctrine of
the immanent Trinity. How should we understand the terms 'being'
and 'person'? Gunton rightly notes that for Torrance we do not begin
thinking about the triune God either with God's oneness or his threeness

but rather with the fact that God is simultaneously one being, three persons. Still, Gunton finds fault with Torrance's use of the term *perichoresis*. Accordingly, he believes that for Torrance *perichoresis* serves to 'hold powerfully together . . . the identity of the divine Being and the intrinsic unity of the three divine Persons'.[1] This Gunton believes is not the usual function of the term; its usual function, he thinks, is to show 'how three distinct persons can yet constitute one God'. Thus, according to Gunton, Torrance believes *perichoresis* led to a new concept of persons in which 'the relations between persons belongs to what they are'. He thus says that its meaning for Torrance is derived mainly from the economy 'rather than reflection on the relation of the eternal persons'.[2]

But is this really what Torrance believes? A close reading of Torrance on his understanding of *perichoresis* shows that his use of the term is intimately connected with the term *homoousion* and that its meaning is strictly governed 'by the mutual indwelling of the Father and the Son and the Spirit'.[3] Torrance notes that Gregory Nazianzen originally used the term to speak of Christ's divine and human natures, but that it was then changed to refer to 'the complete mutual containing or inter-penetration of the three divine Persons, Father, Son and Holy Spirit, in one God'.[4] Further, Torrance insists that while it is through revelation that we know of the 'coinherent relations within the one being of God',[5] still the meaning of this concept was grounded upon the relations within God's being made known in revelation. This is why Torrance insists that

> Just as we take our knowledge of the Father from our knowledge of the Son, so we must take our knowledge of the Spirit from our knowledge of the Son, and in him from our knowledge of the Father: that is, from the inner relations which the Father, Son and Holy Spirit have with one another in the one indivisible being of the Holy Trinity.[6]

Indeed Torrance argues that 'It is on that inner divine basis, and not on any creaturely basis outside of God, that the life and work of Christ

---

[1] Colin Gunton, 'Being and Person: T. F. Torrance's Doctrine of God', in *The Promise of Trinitarian Theology: Theologians in Dialogue with T. F. Torrance* (hereafter: 'Being and Person'), ed. Elmer M. Colyer (Lanham, MD: Rowman & Littlefield, 2001), 125.

[2] Gunton, 'Being and Person', 125.

[3] Torrance, *The Christian Doctrine of God*, 102.

[4] Torrance, *The Christian Doctrine of God*, 102.

[5] Torrance, *The Trinitarian Faith*, 305.

[6] Torrance, *The Trinitarian Faith*, 306.

the incarnate Son of God are to be understood as that of the One Mediator between God and men, who is himself God and man.'[7] Therefore, it is incorrect to suggest that *perichoresis* is understood by Torrance mainly from the economy and not from the relations of the eternal persons. Indeed it is not *perichoresis*, thus understood, that is Torrance's theological criterion but, by his own reckoning, that criterion is the inner trinitarian relations of the Father, Son and Spirit.

How does all of this relate to the understanding of being and person? Torrance follows Gregory Nazianzen in order to avoid any hint of subordinationism and to affirm a view of person that is not to be equated with 'mode of being' as Basil understood this. Of course Gunton opposes Barth's appeal to 'mode of being' rather than person and follows Alan Torrance's view in this matter; a view that we have already discussed in Chapter Eight. Gunton argues for the retrieval of the concept of the person in order to overcome problems in the Church and in the world. Such a concept, he believes, enables theology to emphasize 'the ontological compatibility of the one and the many'.[8] In relation to God, the concept enables recognition that Father, Son and Spirit 'in their interrelatedness make God to be the God that he is'.[9] Here Gunton comes dangerously near to allowing relationality, personally understood, to define who God is as Father, Son and Spirit. Can the term 'person' really do all of this? Or is it not the case that even the term 'person' must receive its meaning from the eternal Trinity? Then the onto-relations of the Father, Son and Spirit would define for us the word 'person' instead of allowing the word 'person' to define both the problem of the one and the many and the inner constitution of God. For Torrance, of course, an onto-relational understanding of the trinitarian persons means 'an understanding of the three divine Persons in the one God in which the ontic relations between them belong to what they essentially are in themselves in their distinctive *hypostases*'.[10] The question that must be asked of Colin Gunton is: Do the Father, Son and Spirit *make* God to be the God he is, or do they reveal the God he is from eternity to eternity in the freedom of his transcendence?

Here, Gunton once more attributes to Barth the suspicion of modalism and attempts to connect this supposed weakness in Barth with T. F. Torrance's analysis by suggesting that, because Torrance

---

[7] Torrance, *The Trinitarian Faith*, 308.
[8] Gunton, 'Being and Person', 126.
[9] Gunton, 'Being and Person', 126.
[10] Torrance, *The Christian Doctrine of God*, 102.

sees the trinitarian persons as relations and because he therefore believes the term 'Father' is not a name for being (*ousia*), that he too is guilty of a kind of modalistic tendency. But this charge neglects Torrance's important distinction between knowing God absolutely and relatively. Speaking of the Father, Son and Holy Spirit relatively refers to them as persons in relation to each other, while speaking of Father, Son and Holy Spirit absolutely refers to their divine being.[11] Torrance's view stems from Athanasius and Gregory Nazianzen and asserts that *ousia* refers to 'being in its internal relations and *hypostasis* as being in its objective relations'.[12] For this reason, the persons must be seen as 'more than distinctive relations, for they really subsist, and coexist hypostatically, in the one Being of God without being confused with one another, for they are *other* than one another'.[13]

It is here that Gunton asks about the nature of that subsistence. As what, he asks, do they really subsist? He rejects Torrance's assertion that Basil identified person with modes of being and he rejects the idea that relation can describe person. But here he was not paying attention to Torrance. Because, while Torrance did say that the persons are relations relatively, he insisted that 'the *Being* of the Godhead is to be understood as fully and intrinsically *personal* as the Father of the Lord Jesus Christ'.[14] Here Gunton wishes to follow Basil and assert that persons are not relations but rather 'are constituted by their relations to one another'.[15] But do we really want to say that persons are *constituted* by their relations? Do they *need* to be constituted this way? Or should we rather not say that the persons subsisting in God are who they are by virtue of their relations? The difference here concerns the implication that we can know *how* God is constituted when in fact we only know that he is constituted as Father, Son and Spirit from revelation. This is where Barth insisted that the *how* of the trinitarian self-revelation could not be explained but could only be accepted and then understood because such knowledge is a miracle that is begun, upheld and completed by God himself in the power of his Spirit.[16]

This is an extremely important insight, recognized by Augustine, emphasized by Athanasius and repeated by Thomas F. Torrance: 'We

[11] Torrance, *The Christian Doctrine of God*, 131, and Torrance, *Trinitarian Perspectives*, 28.
[12] Torrance, *Trinitarian Perspectives*, 28.
[13] Torrance, *Trinitarian Perspectives*, 28.
[14] Torrance, *Trinitarian Perspectives*, 27.
[15] Gunton, 'Being and Person', 126.
[16] See especially *CD* I/1, 475ff.

can no more offer an account of the "how" of these divine relations and actions [than] we can define the Father, the Son and the Holy Spirit and delimit them from one another';[17] indeed Torrance cites Athanasius to stress this point: 'Thus far human knowledge goes. Here the cherubim spread the covering of their wings.'[18] For Torrance, 'just as we cannot comprehend *how* God created the world out of nothing, or *how* he brought Jesus Christ forth from the grave, so we are unable to grasp *how* his redemptive and providential activity makes all things, material as well as spiritual, to serve his eternal purpose of love'.[19] This is not an argument for agnosticism, which both Barth and Torrance reject. Rather it is a recognition that we do not know God as God knows himself and so we cannot intrude into the divine mystery with an explanation and delimitation of the persons of the Trinity.

Furthermore, the difference between Torrance and Gunton here concerns the implication that in Gunton's thought there is implied an element of causality with respect to the fact that it is suggested that their relations cause the divine unity, when in truth the divine unity exists and is manifest in and through the relations. Here, Gunton accuses Torrance of showing little interest in the way in which the persons are distinctly themselves. Yet, as we have just noted, Torrance insists that because we are not God we can only begin to think from a center in God and not from a center in ourselves. We must recognize that this center can be provided only by God in Christ and through the Holy Spirit. But because this is so, we cannot define and delimit the Father, Son and Holy Spirit without trying to redefine God in our own image. Torrance follows Athanasius and speaks in quite distinct ways of the Father as creator, of the Son as reconciler and of the Holy Spirit as the redeemer. But his thinking allows itself to be shaped by revelation rather than a presupposed notion of person. It appears that Gunton's primary concern with Torrance here is to question the traditional Western notion that the works of God *ad extra* are undivided. Yet the twin dangers evident in his objection to Torrance are those of tritheism and adoptionism.

How then are being and person related within the immanent Trinity? Here, Gunton cites Torrance's view that is indebted to G. L. Prestige: 'In precise theological usage *ousia* now refers to "being" not simply as that which is but to what it is in respect of its internal reality, while

[17] Torrance, *The Christian Doctrine of God*, 193, and *CD* I/1, 475f.
[18] Torrance, *The Christian Doctrine of God*, 193.
[19] Torrance, *The Christian Doctrine of God*, 226. Cf. also 233.

hypostasis refers to "being" not just in its independent subsistence but in its objective otherness.'[20] Gunton professes not to know what to make of these formulations and suggests that they tend toward modalism since they imply that God exists one way inwardly and another outwardly. Yet that is exactly opposed to what Torrance intended, namely, that

> while both *ousia* and *hypostasis* describe 'being' as such, in the trinitarian formulation 'one Being, three Persons', Being or οὐσία is being considered in its internal relations, and Person or ὑπόστασις is being considered in its otherness, i.e. in the objective relations between the Persons. In the case of the Father, this would amount to a distinction between the Father considered absolutely, as he is in himself, and the Father considered relatively to the Son, although of course it is one and the same Fatherly Being that is being considered . . .'[21]

Hence, by making a distinction between God's absolute and relative being within the immanent Trinity, Torrance could show that God's oneness is the oneness of being of the God who is three persons, one being. For Torrance, there is no oneness of God that is not the oneness of the being of the Father in the Son and the Spirit who, in virtue of *perichoresis*, mutually interpenetrate each other without dissolution or separation of their distinct onto-relations. Consequently, Torrance did not refer to God's inward and outward relations in this context as Gunton assumes and so he did not present any modalistically tinged notion that God exists in one way immanently and another way economically. Such a conclusion is at variance with Torrance's most basic theological insights. In fact Torrance insists that what God is toward us he is in himself, and that precisely is one God who is equally divine as Father, Son and Spirit *ad intra* and *ad extra*. On this fact rests the validity of the incarnation, reconciliation and redemption.

Gunton believes that Torrance's emphasis on the *homoousion* leads him to stress God's being 'at the expense of the divine *persons*'.[22] Gunton attributes this to his belief that Torrance reads eastern Orthodox theologians too much through western eyes, especially through Augustinian eyes. And, as in other writings, Gunton appears to place these issues in the context of the problem of the one and the many. And that at least raises the question of whether or not we are dealing

---

[20] See Torrance, *The Christian Doctrine of God*, 130, and Gunton, 'Being and Person', 129.

[21] Torrance, *The Christian Doctrine of God*, 131.

[22] Gunton, 'Being and Person', 129.

primarily with God's being and act or with the philosophical problem of the one and the many.

While it must be admitted that the Eastern Fathers are often read through Western eyes, I do not believe this charge is a proper one to level at T. F. Torrance. Gunton argues that Torrance's vision is more patristic than biblical; there is little exegesis of scripture in his trinitarian texts. Indeed, according to Gunton, Torrance's main effort is to choose texts that allow him to unify the immanent and economic Trinity as much as possible. Here Gunton wishes that Torrance would have paid more attention to the 'apparently subordinationist texts of 1 Cor. 15 and some of those in the Fourth Gospel'.[23] But what is the point here? Torrance is very clear for instance that Jesus freely shared our ignorance. And he very clearly rejects Docetism and adoptionism as dualistic attempts to read the New Testament without accepting the 'non-dualist frame of reference deriving from Israel . . .'[24] But he also insists that, while the incarnate Son is subordinate to the Father, such subordinationism cannot be read back into the immanent Trinity.[25] Further, T. F. Torrance is crystal clear about the fact that the human Jesus never exists except as the Word incarnate. Is Gunton in search of a human Jesus here who can be understood without regard for the fact that this man was and is the eternally begotten Son of the Father? Torrance's scriptural exegesis actually makes much of Mt. 11:27 and of Jesus' bodily resurrection not only to stress that what God is toward us he is in himself, but that, if we are to know God in accordance with God's own

[23] Gunton, 'Being and Person', 129.

[24] See Torrance, *Space, Time and Resurrection*, 42. See also *The Christian Doctrine of God*, chapter 3, 'The Biblical Frame'.

[25] Here Torrance differs from Barth, who believes that there was 'a superiority and a subordination' (*CD* IV/1, 201ff.) within God on the basis of which he could say that, in the incarnation, it is God's own obedience that we meet in Jesus' human obedience. Barth's thinking here is indeed intriguing, and he makes every effort to distinguish the immanent and economic Trinity, while avoiding heretical notions of subordinationism and modalism. Still, an ambiguity in his own thought remains as when he describes the incarnation: 'He does not do it [become incarnate] without any correspondence to, but as the strangely logical final continuation of, the history in which He is God' (*CD* IV/1, 203). If the obedience of the Son of God incarnate is the continuation of the history of his obedience in the immanent Trinity, where is the distinction between God's free existence as Father, Son and Spirit who did not need to become incarnate (which Barth also insists upon even in this context) and his free new action *ad extra*? There is an ambiguity here and it may be due to the fact that the element of subordinationism that Barth thinks he can maintain without compromising the equality of the persons in the immanent Trinity is the result of thinking that the Son and Spirit were 'caused' by the Father in the Basilian sense rejected by Torrance. Or it may be due to the fact that Barth has unwittingly read back the Son's incarnate action on our behalf into the immanent Trinity instead of seeing it consistently as a condescension grounded in God's eternal love and freedom.

nature, our knowledge must be grounded in a center in God himself. This is how Torrance could maintain 'the integrity and wholeness of the humanity of the Incarnate Son'.[26] And this commits him to a reading of scripture as a whole in such a way that Jesus, the incarnate Word, is the one who unifies his reading of it. It is for this reason that there is for Torrance no way that scripture can be read to imply subordinationism within the immanent Trinity. This is not just a patristic insight but a biblically based patristic insight.

Gunton wonders whether Torrance reads the *homoousion* back into Athanasius himself in such a way as to compromise the 'particular being of the three persons'[27] as when he writes that 'the fullness of the Father's Being is the Being of the Son and of the Spirit'.[28] Is this statement a valid reading of Athanasius's belief in 'the all-holy Father of Christ beyond all created being'?[29] The first question to be asked of Gunton is whether we want to speak of the 'particular being' of the persons of the Trinity at all. Does this not tend toward tritheism? Torrance insists that the particularity of the Father, Son and Spirit is not the particularity of particular beings but of three uniquely divine persons in the one being of God. This is indeed the gist of his books on the Trinity. Hence Torrance's emphasis in this context is that Father, Son and Spirit are always both together and individually fully God. What is more, if the statement quoted by Gunton is read in context, it is very clear that Torrance does not blur the particularities of the Father, Son and Spirit and does not distort Athanasius. When Torrance said that 'the Father's Being is the Being of the Son and Spirit', he wanted to stress that his understanding of being was not taken from Aristotle, but was instead shaped under the influence of God's self-revelation in Christ, in a manner similar to the way Athanasius thought about God's being. Hence, Torrance was strictly interpreting the being of God following Athanasius's statement that 'It would be more godly and true to signify God from the Son and call him Father, than to name God from his works alone and call him Unoriginate.'[30]

Gunton is also unhappy with the fact that Torrance did not engage more with the work of John Zizioulas so that persons might be seen as beings *in relation to* others rather than simply as relations. This, Gunton believes, would enable theologians to give equal weight to the one and

[26] Torrance, *Space, Time and Resurrection*, 42.
[27] Gunton, 'Being and Person', 131.
[28] See, e.g., Torrance, *The Christian Doctrine of God*, 116.
[29] Gunton, 'Being and Person', 130.
[30] Torrance, *The Christian Doctrine of God*, 117.

the many. But is that really the goal of trinitarian theology? While it is certainly true that all good dogmatics is also ethics, and while it is also true that individualism and collectivism are unacceptable, the question remains as to whether a new understanding of the term 'person' in relation will solve all of this. Do we not need to look exclusively to the person and work of Christ at precisely this point? Can we allow persons in relation to become the subject here with Christ and the Holy Spirit perhaps becoming the predicate? This is certainly a danger at this point.

The final issue to be addressed here concerns T. F. Torrance's understanding of the *filioque*. Gunton sees at least two areas of concern in relation to the western view. First, if we think the Spirit proceeds from the Son as well as from the Father, then the Spirit is seen to be subordinate to the Son and 'is reduced to the margins . . . to do little more than apply Christ's work in the church or to the individual believer'.[31] This leads to 'a failure to do justice to the full humanity of the incarnate Son of God'.[32]

Here, Gunton cites Torrance's important paper on 'The Mind of Christ in Worship: The Problem of Apollinarianism in the Liturgy' to show that Torrance had a healthy concern to stress the fact that Christ's priestly ministry as man offering himself is the focus of our worship. Still, Torrance is criticized for not paying much attention to the detailed Gospel presentations of Jesus' life, death, resurrection and ascension. This is a surprising assertion, especially in light of Torrance's biblical analysis in *Space, Time and Resurrection*. But it is also surprising in light of the fact that what Torrance actually has to say is grounded in and controlled by the biblical revelation itself. Nonetheless, we are told that another problem of the *filioque* is the western tendency toward modalism, that is, in the western search for the One, the question arises as to who or what ultimately unifies our experience; the temptation of the West is to find the unity of all things 'in some deity or divine principle over and above the Triune revelation'.[33]

Here is where the disagreement between Torrance and Zizioulas emerges. Should we follow Zizioulas and say that the Father is the cause of everything, including the triune communion? Or should we say, with T. F. Torrance, that 'we must understand the Triune communion as a whole to be the metaphysical source of unity'?[34] Gunton

---

[31] Gunton, 'Being and Person', 132.
[32] Gunton, 'Being and Person', 132.
[33] Gunton, 'Being and Person', 133.
[34] Gunton, 'Being and Person', 133.

sees this as a question of whether the double procession encourages modalism. Does it?

Gunton wonders that if the Spirit comes from the Father *and* the Son, will we not then wonder what it is that gives the Father and Son *their* underlying unity? In Gunton's view double procession invites us to seek a deeper cause than the Trinity and thus opens the door to modalism. Western minds, he believes, inevitably tend that way. Gunton stresses that neither Torrance nor Barth are actually modalists, but that today we need to stress the persons more in order to overcome any underlying tendency to modalism.

This requires several comments. First, Barth did support the *filioque*, but not because of a modalist tendency and certainly not by thinking beyond and apart from revelation. In fact his main argument in favor of this was to insist that, just as the Spirit proceeds from the Father and Son, so we have no direct mystical access to God that would bypass the Son's incarnate mediation.[35] Indeed, his intention was to safeguard the inseparable relation between the Spirit and the Son in both the economic and immanent Trinity. Barth was sensitive to the fact that the *filioque* was uncharitably added to the creed, yet Barth believed that from the very beginning both East and West did not disagree materially about the procession of the Spirit even when this expression was used. Barth also insisted that passages like Jn 15:26, which speak of the Spirit proceeding from the Father, could not be isolated from other texts that clearly call him the Spirit of the Son. Hence, he explicitly affirmed the *filioque* because for Barth

> statements about the divine modes of being antecedently in themselves cannot be different in content from those that are to be made about their reality in revelation. All our statements concerning what is called the immanent Trinity have been reached simply as confirmations or underlinings or, materially, as *the indispensable premises of the economic Trinity*.[36]

And, as Torrance notes, this was the original intention of the *filioque* clause,[37] even though it had damaging effect because it was unecumenically introduced by the West into the creed. T. F. Torrance

---

[35] Thus, 'if our thinking is not to leave the soil of revelation, a distinction must be acknowledged in the reality of what the Son and the Spirit are antecedently in Themselves' (*CD* I/1, 474). This will lead to a recognition that the Holy Spirit is different from the Son and the Father as well, without being separated from the Father and Son.

[36] *CD* I/1, 479, emphasis mine.

[37] Torrance, *Theology in Reconstruction*, 218–19.

himself partially agrees with Barth's view. While he rejects 'the element of "subordinationism" in his doctrine of the Holy Trinity . . . as a hang-over from Latin theology but also from St Basil's doctrine of the Trinity' he also agreed with Barth that the Nicene *homoousion* should apply to the doctrine of the Holy Spirit. Thus, 'we cannot but trace back the historical mission of the Spirit from the incarnate Son to the eternal mission of the Spirit from the Father. But I would argue that the problem of the *filioque* was created by an incipient subordinationism in the Cappadocian doctrine of the Trinity'.[38] Whatever one's final judgment may be with respect to Barth's view of the *filioque*, Torrance's analysis on this issue deserves careful attention. If Torrance is right, and I think he is, then his suggestion could be the basis of far-reaching ecumenical agreement.

Briefly, Torrance believes that if the *filioque* is set back again on the Athanasian (and 'Cyrilian') basis[39] then the problems associated with it fall away. Torrance believes that, if we accept Athanasius's notion of coinherence, this would lead us to admit that in the Trinity 'no Person is before or after Another, no Person is greater or less, but all three Persons are coeternal and coequal in their substantive relations with one another'.[40] If this is taken seriously then the mission of the Holy Spirit from the Father and the gift of the Spirit by the Son will be governed by the fact that each person is wholly God and that therefore the Holy Spirit 'proceeds from the Father through the Son'. This eliminates both the idea that there is more than one source of deity and the idea that the Son is less than the Father. What Torrance wants to say is that, if we consider the procession of the Holy Spirit from the Father in light of the fact that each person of the Godhead 'is perfectly and wholly God',[41] then we can say 'that the Holy Spirit proceeds ultimately from the Triune Being of the Godhead'.[42] And this must mean that the Spirit 'proceeds from out of the mutual relations within the One Being of the Holy Trinity in which the Father indwells the Spirit and is himself indwelt by the Spirit'. Further, 'since God *is* Spirit, "Spirit" cannot be restricted to the Person of the Holy Spirit',[43] but must also be applied to the eternal communion of the Father, Son and Holy Spirit. Hence the Spirit proceeds from the being of the Father.

---

[38] Torrance, *Karl Barth, Biblical and Evangelical Theologian*, 131–2.
[39] Cf. Torrance, *Trinitarian Perspectives*, 20.
[40] Torrance, *Trinitarian Perspectives*, 20.
[41] Torrance, *Trinitarian Perspectives*, 112.
[42] Torrance, *Trinitarian Perspectives*, 112–13.
[43] Torrance, *Trinitarian Perspectives*, 113.

This eliminates any false notion of causality that would suggest that the Son proceeds from the Person of the Father, and this transcends the rift between East and West. This also eliminates any idea of two ultimate principles in God (Father and Son) and is seen as a procession from mutual relations within the being of God 'who is Trinity in Unity and Unity in Trinity'.[44]

What Torrance opposes here is the Cappadocian conception of God's unity 'as deriving "from the Person of the Father" . . . thereby replacing the Nicene formula "from the Being of the Father . . ."'[45] This thinking does not sufficiently affirm the *homoousion* of the Spirit. Still, the Cappadocians did not think of the Holy Spirit as created. Nonetheless, Torrance believes it was the Cappadocian thinking that actually led Western church leaders to insert the *ex patre filioque* clause unecumenically into the Creed, thus creating the impasse between East and West.[46]

The West assumed that if the Spirit proceeds from the Father and is sent by the Son, then such thinking would suggest that 'the Son would be regarded as subordinate to the Father, as an adopted creature of God, and not really as God of God'.[47] The East believed the *filioque* suggested two ultimate principles in the Godhead and thus opted to speak of the Spirit as proceeding from the Father alone. This was defended on the basis of John's Gospel, which implied a distinction between procession and mission, that is, 'between the *eternal* procession of the Spirit from the Father, and the *historical* mission of the Spirit from the Son'.[48] But this raises the question of whether the sending of the Spirit by the Son has only to do with revelation and faith instead of being 'grounded immanently in the eternal being of God'.[49] If this is the case then that would undercut the *homoousial* relation of the Holy Spirit to God the Father. This thinking, exacerbated by the Basilian and Palamite distinction between the divine being and energies, led both toward agnosticism and dualism, and undermined the Nicene emphasis on the identity of God's being and act; it separated the immanent and economic Trinity.

Hence, Torrance prefers to say, 'the Spirit is from the Father but from the Father in the Son. Since the Holy Spirit like the Son is of the

[44] Torrance, *Trinitarian Perspectives*, 113.
[45] Torrance, *The Christian Doctrine of God*, 186.
[46] In Barth's view this impasse was created more by this action than by any material disagreement.
[47] Torrance, *The Christian Doctrine of God*, 186.
[48] Torrance, *The Christian Doctrine of God*, 186.
[49] Torrance, *The Christian Doctrine of God*, 187.

Being of God, and belongs to the Son . . . he could not but proceed from or out of the Being of God inseparably from and through the Son'.[50] For Athanasius the problem of the double procession of the Spirit did not arise, because he believed it would be irreverent 'to ask *how* the Spirit proceeds from God' since that would have suggested 'an ungodly attempt to intrude into the holy mystery of God's being'.[51] For Athanasius, then, the procession of the Spirit is bound up with the Son's generation and these divine actions exceed and transcend all human thoughts. Therefore, since the Son and Spirit 'are both *of the Being* of the Father . . . the idea that the Spirit derives from the *Being* of the Son just did not arise and could not have arisen'.[52] This then is T. F. Torrance's solution to the problem of the *filioque*. Thus, for Torrance, we can say both that the Holy Spirit proceeds from the Father and the Son and from the Father through the Son as long as monarchy is not limited to the Father; as long as there is no distinction drawn between the underived deity of the Father and the derived deity of the Son and as long as the Holy Spirit is seen to belong 'homoousially with the Father and the Son in their two-way relation with one another in the divine Triunity'.[53] What is so astonishing and helpful about Torrance's proposal is that he simultaneously avoids any hint of modalism or subordinationism.

Hence, the question to be raised to Gunton is: What exactly is it in the notion of person that he adopts from John Zizioulas that leads him to criticize Torrance for modalist leanings? The answer, I suggest, is to be found in the belief that person is more basic than substance or being. If person is believed to be more basic than being, then it strikes me that one will be tempted to explain the *how* of God's triune being when in fact we can only reason in faith from the fact of it which remains a mystery. Further, if person is believed to be more basic than being, then some form of adoptionism in Christology and some separation of the Spirit from the Word will inevitably threaten. It is no accident that, as we have seen throughout this book, adoptionism threatens to weaken much contemporary Christology and thereby lead to some form of self-justification. Nor is it an accident that, even in the most sophisticated Christologies, whenever the Spirit is separated from the Word, then Jesus' activity as the subject of the events of reconciliation

---

[50]   Torrance, *The Christian Doctrine of God*, 188.
[51]   Torrance, *The Christian Doctrine of God*, 188.
[52]   Torrance, *The Christian Doctrine of God*, 188.
[53]   Torrance, *The Christian Doctrine of God*, 190.

and revelation is also called into question. But then the unity of the
Father, Son and Spirit is also called into question. Torrance's thinking
therefore not only has the advantage of healing the wounds that exist
between East and West, but it helps theologians realize that the strength
of trinitarian theology rests, as it always has, upon the fact that Jesus
Christ is the eternally begotten Son of the Father and that this takes
place in the unity of the Holy Spirit. It is not then to be found in his
human activity within history except as that human activity is the
activity of the Word of God incarnate.

Selected Bibliography

ACHTEMEIER, ELIZABETH. 'Exchanging God for "No Gods".' *Speaking the Christian God: The Holy Trinity and the Challenge of Feminism.* Ed. Alvin F. Kimel, Jr. Grand Rapids, MI: Eerdmans, 1992. 1–16.

AQUINAS, ST THOMAS. *Summa Theologica: Complete English Edition in Five Volumes.* Trans. Fathers of the English Dominican Province. Westminster, MD: Christian Classics, 1948.

ATHANASIUS. *Four Discourses Against the Arians* 1.34. *A Select Library of Nicene and Post-Nicene Fathers of the Christian Church Second Series.* Trans. and ed. Philip Schaff and Henry Wace. Edinburgh: T&T Clark, 1987.

———. *Letters of Saint Athanasius Concerning the Holy Spirit.* Trans. C. R. B. Shapland. London: The Epworth Press, 1951.

———. *Athanasius, Select Works and Letters* in *A Select Library of Nicene and Post-Nicene Fathers.* Trans. and ed. Philip Schaff and Henry Wace, Vol. 4. New York: Charles Scribner's Sons, 1903. *Epistle of Athanasius Concerning the Arian Bipartite Council Held at Ariminum and Seleucia.*

AUGUSTINE. *The Trinity.* Trans. Edmund Hill, OP. Ed. John Rotelle, OSA. New York: New City Press, 1991.

BALTHASAR, HANS URS VON. *The Theology of Karl Barth: Exposition and Interpretation.* Trans. Edward T. Oakes, SJ. San Francisco: Ignatius Press, 1992.

BARTH, KARL. *Ad limina apostolorum: An Appraisal of Vatican II.* Trans. Keith R. Crim. Richmond, VA: John Knox Press, 1968.

BARTH, KARL. *Anselm: Fides quaerens intellectum. Anselm's Proof of the Existence of God in the Context of his Theological Scheme.* Richmond, VA: John Knox Press, 1960.

————. *Church Dogmatics.* 4 Vols. in 13 parts:

Vol. 1, part 1: *The Doctrine of the Word of God.* Ed. G. W. Bromiley and T. F. Torrance. Trans. G. W. Bromiley. Edinburgh: T&T Clark, 1975.

Vol. 1, part 2: *The Doctrine of the Word of God.* Ed. G. W. Bromiley and T. F. Torrance. Trans. G. T. Thomson and Harold Knight. Edinburgh: T&T Clark, 1970.

Vol. 2, part 1: *The Doctrine of God.* Ed. G. W. Bromiley and T. F. Torrance. Trans. T. H. L. Parker, W. B. Johnston, H. Knight and J. L. M. Harie. Edinburgh: T&T Clark, 1964.

Vol. 2, part 2: *The Doctrine of God.* Ed. G. W. Bromiley and T. F. Torrance. Trans. G. W. Bromiley, J. C. Campbell, Iain Wilson, J. Strathearn McNab, Harold Knight and R. A. Stewart. Edinbugh: T&T Clark, 1967.

Vol. 3, part 1: *The Doctrine of Creation.* Ed. G. W. Bromiley and T. F. Torrance. Trans. J. W. Edwards, O. Bussey and Harold Knight. Edinburgh: T&T Clark, 1970.

Vol. 3, part 2: *The Doctrine of Creation.* Ed. G.W. Bromiley and T. F. Torrance. Trans. Harold Knight, G. W. Bromiley, J. K. S. Reid and R. H. Fuller. Edinburgh: T&T Clark, 1968.

Vol. 3, part 3: *The Doctrine of Creation.* Ed. G. W. Bromiley and T. F. Torrance. Trans. G. W. Bromiley and R. J. Ehrlich. Edinburgh: T&T Clark, 1976.

Vol. 3, part 4: *The Doctrine of Creation.* Ed. G.W. Bromiley and T. F. Torrance. Trans. A. T. MacKay, T. H. L. Parker, Harold Knight, Henry A. Kennedy and John Marks. Edinburgh: T&T Clark, 1969.

Vol. 4, part 1: *The Doctrine of Reconciliation.* Ed. G.W. Bromiley and T. F. Torrance. Trans. G. W. Bromiley. Edinburgh: T&T Clark, 1974.

Vol. 4, part 2: *The Doctrine of Reconciliation.* Ed. G. W. Bromiley and T. F. Torrance. Trans. G. W. Bromiley. Edinburgh: T&T Clark, 1967.

Vol. 4, part 3: *The Doctrine of Reconciliation.* First Half. Ed. G. W. Bromiley and T. F. Torrance. Trans. G. W. Bromiley. Edinburgh: T&T Clark, 1976.

Vol. 4, part 3: *The Doctrine of Reconciliation.* Second Half. Ed. G. W. Bromiley and T. F. Torrance. Trans. G. W. Bromiley. Edinburgh: T&T Clark, 1969.

Vol. 4, part 4: *The Doctrine of Reconciliation.* Fragment. *Baptism as the Foundation of the Christian Life.* Ed. G. W. Bromiley and T. F. Torrance. Trans. G. W. Bromiley. Edinburgh: T&T Clark, 1969.

Vol. 4, part 4: *The Christian Life.* Lecture Fragments. Trans. G. W. Bromiley. Grand Rapids, MI: Eerdmans, 1981.

———. *Credo.* Trans. Robert McAfee Brown. New York: Charles Scribner's Sons, 1962.

———. *Deliverance to the Captives.* Trans. Marguerite Wieser. New York: Harper & Row, 1959.

———. *Ethics.* Ed. Dietrich Braun. Trans. Geoffrey W. Bromiley. New York: Seabury Press, 1981.

———. *Evangelical Theology: An Introduction.* Trans. Grover Foley. Grand Rapids, MI: Eerdmans, 1963.

———. *The Göttingen Dogmatics: Instruction in the Christian Religion Volume One.* Trans. Geoffrey W. Bromiley. Grand Rapids, MI: Eerdmans, 1991.

———. *The Holy Spirit and the Christian Life.* Foreword by Robin W. Lovin. Trans. R. Birch Hoyle. Louisville, KY: Westminster/John Knox Press, 1993.

———. *The Humanity of God.* Trans. Thomas Wieser and John Newton Thomas. Richmond, VA: John Knox Press, 1968.

———. *Letters 1961–1968.* Ed. Jürgen Fangemeier and Hinrich Stoevesandt. Trans. and ed. Geoffrey W. Bromiley. Grand Rapids, MI: Eerdmans, 1981.

———. *Prayer.* Ed. Don E. Saliers. Trans. Sara F. Terrien. Philadelphia: Westminster Press, 1985.

———. *Protestant Theology in the Nineteenth Century: Its Background and History.* Valley Forge, PA: Judson Press, 1973.

———. *Theology and Church (Shorter Writings 1920–1928).* Trans. Louise Pettibone Smith. With an Introduction (1962) by T. F. Torrance. London: SCM Press, 1962.

BAUCKHAM, RICHARD J. 'Moltmann's Messianic Christology.' *Scottish Journal of Theology* 44 (1991), 519–31.

———. *The Theology of Jürgen Moltmann.* Edinburgh: T&T Clark, 1995.

BIGGAR, NIGEL (ed.). *Reckoning with Barth: Essays in Commemoration of the Centenary of Karl Barth's Birth.* London: Mowbray, 1988.

BURGHARDT, WALTER J., SJ. *Long Have I Loved You: A Theologian Reflects on his Church.* New York: Orbis Books, 2000.

BUSCH, EBERHARD. *Karl Barth: His Life from Letters and Autobiographical Facts.* Trans. John Bowden. Philadelphia: Fortress Press, 1976.

BROMILEY, GEOFFREY W. *Introduction to the Theology of Karl Barth.* Edinburgh: T&T Clark, 1995.

CARR, ANNE. 'Theology and Experience in the Thought of Karl Rahner.' *Journal of Religion* 53 (1973), 359–76.

———. *Transforming Grace: Christian Tradition and Women's Experience.* San Francisco: Harper & Row, 1988.

CHADWICK, HENRY. *The Early Church.* New York: Penguin, 1967.

CLARKSON, JOHN F., SJ, et al. (trans. and eds). *The Church Teaches: Documents of the Church in English Translation.* London: Herder, 1955.

COFFEY, DAVID. *Deus Trinitas: The Doctrine of the Triune God.* New York: Oxford University Press, 1999.

———. 'The "Incarnation" of the Holy Spirit in Christ.' *Theological Studies* 45.3 (September 1984), 466–80.

———. 'The Theandric Nature of Christ.' *Theological Studies* 60.3 (September 1999), 405–31.

COLYER, ELMER M. *How to Read T. F. Torrance: Understanding His Trinitarian and Scientific Theology.* Downers Grove, IL: InterVarsity Press, 2001.

———. *The Promise of Trinitarian Theology: Theologians in Dialogue with T. F. Torrance.* Lanham, MD: Rowman & Littlefield, 2001.

CUNNINGHAM, DAVID S. *These Three Are One: The Practice of Trinitarian Theology.* Oxford: Blackwell, 1998.

DALY, MARY. *Beyond God the Father: Toward a Philosophy of Women's Liberation.* Boston, MA: Beacon Press, 1985.

DAVIS, STEPHEN T., Daniel Kendall, SJ and Gerald O'Collins, SJ (eds). *The Trinity: An Interdisciplinary Symposium on the Trinity.* Oxford: Oxford University Press, 1999.

DEL COLLE, RALPH. *Christ and the Spirit: Spirit-Christology in Trinitarian Perspective.* New York: Oxford University Press, 1994.

DINOIA, J. A., OP. 'Karl Rahner.' *The Modern Theologians*, Vol. 1. Ed. David F. Ford. Oxford: Blackwell, 1989.

DYCH, WILLIAM V., SJ. *Karl Rahner.* Collegeville, MN: The Liturgical Press, 1992.

———. 'Theology in a New Key.' *A World of Grace: An Introduction to the Themes and Foundations of Karl Rahner's Theology.* Leo J. O'Donovan, SJ (ed.). New York: Crossroad, 1981.

FARROW, DOUGLAS. *Ascension and Ecclesia: On the Significance of the Doctrine of the Ascension for Ecclesiology and Christian Cosmology.* Grand Rapids, MI: Eerdmans, 1999.

FERGUSSON, DAVID A. S. 'Interpreting the Resurrection.' *Scottish Journal of Theology* 38 (1985), 287–305.

FEUERBACH, LUDWIG. *The Essence of Christianity.* Trans. George Eliot. Introduction by Karl Barth. Foreword by H. Richard Niebuhr. New York: Harper Torchbooks, 1957.

FOLEY, GROVER. 'The Catholic Critics of Karl Barth in Outline and Analysis.' *Scottish Journal of Theology* 14 (1961), 136–51.

FORTMANN, EDMUND J. *The Triune God: An Historical Study of the Doctrine of the Trinity.* Philadelphia: Westminster Press, 1972.

FRYE, ROLAND M. 'Language for God and Feminist Language: Problems and Principles.' *Scottish Journal of Theology* 41.4 (1988), 441–69.

———. 'Language for God and Feminist Language: Problems and Principles.' *Speaking the Christian God: The Holy Trinity and the Challenge of Feminism*, Alvin F. Kimel, Jr (ed.). Grand Rapids, MI: Eerdmans, 1992, 17–43.

GALVIN, JOHN P. 'The Invitation of Grace.' *A World of Grace: An Introduction to the Themes and Foundations of Karl Rahner's Theology.* Ed. Leo J. O'Donovan, SJ. New York: Crossroad, 1981. 64–75.

GILSON, ETIENNE. *God and Philosophy.* New Haven: Yale University Press, 1979.

GREGORY OF NYSSA. *Against Eunomius Book I*, §42. *Select Writings and Letters of Gregory, Bishop of Nyssa.* Trans. William Moore and Henry Wilson. *Nicene and Post-Nicene Fathers of the Christian Church.* Grand Rapids, MI: Eerdmans, 1988.

GRENZ, STANLEY J. and ROGER E. OLSON. *20th Century Theology: God and the World in a Transitional Age.* Carlisle: Paternoster Press, 1992.

GUNTON, COLIN. *Becoming and Being: The Doctrine of God in Charles Hartshorne and Karl Barth.* London: Oxford University Press, 1978.

———. 'Being and Person: T. F. Torrance's Doctrine of God.' *The Promise of Trinitarian Theology: Theologians in Dialogue with T.F. Torrance.* Ed. Elmer M. Colyer. Lanham, MD: Rowman & Littlefield, 2001.

———. *A Brief Theology of Revelation.* Edinburgh: T&T Clark, 1995.

———. *Christ and Creation.* Grand Rapids, MI: Eerdmans, 1992.

———. *The Actuality of Atonement.* Edinburgh: T&T Clark, 1994.

———. *Theology through the Theologians: Selected Essays 1972–1995.* Edinburgh: T&T Clark, 1996.

———. *The One, the Three and the Many.* Cambridge: Cambridge University Press, 1993.

———. *The Promise of Trinitarian Theology.* Edinburgh: T&T Clark, 1991.

———. *The Promise of Trinitarian Theology.* Second edn. Edinburgh: T&T Clark, 1997.

———. *The Triune Creator: A Historical and Systematic Study.* Edinburgh Studies in Constructive Theology. Grand Rapids, MI: Eerdmans, 1998.

———. 'Two Dogmas Revisited: Edward Irving's Christology.' *Scottish Journal of Theology* 41 (1988), 359–76.

———. Review of Ted Peters, *God as Trinity. Theology Today* 51.1 (1994), 174–6.

———. *Yesterday and Today: A Study of Continuities in Christology.* Grand Rapids, MI: Eerdmans, 1983.

——— (ed.). *God and Freedom: Essays in Historical and Systematic Theology.* Edinburgh: T&T Clark, 1995.

——— (ed.). *The Cambridge Companion to Christian Doctrine.* Cambridge: Cambridge University Press, 1997.

——— (ed.). *The Doctrine of Creation: Essays in Dogmatics, History and Philosophy.* Edinburgh: T&T Clark, 1997.

HANSON, R. P. C. *The Search for the Christian Doctrine of God.* Edinburgh: T&T Clark, 1988.

HARNACK, ADOLF VON. *History of Dogma.* Vols I, III and VI. Trans. Neil Buchanan. New York: Dover, 1961.

HERON, ALASDAIR I. C. *A Century of Protestant Theology.* Philadelphia: Westminster Press, 1980.

———. *The Holy Spirit in the Bible, the History of Christian Thought, and Recent Theology.* Philadelphia: Westminster Press, 1983.

HICK, JOHN. *The Metaphor of God Incarnate: Christology in a Pluralistic Age.* Louisville, KY: Westminster/John Knox Press, 1993.

HILARY OF POITIERS. *On the Trinity. A Select Library of Nicene and Post-Nicene Fathers of the Christian Church Second Series,* Vol. IX. Trans. Philip Schaff and Henry Wace. Grand Rapids, MI: Eerdmans, 1997.

HILL, WILLIAM J. *The Three-Personed God: The Trinity as a Mystery of Salvation.* Washington, DC: The Catholic University of America Press, 1982.

HUNSINGER, GEORGE. *Disruptive Grace: Studies in the Theology of Karl Barth.* Grand Rapids, MI: Eerdmans, 2000.

———. *How to Read Karl Barth: The Shape of his Theology.* New York: Oxford University Press, 1991.

———. Review of Jürgen Moltmann, *The Trinity and The Kingdom. The Thomist* 47 (1983), 124–39.

IMHOF, PAUL, and HUBERT BIALLOWONS (eds). *Karl Rahner in Dialogue: Conversations and Interviews 1965–1982.* Trans. Harvey D. Egan. New York: Crossroad, 1986.

JENSON, ROBERT W. *God According to the Gospel: The Triune Identity.* Philadelphia: Fortress Press, 1982.

———. *God after God.* New York: The Bobbs–Merrill Company, 1969.

———. *Systematic Theology Volume 1: The Triune God.* New York: Oxford University Press, 1997.

JOHNSON, ELIZABETH A. *She Who Is: The Mystery of God in Feminist Theological Discourse.* New York: Crossroad, 1992.

JOHNSON, WILLIAM STACY. *The Mystery of God: Karl Barth and the Postmodern Foundations of Theology.* Columbia Series in Reformed Theology. Louisville, KY: Westminster/John Knox Press, 1997.

JÜNGEL, EBERHARD. *God as the Mystery of the World: On the Foundation of the Theology of the Crucified One in the Dispute between Theism and Atheism.* Trans. Darrell L. Guder. Grand Rapids, MI: Eerdmans, 1983.

———. *The Doctrine of the Trinity: God's Being Is in Becoming.* Trans. Horton Harris. London: Scottish Academic Press, 1976.

———. *Theological Essays.* Trans. and ed. J. B. Webster. Edinburgh: T&T Clark, 1989.

KASPER, WALTER. *The God of Jesus Christ.* Trans. Matthew J. O'Connell. New York: Crossroad, 1986.

KAUFMAN, GORDON D. *An Essay on Theological Method.* Atlanta: Scholars Press, 1990.

———. *God – Mystery – Diversity: Christian Theology in a Pluralistic World.* Minneapolis: Fortress Press, 1996.

———. *God The Problem.* Cambridge, MA: Harvard University Press, 1972

———. *In Face of Mystery: A Constructive Theology.* Cambridge, MA: Harvard University Press, 1993.

———. *Systematic Theology: A Historicist Perspective.* New York: Charles Scribner's Sons, 1968.

———. *Theology for a Nuclear Age.* Philadelphia: Westminster Press, 1985.

———. *The Theological Imagination: Constructing the Concept of God.* Philadelphia: Westminster Press, 1981.

KELLY, J. N. D. *Early Christian Doctrines.* New York: Harper & Row, 1978.

KIMEL, ALVIN F., JR (ed.). *Speaking the Christian God: The Holy Trinity and the Challenge of Feminism.* Grand Rapids, MI: Eerdmans, 1992.

KNITTER, PAUL F. *No Other Name? A Critical Survey of Christian Attitudes toward the World Religions.* New York: Orbis, 1985.

KNOX, JOHN. *The Humanity and Divinity of Christ: A Study of Pattern in Christology.* New York: Cambridge University Press, 1967.

LACUGNA, CATHERINE MOWRY. *God for Us: The Trinity and Christian Life.* San Francisco: HarperSanFrancisco, 1991.

LaCugna, Catherine Mowry (ed.). *Freeing Theology: The Essentials of Theology in Feminist Perspective.* San Francisco: HarperSanFrancisco, 1993.

——. 'The Trinitarian Mystery of God.' *Systematic Theology: Roman Catholic Perspectives.* Ed. Francis Schüssler Fiorenza and John P. Galvin. Minneapolis: Fortress Press, 1991. 151–92

Lane, Dermot A. *The Reality of Jesus.* New York: Paulist Press, 1975.

Leonard, Ellen. 'Experience as a Source for Theology.' *Proceedings of the Forty-Third Annual Convention of the Catholic Theological Society of America.* Ed. George Kilcourse. Toronto, 43 (1988), 44–61.

Lewis, Alan E. *Between Cross and Resurrection: A Theology of Holy Saturday.* Grand Rapids, MI: Eerdmans, 2001.

Macquarrie, John. *Jesus Christ in Modern Thought.* Philadelphia: Trinity Press International, 1990.

Martin, Francis. *The Feminist Question: Feminist Theology in the Light of Christian Tradition.* Grand Rapids, MI: Eerdmans, 1994.

McBrien, Richard P. *Catholicism Completely Revised and Updated.* San Francisco: HarperSan Francisco, 1994.

McCormack, Bruce L. *Karl Barth's Critically Realistic Dialectical Theology: Its Genesis and Development 1909–1936.* Oxford: Clarendon Press, 1995.

——. 'Divine Revelation and Human Imagination: Must we Choose between the Two?' *Scottish Journal of Theology* 37.4 (1984), 431–55.

——. 'Grace and Being: The Role of God's Gracious Election in Karl Barth's Theological Ontology.' *The Cambridge Companion to Karl Barth.* Ed. John Webster. Cambridge: Cambridge University Press, 2000. 92–110.

McFague, Sallie. *Models of God: Theology for an Ecological Nuclear Age.* Philadelphia: Fortress Press, 1987.

——. *The Body of God: An Ecological Theology.* Minneapolis: Fortress Press, 1993.

McGrath, Alister E. *Thomas F. Torrance: An Intellectual Biography.* Edinburgh: T&T Clark, 1999.

Molnar, Paul D. *Karl Barth and the Theology of the Lord's Supper: A Systematic Investigation.* New York: Peter Lang, 1996.

MOLNAR, PAUL D. 'Can We Know God Directly? Rahner's Solution from Experience.' *Theological Studies* 46 (1985), 228–61.

———. 'The Function of the Immanent Trinity in the Theology of Karl Barth: Implications for Today.' *Scottish Journal of Theology* 42 (1989), 367–99.

———. 'The Function of the Trinity in Moltmann's Ecological Doctrine of Creation.' *Theological Studies* 51 (1990), 673–97.

———. 'Is God Essentially Different from His Creatures? Rahner's Explanation from Revelation.' *The Thomist* 51 (1987), 575–631.

———. 'Experience and Knowledge of the Trinity in the Theology of Ted Peters: Occasion for Clarity or Confusion?' *Irish Theological Quarterly* 64 (1999), 219–43.

———. 'Moltmann's Post-Modern Messianic Christology: A Review Discussion.' *The Thomist* 56 (1992), 669–93.

———. 'Reflections on Pannenberg's Systematic Theology.' *The Thomist* 58 (1994), 501–12.

———. 'Some Dogmatic Consequences of Paul F. Knitter's Unitarian Theocentrism.' *The Thomist* 55 (1991), 449–95.

———. 'Some Problems with Pannenberg's Solution to Barth's "Faith Subjectivism".' *Scottish Journal of Theology* 48 (1995), 315–39.

———. '*Deus Trinitas*: Exploring Some Dogmatic Implications of David Coffey's Biblical Approach to the Trinity.' Forthcoming in *Irish Theological Quarterly*.

MOLTMANN, JÜRGEN. *God in Creation: A New Theology of Creation and the Spirit of God.* Trans. Margaret Kohl. New York: Harper & Row, 1985.

———. *History and the Triune God: Contributions to Trinitarian Theology.* Trans. John Bowden. New York: Crossroad, 1992.

———. *The Spirit of Life: A Universal Affirmation.* Trans. Margaret Kohl. Minneapolis: Fortress Press, 1993.

———. *The Trinity and the Kingdom: The Doctrine of God.* Trans. Margaret Kohl. New York: Harper & Row, 1981.

———. *The Way of Jesus Christ: Christology in Messianic Dimensions.* Trans. Margaret Kohl. San Francisco: HarperCollins, 1989.

NEUNER, JOSEPH, SJ, ROOS, HEINRICH, SJ and RAHNER, KARL, SJ (eds). *The Teaching of the Catholic Church.* Cork: The Mercier Press, 1966.

The New Testament of the New Jerusalem Bible with Complete Introductions and Notes. Garden City, NY: Image Books, 1986.

O'DONOVAN, LEO J., SJ (ed.). 'A Journey into Time: The Legacy of Karl Rahner's Last Years.' *Theological Studies,* 46 (1985), 621–46.

———. *A World of Grace: An Introduction to the Themes and Foundations of Karl Rahner's Theology.* New York: Crossroad, 1981.

OLSON, ROGER. 'Wolfhart Pannenberg's Doctrine of the Trinity.' *Scottish Journal of Theology* 43 (1990), 175–206.

PAGELS, ELAINE. *The Gnostic Gospels.* New York: Random House, 1979.

———. 'The Gnostic Jesus and Early Christian Politics.' University Lecture in Religion at Arizona State University. 28 January 1982.

PANNENBERG, WOLFHART. *Faith and Reality.* Trans. John Maxwell. Philadelphia: Westminster Press, 1977.

———. *An Introduction to Systematic Theology.* Grand Rapids, MI: Eerdmans, 1991.

———. *Jesus – God and Man.* Second edn. Trans. Lewis L. Wilkins and Duane A. Priebe. Philadelphia: Westminster Press, 1977.

———. *Systematic Theology, Volume 1.* Trans. Geoffrey W. Bromiley. Grand Rapids, MI: Eerdmans, 1991.

———. *Systematic Theology, Volume 2.* Trans. Geoffrey W. Bromiley. Grand Rapids, MI: Eerdmans, 1994.

PETERS, TED. *God as Trinity: Relationality and Temporality in Divine Life.* Louisville, KY: Westminster/John Knox Press, 1993.

RAHNER, KARL, SJ. *Foundations of Christian Faith: An Introduction to the Idea of Christianity.* Trans. William V. Dych. New York: A Crossroad Book, Seabury Press, 1978.

———. *Hearers of the Word.* Trans. Michael Richards. New York: Herder & Herder, 1969.

———. *Spirit in the World.* Trans. William Dych, SJ. New York: Herder & Herder, 1968.

RAHNER, KARL, SJ. *Theological Investigations*. 23 vols:

Vol. 1: *God, Christ, Mary and Grace*. Trans. Cornelius Ernst, OP. Baltimore: Helicon Press, 1961.

Vol. 2: *Man in the Church*. Trans. Karl-H. Kruger. Baltimore: Helicon Press, 1966.

Vol. 3: *Theology of the Spiritual Life*. Trans. Karl-H. Kruger and Boniface Kruger. Baltimore: Helicon Press, 1967.

Vol. 4: *More Recent Writings*. Trans. Kevin Smyth. Baltimore: Helicon Press, 1966.

Vol. 5: *Later Writings*. Trans. Karl-H. Kruger. Baltimore: Helicon Press, 1966.

Vol. 6: *Concerning Vatican Council II*. Trans. Karl-H. Kruger and Boniface Kruger. Baltimore: Helicon Press, 1969.

Vol. 7: *Further Theology of the Spiritual Life 1*. Trans. David Bourke. New York: Herder & Herder, 1971.

Vol. 8: *Further Theology of the Spiritual Life 2*. Trans. David Bourke. New York: Herder & Herder, 1971.

Vol. 9: *Writings of 1965–1967 1*. Trans. Graham Harrison. New York: Herder & Herder, 1972.

Vol. 10: *Writings of 1965–1967 2*. Trans. David Bourke. New York: Herder & Herder, 1973.

Vol. 11: *Confrontations 1*. Trans. David Bourke. New York: Seabury Press, 1974.

Vol. 12: *Confrontations 2*. Trans. David Bourke. New York: Seabury Press, 1974.

Vol. 13: *Theology, Anthropology, Christology*. Trans. David Bourke. London: Darton, Longman & Todd, 1975.

Vol. 14: *Ecclesiology, Questions of the Church, the Church in the World*. Trans. David Bourke. New York: Seabury Press, 1976.

Vol. 15: *Penance in the Early Church*. Trans. David Bourke. New York: Seabury Press, 1976.

Vol. 16: *Experience of the Spirit: Source of Theology*. Trans. David Morland. New York: Seabury Press, 1976.

Vol. 17: *Jesus, Man, and the Church*. Trans. Margaret Kohl. New York: Crossroad, 1981.

Vol. 18: *God and Revelation*. Trans. Edward Quinn. New York: Crossroad, 1983.

Vol. 19: *Faith and Ministry.* Trans. Edward Quinn. New York: Crossroad, 1983.

Vol. 20: *Concern for the Church.* Trans. Edward Quinn. New York: Crossroad, 1986.

Vol. 21: *Science and Christian Faith.* Trans. Hugh M. Riley. New York: Crossroad, 1988.

Vol. 22: *Humane Society and the Church of Tomorrow.* Trans. Joseph Donceel, SJ. New York: Crossroad, 1991.

Vol. 23. *Final Writings.* Trans. Joseph Donceel, SJ and Hugh M. Riley. New York: Crossroad, 1992.

———. *The Church and the Sacraments,* Quaestiones disputatae, 9. Trans. W. J. O'Hara. New York: Herder & Herder, 1968.

———. *The Trinity.* Trans. Joseph Donceel. New York: Herder & Herder, 1970.

——— and JOSEPH RATZINGER. *Revelation and Tradition.* Quaestiones disputatae, 17. Trans. W. J. O'Hara. New York: Herder & Herder, 1966.

——— and HERBERT VORGRIMLER. *Theological Dictionary.* Ed. Cornelius Ernst, OP. Trans. Richard Strachan. New York: Herder & Herder, 1965.

——— and KARL-HEINZ WEGER. *Our Christian Faith Answers for the Future.* Trans. Francis McDonagh. New York: Crossroad, 1981.

RATZINGER, JOSEPH CARDINAL. *Principles of Catholic Theology: Building Stones for a Fundamental Theology.* Trans. Sister Mary Frances McCarthy, SND. San Francisco: Ignatius Press, 1987.

Review Symposium on Catherine Mowry LaCugna's *God for Us: The Trinity and Christian Life. Horizons* 20.1 (1993), 127–42.

RUSCH, WILLIAM G. (ed. and trans.). *Athanasius's Orations against the Arians,* in *The Trinitarian Controversy, Sources of Early Christian Thought.* Philadelphia: Fortress Press, 1980.

SCHWEIZER, EDUARD. *Jesus.* Trans. David E. Green. Atlanta: John Knox Press, 1971.

SCHWÖBEL, CHRISTOPH (ed.). *Trinitarian Theology Today: Essays on Divine Being and Act.* Edinburgh: T&T Clark, 1995.

SENG, KANG PHEE. 'The Epistemological Significance of ὁμοούσιον in the Theology of Thomas F. Torrance.' *Scottish Journal of Theology* 45 (1992), 341–66.

SYKES, S. W. (ed.). *Karl Barth: Centenary Essays.* New York: Cambridge University Press, 1989.

THOMPSON, JOHN. *Modern Trinitarian Perspectives.* New York: Oxford University Press, 1994.

——. *The Holy Spirit in the Theology of Karl Barth.* Allison Park, PA: Pickwick Publications, 1991.

TILLICH, PAUL. *The Shaking of the Foundations.* New York: Charles Scribner's Sons, 1948.

TORRANCE, ALAN. *Persons in Communion: Trinitarian Description and Human Participation.* Edinburgh, T&T Clark, 1996.

TORRANCE, JAMES B. *Worship, Community and the Triune God of Grace.* Downers Grove, IL: InterVarsity Press, 1996.

TORRANCE, THOMAS F. *Christian Theology and Scientific Culture.* New York: Oxford University Press, 1981.

——. *The Christian Doctrine of God, One Being Three Persons.* Edinburgh: T&T Clark, 1996.

——. 'The Deposit of Faith.' *Scottish Journal of Theology* 36 (1983), 1–28.

——. 'Ecumenism and Rome.' *Scottish Journal of Theology* 37 (1984), 59–64.

——. *God and Rationality.* London: Oxford University Press, 1971; reissued Edinburgh: T&T Clark, 1997.

——. *The Ground and Grammar of Theology.* Charlottesville: University Press of Virginia, 1980; reissued Edinburgh: T&T Clark, 2001.

——. 'Karl Barth and the Latin Heresy.' *Scottish Journal of Theology* 39 (1986), 461–82.

——. *Karl Barth, Biblical and Evangelical Theologian.* Edinburgh: T&T Clark, 1990.

——. *Preaching Christ Today: The Gospel and Scientific Thinking.* Grand Rapids, MI: Eerdmans, 1994.

——. *Reality and Evangelical Theology.* Philadelphia: Westminster Press, 1982.

——. *Space, Time and Incarnation.* London: Oxford University Press, 1969; reissued Edinburgh: T&T Clark, 1997.

TORRANCE, THOMAS F. *Space, Time and Resurrection*. Grand Rapids, MI: Eerdmans, 1976; reissued Edinburgh: T&T Clark, 1998.

——. *Theology in Reconciliation*. London: Geoffrey Chapman, 1975.

——. *Theology in Reconstruction*. London: SCM Press, 1965.

——. 'Toward an Ecumenical Consensus on the Trinity.' *Theologische Zeitschrift* 31 (1975), 337–50.

——. *The Trinitarian Faith: The Evangelical Theology of the Ancient Catholic Church*. Edinburgh: T&T Clark, 1988.

——. *Trinitarian Perspectives: Toward Doctrinal Agreement*. Edinburgh: T&T Clark, 1994.

TRACY, DAVID. 'Approaching the Christian Understanding of God.' *Systematic Theology: Roman Catholic Perspectives*. Ed. Francis Schüssler Fiorenza and John P. Galvin. Minneapolis: Fortress Press, 1991. 133–48.

——. 'Trinitarian Speculation and the Forms of Divine Disclosure.' *The Trinity: An Interdisciplinary Symposium on the Trinity*. Ed. Stephen T. Davis, Daniel Kendall, SJ and Gerald O'Collins, SJ. Oxford: Oxford University Press, 1999. 273–93.

VAN BEECK, FRANS JOSEF, SJ. 'Trinitarian Theology as Participation.' *The Trinity: An Interdisciplinary Symposium on the Trinity*. Ed. Stephen T. Davis, Daniel Kendall, SJ and Gerald O'Collins, SJ. Oxford: Oxford University Press, 1999. 295–325.

VORGRIMLER, HERBERT. *Understanding Karl Rahner: An Introduction to his Life and Thought*. New York: Crossroad, 1986.

WAINWRIGHT, ARTHUR. *The Trinity in the New Testament*. London: SPCK, 1980.

WEBSTER, JOHN. *Barth's Ethics of Reconciliation*. Cambridge: Cambridge University Press, 1995.

——. *Barth's Moral Theology: Human Action in Barth's Thought*. Edinburgh: T&T Clark and Grand Rapids, MI: Eerdmans, 1998.

—— (ed.). *The Cambridge Companion to Karl Barth*. Cambridge: Cambridge University Press, 2000.

WISEMAN, JAMES A., OSB. '"I Have Experienced God": Religious Experience in the Theology of Karl Rahner.' *American Benedictine Review*. March (1993), 22–57.

WONG, JOSEPH H. P. *Logos-Symbol in the Christology of Karl Rahner.* Rome: Las-Roma, 1984.

ZIZIOULAS, JOHN D. *Being as Communion: Studies in Personhood and the Church.* Foreword by John Meyendorff. Contemporary Greek Theologians, 4. Crestwood, New York: St Vladimir's Seminary Press, 1993.

Index of Names

Index of Subjects

Lightning Source UK Ltd.
Milton Keynes UK
UKOW06f1130250116

267064UK00001B/122/P